# MAROONED

# MAROONED

*Jamestown, Shipwreck, and a*
*New History of America's Origin*

# JOSEPH KELLY

BLOOMSBURY PUBLISHING
NEW YORK · LONDON · OXFORD · NEW DELHI · SYDNEY

BLOOMSBURY PUBLISHING
Bloomsbury Publishing Inc.
1385 Broadway, New York, NY 10018, USA

BLOOMSBURY, BLOOMSBURY PUBLISHING, and the
Diana logo are trademarks of Bloomsbury Publishing Plc

First published in the United States 2018

ISBN: HB: 978-1-63286-777-3; eBook: 978-1-63286-779-7

Library of Congress Cataloging-in-Publication Data
Names: Kelly, Joseph, 1962– author.
Title: Marooned : Jamestown, shipwreck, and a new history of America's origin /
Joseph Kelly.
Description: New York : Bloomsbury Publishing, 2018. | Includes
bibliographical references.
Identifiers: LCCN 2018003587| ISBN 9781632867773 (hardcover) |
ISBN 9781632867797 (ebook)
Subjects: LCSH: Jamestown (Va.)—History—17th century. | Frontier and pioneer
life—Virginia—Jamestown. | Virginia—History—Colonial period, ca. 1600-1775.
Classification: LCC F234.J3 K449 2018 | DDC 975.5/4251—dc23
LC record available at https://lccn.loc.gov/2018003587

2   4   6   8   10   9   7   5   3   1

Typeset by Westchester Publishing Services
Printed and bound in the U.S.A. by Berryville Graphics Inc., Berryville, Virginia

To find out more about our authors and books visit
www.bloomsbury.com and sign up for our newsletters.

Bloomsbury books may be purchased for business or promotional use.
For information on bulk purchases please contact Macmillan Corporate and
Premium Sales Department at specialmarkets@macmillan.com.

*For William and Mary Lou Kelly*

# CONTENTS

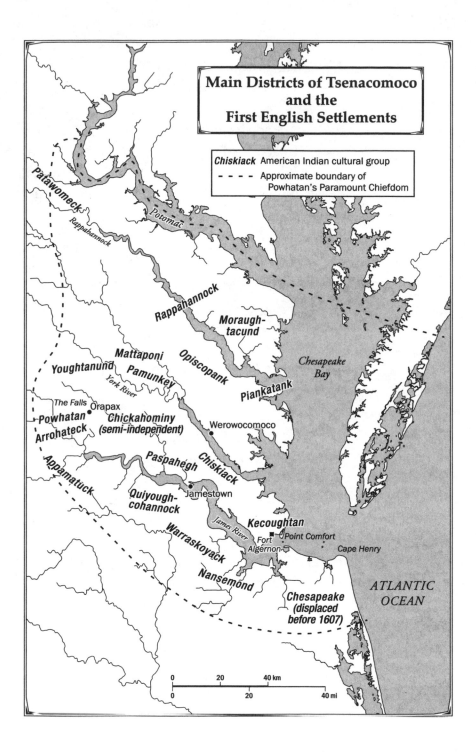

## Main Districts of Tsenacomoco and the First English Settlements

*Chiskiack*  American Indian cultural group

- - - -  Approximate boundary of Powhatan's Paramount Chiefdom

Patawomeck

Potomac

Rappahannock

Rappahannock

Moraugh-tacund

Opiscopank

Chesapeake Bay

Mattaponi

Youghtanund

Pamunkey

York River

Piankatank

The Falls

Orapax

Powhatan

Chickahominy (semi-independent)

Werowocomoco

Arrohateck

Appamatuck

Paspahegh

Chiskiack

Quiyough-cohannock

Jamestown

Kecoughtan

Warraskoyack

James River

Fort Algernon

Point Comfort

Cape Henry

Nansemond

ATLANTIC OCEAN

Chesapeake (displaced before 1607)

| 0 | 20 | 40 km |

| 0 | 20 | 40 mi |

✿

# In the Beginning

**A storm at sea.** Waves swelling higher than the ship's deck and wind like an ax chopping off their caps and throwing water at the heavens. So much seawater in the air, it seems it will drown the lightning. The sky pours down "stinking pitch," sulfurous smell, and thunder. A "brave vessel" full of "noble creature[s]" climbing the waves and sliding into the troughs, its seams barely holding together.

So opened Shakespeare's *Tempest* in a cold London theater in the winter of 1611.

It was a true story. To use today's common language, Shakespeare ripped this scene from the headlines. Only there were no headlines in 1611. Newspapers had not been invented. The first English-language periodical, a weekly broadsheet, was printed ten years later, ironically enough in Dutch-speaking Amsterdam. News of great events circulated the streets of England's towns in more entertaining, less dependable channels: pamphlets, sermons, songs, notices posted in town squares, private letters passed around from one reader to another. And rumor. Buzzing like the crowd noise preceding a play, the cacophonous, often contradictory, sailors' stories seeped up from the docks of London, Southampton, and Plymouth. And plays, even those as fantastical as *The Tempest*, dramatized the rumors and publicized what was going on in the world.[1]

This story of storm, wreck, and redemption was the talk of England. Although a century had passed since Columbus first crossed the Atlantic, the open sea still preyed on the sailor's psyche in a way that coast-hugging Europeans had never felt. When a storm came on the western ocean, there was no chance of running to harbor. Voyagers were beyond the frontiers of civilization, encroaching on spaces unlit by Christianity, where dark forces reigned. Anything could happen.

At the height of Shakespeare's play, a few noblemen come on deck demanding to speak with the ship's master.

"[Y]ou marre our labour," the boatswain answers. "Keepe your Cabines: you do assist the storme."

The words sound like revolution. At least on the surface, the seaman seems to be a leveler who favors meritocracy over aristocracy.

"You are a Counsellor," the boatswain tells Gonzalgo, "if you can command these Elements to silence . . . vse your authoritie: If you cannot . . . out of our way I say."

Gonzalgo warns him, "remember whom thou hast aboord."

"None that I loue more than my selfe," replies the sailor. "[W]hat cares these roarers for the name of King?"

Such stuff might embolden the "common sort" to check their supposed "betters." One might think so, until it is remembered that the common sort was not in the play's audience. *The Tempest* premiered in the elegant, enclosed Blackfriars Theatre. The more democratic and open-air Globe Theatre was always crowded with groundlings, who stood in the pit chewing their sausages. But tickets to the indoor, winterized Blackfriars Theatre were pricier. London's aristocracy sat in their boxes dressed in finery, and the guildsmen and craftsmen and professionals, up to perhaps a thousand patrons, filled the rest of the audience. Rich though they were, they were as eager as any to see onstage what they'd heard about in rumor: what had happened to the *Sea Venture*.

The players wobble-strut on the stage as if on the heaving and tossing deck of that ship, while the master and boatswain shout instructions into the noise of the wind.

"Take in the toppe-sale!"

At all cost they must keep steerageway. They catch just enough wind to point her bow into those rising seas. If a wave should take them broadside, it might roll the top-heavy ship till the masts kissed the water, and she would not rise again.

"Lay her a hold, a hold, set her two courses off to Sea again, lay her off!"

All labor for naught! The ship does not roll but its very boards come apart, letting in the sea like a sieve. The scene ends with mariners flooding the stage, clothes dripping with salt water, crying in despair and fear: "We split, we split!"

"Farewell my wife, and children," the sailors wail.

"Farewell, brother!"[2]

Elizabethan theater might have skimped on props and sets and special effects when judged by the standards of our own blockbuster action films. It had to rely on the words of the actors to paint the scene. As Shakespeare himself put it, the breath of those who watched the play must fill the ship's sails with wind. But Shakespeare's words! They whipped up gales in the minds of the viewers. The patrons quaked under the shock of thunder and lightning.

A ship full of a hundred and fifty souls split at sea, in the midst of the most terrible storm, and yet every person lived! This was England's most shocking, unbelievable news.

More than a year earlier, on the fifteenth of May, 1609, the *Sea Venture* set sail from London, the "admiral" of an impressive fleet. The *Diamond*, the *Falcon*, the *Blessing*, the *Lion*, and the *Unity*, as well as a pinnace (a shallow-draft boat designed for coastal exploration) too small to be named, sailed behind her, headed to Virginia, the third and by far largest resupply of two-year-old, fledgling Jamestown,

England's tiny, rough-hewn, and hungry little campsite, its only toehold on the vast American continent. The flotilla was the largest and most expensive and most promising overseas expedition that England had ever organized, and the six hundred people crowded into the vessels would triple or quadruple the population of the colony. It seemed that all England applauded their departure. "Crowds of London's ever-curious spectators," one historian explains, "lined the river's banks and cheered as the seven ships, sails billowing, flags flying, glided past them on the spring afternoon."[3] Several weeks later, after a stop at Plymouth increased the fleet to nine vessels, they left England's toe, the very westernmost tip of the nation, following the setting sun into the newly charted seas of the vast North Atlantic. Seen from the land's end, they disappeared into oblivion, as if a curtain shut upon them. No one in England would hear from the fleet for ages. No one expected to. Ships that sailed west into the Atlantic reappeared, if they ever did, almost miraculously, many months or even years later.

This time the Atlantic was quiet. Each morning from the second of June to July twenty-third, 1609, the sun rose in a clear sky off the stern, and it chased the squadron all morning long, till in the afternoon and evening the ships chased the setting sun toward Virginia. The seas were calm. It was a relief to Sir George Somers, admiral of the fleet, who did not know what to expect. Previous English expeditions followed the winds south, island-hopping to the Canaries, then the West Indies, and thence to Jamestown. But the Virginia Company had recently scouted a quicker, "more direct line," a northern passage that avoided the Caribbean's hazard of Spanish ships, and Somers followed this unfamiliar route. The month and a half of fair breezes and clear skies seemed to justify the gamble. They made such good time that one of the pinnaces could not keep up. The flagship, the *Sea Venture*, had to tow it across the Atlantic.

The *Sea Venture* was a three-hundred-ton merchant ship about a hundred feet long that had been designed to carry English wool to Dutch dyers. It was broad and "chubby," which suited Holland's trade but made it ungainly on the wide Atlantic Ocean. Fore and aft, high superstructures—wooden castles piled in the style of the carrack, the most common type of oceangoing vessel in the sixteenth century—rose above the deck. These structures made such ships top-heavy, and the tall forecastle prevented carracks from sailing very efficiently when facing contrary winds. The Spanish and the English both had fixed the defect by developing the galleon, which lowered the forecastle, but the *Sea Venture* was built according to the older design. Further harming her balance were the sixteen cannons mounted on the upper deck. Normally these heavy weapons would have been below the open-air deck and above the hold, but that in-between area housed many of the colonists and their gear in tightly crowded makeshift cabins.[4]

The fleet was just over a week's sailing from Virginia when the sunny days disappeared. In the midst of the Atlantic's emptiness, alone in the world, not another human being anywhere for a thousand miles, dark and terrifying clouds sped in from the northeast. It was the front edge of a gale, a storm that blew worse and longer than even the maddest storms in the familiar waters of northern Europe, the Barbary Coast of Africa, the Levant, or the Adriatic.[5]

The fleet was overtaken by a hurricane. Most ships were demasted. They limped into Jamestown one by one, their holds leaky and their supplies sodden and of little use to the colony. All the ships survived save the flagship, the *Sea Venture*, the biggest and best supplied of them all, containing not only George Somers but also Sir Thomas Gates, the new governor, and the lion's share of provisions. She had disappeared without a trace, swallowed by the storm and presumed to have been swallowed by the sea. So came the news from Virginia. The wives and parents and children of

the dead had their mourning. The directors of the Company reckoned their losses. The morale of the nation suffered its blow and
moved on.

A year later, a miraculous rumor started to circulate around the
docks of England's port cities. Everyone on the *Sea Venture* had been
saved. Had no one drowned? All were plucked somehow from a
sinking ship in the middle of a hurricane in the middle of the wide
Atlantic. The fantastic story sped through the chattering streets of
London.

Shakespeare did not get the story from rumors. He had the most
credible source: a narrative letter dozens of pages long and hand-
penned by an eyewitness, a survivor of the *Sea Venture* foundering.
It told a harrowing tale of heroic deeds and base mutinies. Written
by a gentleman named William Strachey, this remarkable document was, ostensibly, a private missive to some unidentified "Excellent Lady," but it quickly circulated among London's literary
crowd in manuscript—as Strachey knew it would—and through the
finer houses and government offices of England. Shakespeare read it.
The famous playwright was Strachey's friend. They had probably
shared drinks at the Mermaid Tavern, if not jokes and jibes. And so
at the very end of his career, on the edge of retirement, England's
greatest playwright found himself with what we would call today a
"scoop": the story of the founding of a brave new world.


EXODUS AND JEREMIAD

We typically think of myths as the superstitions of ancient societies,
like the Olympian gods of Greece, Rome's pantheon, the Vikings'
Thor, and the faerie people of Ireland. But modern nations need
myths too. About fifty years ago, Warren Susman, who described
himself as a historian of "the enormous American middle class,"
explained how myths unify complex modern societies, justify the

existing social order, and reinforce basic values. One could hardly imagine a more prosaic people than the American middle class. And yet it, too, uses myth to sanctify communal goals. This is what Joseph Campbell calls the "sociological function" of myth.[6]

The most important modern myths narrate the nation's founding, and in the American consciousness that has meant the Pilgrims. If you studied history at an American high school or in your college days you read any of the half dozen big anthologies of American literature, you will probably contend that the United States of America started at Plymouth Rock.[7] But the Pilgrims' story has not always been our founding myth. Northern states began disseminating the Pilgrim myth right about the time of the Civil War, and the last hundred years have cemented the Pilgrims into the shape of our forefathers. Thanksgiving themes about religious fidelity in the face of ocean storms and winter starvation, about racial generosity and the reward of good harvests, gourds of plenty on outdoor tables heaped with food, go back only to about World War I. About a hundred years ago, the Pilgrims became the myth of our beginning.

Their story is an Exodus.

Take, for example, the 1988 Peanuts version, "The Mayflower Voyagers," which was the first episode in the children's miniseries *This Is America, Charlie Brown*. Snoopy and Linus and Lucy explain the familiar motifs: persecuted Pilgrims flee from England as the Israelites fled from Egypt; during the Atlantic passage, storms try their faith and endurance; disease and hunger stalk their first winter. The TV program also features the generosity of Native Americans and the racial harmony of the Thanksgiving feast, themes absent and even contradicted by some pre–civil rights era narratives. Underlying all, like a droning rhythm, is the suggestion that the settlers' progress was a series of "miracles," an understated but unequivocal indication that the Pilgrims, and by extension all Americans, are God's chosen people.[8]

The image of a "shining city on a hill" emblemizes this religious explanation of American exceptionalism. Ronald Reagan, borrowing from John F. Kennedy, popularized that image of America in the 1980s. Very reasonably, he imagined the United States to be the land of liberty and opportunity, as compared to the totalitarian regimes behind the Iron Curtain; the Pilgrims walked their gauntlet of trials, Reagan explained, but "that small community . . . prospered and . . . went on to become a beacon to all the oppressed and poor of the world."[9] The connection between the modern United States and the shining city on a hill goes all the way back to John Winthrop, the Puritan founder of the Massachusetts Bay Colony, who used the image in a sermon he preached on the *Arbella* as it crossed the Atlantic in 1630. Winthrop struck a bargain: If God would guide the *Arbella* through its trials and, most especially, if He would spare it from shipwreck, the colonists promised to obey His will, love each other, and avoid "pleasure and profits." Docility, obedience, and keeping to one's appointed place prop up Winthrop's notion of a good society.

Such are the spit and polish on the Puritans' hilltop city. Fidelity. Resistance to corruption. Inoculation against contaminating influences. These are the essence of Exodus. God's people must stay virtuous. They must resist the temptation to worship false gods, like the golden calf that led astray the people of Moses. Though the trials of the desert last forty years, they must stay pure so they might enter and dwell in the Promised Land. And such is the substance of the opening chapters of William Bradford's *Of Plymouth Plantation*, which recount the Pilgrim's exile in Holland. Fear that their own children were falling away from the faith and assimilating to Dutch culture drove the Pilgrims to America, where they might live wholly righteous lives removed from the influences of mammon. Such is the theme as they enter the Promised Land, the land of heathens. They must keep vigilant inside their citadel of faith, lest they break their promise to God. Under this template, becoming Americanized means no more than listening to Squanto explain how to plant corn. God forbid the Pilgrims might learn more from the Indians, for the devil lives in their wild woods, as Nathaniel Hawthorne's Young Goodman Brown reminded us in the nineteenth century.

But the chosen people never keep their faith. They forget. They backslide. They must be reminded. So the inevitable sequel to every Exodus is the Jeremiad. Like the Old Testament prophet, Jeremiah, someone must stand up and harangue the people. The last half of Bradford's narrative, written in the second generation after the *Mayflower*, warns a backsliding people that they must return to the faith of their fathers. They must abandon the conceits and attractions of a prosperous Massachusetts and conform again to the strict founding dogma.

In 1978, Sacvan Bercovitch first suggested that the Pilgrims' experience defines America. His seminal book, *The American Jeremiad*, argues that nostalgia for the faith of our fathers, and the disapproval of modern apathy and backsliding, together constitute *the* characteristic form of American literature. In truth, scholars as far back as the 1930s pioneered this idea that American intellectual history began with the Puritans. James Truslow Adams's hugely influential 1931 history, *The Epic of America*, popularized the concept of the "American Dream" and held that the Mayflower Compact originated a distinctly American society. "The novel situation of being free from all laws whatever," Adams explained, "faced the Pilgrims even before they landed from the *Mayflower* . . . Some government was needful . . . They simply avoided the possible dangers of anarchy or an iron dictator by agreeing to abide by the expressed *common* will." Following Adams, English professors have told several generations of college students that the Puritans, especially Bradford and

Winthrop, are the foundation of the national canon. Their books, exodus tales and jeremiads, have become the sacred texts of the American people.[10]

My book is hardly the first to trouble the Puritan myth. Debunking Pilgrims is something of a cottage industry. For instance, a full chapter of James Loewen's *Lies My Teacher Told Me: Everything Your American History Textbook Got Wrong* exposes "the truth about the First Thanksgiving" like an episode of *60 Minutes*. Howard Zinn's *People's History of the United States* corrects a thousand myths of American history, including the Puritans. Even Nathaniel Philbrick, today's most popular chronicler and one might say *booster* of Massachusetts history, wants to demythologize. He remembers that, "like many Americans," he "grew up taking this myth of national origins with a grain of salt." One of his aims in the bestselling *Mayflower: A Story of Courage, Community, and War* was to explode the stereotype of the school-textbook Pilgrims sporting "wide-brimmed hats and buckled shoes," those two-dimensional images that "symbolize all that is good about America." In their place, Philbrick offers a complex, historically accurate, three-dimensional portrait of "real-life Indians and English": men and women who were "too smart, too generous, too greedy, too brave—in short, too human—to behave predictably." But for all that, Philbrick falls back into the shallow grooves of the Pilgrim myth, and his *Mayflower* ends up reassuring readers with undisturbing dogma: "There is a surprising amount of truth," he concludes, "in the tired, threadbare story of the First Thanksgiving." Philbrick's later book, *Bunker Hill: A City, a Siege, a Revolution*, treats the Enlightenment ideals of the American Revolution as if they came at the end of a Pilgrim's progress, painting Boston in 1776 as the fulfillment of Winthrop's "City on the Hill."[11] Despite my very high esteem for Nathaniel Philbrick, my book disputes his conclusions.

Perhaps in response to Philbrick's bestseller, the television comedy *The Simpsons* mocked the notion that Pilgrims were the root of American values. Constance Prudence Chastity Goodfaith (also known as Marge Obedience Temperance Sexwon't) shoos Bart and Lisa onto the *Mayflower*, exclaiming, "Hurry, my little puritans. We must flee England and its insufficiently puritanical ways." So much for Exodus. The Simpsons do not flee oppression; they seek a place where they can freely oppress. The vignette is satire, and, like the best satire, Marge's line might have been lifted verbatim from *Of Plymouth Plantation*, which positively crowed that the city on a hill was *less* free than England: "wickedness," Bradford bragged, was "here more stopped by strict laws" than in the mother country. He had no problem with tyranny so long as it was some bona fide Puritan who was bossing people. Social mobility? John Winthrop's sermon on the *Arbella* commands the poor to keep in their place and be satisfied with their lot. Freedom of religion? The trial of Mrs. Anne Hutchinson and her subsequent exile demonstrate how the Puritans abhorred that idea. Devotion to the truth? People who hunted witches can hardly be held up as purveyors of rational inquiry. If Plymouth was exceptional, what set it apart was its faith in authority. According to Bradford and Winthrop, righteousness, not liberty or equality, made Massachusetts a beacon to others, a "Citty upon a Hill," with "the eies of all people . . . uppon us."[12]

But the historical inaccuracy beneath the Pilgrim story is not the only issue. As Benedict Anderson reminded us thirty-five years ago, nations are "imagined" communities. What matters is not so much what the historians would call legitimate or accurate history, although by all means we ought to drive out error wherever we find it. More important in defining a nation is what Ernest Renan called "a rich legacy of memories," a community's sense of shared deeds, the suffering and glories of our grandmothers and grandfathers. Memory, as we all know, selects and discards and distorts, and even though it should strive to be objective, it still must witness each scene from one angle. Such is the nature of myth. Both Renan and Anderson (and

Donald Trump, for that matter) understood that cultural phenomena like Lin-Manuel Miranda's *Hamilton* or D. W. Griffith's *Birth of a Nation* contribute more to our collective memory than any historian can. It comes as no surprise, then, that American Studies programs in our universities tend to be collaborations between departments of history and English. English professors study the *imaginative* artifacts of our culture—our novels and films and comic books. The recent debates about Confederate monuments in the South are not just about *history*: they are about communal *memory*. The historians might tell us that the Puritans hated democracy and that they loved to persecute people who did not worship in their particularly esoteric way, but if our imaginative culture only remembers that they fled religious persecution, Pilgrims might still give us at least a part of that legacy we require. The deep problem lies elsewhere, in the very structure of their myth, with exodus itself and with jeremiads. Those stories no longer serve. Perhaps they never should have served. They have always been the wrong myths on which to erect our national consciousness.

## MAROONS AND CASTAWAYS

Jamestown has long competed with Plymouth as our origin myth. If *Peanuts* proffered its "Mayflower Voyagers," Disney produced the hugely popular *Pocahontas*. That film is not without its problems. Conforming to a dangerous tradition, it dramatizes colonization as a contest between a European man (John Smith) and a native (Kocoum) for the heart of an indigenous woman (Pocahontas), who symbolizes the land. But even so, *Pocahontas* is a more appropriate myth of the nation's birth. For one thing, Native Americans, however romanticized, are at the center of the story, and the notions of American identity that the film inculcates in young viewers are defined not by retaining cultural purity and resisting outside influences but by miscegenation, cultural impurity, and the need to form a middle ground between Europe and Native America.

Yet *Pocahontas* is an outlier, one of the few positive representations of the encounter on the Chesapeake. More often, Jamestown is the redheaded stepchild among America's progeny. Although none could deny it is a full thirteen years older than Plymouth, the plantation on the James River has been America's shameful southern misbirth compared to the northern golden child of Plymouth. Virginia's first colonists have been cast as our regretted start. If the Pilgrims and their city on a hill are the American utopia, Jamestown has been the dystopia, remembered for its greedy, idle, unruly cannibals. "Jamestown," Karen Ordahl Kupperman declares in her recent history of the colony, "makes us uncomfortable."[13] And so the several recent historical treatments of Jamestown—at least five significant books have come out since the 2007 anniversary of the colony's founding—struggle to justify themselves in the shadow of the Pilgrim myth. Kupperman herself declares that Jamestown's "contribution" to American history was to develop the prototype for the more successful plantations in Massachusetts.[14] This book argues otherwise. Jamestown was no Exodus. No Jeremiah rose up to harangue the present day. And yet, the true stuff of our national birth can be found in the Jamestown narratives. I say *can be found* because we have overlooked the most important parts of the Jamestown story. That's not surprising, really, when we consider who wrote the Jamestown narratives, what their prejudices were, what axes they had to grind. The true story of what happened at Jamestown has been buried deep. The evidence is still there. It has been there all along, hidden, waiting to be mined. The texts have to be cracked open. The rich veins of ore that stud the Jamestown stories have to be smelted before we can cast the iron base of our nation.

Hundreds of letters, reports, narratives, court records, charters, and such concerning the first years of Jamestown still survive. Editors started collecting these sources right away, the first being Samuel Purchas, whose 1625 *Hakluytus Posthumus: Or, Purchas His Pilgrimes* contained dozens of items, including Strachey's narrative. George Percy's *True Relation of the Proceedings and Occurances of Moment Which Have Happened in Virginia from the Time Sir Thomas Gates Shipwrecked upon the Bermudes Anno 1609 Until My Departure out of the Country Which Was in Anno Domini 1612*, which contains our most vivid picture of the "starving time," was not rediscovered until 1922. Otherwise, the key texts have been published and readily available to historians for hundreds of years. In 1890, Alexander Brown published an edition of early texts in his two-volume *Genesis of the United States*, an authority still often cited today. Edward Wright Haile's 946-page *Jamestown Narratives: Eyewitness Accounts of the Virginia Colony* (1998), one of the more recent editions, selects fifty-eight distinct texts, running from one-page letters to Smith's 135-page *General History*. James Horn's Library of America edition (2007), *Capt. John Smith: Writings, with Other Narratives of Roanoke, Jamestown, and the First Settlement of America*, reduces that number to fifteen crucial texts.[15]

Three figures tower over all the other sources: John Smith and George Percy, original colonists who each became president of Jamestown; and William Strachey, who arrived in the Third Supply and became the colony's secretary. Their narratives are longer, more detailed, vivid, and compelling than the others, and they have stamped their impressions on history. It is not that we read the narratives naively. Readers have never taken them at face value. No historical text is entirely neutral or objective. Even the barest "facts" of a church registry or testamentary will require analysis. What does it mean, for instance, that Shakespeare left his second-best bed to Anne Hathaway? The best literary historians are still unsure. Narratives require even more interpretation, because storytellers, even those who strive for honesty, paint with their personal palate, their likes and dislikes and predilections. And each narrative's purpose and audience select certain facts for notice and assign others to oblivion. The writer reporting on a territory's marketable commodities sees the land differently from the soldier worried about Indians. Readers of the Jamestown narratives have not been inattentive to these influences. They regard the narratives with a judicious eye. John Smith's self-aggrandizing "history" has elicited special skepticism. The most spectacular example is the caution with which historians approach the famous vignette of young Pocahontas saving Smith from execution.

For four hundred years, we have known the particular prejudices and even grudges that distorted these writers' points of view. They each needed to flatter particular men, exaggerate the flaws of their personal enemies, maximize their own praise, and minimize their blame, so they used their pens as they used their swords—as weapons of preservation and tools of advancement. The first president, Edward Maria Wingfield, wanted to paint Smith as a mutineer; Smith, part of the coup d'état that toppled Wingfield, drew him as an incompetent leader; Percy succeeded both and undermined both; and Strachey inflated the character of his own patron, Governor Thomas Gates. We know that these intrigues snaked their way into the narratives, and so we read all with suspicion.

Almost all. This laudable skepticism has managed to overlook one important fact. Except for the very rare exception, the history of Jamestown was recorded by upper-class gentlemen who were high-ranking executives of the Virginia Company.[16] Despite their petty differences, these writers stand united by class prejudice. They looked at the common settler, the Company's low-level employees, the way management regards labor, as a resource to be manipulated. Almost from the first day of landing in America, the Company men found that their workers were discontent. Within months the settlers stopped doing what they were told. They stopped working for the Company's profit. Made desperate by circumstances on the American frontier, the common settlers had the temerity to claim the right of self-determination, which the narratives all condemn as mutiny. The historical texts characterize the settlers as idle, lazy, sensuous, given to drink and greed, mutinous in thought and deed—in a word, *ungovernable*. Though attentive to how the incessant backstabbing distorted Jamestown's narratives, historians have missed the ideological perspective of the Company men. They uncritically accept that Jamestown's settlers were unruly. And so a reader as sensitive to nuance as Kupperman can still claim that Jamestown was a false start whose importance to American history is subordinate to the governable and well-governed Pilgrims at Plymouth Plantation.

This book reverses the habitual point of view. It looks at Jamestown through the eyes of the idle, the discontented, the unruly renegade mutineers. They did not record their own thoughts and impressions. They did not write about their adventures and justify their deeds and inscribe the faults of their oppressors. They never told their story. Nevertheless, it has been in front of us for four hundred years. It's in the margins of Smith's *General History of Virginia, New England, and the Summer Isles*. It lurks behind the text of George Percy's *True Relation*. And imprisoned in William Strachey's *True Reportory* are the voice and words of the most important unacknowledged founding father of our country.

The man we might call the first true American was a commoner by the name of Stephen Hopkins, a settler headed to Jamestown but shipwrecked on a desert island. Into the ears of his fellow castaways he whispered the same ideas that Thomas Jefferson later immortalized in the Declaration of Independence. Carrying the torch of these ideas, he tried to lead a group of volunteer settlers into the wilderness, and for this crime Hopkins was sentenced to death. He talked his way out of that fate, and, remarkably, history finds him ten years later with the Pilgrims on their voyage, a signatory of that remarkable document we call the Mayflower Compact. It is almost by accident that we know anything at all about Stephen Hopkins and his enlightened political philosophy. It is as if our record of the Sermon on the Mount came from the disapproving pen of Pharisees. Strachey meant to vilify Hopkins, and when history has deigned to remember him, it has treated him as a villain. But if we turn the lens slightly to eliminate Strachey's prejudice, the real picture snaps into clear focus. Hopkins appears as a new *Homo politicus* forged by the experience of the castaway. He is not the first hero of this tale, but Hopkins is almost unique because most of the common settlers left behind no record of their adventures and only the barest trace of their existence. We will not pick up the thread of his life until nearly halfway through the book, after we recover the stories of dozens of others, the anonymous deserters, renegades, and castaways of Jamestown. No fewer than fourteen separate uprisings were recorded in the first few years of Virginia. Some were small-scale resistance, on the order of a few individuals; others were so widespread that the Company hammered them down with peremptory military justice. The narratives call them "mutinies," but the men involved were not really trying to overthrow any authority. They wanted to maroon themselves in the wilderness, and their stories dramatize the origins of the democratic virtues, the unalienable rights of freedom and equality.

The English word *maroon* did not yet exist in 1607. The Spanish word from which it derives, *cimarrón*, was first coined to describe domesticated cattle brought to Hispaniola that escaped into the wild parts of the island. Most scholars today accept some form of this derivation, which dates at least to 1535, just forty years after Columbus landed on Hispaniola. By 1540, *cimarrón* was applied to Africans who, like the chattel before them, fled to the remote, wild places behind Spanish coastal colonies. *Maroon* first appeared in English in 1666 when John Davies, translating a history of Barbados, wrote that slaves, like those animals, would "run away and get into the Mountains and Forests, where they live like so many Beasts; then they are call'd

Marons, that is to say Savages."[17] Sometimes, these escapees formed
new communities in the wilderness, a phenomenon that anthropologists call *grand marronage*. *Cimarrón* and eventually the shortened
word, *maroon*, carried a heavy metaphoric or perhaps even literal sense
that these fugitives devolved to an animal ferocity, wildness, and
savagery. That is to say, they left civilization to live like Native
Americans.[18]

Indians were often midwife to marronage. Siouan tribes or Yuchi
Indians living on South Carolina's coast helped the first maroons on
the soil of what is today the United States. In 1526, five hundred
Spanish with one hundred African slaves settled near the mouth of
the Pee Dee River. The summer "seasoning," mosquito-borne illnesses
like yellow fever, began to carry off the settlers. In the midst of this
crisis, several slaves escaped into the hinterland, taking refuge among
the Indians, and when in October the 150 surviving Spanish abandoned the settlement and sailed for Hispaniola, they left behind
those escapees. Eighty years before Jamestown, the first inter-
continental settlers on the East Coast of the United States were
maroons: Africans who had escaped Spanish slavery.[19]

Although maroons escaped from slavery, it was no Exodus. No
God tendered them a land of milk and honey as reward for keeping
faith. They retained no orthodox hegemony. They were heterodox.
Typically, they came from various districts in Africa, and although
they might share a creole language and common suffering, they shared
little else. They entered no promised land. The wildernesses to which
they fled were not their natural element, though the Europeans often
thought they were. The mountains of Jamaica were just as inhospitable to Africans as they were to Europeans. The jungles of Suriname
and the swamps of Carolina posed the same dangers for blacks as
for whites. These places terrified the escaped slaves as they would
terrify you or me were we suddenly hurled into them with only the
resources we could steal and carry. Maroons embraced these dangers

Maroons in Suriname, 1899.

in desperation, preferring them to the certain dangers and degradations of slavery. They pledged faith to each other, formed communities according to their own liking, and kept sacred above all else the principal of freedom.[20]

According to the anthropologist Richard Price, even hundreds of years after their escape from bondage, "freedom" still defines maroon communities. *Choosing freedom* is the pillar of their identity. Maroons are the people who escaped slavery; who braved the snakes and alligators and cats of jungle, swamp, and mountain; who had the courage to risk the retributive torture of pursuing whites—all for freedom. Maroon identity, Price tells us, "is predicated on a single opposition: freedom versus slavery." No other mode of society identifies so strongly with the unalienable human right of self-determination.[21]

To borrow a title from the naturalized American, Christian existentialist Paul Tillich, maroons display better than anyone the *Courage to Be*. Martin Luther King Jr. wrote his dissertation on the philosophy of Paul Tillich and applied it to the existential experience of African Americans. Suffering under the penal laws of Jim Crow, they valued freedom as the defining human identifier. And so, in his "Letter from a Birmingham Jail," MLK, quoting Tillich, identifies segregation as an *existential* crime and, borrowing from Saint Thomas Aquinas, defines unjust laws as those *degrading the human personality*. Scholars are just beginning to catch on to how important maroons are to our conception of freedom. The philosopher Neil Roberts, for instance, suggests that marronage exemplifies the "supreme ideal of freedom" and that to understand "freedom" we must understand the psychological experience of flight from bondage and the subsequent reconstruction of civil society. For Roberts, the maroon is the lens through which we can understand freedom, which is not a static condition but "perpetual, unfinished, and rooted in acts of flight." In this spirit, Isaac Curtis studies the "masterless peoples" of the historic Caribbean, not only maroons but also pirates. These societies were "remarkably egalitarian" on the whole and sometimes democratic, especially compared to the societies from which maroons escaped and pirates plundered. In the "bizarre and horrifying world" of pirates, Sarah and Paul Robinson write (perhaps too enthusiastically but with general accuracy), "genuine democracy flowered, far beyond what existed in the budding democracy movement of the day." And Sylviane Diouf's *Slavery's Exiles: The Story of the American Maroons* has begun to nudge historians towards recognizing that maroons—"people in the hidden wilds"—are central to our history.[22]

The first Englishman to meet a genuine maroon was a red-bearded corsair not yet thirty years old. Cruising the coast of Spanish Panama, he hoped to loot the mule trains that hauled heavy bars of Peruvian silver over the isthmus for loading on the treasure ships. In 1572 this pirate was better known in Panama than in his native Plymouth. His name swept up and down the coast and carried eventually inland, via murky lines of communication, from the mouth of one

slave to the ear of another, till finally it reached the villages of a mysterious people living in the impenetrable jungles of Panama's interior. His notorious enmity for the Spanish made these maroons (or
*Symerons*, as they were called in the narratives) seek out the obscure
sailor from Devonshire, the man known as Francis Drake.[23]

Drake lived with the *Symerons* for months. He admired their
remarkable woodcraft as they stalked the Spanish convoys. He fought
side by side with them till finally he got his silver and the maroons
got their iron, a metal far more valuable to people carving a society
out of the wilderness. For a time Drake's maroons were crucial to
England's overseas strategy, the linchpin of a plan drawn up by
an Oxford cosmographer named Richard Hakluyt. Under English
protection and transported by Drake, hundreds of maroons disappeared at Sir Walter Raleigh's settlement at Roanoke, yet another
mystery of the "lost" colony. A generation later the very same Richard
Hakluyt, by then an old man, was one of the few names on the Virginia
Company's charter. Although liberated slaves were no longer at the
center of England's plans for America, Jamestown produced its
own maroons: white Englishmen escaping the slave-like conditions
imposed by the joint-stock corporation that governed them.

We do not often acknowledge it, but our more common use of
the word *maroon*, not as a noun but as a transitive verb, retains much
of the original sense. It was first applied to whites metaphorically: one
was castaway, as Robinson Crusoe was *marooned* on his desert island,
or deliberately exiled to a wilderness, the way one of Roanake's ships
*marooned* Englishmen on Jamaica. To be marooned in this sense is to
be an unwilling victim either of circumstance, like shipwreck, or of
punishment. Its first application to whites came in 1699 when William
Dampier, a logger on the Campeche coast of Mexico, wandered from
a hunting expedition and lost his way. "I began to find," Dampier
explained in his memoir, "that I was (as we call it, I suppose from the

Spaniards), Marooned, or Lost, and quite out of the Hearing of my Comrades Guns." He lived on "Wild-Pines" and suffered clouds of mosquitoes before he was rescued a couple of days later.[24]

The analogy is clear: to be marooned is to be *like* escaped slaves, lost in the wild and reduced to a life not much higher than that of animals. But there is a crucial difference. If Panama's *Symerons* fled into the wilderness, Robinson Crusoe was cast into it. Jamestown's settlers experienced both senses of the word: they *were* marooned and they *chose to become* maroons. Shipwrecked, cast away, abandoned, they were marooned in the more modern sense of the term. But the settlers of Virginia passed through a psychological experience similar to the *Symerons* of Panama. They fled into the woods and there discovered freedom.

American ideals did not begin with a covenant between God and his chosen people, a bargain by which a faithful people avoided shipwreck and entered the promised land. Altogether, the Exodus story is too antiseptic. Bone-dry boots stepped ashore at Plymouth Rock. The Puritans might have been immersed in a strange land and surrounded by exotic people, but somehow they remained impervious, unwetted. They were waterproof. These Old World zealots were hardly touched by their encounter with America, against which they inoculated themselves as if against the devil.[25] Our true birth was a plunge and a forgetting: wrecking on the rocks, dunking in the brine, floating away from solid decks, loosed from the timbers of the Old World, set loose from old bindings, stumbling ashore drenched and dripping. Then salvage begins. Americans are castaways, maroons, and we began on a reef in the mid-Atlantic.

THE TEMPEST

On the evening of July 28, 1609, William Strachey reported, "a dreadful storm and hideous began to blow." Winds scattered the fleet apart. Ships lost sight of each other. All day long and then all night without a break the winds blew so hard, they seemed to lift the waters up out of the sea, and, freed from the mountainous swells, the sea spray battled with the sky. It didn't rain in sheets as heavy rains fall on land: "The waters like whole rivers did flood the air." Seasoned sailors were terrified. The women and passengers were beyond hope, and their prayers "dround in the windes, and the windes in thvnder. Prayers might well be in the heart and lips, but drowned in the outcries of the Officers: nothing [was] heard that could give comfort, nothing seen that might encourage hope." Sails were of no use. Eight men together could hardly handle the tiller.[26] They kept no course. The storm drove them northeast and then northwest. It hardly mattered. There was nothing to crash into. Nothing but empty ocean. They struggled to face the ship into rising waves.

The seams between the hull's planks began to split. The oakum that sealed the planks spewed, and as the sailors fought the raging sea outside, salt water seeped into the bottom of the ship, three feet, four feet, five feet deep. They worked the pumps, but the pumps did no more than slow the deepening water. Master and mate, boatswain, cooper, carpenters—all searched with candles below the decks, plugging the seeping leaks where they found them. They stuffed strings of salted beef into one large opening seam in the gunners' room. But still the waters continued to rise inside the ship. Distinctions of class disappeared. Gentleman adventurers "such as in all their life times had never done [an] hour's work before" traded shifts with the mariners, equal except that the veteran sailors stripped themselves naked to better work in the deluge. Three days the storm blew, and through four long nights they worked to keep the leaking ship afloat.

They lost hope. They were foundering in the middle of the wide Atlantic, weeks of fair sailing from any landfall. Their labors did no more than delay by a few hours the inevitable swamping of the ship, when each person would float away in cold ocean swells. They knew

Wreck of the *Sea Venture* off Bermuda, 28th July 1609.

this, but still they pumped. What else was there to do? They could quit working and drown. Or they could keep working the pumps and postpone the drowning a few more hours. Such is our instinct for life, Strachey wrote in his *True Reportory* that we labor beyond endurance to extend it half a day. They worked "beyond . . . reason." They worked to delay the inevitable end that rushed toward them, when the sea would extinguish their candle. Those last precious hours before drowning were all they had, and they exhausted themselves desperately to extend the interval of life.

One gigantic wave swamped the entire deck from "sterne to stemme" in a "garment or a vast cloude" of frothing water, and it stopped the ship short with a shudder as if a net had caught her. The helmsman was flung from the whipstaff and was nearly broken in two. Strachey thought the ship was "alreadie in the bottome of the Sea." Over the side went their luggage in trunks and chests. They tossed butts of beer, oil by the hogshead, cider and wine and vinegar, and finally the cannons. They started to cut away the mainmast to lighten the ship further. None of it helped. Still the waters rose, and still they pumped, staving off the inevitable. Finally, beyond the ends of endurance, they decided to shut up the hatches and commend their souls to God and the ship to the "mercy of the Sea." All was lost.

"Land!" the admiral cried.

Land! In the middle of the wide Atlantic Ocean!

Strachey rushed to the rail with all the worn-out sailors and settlers, peering to where the hands pointed. Between the bars of rain he could just make out a long, low-lying shore and the branches of trees shaking in the wind.

## CHAPTER ONE

### Renegades

**Two years earlier, in 1607,** three English ships carrying about a hundred settlers and scores of crewmen were sailing for Chesapeake Bay. First they had to find the continent. A sailor threw out a sounding line a hundred fathoms long, but it found no bottom. Nor the next day, or the day after that. At four in the morning on the twenty-sixth of April, 1607, someone sighted land, a rough-edged tree line barely above the horizon. By daylight they found that their navigation had been perfect: the mouth of the bay gaped in front of them. They sailed in that copious opening and threw down their anchors, lowered boats, rowed ashore. About three dozen men laden with the gear of battle climbed over the side, splashing through the ankle-deep water to dry land. They spent the day wandering inland with little purpose other than to make contact, to reconnoiter, to begin mapping what one might call the lower jaw of the bay's mouth. They wandered through meadows and meandered between "goodly tall Trees" and crossed freshwater creeks. The land "ravished" their eyes. There was no sign of any human beings.

At nightfall, when they were climbing wearily back into the boats, suddenly out of the tall grass "savages" swept down the slope like bears. A rain of arrows. Most that found their targets glanced harmlessly off steel armor. The Indians were close enough for pistols, and a hastily organized volley of shot came from the English, loud and smoky, and chased the savages away as suddenly as they had appeared. Only a few arrows found flesh. A sailor, Matthew Morton, who would not have been protected by any armor, was hit in two "very dangerous" places. And an arrow pierced both hands of Captain Gabriel Archer, which he had probably raised to protect his face.[1]

For the next several days, parties of "gentlemen and soldiers" came ashore in various places for forays into the eerily silent woods. They saw no more Indians. They came to a fire where someone had obviously been roasting oysters, "very large and delicate in taste," but no one was there. The English helped themselves. The third day "some gentlemen" crossed a vast expanse of ground, five miles across with not a bush nor a tree. But they found no human beings, only a gigantic dugout canoe forty-five feet long. They again helped themselves to a feast of oysters and mussels, recently abandoned, opening as many as they liked and stealing the pearls inside. They found grass fires but no people. Fields with strawberries four times the size of English strawberries. But no people. They erected a cross near where they had landed on the first day, when they'd been attacked, which they named Cape Henry.

They finally saw some Indians on the fourth day. Five men stood onshore staring across the water at the ships. The English rowed their shallop toward them, and after some gestures of peace on both sides the English came ashore and followed their hosts to the town called Kecoughtan. All sat down on mats and shared food, and they smoked tobacco from long earthenware pipes. News of this encounter must have traveled upriver, because in the next two weeks the English found similarly friendly greetings in four towns well spaced apart. At Paspahegh, the villagers shared meals and ritual dances. The weroance, or chief, of Rapahanna "entertained" them "in so modest a proud fashion" that they imagined him a "prince of civil government, holding his countenance without laughter or any such ill behavior." Farther upriver, at Appamattuck, they encountered "warlike" men "with swords at their backs beset with sharp stones and pieces of iron able to cleave a man in sunder." But after some gesture diplomacy, these, too, were satisfied to let the English "land in quietness."²

Sometime in these early days, perhaps the night of that first skirmish on the southern shore of the Chesapeake, the one-armed Captain Christopher Newport broke the seal on a box and lifted out a sheaf of papers. Probably this ceremony was witnessed by as many of the more prominent settlers as could crowd into his little cabin on the *Susan Constant*. No one knew what was written there, not even Captain Newport, but all had agreed to abide by the instructions. The gentlemen looked at each other tensely, for the passage across the ocean had riven many of them into rival factions. Who would be empowered? Who would not? Despite their growing enmities, all would be ruled by those papers. Names were read aloud: the seven members of a governing council. The captains of each of the three ships were appointed: Newport, Bartholomew Gosnold, and John Ratcliffe. And then came the soldiers: George Kendall, John Martin, and Edward Maria Wingfield. To the horror of some and the relief of others, the seventh name belonged to the blunt and divisive John Smith, who was at that moment chained belowdecks, a condemned prisoner.

## THE VIRGINIA COMPANY

English shipping, which had slumbered under most of the Tudor monarchs, was awakened by the demise of the Spanish Armada in 1588. By the end of Queen Elizabeth's reign, England had become a hive of maritime activity, its ships flying nearly everywhere from its honeycomb of ports and havens, swarms of bees feeding on the nectar of foreign trade. The first almost false start of this explosion of activity came in 1555, when the Company of Merchant Adventurers to New Lands, which sought a northeast passage to China, accidentally found a route to Moscow. The company reformed itself as the "Muscovy" or "Russian" Company, wrote up a governing charter, and made it legal and binding by persuading Queen Mary to stamp it with her seal. The Muscovy Company charted the sea and river routes to the czar's capital. More importantly, they pioneered capitalism. The company's fortunes waxed and waned, and no one followed the trail it blazed—at least, not at first. But after the English defeated the Armada, activity picked up. Europe's best cosmographer, the scholar, researcher, compiler, editor, and writer Richard Hakluyt, published his manifesto, *The Principall Navigations, Voiages, and Discoveries of the English Nation.* That compendious history inspired a generation of sailors and merchants, and in 1592 a few hundred commercial men pooled together to form the Levant Company, which purchased ships, financed ambassadors and agents, and carried English textiles through the Mediterranean Sea to newly acquired depots in Aleppo and other Turkish ports. On the last day of the sixteenth century, a similar consortium organized what came to be called the East India Company.

These were the first "corporations" in the sense that we understand today. Stockholders pooled their capital to underwrite enterprises that were too expensive for any individual to finance or too risky for any individual to hazard. The risk of losing a ship in the perilous sea routes through the Mediterranean and through Europe's northern seas to Russia were spread among individual investors, who each owned just a slice of a voyage. The incorporators wrote rules that spelled how they would govern themselves, and the English crown officially "chartered" those rules, giving them binding power. Start-up costs were huge. Captains had to discover the best winds and currents and how to avoid pirates. Employees known as factors had to develop contacts. The merchants had to figure out the right commodities to ship out and ship in. These companies bought ships, hired crews, armed escorts, paid factors in distant locales, paid the salaries of ambassadors. All this was accomplished more or less by trial and error, and those who suffered early mistakes needed to be assured of reaping the rewards of eventual success, so the monarchs— Mary, Elizabeth, and finally James—granted "concessions," or monopolies, giving each company the exclusive right to develop a particular market.

At the center of many of these corporations was Thomas Smythe, the "Pierpont Morgan of his time." He's one of the most neglected men in the story of English exploration. Swashbucklers like Francis Drake and courtiers like Walter Raleigh get all the notice. Poets wrote odes about the corsairs. Pamphlets pumped their glory or blame, and balladeers sang in the streets about pirates. These men of action had shields, or "targets," that bore not only their newly blazoned escutcheons but the real dents and scuffs of Spanish pike and sword. Smythe did not follow their route to success and fame. He started life fairly well-off. His father, also named Thomas, married the daughter of London's Lord Mayor and secured the lucrative job of the collector of the queen's customs. The children of "Customer" Smythe grew up rich, and the second Thomas, Customer's third son, was raised to the manner of commerce and government bureaucracy. He attended Oxford. In 1591, like his father before him, Smythe was collecting England's custom fees. At the age of twenty-one, he understood the value of these new instruments of commerce, joint stocks, and he ventured a portion of the family fortune as one of the "incorporators" of the Levant Company. Six years later he became one of the principals of the Muscovy Company, serving, eventually, as English ambassador to that country. By 1606, Smythe was the most prominent of the hundreds of merchants investing in these corporations. He was the businessman par excellence. He had the perspicacity of the venture capitalist, the organizational know-how of the chief operating officer, the exactitude of the treasurer, the connections of a government liaison, and the lobbyist's suavity. He connected merchants to ship captains, victualers to investors, cosmographers to government ministers, soldiers to schemers, each to the other. When King James came to the throne, Smythe purchased his knighthood in a transaction that stirred no one's imagination. Bards don't sing about the countinghouse and bills of exchange. Excisers make poor ballad fodder. Business bores.

And as a result, exactly *how* the Virginia Company formed is still a mystery. Some accounts credit Sir John Popham, lord chief justice of England, who summoned interested parties to a summit in 1606, and the story may be true. He was the driving force behind a group associated with the port of Plymouth and England's West Country. But another faction centered in London was headed by Smythe.[3] Without any great notice, these two groups drafted the first constitution for English America. First came a royal license creating the Virginia Company (April 10, 1606), which historians have dubbed the "First Charter." Then came the king's more detailed "Instructions" for the Company (November 10, 1606), which identified the real powers behind the company, the fourteen men whom the king appointed to the Company's "council," or board of directors. Half were Plymouth men and the other half came from London, and the instructions split Virginia into two spheres of operation, with the north governed by Plymouth and the south by London. Some men in the London branch were public figures (William Wade, lieutenant of the Tower of London, for instance); some were high-placed aristocrats (Lord Salisbury's proxy, Walter Cope), and others were East India Company merchants, like Smythe. These men drafted "Orders for the Council," promulgated on December 10, 1606, which were directives for the council that would govern on the ground in the southern part of Virginia. Ultimate authority rested in the king, but in practice it devolved to those he appointed to the Company's council, who wrote "laws ordynaunces and instructions" for the people who actually went to North America. Together, all of these documents—the First Charter, the king's instructions, and the London council's instructions to the colony's council—formed Virginia's "constitutions." The men who drafted these constitutions did not know they had done anything revolutionary. Even Smythe did not know it. All they meant to do was write up another charter, like those that governed previous trading companies. In truth, the bulk of the fine print spelled out the usual rules of trade: the king would get 20 percent of the gold and silver and 7 percent of the copper mined in America; a tariff would be assessed for five years; all exports would be consolidated in Company storehouses in London or Plymouth; private trade could not begin till 1612.

The Levant, Muscovy, and East India companies had also figured out how a large group of equals might make corporate decisions. The mechanism was majority rule within representative councils, and the Virginia Company replicated that practice. In disputes among councillors, the "most part" would prevail over the lesser part. The "most part" of the Virginia Company council would appoint the members of the London and Plymouth branches. The "major part" of each branch council would elect a president, who would lead the colony for a term of one year unless the "major part" of the council voted to remove him from office. Under the London branch's particular directions, the president of the colony was really just the first among the colonial councillors. When opposing sides had an "Equality of Voices" in council, the president voted a second time to decide the issue.

At least at the level of the incorporators, consent of the governed was implicit. The original Virginia Company council was appointed by the king. We don't know how those names were compiled in the first place, but it is likely that James just rubber-stamped the names that the chief incorporators handed him. They had probably been elected by shareholders. The act of investing money in the Company might be considered the bestowal of consent. Each "adventurer" was bound to the rules of the Company. If one disliked the council or the rules of government, he could simply refuse to buy shares. Similarly, the Company's fourteen councillors swore an oath, a freely given public declaration, that bound them to the First Charter and the king's Instructions. One might refuse to take the oath and thus refuse to join the council. Such a person, of course, would then not be bound by the Company's practice of majority rule, but neither could he exercise the Company's powers.[4]

In these matters, the Virginia Company did not depart from previous practice. It differed in that it allowed for another category of "adventurers." These were the people who signed up to populate the colony. They invested themselves, an act that gave at least tacit consent to be governed by the Company's councils. What they did not really understand was that the corporation had the right to kill them.

## TRANSPORTATION

So many English ships had crossed the Atlantic by this time that provisioning was nearly routine. To trade with the "naturals" the English would have packed barrels full of "iron hatchets, saws, knives, rosaries, little bells, and other similar trifles which [the Indians] esteem very highly." The Indians loved to ornament their bodies with copper earrings, nose rings, and piercings of their lips. The English knew what a crew would need in the way of victuals for a trans-Atlantic voyage. But even to as seasoned a merchant-trader as Thomas Smythe, most of this outfitting was new. The English had been sending groups of settlers to Ireland for years, but Ireland was not far from resupply. Nothing like this had been attempted in over twenty years, not since Sir Walter Raleigh outfitted settlers for Roanoke. The settlers needed enough food and drink to last till the first resupply, which would not come for six to twelve months. Carpenters had to be recruited for the voyage. Workmen had to be recruited. Tools bought and stowed for the building of a "Storehouse and those Other

Rooms of Publick and necessary Use," not to mention the sleeping quarters. Tools to dig trenches and build earthen walls. Cannons would be mounted inside the earthen fort. Picks and the like for mining. Weapons for the armory. A forge: they must carry over the ocean an entire blacksmith's shop, and a smith or two.[5]

Late in November, two ships came up the Thames for this provisioning, the *Susan Constant*, of about 120 tons, and the smaller *Godspeed*, Bartholomew Gosnold, captain. The first night at anchor, the crew of the *Susan Constant* "sate tiplinge and drinkinge," and when the tide turned they did not notice the ship swinging about on its line until it crashed down on a smaller ship, splintering its bowsprit and wrecking the sheet anchor. It was not an auspicious start, and as Captain Newport, the Company's choice as admiral, disentangled the ships, the London branch of the Company found itself tangled in a minor lawsuit. But Thomas Smythe could untie such knots, and on the tenth of December orders from the London branch council came aboard giving Newport "Sole charge and Command" over crews and passengers and over all the Company's stores while the ships were at sea. Nothing was unusual about giving such dictatorial powers to a sea captain. But the next instruction was unique: a secret "instrument" was put into Newport's care, a box not to be opened till Newport put the settlers ashore in Virginia. Only then would be revealed whom the Company appointed to the colonial council, the men who would govern the colony.[6] In late December, these two ships and a twenty-ton flyboat called *Discovery*, captained by John Ratcliffe, sailed down the Thames. They slipped out of port without fanfare, drawing so little attention that they were gone a month before the Spanish ambassador learned what they were up to.

A full count of the settlers ran to 104 people. Forty-eight were "gentlemen" with no clear qualification for colonizing—that is, no recorded skill or role. Counting the six councillors, the number rises to fifty-four. Many of these, presumably, had been soldiers at some point in their lives, although by no means did being a gentleman in King James's time mean, as it once did, that you were trained in the military arts. Only three commoners are identified as soldiers—one of these moonlighting as a tailor and one a bricklayer— along with one sergeant and one drummer. The London instructions called for about fifty soldiers, so most of the gentlemen must have assumed military or paramilitary duty.[7] The colony had one fisherman, several carpenters, two surgeons—one of these a gentleman, one a commoner—a couple of bricklayers, and a mason. One settler was a sailor by profession. One a barber. Thirteen others were mere "laborers," workers who had mastered no trade. Also, there were a handful of "boys." "Divers others," fifteen in all, were not recorded by name or profession, but their very lack of noteworthiness probably means they were common laborers.[8] Christopher Newport set their course for the Canary Islands.

❧

The old captain knew his business. Born in 1561 to a mariner turned pub owner, Newport grew up in Harwich with the sea as frontyard and playground. At the age of nineteen he crossed the Atlantic on a rare English voyage to Brazil. A violent and tyrannical captain persuaded Newport and two friends to jump ship, employing the sailors' final expression of self-determination, one of a thousand examples of desertion in American waters.[9] By the age of twenty-six, Newport commanded his own vessel. He sailed with Sir Francis Drake in 1587, fought the Spanish Armada the next year from the deck of the *Thomas*, and, following Francis Drake's example, turned privateer in the Caribbean. Sir Walter Raleigh hired him to captain the *Little John*, part of a fleet meant to rescue the lost Roanoke settlers. On the way out Newport captured his first prize, a small ship carrying cinnamon and wine. Near Jamaica, the *Little John* exchanged several cannonades with a Spanish ship, closed completely, and tangled their rigging, and the English pirates boarded the Spanish ship. Swords flashed, small arms crackled, the smoke from gunpowder and the noise of desperate hand-to-hand fighting clouded the air. Though outnumbered, the Spanish fought hard. Newport's lieutenant and four other English perished in the melee, while another fourteen received some cutlass gash or a pistol ball. In the thick of the fight a Spaniard came at Newport. His sword flashed swift as lightning. Newport's right arm was "strooken off" clean. The bloody limb fell on the deck, deader than a ten-pound eel hauled out of the depths.[10]

The Spanish ship sank before they could pull out the barrels full of silver, and all they got was a little supply of cochineal, a red dye. It might have seemed a poor bargain in the short term: a right arm for the little lucre stolen from the Spanish on this cruise. But Newport was in it for the long haul, and privateering paid dividends two years later in 1592. Commanding the brand-new *Golden Dragon*, Newport had already "sacked four towns and two ships, and captured a total of eight prize ships" when he teamed up with another fleet of ships commissioned by Sir Walter Raleigh. Together they came across the massive, 1,600-ton Portuguese treasure ship *Madre de Deus*, carrying on its four decks 600 men, 850,000 pounds of pepper, 537 tons of "cloves, cinnamon, and nutmeg . . . large quantities of ambergris . . . pearls, silk, ivory, silver, rubies, and gold," besides four hundred slaves chained below.[11] Like hyenas harassing a lion, the English ships peppered the Portuguese and boarded her several times, the one-armed Newport in the vanguard, but the *Madre de Deus* kept fighting. One English ship was demasted and dead in the water. Another had six feet of water in the hold. But after a day and night of hard fighting, the Portuguese struck their colors. The dead and living wounded littered the ship in tangles of limbs and blood and gore.[12]

Newport had the honor of sailing the *Madre de Deus* back to England, gliding into Dartmouth's harbor on September 7, 1592, with the largest ship anyone in England had ever seen. The queen's share amounted to ninety thousand pounds, by far the largest, and the investors had to be paid, but Newport's portion was enough to set him up in a fine house and garden on Tower Hill in London, where he installed his third wife, Elizabeth, and his four children. Feared by the Spanish and the Portuguese, the one-armed captain commanded the respect of English investors, who now competed to install him in their own ships. All in all, Newport had nine more cruises in the next ten years. Most spectacularly, in 1602, he seized some Spanish frigates coming from Cartagena, and the loot of gold tallied into the millions, far more even than the *Madre de Deus* ten years earlier. When King James made peace with Spain, some of Newport's colleagues turned pirate, cutting themselves off from England. But Newport, at forty-four and very comfortably set up in London, turned honest merchant in the West India trade. He presented two alligators to King James, who had a fancy for exotic creatures. The gift was less subtle than effective: Newport was soon appointed one of the "principal masters" of the British Navy.[13]

Though two other notable mariners—Bartholomew Gosnold and Sir George Somers—were among the Company's directors, Newport's experience made him invaluable. According to "legend," as Newport's biographer calls it, when Gosnold gathered several friends to his Suffolk manor, Otley Hall, to plot the colonization of Virginia, Newport was chosen to admiral the three-vessel fleet.[14] No one knew the West Indian islands better than he did, and his talent for leadership was obvious. In the résumé of Newport's life, shuttling back and forth from Virginia should have been an easy assignment.

❧

By the time the ships reached the Canaries, one of the soldiers, John Smith, had attracted a large enough following among the settlers to be suspected of plotting to set himself up as a king in Virginia. Historians tend to name Edward Maria Wingfield as the man who denounced Smith. Wingfield was an experienced colonizer. When he was just nineteen, he helped his uncle, the constable of Dublin Castle and privy councillor for Ireland, settle English farmers in the province of Munster, and it was in Ireland that he met John Popham. These credentials were enough to make Wingfield one of the seven people named on the Company's first charter. He was of an older generation than most settlers (for example, Bartholomew Gosnold was his nephew), and by this virtue and by his having servants with him he began the voyage with a certain cachet. His accusations carried weight. But Newport was in charge, and his reaction—restraint rather than summary execution—indicates that he discredited the charges but could not entirely dismiss them.[15] Probably Smith was kept shackled and isolated, lest his golden tongue continue to sway hearts and minds.

On the twenty-third of February, Newport's squadron landed in the West Indies, and at Dominica most of the passengers got their first look at Native Americans. George Percy, son of the Earl of Northumberland, watched in fascination as a crowd of canoes surrounded the ships and the Indians climbed up on the decks carrying pineapples, potatoes, tobacco, and plantains to trade for knives and hatchets. The exotics were "very strange to behold," naked, their bodies painted red with some mosquito repellent. Percy reported that they were "Canibals" because they "will eat man's flesh." Not only that, but he went on to say that "they worship the devil for their god, and have no other belief." Percy's observations have a curiously tolerant tone, and the English were hardly shy about trading with devil-worshipping man-eaters. After all, both the Dominicans and the English hated the Spanish, and that was the main thing. They might have "barbarous" customs "like dogs," but a certain fondness creeps into Percy's account, as one might express for intelligent animals. Next he describes a thresher shark and a swordfish teaming up to chase a whale. It was all of a piece, painted

Indians eating people and sharks eating whales—the fauna of
the New World. Percy's first impressions were paradoxical, and we
might guess that the Dominicans understood the English better
than the English understood the Dominicans.[16]

For six days the settlers camped on Nevis, recuperating from the
voyage in the hot and cold springs, hunting, fowling, fishing, feasting.
They glimpsed people, who flitted like shy deer through the woods.
A gallows was erected to hang Smith, but Newport apparently
prevented the execution, and Smith continued the voyage under
arrest. He was still in irons when they watered at Puerto Rico, and
when the ships sailed into the Chesapeake, John Smith's life still hung
in the balance between Newport's restraint and Wingfield's zeal. It
was his appointment to the council that probably saved his life. Wingfield still hated him, but Newport struck off his shackles, and the
pall of condemnation finally disappeared.[17]

## CORPORATE DECISIONS

The English reconnoitered the lower James River for a couple of
weeks, looking for a likely place to plant their colony. Captain Gosnold
preferred a piece of high ground jutting out into the river, which
provided a natural haven for shipping. The land itself was full of wild
turkey and "excellent good timber" supporting "vines in bigness of
a man's thigh," as George Percy described it. But Gosnold's uncle,
Edward Maria Wingfield, preferred a spot a few miles farther up the
river, almost an island, surrounded by swamp and marsh. Connected
to the mainland by a narrow causeway, it seemed highly defensible.
Best of all, the river carved out a natural deepwater slip where the
"ships do lie so near the shore that they are moored to the trees in six
fathom water."[18] Although this was the first momentous decision
required of the government, neither Percy's account nor John Smith's
indicate how or even if the council made the decision. There was no

formal vote to determine the will of the "major part." Perhaps the decision was unremarkable. Informal discussion and persuasion probably led to consensus. Or perhaps youth merely deferred to age. To everyone's later misfortune, Wingfield's view prevailed, and on the thirteenth of May, 1607, the ships tied up to the trees at the site that would be first called James Fort and then James Towne.[19]

Six of the councillors—everyone but John Smith—elected their president: Edward Maria Wingfield. Following the Company's orders, Wingfield swore his own oath in front of these councillors, and immediately thereafter President Wingfield administered an oath to the councillors themselves. No fewer than "twenty of the Principal Persons adventurers"—that is, *gentlemen* who had purchased shares in the Company—were required to witness these oaths. Gathered in some commodious grove or meadow, those settlers of inherited, earned, or purchased rank listened to Jamestown's councillors and president promise to follow the king's instructions and to follow the Company's instructions—to abide by Virginia's "constitutions." There might have been no mechanism by which the "principal Persons adventurers" could hold the councillors to account, should those councillors abuse their constituted powers. The gentleman witnesses were not given the authority to depose any of these governors. But they had considerable *moral* authority.[20]

At least half the colony was not required to attend this ceremony. The commoners were already lifting barrels from the ships' holds by rope and tackle, swinging them with care onto the shore, lining them up in neat rows. Already the picks had been found among the cargo and distributed, and men were ranged along the three converging lines that had been scored in the earth, a long triangle that marked where the palisade would go. They were digging the first trench and raising an earthen redoubt.

The strange land must have unnerved them. Ancient trees towered, and the sounds of exotic birds and the incessant rhythm of exotic insects droned in the ears. They were relieved from the heat only when the sun went down. They slept outdoors, under the stars. Beyond the flickering light of the campfire, a continent lurked. Nevertheless, after so many weeks at sea, a day of hard digging in the resisting earth would have exhausted the laborers, and we can imagine that no matter how frightening the place was, once they fell asleep, they slept soundly—at least, until midnight. Alarms were shouted! The commoners were awakened by the clanking sounds of gentlemen buckling on their swords and scrambling into the forms of battle. Fifty soldiers had been roused by silent apparitions. Some saw them, some did not. Gliding down the black river, Indians in their dugout canoes were glimpsed in the starlight. The "savages" took a long, silent look at the camp before slipping back into the darkness. If the commoners were frightened—and it is hard to imagine that such a vision would not unnerve a common laborer or a tailor or a bricklayer come from London—the competent, businesslike deployment of the armored gentlemen would have been reassuring.[21]

Because they depended upon these gentlemen for their protection, the commoners had all the more reason to worry about the visible rift growing between them. The issue was John Smith. Wingfield would not swear him onto the council. Disaffected with Wingfield's high-handedness, a group of gentlemen thought that excluding Smith from the council was a "preposterous proceeding." Men were grumbling against Wingfield and already cherishing a "grudge."[22] Newport defused the time bomb. He left Wingfield to the business of erecting a fort while he sailed off to explore the James River, and in addition to four mariners and fourteen sailors he took four of the gentlemen and John Smith. The explorers went as far as the river was navigable, practicing diplomacy, surveying the country, and looking for potential mines. Smith began his study of the Algonquians, as the English were "kindly" treated to feasts of "strawberries, mulberries, bread, fish, and other [of] their country['s] provisions." Captain

The Tsenacomocoan view of the construction
of Jamestown's palisade.

Newport spread bells, pins, needles, glass beads, and goodwill "in all places," and Smith carefully observed how this "liberality" affected the Indians. The explorers went upriver till their progress was stopped by the falls, near the Indian town of Powhatan, and they sailed back down river with barrels full of rock and the beginnings of native alliances.[23]

On May 27, the day before Newport's explorers made it back and in contrast to their reception in the towns on the upper reaches of the James River, a couple of hundred Indians assaulted Jamestown. The fort was not finished. Indeed, Newport found that it had hardly been begun, and so the arrows had come pouring into the tents. The soldiers scrambled to arms and repulsed the assault, and for an hour the two sides exchanged fire, arrows from one side, firearms from the other. A cannon from one of the ships raked the long grass in front of the earthworks with small shot, and the Indians finally withdrew. Two colonists were killed. Ten others were wounded. The commoners must have been more troubled than before.[24]

President Wingfield fought bravely. An arrow passed through his beard at the height of the fighting, but the remnants of his prestige suffered a fatal blow. He should have been prepared. Signs of Indian hostility had been growing for days, and yet the English were taken unawares. Captain Newport took charge of the situation and ordered his sailors to help finish the fort. Work on the palisade quickened. But the skirmishes continued. On the thirtieth, a gentleman, Eustace Clovell, straggling outside the fort was ambushed by Indians hiding in the long grass. Six arrows found their mark before he was dragged back inside the walls, and for the next week the colonists listened to his slow death agony. On the fourth of June, a laborer was relieving his bowels outside the fort when Indians again hidden in the grass "shot him in the head." In the midst of this crisis, Wingfield had the workers sawing timber into clapboard to ship back to England. After Clovell was shot but two days before he died, the "principal men" had had enough. In formal petition—the only instrument of their moral authority—they demanded reforms from the council. Chief among those demands: the installation of John Smith on the council.

Still the council dawdled. Not until the tenth of June, four days after the gentlemen's petition, were they moved to action, and then only because of the emotional pleas of Captain Newport, who was about to take the two big ships back to England. The last thing he wanted was to report back in London was that he had left Jamestown in civil strife. He spoke fervently to both the council and the petitioning gentlemen, pleading for their unanimity and amity. Both sides compromised. The council accepted Smith and swore him in that day. The faction of gentlemen petitioners "subscribed an obedience to our superiors." *Subscribed* here probably does not carry its literal sense, that they signed an oath, but the effect was the same. Although no mechanism for such an action had been designed or even contemplated by the Company, on June, 10, 1607, the gentleman of Jamestown willingly consented to their government, and the government conceded it must attend to the will of at least a portion of the "better sort" of people it governed. The living symbol of these reciprocating bonds of obligation was John Smith. The following day, with Smith on the council, the council handed down "Articles and orders for *gentlemen* and soldiers [who] were upon the court of guard." More than a month after their arrival, at least as far as the gentlemen were concerned, "content was in the quarter."[25] The commoners were not yet complaining.

The Company was given license to "take and leade" only English subjects "as shall willinglie accompanie them" to North America, so we know that most of the commoners, at least theoretically, consented to go. (The servants of rich men like Wingfield and John Martin might have had less say in their own fates.) At least theoretically, the Virginia constitutions guaranteed them the same "liberties, franchises and immunities" that they enjoyed in England. Any of their children born in America would be treated as if they were born in England. The king's Instructions required that all permanent residents of the colony swear the "usual oath of obedience to us."[26] There is no record of a similar oath—such as that sworn by the council members—promising to abide the Company's governors. Nevertheless, by setting foot onto the deck of one of the Company's three ships in the river Thames, each settler implied he understood that he was subjecting himself to the Company. The act of coming on board the ships was as effective as signing one's name on a piece of paper. While at sea, everyone took orders from Captain Newport. Once they landed in Virginia, everyone understood that authority would be vested in the colonial council and its president.

The council was given the power to execute normal criminal justice. Anyone who committed murder, manslaughter, incest, rape, or adultery would be tried by the council and president before a jury of twelve honest men. Whether or not these rules were read to the common settlers, their assent might be presumed. Other laws might have troubled them: crimes and misdemeanors, including drunkenness and vagrancy, required no jury. These would be adjudicated by the "greater number" of the council, which was authorized to mete out fit punishments. What could have been meant by vagrancy is hard to figure when property and housing were all held in common, and it might have given an impecunious laborer some worry. Ideological crimes were to be taken seriously. Just because you found yourself in a distant wilderness did not mean you could "seeke to withdrawe" yourself from the Church of England. Consent was hardly at issue here: in England everyone was already required to live under such obligations. But the king also outlawed rebellion, mutiny, and sedition *against the Company*. Disobedience to the colonial council could mean a sentence of death. (As we shall see, this power was not idle.) Everyone understood the authority of a ship's captain at sea. But did they understand that a handful of Company men exercised the same authority on land? That they could be put to death, for instance, for refusing to saw clapboard? On Friday the twelfth, the day after John Smith was sworn in and peace was made among the gentlemen, the laborers cut down a second great tree, and under Wingfield's instructions began their clapboard manufactury. On Saturday another Englishman took an arrow in the chest. As the fort neared completion, as it became more evident that the settlers were divided into two classes—gentlemen soldiers and laborers—the common settlers were beginning to worry about the Company's priorities.[27]

## DISSENSION AND DESERTION

Virginia was not England's first encounter with the wilderness. There was Ireland, and the first settlers of America comprehended the experience in terms of their long settlement and warfare in that country. In the 1500s the Irish populace divided into two categories. Those who submitted to Henry VIII's sovereignty were metaphorically (and most were literally) living within the "Pale," the fortified base closest to England's beachhead on Ireland's east coast. Beyond the Pale lived "the King's Irish enemies," to use the sixteenth-century term, who were by far the majority of the population. When Henry VIII tried to impose his centralized form of government and the Protestant church on reluctant Irish lords, he started a long war that would chew up several armies, several monarchs, and several generations of Englishmen. In theory, England had ruled Ireland ever since King Henry II's invasion in the twelfth century. But some historians call the sixteenth-century Tudor conquest of Ireland a *rediscovery*. "For the men on board the ships," William Kelly writes of some English soldiers sent to fortify the north coast of Ireland in 1600, "this was *terra incognita*, a land so unknown they might well have been in the Americas." One Englishman living in Ireland, the famous poet Edmund Spenser, whose epic *The Faerie Queene* celebrated Queen Elizabeth's enlightened rule, thought the native Celts were barbarous tribes of uncivilized, uncouth primitives. Ancient Gaels, he hypothesized, had migrated to Ireland from "cold caves and frozen habitation," from some ancestral land of "continual frost." Though nominally Catholic—which was bad enough to the Tudor Englishman—the Irish seemed more pagan than Christian. The English thought of them as wild animals, cannibals, sexual debauchers, incestuous nomads following herds and living in hasty hovels. Some thought Ireland was a time capsule, a pocket of Europe that had never become civilized, a people still living according to the customs of prehistoric man. When Shane O'Neill, the Irish king of Ulster and the son of the Earl of Tyrone, came in embassy to Elizabeth's court, Londoners marveled at the terrifying barbarian, who traveled (according to a contemporary English description) with a retinue of soldiers "armed with battle-axes, bare-headed, with flowing curls, yellow shirts dyed with saffron . . . large sleeves, short tunics and rough cloaks." The crowds stared in awe and "much wonderment as if they had come from China or America." The analogy with Native Americans was irresistible.[28]

Worse than the physical threat was the call of the wild that might infect the civilized English colonists. So-called primitives have their appeal—an exotic, intoxicating siren song, a virus that infects the civilized soul. Dragged against his will from the shires of England, harried by a brutal army discipline, huddled inside the walls of his garrison fortress, might the lowly English conscript listen to that wild, haunting song calling from the mists and woods?[29] The typical English foot soldier serving in Ireland was wet, cold, hungry, and scared. Most were posted to some garrison, typically a castle, where the soldiers were safe from the natives. But inside the walls was misery. The foot soldier made eight pence a day from which he was supposed to buy his commissary rations: his daily bread (one pound), butter (one-sixth of a pound), and cheese (one-third of a pound). Every week six men shared two pounds of salted beef or fish or pork or bacon, and for vegetables the soldier enjoyed a pint of peas every two weeks. They imported English beer to drink, or Irish whiskey, at any rate something with alcohol, because pure water would unhinge the sphincter. In reality, the supply lines were so corrupt that food arrived spoiled if at all. Profiteers in England and Dublin fattened while the soldiers starved. Garrisons were often expected to supply themselves through plunder: corn and cows stolen from natives.[30]

To take one well-documented example, four thousand men sailed up the river Foyle on the far north of Ireland, landed, and garrisoned themselves near today's still troubled town of Derry. Conditions were horrible. Morale bottomed out. Soldiers refused to work, and broke their shovels rather than dig their earthworks. Within a year, only 1,500 were fit for duty. Most were killed by dysentery. The soldiers ingested food or water contaminated with bacteria or parasites, which colonized their intestines, eating away at the lining. High fevers shivered their bodies while bloody, unbelievably foul-smelling diarrhea leaked continually from their bowels, smearing the camp with contagions. Weakened by malnutrition, more soldiers died of disease than in combat. In 1599, the Irish council grieved "to see the poor state of the soldiers, 'like prisoners half-starved for want of cherishing.'" Everyone in England knew what was going on in Ireland. After half a year, the queen refused to send any more men to the Foyle outpost, complaining that "to raw men such a place will rather serve now for a grave than a garrison."[31]

This was England's Vietnam. The English soldiers were prisoners caged in their castles, while the native Irish roamed free. The English went out on "journeys" or periodic raids through the hostile countryside. Slow-marching columns of heavily encumbered armies lumbered out the gates of their safe zones into vast expanses of "what for the English was the wilderness." They faced lightly clad, fast moving, hit-and-run insurgents who knew the terrain, who had lived in these forests and bogs all their lives. Lightning attacks, and then the Irish were gone again, melting into the wilderness. The worst of these ambushes came in 1598, when the English tried to resupply a garrison outpost in Ulster. The English mustered four thousand for the expedition. Fewer than two thousand struggled back to their base in Armagh. Their marshal was killed, so a junior officer, Edward Maria Wingfield's older brother, Thomas, led the bedraggled remnants home. Hundreds of soldiers—Irishmen under English arms—deserted and joined the king's Irish enemies. The native seemed perfectly suited to the wilds. Trailing behind each English column were long, vulnerable lines of supply, while the Gael wandered at will, living off the land. At home in the bogs and forests, the Irish soldier, draped in his capacious mantle, seemed impervious to the rain and cold. It may seem odd to us that Elizabethans thought Ireland's cold and wet and boggy lowlands and its dense forests were like a distant continent and foreign climate. Isn't London the city of fog and damp? Nevertheless, that was how Elizabethans experienced Ireland:

as fantastic, wild, intimidating, and as inscrutable as the Iowa farm boy of eighteen found the jungles and rice fields in the Mekong Delta.[32]

It was pretty clear to these conscripts that the higher-ups just did not understand what was going on in Ireland. They needed tactics that matched those of the Irish. They needed equipment suited to the terrain and climate. Forget English shoes and cloaks. What was needed were the crude, durable Irish brogues and most especially that gigantic, versatile garment, the Irish mantle, that served as roof and walls against the cold and wet. Back in London, Sir Robert Cecil disapproved. It was a contagion: by donning the Irish mantle, Cecil insisted, "our English shall become in apparel barbarous." By 1600 common sense prevailed, but Cecil's objection indicates London's persistent worry. English armies might melt away. English soldiers might abandon their posts. Just walk away into the woods.[33]

English soldiers deserted everywhere. Baron Mountjoy, Elizabeth's lord deputy of Ireland, was obliged to issue special directives against fornication with natives, harboring the enemy, selling one's arms, breaking ranks, and desertion. When Cecil accused him of being too soft, Mountjoy wrote back testily that he had just hanged sixteen English deserters. The Irish welcomed deserters, figuring it cost less to smuggle them back into Scotland than it did to kill them. The scheme was so successful that Queen Elizabeth appealed to King James of Scotland, who forbade his own subjects from helping these refugees of war resettle in his kingdom. It is not really clear what happened to the successful deserter. We have no direct record of their lives. The best evidence we have comes from these lofty attempts to outlaw or regulate their behavior. Some who abandoned that beleaguered garrison on the river Foyle walked into Irish camps and accepted free passage to Scotland. That the Irish could successfully publicize such an offer to the common garrison soldier tells us something of how porous the wall was between English and locals. No wonder Mountjoy had to ban fornication, which suggests that at least some English soldiers started Irish families. Some few even joined the Irish rebels and fought against the English. The nervous anxiety of poets like Spenser and statesmen like Cecil suggests that English soldiers were going native in alarming numbers.

Desertion is a ubiquitous phenomenon of war. It fills our literature. In World War I, Hemingway's Frederic Henry deserts in *A Farewell to Arms*. In World War II, Joseph Heller's Yossarian constantly fantasizes about desertion in *Catch-22*. Tim O'Brien's *Things They Carried* and *Going After Cacciato* explore desertion in Vietnam. Tens of thousands of American soldiers deserted each year during that conflict, most before they shipped out, but at least some of them deserted "in country," melting into Vietnamese society. Despite all of this cultural attention, very few scientists have studied the phenomenon. In 2002 the U.S. Army Research Institute issued a report, *What We Know About AWOL and Desertion: A Review of the Professional Literature for Policy Makers and Commanders*, which says that we do not know much. Very few of the deserters in that study actually left their posts in a war zone; most of the evidence comes from peacetime desertions stateside.[34] The report seems pitifully unequal to the task (for instance) of explaining the psychology behind the Bowe Bergdahl case in Afghanistan, in which an infantryman abandoned his post in hostile territory—just walked away into a desert controlled by the Taliban. You have to go all the way back to the Allied invasion of Italy in World War II to find a scientific study of combat desertion, an oft-cited paper by the army psychologist Arnold M. Rose that compared deserters to what he called "normals," or soldiers from the same units who did not go AWOL.

The men Rose studied did not desert for a specific reason, as they often did in the peacetime study. Desertion was a way of coping with a horrible environment, which surrounded the soldier's psyche like an atmospheric condition. Combat stress, especially a train of days of unrelieved battle, contributed. "Specific cases of mistreatment" by one's superiors could poison morale, cases in which officers administered what seemed to be arbitrary and officious discipline that was absurd in the context of lethal danger from the enemy. Rose cited a case in which a sergeant, fresh from combat, was "busted" by an officer for failing to polish his tin cup. Notably, the deserter was not the sergeant but someone else in his unit who witnessed the injustice. Lost confidence in the chain of command, a sense that officers have little interest in the foot soldiers' fate, disillusionment with the cause, a lack of hatred for the enemy—all of these hang like fog over the forward foxhole. The deserter is no more scared than other soldiers, but he thinks he is. He thinks other people are braver. He is more inclined to think he is going to be killed.

Strangely, the deserter is more likely to be a volunteer than a draftee. Rose speculated that volunteers found the reality of combat life to be far worse than what they expected, while the conscript had no illusions in the first place. The deserter slept less and ate less than "normals." Surprisingly, neither the initial shock of battle nor excessive exposure led to desertion in the Italy campaign. Most deserted between two and five months into their combat. Perhaps most surprising of all, the "normals" did not much resent deserters. They sympathized, and saved their scorn for people who faked medical conditions to avoid combat. In some cases deserters were even considered heroes, as if desertion expressed the communal disgust for the absurd and inhumane ways of the army. In sum, Rose found that all soldiers breathed the atmosphere of injustice and absurdity permeating combat life, but this pall most affected those soldiers who were sensitive and nervous.[35]

The differences between Americans in Italy in the 1940s and Brits in Ireland around 1600 are so plentiful that a strong dose of common sense has to shade the light of comparison. For one thing, American deserters were not trying to melt into the Italian village or city. They expected to be caught and punished. Desertion was an impermanent solution to the conditions of army life in combat. By contrast, Elizabethan deserters knew they would be hanged if they were caught. They meant either to live with the Irish or resettle in Scotland. Or perhaps they did not even think that far ahead—they just wanted to escape the hell of malnutrition, disease, and arbitrary injustice that was life in a remote English garrison. So it seems the attractiveness of life among native peoples must have played some role in 1600 that it did not in 1943. (It played a role in Vietnam, where at least a few American deserters stayed permanently.)[36] But armies are armies, and at least some of the stresses of combat and even of military life are probably universal. Whether escape is temporary or permanent, desertion is a rational response to the dangers and absurdity of life in an army during war. The culture of the particular army and the dangers of the particular war might darken the psychic storm clouds. We know that the English soldiers in Ireland suffered terribly dispiriting conditions.

James Fort was an Irish garrison set down in America. The numbers were smaller: the fort on the Foyle had four thousand soldiers, while the fort on the James had barely a hundred souls altogether. But the enemy in Virginia was less terrifying. In addition to their traditional battle-axes, spears, and bows, the Irish rebels had modern weapons from Spain or smuggled from Scotland and England: pikes and firearms like muskets and calivers.[37] By comparison, Native Americans fought with sticks and stones. That is not to say their arrows were not dangerous. About a week after the English started building the fort, forty warriors from the Paspahegh villages just upriver from Jamestown and on whose land they were squatting offered a deer as a token of friendship. While they lingered in the fort, sizing up the defenses, one of the English set up a demonstration of arms. He hung a wooden shield on a tree, and one of the warriors notched his arrow to the leather string of his hazelwood bow and let fly. The English were very impressed to see the arrow pierced the shield, which even a pistol could not do. But then the Englishman hung up a steel shield. This time, the arrow splintered harmlessly, and the Indian pulled out another arrow and bit it "in a great rage" before stomping off.[38] Clear to both English and Indian was that native weapons might be effective in ambush. Half a dozen arrows might bring a man down, and then the Indians could leap upon him and bash in his skull. Proper battles were another matter, and anyone who had faced the army of Tyrone in Ireland would smile at the primitive weapons and tactics of Virginia's "naturals." Englishmen could "journey" through the American wilderness with little fear, even when their numbers were relatively small—say a dozen or twenty well-armed men. If the English exercised reasonable caution, they had little to fear from the natives.

Wingfield was familiar with garrison duty, having served in both Drogheda and Dundalk in Ireland, and he was himself in the field facing the dreaded barbarian, Hugh O'Neill, the Earl of Tyrone.[39] Native Americans must have seemed feeble by comparison. A week after the big Indian attack was repulsed, the triangular palisade was up. The cannons were then mounted on the bulwark at each corner, and the surrounding long grass was mown down. James Fort became virtually impregnable. So long as they were fed and so long as no disease plagued the fort, the experienced soldier knew his garrison duty would be child's play.

But life was different for the commoners. No armor graced their modest wardrobes. They did not know how to use a pike or wield a sword, let alone fire a musket. They were not soldiers. They had not expected to live inside a garrison. Their first days in America were disorienting and scary, and if they were grateful for the troop of haughty gentlemen soldiers, that soon changed. Captain Newport and the ships left on June 22, 1607, leaving the colonists on Jamestown Island "verie bare and scantie of victualls." He promised to return by December, but the colony had provisions that would last only till about the first of October. Without the steadying weight of Newport's presence, things began to spin out of control. The squabbling council neglected the colonists' "own good and safety." Ill-fed as they were, exhausted from sentinel duty or imposed labor, living on the edge of a swamp with no source of clear freshwater, the English began to sicken. The air of Jamestown Island thickened into summer. Fetid smells rose from the swamps. Mosquitoes infiltrated the fort with the humid night air. The sweaty men who gave orders began to stink of dissension and cabal. The atmosphere of desertion descended.

Six weeks after Newport left, the deaths began. John Asbie on the sixth of August died of the "bloody flix." The veterans of Irish wars could interpret these signs of dysentery. Another laborer, George Flowre died three days later "of the swelling." A week later the gentlemen began to die. Francis Midwinter went first. Then the councillors got sick: Martin, Smith, then Gosnold and Ratcliffe. Even today, scholars are not sure exactly what disease plagued the fort. Malaria has been ruled out. Typhoid and pellagra are candidates. A diet of nothing but corn would cause pellagra, a vitamin deficiency that manifests in muscle pain, apathy, and despair, which were symptoms reported at Jamestown. Whatever it was, so many people sickened that "the living were scarce able to bury the dead." But bury them they did, a weary train of funerals held within the palisade, lest the Indians see the thinning of their ranks. James Fort became a necropolis.[40]

Bartholomew Gosnold's death shattered the colony. Loyal friend of John Smith, loyal nephew of President Wingfield, Gosnold had knotted the council's factions together. Wingfield attributed a "great part" of the government's "good success" to Gosnold, and on August 22, 1607, he was "honourably buried" and mourned by everyone. The sick and indolent roused themselves to fire volley after volley of small shot from the cannons. As the echo of the guns died in the forest to one side and on the open water to the other, the knot of concord unwound. The factions of the council resumed eyeing each other's throats. President Wingfield "committed" Kendall "to prison" for sowing discord. He then informed the rest of the council that he and Gosnold had been secretly reserving sack and aqua vitae "and other preservatives for our health" against "such extremities as might fall upon us." Smith and the other councillors were outraged and suspected that Wingfield and his "associates" treated the public stores as a private stock. Wingfield confronted Smith, called him a liar, and said it was beneath the dignity of a gentleman to associate with him.[41]

As the gentlemen played their intrigues, squabbled over a keg of wine, and bristled at affronts to their conceit, as the sick crouched under rotting tents and the death toll rose, as the honeycomb of graves crowded the parade ground inside the fort, the gentlemen soldiers grew more and more frightened of the Indians. Wingfield thought they could survive only so long as they hid their "weakness carefully from the savages." Percy expected the devil-worshippers to swarm over the walls at any moment and overwhelm the garrison. Smith was braced for the assault.[42]

Curiously, as terror spread through the soldiers, fear fell like scales from the eyes of the common settlers. They made friends with the Indians. Evidence of familiarity, trade, intercourse, and friendships lurks on the edges of the narratives. John Smith tells us that in May, before Newport sailed back to England, they left "a mariner in pawn with the Indians for a guide of theirs." This man lived with the Indians at least for several days, but we never hear about him again. His return was not worth noting. Barely a week after they had landed at Jamestown, Percy and three or four others followed a path that reminded Percy of a wilderness trail in Ireland till they came to a "savage town," where they stayed for "a while" to eat strawberries. One of the villagers showed them round the gardens and gave them tobacco. The episode suggests how normal it was for English to wander from the camp, meet Indians, and exchange pleasantries and tokens of friendship.[43]

The English appointed a "cape merchant," an official through whom all trade was supposed to flow, but the palisades held European goods about as well as a sieve holds water. Even before Newport departed for England, Wingfield was already complaining that sailors and settlers alike were heading into the woods to harvest sassafras, which had medicinal purposes back in England. They spoiled Company tools, and the commoners were stealing their own labor, which belonged to the Company, all for private gain, because the sassafras was smuggled onto the ships. Wingfield complained that the smuggled supply would ruin the Company's profit by flooding the market and driving down prices.[44] We know that later a black market flourished beneath the supposed monopoly on trade that the Company tried to impose. The Indians were fascinated with the littlest thing—a bead, a button, a mirror, a razor, a knife, a cup—and the common Englishman was eager to trade for food.

Even the odd ambush on the stray Englishman, which obviously betokened the hostility of some Indians, indicated the friendliness of others. It would have been a bold Englishman indeed to defecate outside the palisade if he thought the woods were full of nothing but hostiles. Two sailors were ambushed on a Saturday. On Sunday, two unarmed Indians came into camp, one of whom had already befriended the English. He named four tribes that wanted peaceful relations, and he warned them against five others.[45] Throughout the summer, the English were communicating with Indians far more promiscuously than conscripts in any Irish garrison communicated with the natives of that country.

By early September, fewer than six of the gentlemen soldiers were well enough to stand guard duty on the bulwarks. Swellings, fluxes, and burning fevers assailed them. The daily ration for five men had sunk to a can of barley soaked in water. They had not yet dug a well, so their water came from the river, salty at high tide and slimy at low. Skirmishes with the Indians continued. All in all, forty-six of their company died by the end of the year. As early as August, colonists were slipping through the palisade and walking into the woods to go live with the Indians.

President Wingfield decreed that the English settlers needed "passports" to "travel abroad" in Virginia, a policy he learned in the Irish wars: only a passport might allow soldiers to leave their garrison. But it didn't work. People left at will. Wingfield called them "runagates," which, according to a 1611 dictionary, was someone who had "renounced his religion or country." In a report published in 1614, Samuel Purchas called Wingfield's renegades "fugitiues," as if leaving the garrison were a crime, and in the eyes of the Company it was a crime, for they had deserted. They were doing the same thing that those foot soldiers on the river Foyle had done when they walked away from their garrison a couple of years earlier.[46]

We have no record from the point of view of the renegades themselves. We do not know if they thought they had renounced anything. It seems unlikely. It is doubtful they even imagined they were deserters. They were not soldiers. They had no place in any military command. Fugitives? Fugitives from what? Were they not free Englishmen? Did free men need permission to walk beyond a palisade?

The bricklayers and tailors and common laborers must have felt abandoned by the Company. Even if Newport were to keep his promise, he was not returning till December. Each day in August the starving in Jamestown buried the dead. They would never make it to December. They could stay in the garrison and consign their fate to the Company's squabbling leaders, or they could take their lives into their own hands. Some went to the Paspahegh villages closest to Jamestown, which had at times been hostile and at times friendly. Others escaped to several villages farther away, drawing on connections they must have made in June and July. William White, a laborer, went about ten miles up and across the river to live with the Quiyoughcohannock.

White was one of thirteen men named as "laborers." His story was probably not unique, but it is the only testimony we have from the mouth of a commoner who deserted Jamestown. He had been welcomed into the Indian village and lived with them long enough to study their customs. For instance, White reported that everyone older than ten years bathed every morning in the river and paid homage to the rising and setting sun. He learned something about their theology, and they even allowed him to witness an elaborate fertility rite, days of dancing and ritual, painted bodies, chant and song, at the center of which was a mock sacrifice of fourteen of the village's "well fauoured children" to the god Oke. (Percy, stubbornly prejudiced, glossed all references to Algonquian gods with a knowing aside: the "Diuell.")[47]

The common settlers, apparently, were less frightened of the Indians than of staying in the fort. That should come as no surprise. Discipline in Jamestown was so shattered, the chain of command proved itself so detached from reality and indifferent to the welfare of the commoners, that there was very little to hold anyone inside the fort. Even if he disapproved, Wingfield seems to have done nothing to stop people from leaving. Desertion seems rational enough. "In that extremitie of miserie" that was James Fort, one account reported, deserters were attracted to the "plentie" they found in the native villages. Nevertheless, men like Wingfield and Percy could not comprehend it. You might as well hurl your soul into damnation. As late as September, Percy still thought of the Indians as "vild and cruel pagans" thirsting for English blood.[48] Perhaps they did—for some English blood. Just as the English could appreciate that some tribes were friendlier than others, so the Indians must have comprehended that two kinds of English populated the fort. There were soldiers, and there were men who had no armor and no weapons and posed no threat. If Percy was still regarding Indians as monsters, it seems that by August the commoners among the English had good reason to think otherwise.

Percy was not alone. Wingfield thought the Indians would have slaughtered the English if they had discovered how weak the colony was in August and September. But the Indians knew exactly how vulnerable the fort was. They might not have been able to see over the palisade. They couldn't count the graves. But who needed to see inside the fort when skin and bones stumbled through the woods begging for food and shelter? The condition of the "renegades" would have taught the Indians all they needed to know about the enfeebled fort. The Indians must have known they could easily overwhelm the English. Despite the tenacity of this prejudice among the soldiers— that the "savages" thirsted for their blood—most evidence points to the extraordinary goodwill of the natives. They treated the deserters well, feeding them, housing them, and welcoming them into the circle of village life, ritual, and custom. Even Wingfield was obliged to concede that "we found them no cannibals."[49]

By mid-September, the house of cards could have been knocked over with slightest breath of hostility. Thirty or forty warriors climbing over the palisade at dawn would have surprised the garrison and easily dispatched its invalid defenders. The Indians did approach the fort. They came to the very gate of the palisade. But they did not climb over, carrying those wretched wooden swords studded with sharp shells. The Indians brought food. They carried bread, corn, fish, and meat "in great plenty." John Smith was so shocked, he thought that God must have moved the Indians to bring them corn. To Percy, this beneficence was so unexpected, so inexplicable, so out of native character, that only God's intervention could explain it. "It pleased God . . . to send those people which were our mortal enemies to relieve us with victuals," he explained. The gesture made so little sense to the Company's men that they thought it was a miracle. Wingfield, too, thought their deliverance was part of God's generosity, which chose to manifest itself through the most unlikely of instruments, the hostile Indians.[50]

A good portion of American identity has been attributed to this kind of willful misunderstanding. Up and down the Atlantic seaboard, the English colonists found themselves faced with hostile Indians, and such danger fostered a garrison mentality. Beyond the palisade, the thinking went, the forces of the devil, the "cruel pagans," roamed in the dark woods. And such an attitude naturally contributed to a sense that the people *inside* the palisade were God's chosen. Adjusting one's mind to this condition "Americanized" the European. As one historian put it, "a defensive garrison mentality . . . reinforced the colonists' sense of being a chosen if momentarily abandoned people."[51] Thirteen years before the Pilgrims, Englishmen were already placing themselves at the center of an eschatological history. At least in regard to the people who recorded the early history—Percy, Wingfield, and Smith—this seems to be true. But this thesis about American identity ignores that there is a second, very different kind of "garrison mentality" among many foot soldiers, especially in garrisons that deteriorate as thoroughly as Jamestown did. Those who deserted the fort did not see the Indians as devils, nor did they see themselves as God's chosen people.

The deserters certainly felt abandoned, but they did not retreat into the fortress of self-righteousness. They saw their Indian neighbors as collaborators, benefactors, a way out of the hell that "civilization" had become. They knew who saved the fort, and it wasn't God. The deserters persuaded the Indians to come to the Englishmen's aid. The supposedly miraculous generosity of the Indians coincided with the return of several deserters, a fact that none of the Company's men appreciated. It must have been their good embassy and friendliness or simply their pleas to common humanity that moved the Indians to share their stores of food. These men were no renegades. They had not renounced Christianity for paganism. They had deserted Jamestown merely to save themselves. They took command of their own lives, claimed the right to determine their own fates, and they saw surer survival in places like Quiyoughcohannock than in James Fort. The suffering did not end with their return. Englishmen still died, three more within the week of the Indians' gift. But the "extremitie of miserie" was over.

### THE FIRST TRIUMVIRATE

While hunger would return in periodic intervals for the next several months, the native bounty revived the English gentlemen sufficiently to resume their intrigues. Captain Ratcliffe brandished trumped-up charges against President Wingfield. Backed by the remaining councillors, John Smith and John Martin, he ordered the president's arrest. Wingfield's sword stayed in its scabbard. His personal retainers put up no fight. On the way to the pinnace, which was serving as a makeshift jail, he quoted the colony's constitutions, insisting this proceeding was illegal, a coup d'état, and that the council had made itself a tyrannical "triumvirate."[52] The pinnace was tied to a tree on the bluff just a stone's throw from the palisade, and Wingfield joined the councillor that he himself had arrested, George Kendall. But the triumvirate set Kendall free to move out of the boat and into the fort, although he was not allowed to carry a weapon, a continual humiliation for someone of his status. Smith, who at Wingfield's insistence had spent so many weeks manacled belowdecks in the *Susan Constant*, must have relished the irony.

President Ratcliffe and Martin, two of the remaining four councillors, again took ill, so John Smith was assigned to the all-important position of "cape merchant." The cape merchant was supposed to direct trade—a kind of customs officer charged with enforcing the

Company's monopoly and supervising public supplies. On paper,
the cape merchant assured the
Company of the lion's share of
Virginia's resources. In reality, with
the colony near extinction, the cape
merchant was in charge of finding
food. So Smith sailed downriver to
Kecoughtan, the Indian village at
the tip of peninsula where the James
River converges into Chesapeake
Bay. Eighteen houses occupied three
acres of ground surrounded by farms
and a pleasant plain. Smith secured
sixteen bushels of corn. A couple of
canoes approached the English from
across the five miles of water at the

President Wingfield's
deposition in Jamestown as
illustrated in Willian Cullen
Bryant's 1876 *A Popular
History of the United States.*

mouth of the river to ask if they could trade next. All in all, Smith
brought thirty bushels of corn back to the garrison. Trade missions
upriver to the mercurial Paspaheghs were less successful. A grudging
trade session nearly ended in a melee and yielded but ten more bushels.[53]

By this time, perhaps because of Smith's increased authority, the
rotting tents had been replaced with cabins. Nevertheless, the old
mood of indiscipline lingered in the camp. According to Smith,
"most of our chiefest men" were "either sick or discontented," while the
rest of the garrison were "in such despair as they would rather starve
and rot with idleness, than be persuaded to do anything for their own
relief without constraint."[54] Historians used to find a facile lesson
about aristocratic greed and privilege in the idleness at Jamestown.
Gentlemen would rather starve than work. They drew this moral to
celebrate the social leveling of American democracy, and that interpretation of events tended to lionize Smith as the "first American," a

self-made man preferring meritocracy to aristocracy. In 1979, Karen Ordahl Kupperman's fine study of the garrison's poor diet complicated that story. She asserted, quite persuasively, that despair and lethargy were symptoms of malnutrition. Behavior so clearly at odds with their own interests and at odds even with their self-preservation were symptoms of disease brought on by a corn-dominated diet.[55] But neither of these interpretations takes into account the sharp distinction in rank between the gentlemen soldiers and the other settlers, between Smith's "chiefest men" and those he called "the rest." Two different kinds of "idleness" plagued the fort. The idleness of the gentlemen soldiers conformed to English army discipline, which separated officers from foot soldiers. Their discontentedness might have displeased Smith, but he tolerated it. In the summer of 1607, only "the rest" of the settlers, the commoners, were "constrained" to work. *Constrained* here means *coerced*. These common laborers suffered the virtual slavery that English conscripts suffered in remote Irish garrisons, and their "idleness," like the broken shovels and desertions in Ireland, repudiated the Company's authority over their lives. The common settlers might have freely agreed to join the Virginia expedition, but they never signed up for the miseries of James Fort. They were not foot soldiers. They never consented to military discipline. And they never imagined that they would be the Company's slaves.

Had Smith been in charge from the beginning, things might have gone another way. Had the council followed sensible policies that provided a measure of comfort, safety, and food, the summer's squalor might have been avoided. The settlement would have resembled a town more than a garrison. Then the atmosphere of desertion would not have settled upon the lowest inhabitants. They might have retained some confidence in the councillors and in the "principal men," the gentlemen, that the council seemed to serve. By September things had deteriorated too far. Not even Smith, talented and resourceful as he was, could restore respect for the Company. To many commoners he was hardly distinguishable from the other conniving, conspiring, backstabbing, incompetent gentlemen who were the Company's officers.

Ratcliffe recovered. Martin recovered. And meanwhile Smith explored the Chickahominy River. This "discovery" was a sort of insubordination. He had been told to go up the James River all the way to its head in order to trade with Powhatan, the highest village they had visited with Captain Newport back in May. But Smith turned into the Chickahominy where it emptied into the James, went up that tributary, and discovered nearly a dozen villages full of Indians so eager to trade that they swarmed the English with their canoes. Shallow drafted as it was, the oceangoing pinnace proved too big for the Chickahominy, running aground near the mouth of the river. Smith and eight others went up in the barge, a small vessel they could use to ferry cargo to the larger boat. Hundreds of Indians poured out of their village, delighted with the sight of the nine Englishmen rowing up their river. They begged the English to fire off their guns so they could hear the thunder and see the birds burst from the trees into the sky, their clouds of wings wheeling on the echoes of the shots. Smith made the journey twice, bringing back "7 or 8 hogs-heads" of corn, which blunted the accusations of cowardice. Some, apparently, still grumbled that he was too scared to go up to Powhatan.[56]

Those grumblers almost certainly were other gentlemen soldiers. One faction, headed by President Ratcliffe and Captain Archer, wanted to sail the pinnace back to England to get supplies, leaving a further-diminished garrison in Virginia. The other group, headed by councillors Smith and Martin, wanted the pinnace to trade upriver and support further explorations. While these groups debated, dissension among the lowly commoners was coalescing into a plan of rebellion. The details of this plot were never recorded, but we can surmise that the mutineers would have taken the pinnace by force and fled the colony, perhaps to the Spanish West Indies. But a stray spark lit the fuse of rebellion before their muskets were ready.

President Ratcliffe strode up to the blacksmith one day in late November to harangue him for some "misdemeanor." The smithy, James Read, had no patience for the man's bloody cursing. Seven months in Virginia, and nearly half the colony dead and buried, a miserable diet of corn and more corn, and all the labor done by workingmen while their betters did nothing but fight over who got to give the orders. What was the real difference between a workingman and this embroidered gentleman? The flux bled all, rich or poor, did it not? James Read would have no more of it. The blacksmith cursed the president. Words spiraled higher. Ratcliffe, a soldier, may or may not have been armed. Read certainly was, with the tools of his trade, a great heavy hammer or tongs. He threatened to strike or actually tried to strike the president, but before he could do much more than raise an arm, he was grabbed by some men of the court of guard. Read was not much concerned. What could Ratcliffe do to him when so many sympathized with the common cause? He smiled through his hasty trial. A jury of gentlemen returned a verdict of guilty and a sentence of death. Even as he approached the ladder he would climb to the hangman's noose, Read expected to be rescued. He knew that the discontented would rise up. Almost to the last minute he was unrepentant and defiant. But when he put his foot upon the ladder, he realized that he had miscalculated the courage of his confederates. No one spoke up for him. No gang of mutineers swarmed between him and the executioners. Finally, fear betrayed him, and then Read broke down. He would not give his life for men who would not risk theirs. He begged Ratcliffe to forgive him. Confessions poured out of him. He revealed a conspiracy, and at its center was the deposed councillor, George Kendall. Ratcliffe hastily conducted another trial and pronounced another sentence of death. The rest of the would-be mutineers, including the pardoned blacksmith, dirty and hungry and dispirited, watched the court of guard grimly proceed. Kendall was no commoner to be hoisted up a ladder and hanged. He was a gentleman. The other gentlemen stood him up against a squad of muskets, and they fired a volley into his chest.[57] Thus to mutineers. Thus to anyone who would challenge the president. Henceforth, do what you are told. Read went back to the forge, humbled, his head down, hammer clanging on anvil.

There was much work for him to do. John Smith needed him to manufacture more iron and copper goods for trading on the Chickahominy River. Just a day or two after Kendall's execution, Smith and eight bargemen went upriver a third time, beyond the dozen villages, all the way to Apocant, the "highest town" on the Chickahominy, where the stream was only six feet deep at low tide. They sawed through a tree trunk that had fallen across the water and continued on. They found no villages above Apocant, "only a vast and wild wilderness." Smith thought they were on the verge of finding the river's source, which he thought might be a lake, and so he pushed on. Even the barge was too big, so he hired a canoe with two Indian guides and sent the barge back down to Apocant with seven of the men. Smith, two English, and two native guides paddled farther up the narrow and shady stream.[58]

The bargemen waited. They had orders not to go ashore. The townspeople of Apocant must have wondered at that sudden unfriendliness. No doubt they rowed out to the barge in their own canoes. But they could talk only with gestures and a few quicklearned words. John Smith, a gifted linguist, was already picking up the language, but he was gone. Maybe the bargemen engaged in some private trading. If they kept it discreet, Smith, the cape merchant, might not notice when he returned. The seven men still waited. But

John Smith never came back out of the vast wilderness. When the bargemen could wait no longer, they rowed back downstream to the James River and thence to the fort.

Only two councillors remained. Newport was in England. Gosnold had died. Wingfield was deposed. Kendall had been killed. And now John Smith was gone. John Ratcliffe and John Martin pondered the situation. Smith was either dead, ambushed somewhere in the hinterland, or had done what so many of the commoners already had: gone renegade.

## CHAPTER TWO

### Tsenacomoco

**The day the English arrived** on the Chesapeake, messengers from the Nansemond district on the south side of the Powhatan River and from the Kecoughtan district on the north side rushed to report what they had seen. They followed well-worn paths between villages till they came to the Pamunkey River, and the villages there ferried them across the water in dugout canoes. After half a day of travel, they came into Werowocomoco, the "town of the weroance," the highest chief of all, Wahunsonacock. They found Wahunsonacock in his everyday attire, which is to say wearing nothing but a small apron in front and with his naked buttocks behind. Rich ornaments in his ears or fastened in his hair might have marked him as a man of rank. Unlike other men, he wore his hair unbraided, and he allowed the few sprouting hairs on his lip and chin to grow. Except for these distinctions, he dressed no differently from any warrior. But there was no mistaking him. Tall, strong-limbed, gray-haired, he carried a sour look on his round face, and everyone who saw him feared to ignite the slightest displeasure in his eye. The glamour of a demigod hung about his shoulders. He had been raised from childhood to be a weroance, and so his posture and bearing bespoke authority. Nobility shone from him. He expected deference. He expected obedience. Both were given to him spontaneously.[1]

The message was quick to deliver.

*European ships are in the bay. They have landed in Nansemond. They were roaming this very day over the district of Kecoughtan.*

Had there been any contact?

*A brief skirmish, in which they fired their guns*, Wahunsonacock would have learned, *but otherwise we have kept out of sight.*

It was the type of news that came perhaps twice in a decade: not so unusual as to be shocking, but rare enough to alarm the entire country. Europeans required handling. They often killed or kidnapped people. On the other hand, they had valuable tools they might trade. Wahunsonacock would have summoned his advisors. It would have taken a day or two for representatives from the several districts to travel to Werowocomoco, and of course we have no record at all of Wahunsonacock's council, but using other narratives and anthropological evidence we can reasonably imagine some aspects of the scene. Advisors coming into the capital would have first encountered one of his personal corps du guard. Four outer sentries stood an arrow's shot away from the chief, and "forty or fifty of the tallest men his Country doth afford" stood nearer to him. These might not have attended him daily, but the arrival of the ships would have warranted their deployment. The advisor arriving in Werowocomoco would have been led into a big house and would wind his way through curving corridors forty or fifty yards long before coming to the inner chamber where the chief conducted official business.[2]

Several of Wahunsonacock's brothers and sons and sons-in-law would have been there. Opitchapam, heir to the throne, the man whom Powhatan had installed as chief of the numerous Pamunkeys, who lived high on the freshwater of that river, beyond the salty tides. Opechancanough, the next brother in line, and chief of the Youghtenunds, lived even farther up river, on the frontier, and thus was among the most militant and vigilant of the Powhatans. He was the Powhatan's war chief. Kekataugh was a third brother and heir who would die young. The weroances of other principal towns would have been there, especially Nansemond, Kecoughtan, and Paspahegh.[3]

Reclining on a bench heaped with mats, Wahunsonacock was flanked by his wives, one at his feet and another at his head. Winganuske, one of "a dozen wives" who lived in Werowocomoco, was perhaps no more than twelve or thirteen years old: Powhatan girls were marriageable as soon as they first menstruated. She

Wahunsonacock sitting in state. Detail from John Smith's *Generall Historie*, 1624.

"must have had some charisma," the anthropologist Helen Rountree suggests, for she charmed Wahunsonacock so successfully that he did not later discard her as he dismissed most other wives eventually. Her brother, Machumps, was probably there, and another promising youth, an intellectual protégé called Namontack. Powhatan trusted Namontack's loyalty as if he were kin, and the boy's intelligence, subtlety, and circumspection prompted Wahunsonacock to school him in the craft of diplomacy. Neither of these young men was old enough or experienced enough to contribute to the public debate, but they were close enough to the chief to hear the various advice and to watch the great ruler's frowning face as he listened to the troubling news. One after another, from youngest to oldest, the councillors had their say, priests with their skills of divination commanding even more attention than the chiefs. As each person spoke, everyone listened attentively. No one interrupted. The rules were as rigid, though simpler, than *Robert's Rules of Order*. Every councillor had his say.[4]

Wahunsonacock considered it all carefully, for his decisions in the coming weeks would affect the lives of a nation.

## TSENACOMOCO

Europeans arriving to settle in America imagined they had landed in a wilderness. The narratives of the Jamestown and Plymouth Plantations bear this out, and their first impressions lasted. As late as the 1960s, the Wilderness Act declared that Indians left no trace on the land: "the imprint of man's work" was so slight as to be "substantially unnoticeable."[5] Our own propaganda uses Indians to symbolize perfect human harmony with nature, an example of how people can share in the bounty of a wilderness without altering it.

In 2005, Charles C. Mann, a writer for *Science* magazine and a science correspondent for the *Atlantic Monthly*, detonated a bomb under the wilderness myth. He published a book he titled *1491: New Revelations of the Americas Before Columbus*, which references the last year before that mingling of flora and fauna, microbes, diseases, gold, and gunpowder that we now call the "Columbian Exchange." Mann's thesis was simple and provocative: the continents of North and South America and the islands of the Caribbean that looked so wild to European settlers were in reality "completely humanized landscape[s]." The supposedly "primeval" forest "was not the vast, silent, unbroken, impenetrable and dense tangle of trees beloved by so many writers in their romantic accounts of the forest wilderness," according to the natural historian, Michael Williams. To take Virginia, for example, Williams tells us that "selective Indian burning" created unnatural forests of "large, widely spaced trees, few shrubs, and much grass and herbage." Meadows of "blackberries, raspberries, and other gatherable foods," explained William Cronin, even the gigantic strawberries that George Percy marveled at as he tramped through the woods on April 26, 1607, flourished because Indians were managing the forests.[6]

According to Mann, later Europeans did encounter genuine wilderness, but that was because early contacts annihilated nearly one hundred million Native Americans. Old World diseases and conquistadors so obliterated native communities that the New World forests looked much wilder in 1750 than they had two and a half centuries earlier, in 1492. Native Americans were what Mann calls a "keystone species," the pinnacle stone in the environment's artificial architecture. Indians had regulated the landscape so thoroughly and for so long that an artificial norm had established itself: plants adapted themselves to the human civilization. For instance, vulnerable trees burned out while fire-resistant trees survived in the forests where Indians cleared the underbrush. Populations of animals redistributed themselves according to the pressures of human beings. In the coastal plains of Virginia, for example, human hunting pushed bears nearer to the ocean, while deer flourished farther away, and neither were seen much at all in the more densely populated, middle regions of the Chesapeake.

Whenever Indians suddenly disappeared from a region, the ecological structure collapsed, disorganized itself, and entered a riotous period while natural selection struggled toward a new equilibrium. Species long shaded by human activity flourished in the sudden sunlight. The American passenger pigeon is one example. When one flock flew overhead, "the light of noon-day," the early naturalist John James Audubon wrote, "was obscured as if by an eclipse." Another nineteenth-century ornithologist estimated that one out of every four birds in America was a passenger pigeon. Pioneers took these numbers as a sign of America's magnificent bounty, but the millions upon millions of pigeons were really a sign of riot. A once-humanized ecosystem had collapsed, and nature was in the process of reorganizing the distribution of plants and animals. Forests that had been maintained almost as groves by the Indians suddenly filled up with underbrush, which favored the pigeons, and until some predator established itself, their numbers were uncontained. Europeans settling the continent's interior generally saw the landscape a generation or so after the Indians disappeared. It was not a primeval land undisturbed since the last ice age. It was a suddenly out-of-balance ecology reacting to an absence of humanity.[7]

Mann's book was not really revolutionary. It popularized what had become the new consensus among anthropologists, archaeologists, linguists, historians, geneticists, etc. Beginning in 1970s and 1980s, scholars began to reconstruct history from the perspective of Native Americans—so successfully that, by 2003, Joyce Chaplin could retrospectively identify "new Indian history" as one of "the most important developments in early American history." Mann interviewed many of those scholars and read most of their work. The consensus now is that pre-Columbian America was full of people who had thoroughly tamed the wilderness. The earliest settlers, like the English in Virginia, moved into a landscape that already had been civilized for human habitation. Historians dispute how many people lived in the Americas, and many do not think that it was as high as one hundred million people, but today they agree that the population's impact on the landscape was far greater than we used to believe.[8]

Tsenacomoco, the chiefdom governed by Wahunsonacock, was large by Algonquian standards. It stretched across most of the area surrounding the three southernmost rivers in the bay, what are now called the James, the York, and the Rappahannock, and it extended to the southern bank of the Potomac, although it did not cross that river. The three peninsulas formed by these rivers, called today the Lower or Virginia Peninsula, the Middle Peninsula, and the Northern Neck, were all part of Tsenacomoco, as well as most of the land inward as far as the "fall line." (The fall line is where the effluvial plains along the East Coast give way to the rocky foothills. Rapids and waterfalls make the rivers unnavigable at this point, and so it forms not only a geological but geographic line that runs roughly parallel to the mountains. State capitals from South Carolina to New York sit on the fall line.) Across the bay, Tsenacomoco included the Eastern Shore, that long peninsular barrier between the Atlantic Ocean and the bay itself.

At about six thousand square miles, it was almost twice as big as England's largest county, North Yorkshire, and forty times the size of Rutland, England's smallest county. In 1600, the area that North Yorkshire now encompasses supported over a hundred thousand inhabitants. Rutland had nearly thirteen thousand inhabitants. That's a density of about ninety people per square mile.[9] The low estimates for the population of Tsenacomoco are about the same as Rutland, and the less cautious guesses go as high as thirty thousand. Either way, from an English perspective, the land seemed almost empty. On average, only about three or four people per square mile lived in Tsenacomoco. By North Yorkshire numbers, Tsenacomoco could support ten times the population it did. It makes sense that the English thought they were settling a virtual wilderness. Yet it was not. From the Indians' perspective, Tsenacomoco was full of people.[10]

Those people were living in the Stone Age. Although iron tools like knives and hatches were not entirely unknown, they were rare and obtained indirectly from the Spanish to the south or the French to the north.[11] Other than copper, which the Algonquians obtained in trade from Indians closer to the mountains and which was used ornamentally as a token of high status, Indians on the Chesapeake rarely saw or touched metal. Even stone tools were highly valued, for most of Tsenacomoco was virtually devoid of rocks. Many tools were made of shell or bone. Without plows and pack animals to draw straight lines, tilled fields looked haphazard, each planting done laboriously by hand, a stick-drilled hole, a pile of scraped-up dirt. They manufactured arrowheads out of turkey spurs, oyster shells, bird bills, sharp bone, and deer antlers. They boiled deer antlers down into a gelatinous glue to fix the arrowheads to the shafts. Animals killed on

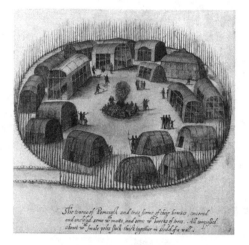

Algonquian village by Theodore
de Bry. An illustration in Thomas
Hariot's 1588 book *A Briefe and
True Report of the New Found Land
of Virginia.*

the hunt—from squirrels to bears—were butchered with fire-hardened
clam shells or beaver teeth. The skins of deer were scraped with shells.
They used deer gut, hemp, bark bast, and other natural fibers to spin
cordage, with which they lashed the beams of their houses and made
bowstrings, fishing lines (with hooks of splintered bone), and even
fishing nets. Baskets of all sorts were woven from corn husks, reeds,
silk grass, and bark. They used coils of clay, "tempered with crushed
shell," to fashion ceramic cooking pots.[12]

By far the biggest objects they manufactured were canoes.
These were massive tree trunks dug out laboriously by burning the
exposed wood with charcoal and then scraping the softened ash
away with stones or shells. The process had to be repeated and
repeated to hollow out the log and round the bottom, but the finished
products impressed even the English. "The biggest canoes," Rountree reports, "were about four feet deep and up to fifty feet long."
Though far clumsier and slower than the birch-bark canoes found in
northern climates, they were remarkably stable and nearly impossible to capsize, even when loaded with forty men. Most canoes were
smaller, with room for ten to thirty men "with baggage." Given the
waterborne nature of native society and how much time went into

their construction, the canoes pulled up on the shore below each village were their most prized commodities—far more valuable, for instance, than their houses.[13]

The houses were roomy and smoky and ingeniously constructed. Saplings between two and four inches in diameter were sunk into the ground in roughly parallel lines, then bent toward each other till they met in an arch and could be lashed together with cords. Horizontal bars were lashed across these arcs for stability, framing an airy and stable scaffold. To finish the job, a thin skin made of mats or bark was tied to the frame. The windiest rain was no bother: Indian houses leaked less than a well-made English house. They were dark inside. No windows. Reed or deerskin flaps covered the square doors at opposite ends. A hole in the roof center let out smoke from the hearth fire, which was always kindled. But the smoke meandered on its way. No chimneys helped draw it outside. The houses ranged from fourteen and a half feet to thirty-one feet on the long axis, and from ten to almost fifteen feet wide. The larger houses had low benches built along the long walls, perhaps for sleeping. The taller houses had overhead platforms or lofts.

Archaeologists have dug up three Indian settlements, one near Jamestown, a "dispersed" village of neighboring Paspahegh Indians. Almost certainly this was a hamlet frequented by English, one of the first places that deserters would have passed through on their way to sanctuary. Forty-eight structures have been found—probably not all of them houses, but enough to call this a prosperous satellite village of Paspahegh's main town, where their chief would have lived. As in most Tsenacomocoan villages, houses were arranged haphazardly, wherever a family chose to build. The structures run for a couple of hundred feet along the bank of the Chickahominy River, near where it feeds into the James River. The village was situated about ten to fifteen feet above the river's high tide on a natural terrace about 150 feet from the water.

On this terrace of land, the Indians cleared not just the under-growth but most of the trees themselves, largely pine, in order to plant fields of corn, beans, and squash. They planted in cycles: after four years the field was left alone, allowing barley, cordage plants, raspberries, and blackberries to grow in the first fallow seasons. Later came cherries, grapes, ground nuts, wild potatoes, sassafras, and persimmon. Below the village and its fields was the marshland, which provided the all-important tuckahoe, a wild potato. Muskrats, raccoons, turtles, and birds were hunted in the marshes, and the Indians harvested reeds to construct their versatile mats, which sheathed the houses and were spread on the ground for sitting and work spaces. Below the marshes was the river, which provided the main line of communication and transport—the Indian highways, so to speak. The Paspaheghs, for instance, ate a lot of oysters, which means they must have traveled ten miles or more downriver to the saltier tidal banks, where they either harvested oysters themselves or traded with their Kecoughtan neighbors. Rivers also provided crabs, crayfish, ducks, geese, beaver, and otter. The Paspaheghs staked weirs in the shallows to catch fish. Analysis of teeth and bones exhumed at this site indicate they ate mostly cultivated plants and seafood: besides oysters, they dined on turtles, catfish, gar, striped bass, and maybe the monstrous sturgeon, which could grow up to 150 pounds. They domesticated no animals other than dogs, so all of their meat came from hunting and fishing.

Above the terrace on which stood the town and fields, the ground rose up another ten to thirty-five feet, where the mature hardwood trees grew. Most villages in Tsenacomoco backed up to deciduous forest upland that provided firewood, cedar bark, acorns, walnuts, hickory, beech, chestnuts, chinquapins, and medicinal herbs. The bark of oaks and elms was used to make shingles, and the saplings provided the scaffolding of their structures. These forests had been cleared by fire. John Smith marveled that a man could ride a horse at a gallop through the forests surrounding the Chesapeake Bay. Twenty years later, another Englishman insisted that an English coach drawn by four horses could easily navigate between the trees. "Parklike" was how the historian Edmund S. Morgan described the woods.[14]

Nuclear families were the foundation of their society. Houses, for instance, belonged to families. Property was owned by both men and women, and although evidence is scant, Helen Rountree argues persuasively that the Tenacomocoan society was not patrilineal. When a father died, his daughters and wives had as big a share of his goods as his sons, and his house itself went to "the wife he liketh best." Nor were families defined as carefully as in English culture. Wives and husbands were not exclusive sexual partners. Maternity was relevant and obvious but paternity was neither. Villages probably were organized at least loosely along some kinship relations, with each village having an animal totem that served—at least in the English interpretation—as a sort of family coat of arms. Men married women from other villages, and wives left their own families to live with their husbands' people. The highest chiefdoms were passed from mother to oldest son, thence to younger brothers, and then to sisters. They passed from one generation to the next through those sisters to their children.[15]

In common parlance, territory was divided among politically distinct "tribes," although anthropologists bristle at the implications of that term. Rountree prefers "group."[16] The Paspahegh group occupied a section of the Lower Peninsula. Farther up the Chickahominy River, they were bound by the group with the same name as the river. Farther down the peninsula, they bumped into Kecoughtan. Over on the other side of the peninsula, hugging the bank of the York River, were the Chiskiak. Across the James River were the Quiyoughcohannock. Each of these groups had its principal town, generally much larger than the village described above. The principal towns had their own councils and chief, who reigned over all the villages and hamlets of the group. A few hundred people might make up the whole group, or a couple of thousand, but not much more than that.[17]

Men did not hold an office by appointment or formal election. (Women were excluded from what we might call public office except when they were chiefs, which was not infrequent.) Authority derived from the prestige a person commanded, and prestige was conferred more or less spontaneously by the people who lived in a group's territory. The first step in gaining that prestige was surviving a rigorous initiation rite, the huskanaw, which lasted weeks or even (as John Smith reported) up to nine months. The ceremony included running a gauntlet, isolation in the woods, and ingestion of hallucinogenic potions. Rountree imagines it was analogous to a vision quest. All boys had to undergo this initiation into manhood. The most promising among them did so at a younger age—some as young as ten years old—while the least brave and worst hunters went through the rite when they were much older. Some few at least seemed to have died during the ordeal, but the survivors were transformed into men. The essence of that transformation was the infusion of a sense of communal responsibility and the dissolution of "prepossessions and unreasonable prejudices" and the ties to friends and family built up through childhood. Leaving behind these "cheats of custom and education" freed up the initiate's reason, which alone "qualified" men to "equally and impartially to administer justice." In other words, mature men were supposed to consider the good of the whole community above any personal affinities.[18]

Some of these men enjoyed higher prestige than others. Perhaps they communed more directly with the spirit world and became priests, authorized to tend to the remains of the dead, which were sequestered in temples before burial. Others proved their worth through cunning and boldness in battle or the hunt. The chief turned to these for counsel before any major decision concerning the community's welfare. One anthropologist, Frederic W. Gleach, called their politics a form of republicanism. No formal elections were held, but a councillor's power derived from his status among the people. The power of the village chief depended on the good opinion of these councillors. He might go against the majority, but he could only do so if he had already banked some political capital. His authority existed only so long as it was respected by his council.

Each town or village commanded a territory large enough to supply all of its inhabitants' needs. Each had its upland forests, its terraced lowlands for its houses and fields, transitional marshland, and riverfronts. In Algonquian society, several villages banded together to form the territorial groups, which on average included five hundred to a thousand people living on about two hundred square miles. Those are averages. Populations living closer to the rivers' fall lines were much denser than those living along the briniest water of the bay. The various groups certainly communicated, trading up- and down-river, since certain foods and shells were more accessible nearer the ocean and stoneware and other foods were more accessible inland. Their pottery suggests that Algonquians shared a general cultural homogeneity, and they enjoyed linguistic ties that also distinguished them from the Iroquoian and Siouan peoples closer to the mountains.

The Algonquian groups living on the Chesapeake are an example of the "traditional" societies that Jared Diamond describes in his recent book, *The World Until Yesterday: What Can We Learn From Traditional Societies?*: premodern people living in "small groups ranging from a few dozen to a few thousand people, subsisting by hunting-gathering or by farming or herding" and without formal or complex government. Everyone knows everyone, and society is organized largely along kinship ties.[19] It is a largely egalitarian society. People have a high degree of liberty, and their world exposes them to frequent violence. According to anthropologists, someone living in a typical traditional society has a higher likelihood of dying violently

than someone living in twentieth-century Germany or Russia, even
when we consider the Holocaust, purges, and the slaughters of
World War II.[20] Without a strong central authority, justice within
a group is settled informally, haphazardly, and often violently, and
each group is more or less in a constant state of war with its neighbors.
Despite cultural homogeneity and however friendly trade might be at
a given moment, each Algonquian group on the Chesapeake had to
regard its neighbors with cautious suspicion. Alliances between two
or even a handful of groups might form under the charisma of a paramount chief and the prowess of a particular district, and they might
even survive that chief's death. But alliances had a provisional character. They were fluid and did not provide the security that is the
main business of more complex civil society. Paspahegh might
suddenly swoop into Kecoughtan territory and raid a village, or some
personal pique might spur some Quiyoughcohannocks to paddle
their canoes across the river and surprise a Paspahegh village,
carrying off women and children. The typical Algonquian lived a
life that was free, equal, satisfying, magnanimous, brutal, and short.

Until Wahunsonacock.

### WAHUNSONACOCK

Wahunsonacock was born in the 1540s in a town called Powhatan.
Near the falls of what is now called the James River, Powhatan was
the last Algonquian town before the unpopulated hunting grounds
that buffered the coastal Algonquians from the Siouan peoples, the
Monacan and the Manahoac, who lived closer to the mountains. Like
Jamestown and like the iconic frontier fort of the American West,
Powhatan was palisaded, but it was not a remote outpost. Algonquians
were more comfortable on freshwater rivers and creeks than on the
open salt water of the Chesapeake Bay, so Powhatan was actually
fairly densely populated.

Algonquian warrior, near Roanoke; the most
detailed images of Algonquians circa 1600 come
from present-day North Carolina, not Virginia.
Tsenecomocoans would have looked very similar.

Every Algonquian village bred its warriors, but along the fall line
warriors were even more vital, and border towns like Powhatan
were known to produce the best. Wahunsonacock was one of these,
the oldest son of the oldest sister of Powhatan's ruling family. His
mother or one of his uncles had accumulated five neighboring
districts, bringing their groups under the leadership of Powhatan's
chief. Through his mother, Wahunsonacock inherited this paramount chiefdom consisting of dozens of villages, six principal towns,
and a few thousand people.[21]

In the English narratives, Powhatan has five meanings. It was
the original name of the James River, the town nearest the river's falls,
the group of people whose capital was that town, the person who was
chief of these people, and all of the people in the paramount chiefdom,
no matter what distinct group they belonged to. The English called
Wahunsonacock "Powhatan" the way Claudius is called "Denmark"
in Shakespeare's *Hamlet* or "Norway" means "the king of Norway" in
*Macbeth*. It was really a title, not a name. To avoid these confusions
and to humanize the much-mythologized chief, I'm using the man's
name, not his title: Wahunsonacock. In this book, *Powhatan* means
the town and the group of people surrounding it, which in 1609 was

governed by Wahunsonacock's son, Parahunt. Wahunsonacock's paramount chiefdom was called Tsenacomoco, and so all the various peoples living in that chiefdom will be called Tsenacomocoans. This last usage requires explanation, because most historians and anthropologists, as well as popular culture, follow the unfortunate custom established by the original English narratives, which use *Powhatan* to refer to *any* Indian belonging to *any* of the groups in Wahunsonacock's paramount chiefdom. That usage suggests a sense of commonality that did not exist. Several of the groups in the paramount chiefdom still exist today and are recognized by the state of Virginia, and none call themselves Powhatans. They are the Mattaponi or Pamunkeys or Rappahannocks or Nansemonds. (Of the other recognized tribes, it's uncertain whether the Patawomeck, who lent their name to the Potomac River at the northern edge of Tsenacomoco, were ever part of that chiefdom. Although the Chickahominy lived in the heart of Wahunsonacock's territory on the Lower Peninsula, they always retained their independence. And the Monacans and Nottoways never belonged.)[22] No Indians thought of themselves as Tsenacomocoans, either, but at least that coinage signifies its own artificiality. It does not suggest any *tribal* cohesion among the various groups.

The English wrote more about Wahunsonacock than about any other Indian in his generation, and in all of those narratives only one, almost offhand, line mentions his father. Ralph Hamor wrote in 1614 that the Spanish drove his father out of the West Indies into the Chesapeake Bay area. Hamor actually met Wahunsonacock, and although his testimony is nowhere corroborated, neither is it contradicted.[23] If what Hamor heard was true, Wahunsonacock was the son of an escaped slave, a maroon, either an Indian from the Caribbean or an African.

The Spanish came into the bay often enough to make it possible, however unlikely, that an escaped Spanish slave took refuge among the Powhatans in Virginia. During their doomed settlement attempt north of Florida in 1526, which marooned over a hundred Africans on the coast of North America, the Spanish sent Captain Pedro de Quejo as far as Virginia. He was looking for people to capture and carry back into slavery in the West Indies, and it's possible someone he kidnapped farther south on the coast escaped ashore in the Chesapeake. While the southern coast, from South Carolina down to Florida, saw Spanish, English, and French ships more or less regularly, and the rich fisheries in the Northeast drew a seasonal ebb and flow of European sailors, the mid-Atlantic coast was relatively untouched. But even here, contact was not unknown. The biography of one remarkable Paspahegh Indian, though highly unusual, demonstrates how Indians were circulating throughout the Atlantic world.

Around 1560, Spanish visiting the James River kidnapped a youth named Paquiquineo, the son of the Paspahegh chief. They brought him first to Mexico, then to Havana, then to Spain and back to Havana. He learned Spanish. He was converted to Catholicism, and so convinced were his captors of his zeal that they rechristened him Don Luís de Velasco. The boy became a prized strategic asset, and in 1570 the Jesuits brought him home to Paspahegh to help convert his countrymen. To their credit, the Jesuit missionaries deplored the violence and cruelty that usually accompanied the missions, so they brought no soldiers with them. It was a brave experiment, but the Jesuits miscalculated the zeal of Don Luís.[24] Only five days into the mission, as the Jesuits described it, Don Luís "fell into evil ways." He abandoned the Spanish. He took off his clothes, going about naked. He had sex with women.[25] In reality, of course, the polyglot Paquiquineo simply preferred to live with his own people rather than with his captors. Eventually, Paquiquineo led a murderous raid on the priests, which spared just one Spaniard, a boy named Alonso de Olmos, who, according to customs of Algonquian warfare, was adopted by the Paspaheghs, and so was marooned for a year and a half among the natives.[26] In 1572 the Spanish were avenged. Florida's governor, Pedro Menéndez de Avilés, sailed to the Chesapeake and recovered the boy. Unable to lay his hands on the priests' killers, the governor kidnapped eight random Indians, baptized them, looped ropes round their necks, and hoisted them to the ship's yardarm. Their strangulating struggles and then their limp bodies, swaying with the roll of the ship, were visible to every Indian spying from shore.[27]

Historians used to speculate that Paquiquineo was Wahunsonacock's father. No one credits that theory today. Yet this episode was only Spain's most spectacular and well-documented contact with the Chesapeake. Any number of visits by Spanish slavers or traders are lost to history, and we know that slaves did escape the Spanish by ducking into Native American villages. If some slave managed to maroon himself in Chesapeake Bay, he would have been a resourceful and courageous individual, and we can well imagine that powerful families would take notice. The sexual liberty of all women in Algonquian society and the fact that women chiefs often took multiple husbands makes it possible that Wahunsonacock was the son of a maroon.

Although he was heir to the chiefdom, Wahunsonacock was raised like all boys. He had a bow in his hands by the age of three. He learned to hunt, fish, and fight. Even as chief, Wahunsonacock was not much different from those he ruled. Algonquian society was not perfectly equal. People could accumulate wealth in the form of beads or furs, and wealthier men might take several wives, each of whom required a bride price and material support. Wealth could buy fancy ceremonial clothing, copper ornaments, and rarer dyes for body paint. But by English standards the Indians were remarkably egalitarian. Tasks were split according to the sexes, and Algonquians had their priests, but for the most part labor was not specialized. As an old man with scores of wives and dozens of subject districts, Wahunsonacock still took pride in sewing his own moccasins. Even in his sixties, like any good husband, he was hunting deer to provide for his own household.[28]

When Wahunsonacock inherited Tsenacomoco, it was wealthy and stable. Each district contributed some particular strength to the whole. The Appamattucks controlled trade routes that were the "conduit[s] to luxury goods" for the whole region. The Youghtanunds and Mattaponis on the Pamunkey River lived on some of the most fertile soil in the entire watershed, and they served as the breadbasket for the James River groups in poor seasons. The formidable Arrohatecks and Powhatans dealt with enemies.[29] Bound together, these several districts made an unusually large, powerful, and stable paramount chiefdom. Districts communicated with each other. Pottery styles indicate that those connections tended to parallel the coast rather than follow the rivers. Groups living on salt water in Chesapeake communicated with groups living on the saltwater sounds of North Carolina. The Indians on Roanoke Island, for instance, were friendly with the Kecoughtans. Women from one district would marry men from another, facilitating this cultural and material exchange. Similarly, the groups along the fall line communicated more with each other than with downriver people. But these cultural exchanges and marriage ties did not lead toward grand, unified chiefdoms. In the long term, even districts that remained very friendly toward each other tended to retain their independence.

No one knows why the chiefdom inherited by Wahunsonacock and centered on the town of Powhatan expanded in the late sixteenth century, but expand it did. This implacable force raced not only along the usual route of communication, from south to north along the fall line but, what is more remarkable, from west to east, from the waterfalls to the sea. Rountree thinks that a drought between 1564 and 1569 probably helped this expansion by destabilizing the region, weakening less resilient groups, exposing them to coercion by the

powerful warriors of the Powhatan and the Arrohateck. First, Wahunsonacock conquered the York River, adding the Chiskiacks. Then
he went down the James River to the Weanocks, whose "useful trade
connections" came under his dominion. In 1594 the chief of the
Kecoughtans died. That district was at the tip of the Lower Peninsula where the York and James come together, and Wahunsonacock
attacked the strategic point with an overwhelming force. He killed
the new chief and many of the warriors and forced the rest of the
Kecoughtans to relocate, moving them into Tsenacomoco's interior.
(In exile, these people retained their identity, and years later Wahunsonacock allowed them to settle open land in Piankatank territory.)
Powhatans colonized Kecoughtan, and Wahunsonacock installed
his son, Pochins, and "a hundred or so loyalists" on the conquered
land. The less bellicose groups on the isolated Eastern Shore, the
Accomacs and Occohannock chiefdoms, came into the fold at some
point, probably through diplomacy. Wahunsonacock conquered the
Chesapeakes either just before or just after the arrival of the English
in 1607, exterminating them mercilessly. He began repopulating
their territory with Nansemonds. Eventually he ruled more than
thirty distinct districts, each with its own capital town and chief,
troop of warriors, cluster of hamlets, marshland, and foraging and
hunting grounds.[30] Never before in Virginia had one man united so
many groups under so large a paramount chiefdom.

The English called the territory ruled by Wahunsonacock
the Powhatan "Empire." Sometimes historians preferred the term
"Powhatan Confederacy" to indicate just how loose the connections
were between the thirty or so groups that constituted Tsenacomoco.
Today we still debate the nature and extent of Wahunsonacock's
power. We know that at certain times Wahunsonacock disrupted
traditional lines of inheritance, installing his own son or brother or
devotee as chief of a district. He extended his patronage into as many
of the districts as possible. He took young wives from every region,

who would live with him till they mothered their first child, when he allowed them to return to their villages and perhaps marry again. We know that Wahunsonacock had the power of life and death over every person in Tsenacomoco: he could and at times did summarily order someone's execution. He could summon the men of the various districts so they would act in concert, hundreds of warriors overwhelming some enemy, as they had conquered the Chesapeakes. But there was no central government; no bureaucracy. Wahunsonacock levied no tax, but people paid him tribute, and he amassed a personal fortune in luxury goods like copper ornaments and beads drilled and polished from shells; useful items like skins and hatchets; and even storable food like corn. These he could bestow as gifts, extending his patronage. He accumulated so many goods that warehouses were constructed to store them.

Even so, as extensive as his powers were, they depended on his maintaining his personal prestige. He might act as a despot, but each decision must be squared in the columns of credit and debit. Would a decision unpopular in one district enhance his reputation among all the people? He had heaped up political capital in a pile far higher than anyone in Algonquian history. And he had a personal retinue of warriors, an inner circle who guarded him. But ultimately his authority, and the unity of Tsenacomoco, rested upon his own glamour, the awe with which he was regarded by his people. If he started spending that capital unwisely, disrespecting traditions or abusing his own patronage system, the pile could dissipate faster than it had accumulated. Such was the nature of his power.[31]

Many aspects of everyday life did not much change under Wahunsonacock's rule. People were occupied with the business of the family and the village. Women farmed and foraged, and men fished as they had before. Men of each hamlet still hunted individually or in small groups in the lands left wild nearest their own houses, the swamps, or the remoter parts of the forest between villages. Villages were still organized by group, under a chief who lived in each district's principal town. Justice was largely served the same way it was before, as a private affair settled between families. But other things changed. Seasonal hunting parties of hundreds of warriors from several districts joined together to roam the wild no-man's-land above the fall line. Such massive, unified hunting parties made the Algonquians too formidable for the Iroquoian or Siouan people to molest them, and they must have forged bonds between districts, acquainting warriors from distant groups with each other, contributing to their sense of being one people.

Older men and women might remember a time when each group fended for itself, when the Wicocomoco guarded themselves against the Sekakawon, the Paspahegh against the Weanock, each district's neighbor a potential enemy. Now, under Wahunsonacock, there was peace. One might paddle up and down the rivers and walk the paths over the spines of the peninsulas without the slightest thought of running into an enemy. Grandparents could hardly recognize the world their grandchildren were born into. Entire generations of youth were growing up in a world that tied the salt wind of the ocean to the freshwater uplands of the fall line. A young man living near the mouth of the bay might cross the territory of ten different groups to find his wife. Without fear of robbery, one hamlet might load a big canoe with salty oysters and pole against the current to trade for deerskins from the higher country or stones suitable for hatchets. News traveled along these networks more swiftly than ever before. Overland paths must have improved, because travelers could move from district to district freely. To the very old, these were amazing times. Nothing in the lore of the Algonquian peoples paralleled the speed with which Wahunsonacock united these districts. The expansion of Tsenacomoco was an incredible feat of political and military genius. If he had had a Shakespeare, Wahunsonacock would be among the most celebrated figures in American history. The cunning of Henry

Bolingbroke; the charm of Prince Hal paired with Hotspur's courage; the ambition of Macbeth but without remorse; Othello's pride—all resided in the bosom of this remarkable man, including Lear's love for Ophelia.

Wahunsonacock had thirty children—twenty sons and ten daughters—living with him and many more scattered throughout Tsenacomoco. He installed one of those sons, Pochins, as the weroance at Kecoughtan town. Another, Parahunt, he made chief of his own hometown, Powhatan, at the James River falls. We know that one daughter was married to a chief, and another, Matachanna, would eventually marry Uttamatomakkin, the great priest. Those are the children we know about. As Napoleon later did on a grander scale, Wahunsonacock used his own family to knot together his conquests, and we can be sure that when any promising child grew up, he or she was installed in some position of authority.

His Cordelia, the beloved daughter, was a slightly built girl named Amonute. In all of Shakespeare there is no one like her. Rountree imagines that the need to compete for her father's attention fed her natural sportiveness, caprice, and insolence, enlarging those parts of her character. Another biographer, Frances Mossiker, called her "frolicsome, mischievous, frisky." She flashed color and light into the brooding worries of the paramount chief: comical, clever, she had a genius for attention, a genius for people. The Powhatan culture allowed parents to express affection more frankly than did English custom, and we can imagine the rapport between this father and daughter was as familiar and intimate as in modern families. Much later, the English captured Amonute and kept her hostage, but her poise and serenity and good humor made her more a guest than a prisoner, till she became as fluent in their culture as her own. The erstwhile prisoner captivated those who held her, commanding their attention, commanding their respect and homage. But back in 1607 she danced naked in the summer, without so much as an apron, for she had not reached puberty, had not yet begun to cover her limbs and breasts with the vivid floral tattoos favored by Tsenacomocoans. It was then, in her prepubescent youth, that this girl earned the playful name that caught her irrepressible personality: Pocahontas.[32]

## SUMMER AND FALL

Pocahontas's entry on the stage of history was still six months away when the English first put spade to soil in Jamestown, when Wahunsonacock held his first council to contemplate how to deal with the strangers. Ironically enough, the English chose to settle in the territory of the Paspahegh, the same people the Spanish had raided in 1560, the same people who had killed the Jesuits, and the people who had suffered Spanish revenge in 1572. That was a long time ago, but it was still remembered, and it might have been Paquiquineo himself, who had seen what the Spanish did in Florida, Mexico, and Hispaniola, who urged Wahunsonacock to slaughter the colony. Let them land on Paspahegh territory, let them begin to settle, let them think we are their friends. Then come upon them in the dark and kill them all and take their weapons as the spoils of war.[33]

But these strangers were not Spanish. They hated the Spanish. And they brought European goods. An iron knife was a treasure to people who sharpened bone by scraping it with a flinty stone, used seashells to butcher deer and cure hides, and tipped their arrows with the spurs of turkeys. A wooden sword, edged as it might be with razor-sharp shell, was no match for a European sword. The advantage European weapons would give them over the Monacans was immense. They could roam at will in the rich hunting grounds above the fall line. Even their Algonquian allies, the Chickahominy, would see the futility of retaining their modicum of independence and come quickly into the fold.[34] Wahunsonacock had a further worry. What if he lost control of the English? The Paspahegh had their private feud with the Weanocks across the river. And what about the Rappahannocks? Might they use English weapons to settle old scores with their neighbors, the Moraughtacunds.[35] Wahunsonacock managed to keep these internecine jealousies and complex webs of vengeance in check. But what might the sudden possession of iron hatchets do to upset that balance? What if some vassal chief of a populous district got it into his head to ally with the English? Close ties of kinship assured the loyalty of the Youghtanunds, the Pamunkeys, the Kecoughtans, and some others. But armed with iron pikes and swords, might not some peripheral district—Nansemond or distant Patawomeck—threaten Tsenacomoco?

Complicating all of these considerations was the incoherence of the English themselves. Most visible and threatening, of course, were the soldiers, the men in armor, the men who came by boat to Indian villages, their weapons clanging loudly when they walked. They were the official conduit of trade, and Wahusonacock could do little more than either allow or ban trade. So long as trade was allowed, each district struck the best deals they could, and the Indians living on the James River had a clear advantage over the other parts of Tsenacomoco. Soon the villagers discovered another category of English, the sailors—barefoot, lightly dressed, and unruly—who traded on better terms. Even the local chiefs had little control over these interactions, because any industrious individuals might paddle canoes out to the ships. The sailors disappeared with the big ships in early summer, but there was yet a third group of English who didn't travel on the river at all. They wore no armor. They carried no weapons. But they wandered the roads of the Lower Peninsula till they came to villages, bearing whatever goods they could smuggle out of the English fort: hoes, hatchets, knives, beads, buttons, cups, kettles. They seemed almost like children, boys, or really not even boys but some other species of humanity, for even mere boys could hunt and fight, while these could do neither. But they were friendly and eager to trade, and it was these starving fugitives who, in July and August, began stumbling into villages.

As these variables waxed and waned, so did Wahunsonacock change his policies. There can be little doubt that Wahunsonacock ordered the general attack on the unfinished fort in May, and just as surely Wahunsonacock authorized feeding the fort in September, what seemed a miraculous salvation to George Percy and John Smith. Rountree attributes the apparent incoherence of Indian behavior to the limits of Wahunsonacock's authority. He might forbid a major assault on the fort, but he could do little to prevent individual Indians from settling individual grievances by ambushing the odd Englishman, especially if it was Paspaheghs who did the killing. Frederic Gleach imagines that Wahunsonacock's authority was substantially greater, and what seemed incoherent was actually canny. He was probing the English, discovering how best to exploit them, how far they could be pushed, and how powerful they might be when they were roused. By late October, Wahunsonacock had settled on a policy of cautious tolerance, and he must have felt that he was in control of the situation. Indian corn and meat helped the garrison edge away from a precipice. Malnourished bodies began to revive. By no means had the suffering ended, but complete oblivion no longer loomed, and the revivification did not seem to threaten Tsenacomoco in any way. The stream of English goods was restarted, flowing through the channel sanctioned by Wahunsonacock himself. It must have seemed to him that his cautious rapprochement with the strangers was the right policy. So long as he kept them contained and dependent, he would reap whatever benefits they could offer.

The forest paths filled up with the fallen leaves. The women gathered nuts: acorns, walnuts, hog peanuts. Tuckahoe and reed roots and skunk cabbage were dug up and stored in baskets. It was fall. The villages were nearly deserted as the women concluded the year's foraging and the men commenced their hunting.[36] A dozen shades of brown drained the vivid colors of the world, and the slanting sun cast long shadows through the naked trees. It was then that the English took one of their boats several times up the Chickahominy River, a tributary of the James, to visit the many villages belonging to that district. They traded hatchets and copper for corn, which was then in abundance after the harvests.[38] The leader of these excursions, an energetic, bold Englishman whom the Indians called "Chawnzmit," began to be known throughout the Lower Peninsula for being particularly friendly with the Chickahominy. This news would have troubled Wahunsonacock. Although the Chickahominy lived in the heart of Tsenacomoco, Wahunsonacock had never conquered them nor had he persuaded them to join the paramount chiefdom. It could disturb the balance of power if the Chickahominy were suddenly better armed than their neighbors.

It was in this atmosphere that hundreds of Tsenacomocoans, led by Opechancanough, Wahunsonacock's younger brother and second in line for the chiefdom, headed to the headwaters of the Chickahominy. Opechancanough was "a man very gracious," according to Samuel Purchas, both with the Indians and the English. Oral tradition that was recorded a hundred years later added that he was a big man whose presence conveyed a nobility that helped him govern "his rude countrymen" with perfect skill. Reading "between the lines" of contemporary accounts, Helen Rountree, who wrote the closest thing we have to his biography, cannot get beyond what she concedes is a two-dimensional sketch. The English found Opechancanough "canny" in negotiations and "fierce" in fights. He was, perhaps, less cautious and quicker to fight than his older brother.[38]

This was backcountry, far from any village or hamlet, the no-man's-land between the Algonquians and the Siouan Indians. They were hunting. Whether deer were their quarry or Englishmen is impossible to say with historical certainty, but the coincidence suggests that Wahunsonacock dispatched his war chief to disrupt

whatever the English were up to. Opechancanough found the boat far
up the river, in a wide, bay-like expanse, just below a narrowing stretch
of the stream that was impassible for the fallen trees. Perhaps half a
dozen men lingered in the boat, wary, no doubt watching the Indians
who watched them from the bank. The boat was beyond arrow shot
from either side of the river, and to take it Opechancanough would
have had to assault it by canoe. Having so many men, he would
certainly succeed, but several warriors were sure to be killed in
the enterprise. As it happened and contrary to Smith's orders,
one of the boatmen was ashore. Opechancanough captured him.
Somehow—whether through someone half-skilled in English or
through rude gesture and sign—the Englishman was questioned.
He revealed nothing. Opechancanough had him tied to a tree near
a fire. His fingers were removed at the joints by sharp shells until he
told them that his chief had gone farther up the river in a canoe. So
Opechancanough followed the river till he came to a little campfire,
where he found an Indian guide and two Englishmen, one a soldier,
one not, both armed with matchlock muskets, both lounging
unawares. Little time was required here. Farther into the woods,
they came at last to a small man in armor, clearly a fighter, clearly a
soldier, and not taken by surprise. He had lashed his Indian guide to
his arm so he could use him as a human shield.

Opechancanough was not deterred. He arrayed his warriors in
a wide arc that closed warily on the soldier, cautiously, as they might
approach a cornered bear, shooting arrows whenever they saw an
opening. One projectile managed to wound his thigh. Others lodged
in his clothing. Wielding a pistol, the Englishman shot and reloaded
and shot again several times, killing two or three and warning the
others to keep their distance. Opechancanough did not tighten the
circle. Time was on his side. He allowed the Englishman to back his
way toward the water, until he got mired in a swampy swale, still

Three images of John Smith's captivity: captured by
Opechancanough, tied to a stake, and bound before an Indian
council. Detail from John Smith's *Generall Historie of Virginia*.

holding his guard as the water's cold quickly penetrated his pants
and then his skin down to the very bone. He could not last long.
Finally he tossed away his weapons and the Indians pulled him
from the water, dragged him to the campfire where the bodies of the
two other Englishmen pierced with arrows were displayed. The
Indians did not kill their final quarry. They warmed him at the fire.
With their own hands they rubbed his numbed legs back to life.[39]

One of the band of Indians, a man named Maocassater, recognized the Englishman, called him Chawnzmit, and greeted him as a
friend. They had met back in early summer, when Chawnzmit had
given him a gift of very valuable beads and other things, for which the
Indian was still grateful. Now, in the cold of December, he returned
the favor, giving the prisoner a mantle to "defend him from the cold."
Soon, Chawnzmit and Opechancanough and several of the Indians
embarked on a long, winding journey across the Middle Peninsula,
unexplored territory for the English, visiting one village, then another,

granting the prisoner an ambiguous status as honored guest—honored, feasted, entertained, but not at liberty to go home.[40]

Opechancanough suggested that Chawnzmit desert the English garrison and join the Tsenacomocoans. Not only would his life be spared and liberty restored, but he would be given ample land to set himself up as an important Indian, enough to support not only himself but several wives as well.[41] The promise of women must have been tempting. Not only had the English lived nearly a year without seeing an English woman, they had grown up in a culture that suppressed rather than expressed sexual impulses, walling in that great river of desire so it might run in one narrow, monogamous channel. English narratives nearly always remarked on the promiscuity of Indian women when compared to Christians, admonishing the "savages" in phrases splendid with envy. To receive all of these benefices, all Chawnzmit had to do in return was teach the Indians how the forty-odd surviving English could be overrun without the Indians losing a comparable number of warriors. Although our histories do not mention it, Chawnzmit might easily have accepted the offer. Plenty of examples close at hand proved that Englishmen might choose life in a Tsenacomocoan village over life in an English garrison. Why wouldn't Chawnzmit maroon himself among the Tsenacomocoans? Unlike most maroons, he would enter Indian society not as a destitute charity case but as an important man with privileges commensurate to his current status in Jamestown.

Wisely, Chawnzmit equivocated. He persuaded the Indians to carry a written note to Jamestown, a three-day walk over a trail now covered in snow. Besides alerting the garrison that John Smith was indeed alive and living with the Indians, the note instructed them to deliver certain goods to a certain place in the woods. The English did as instructed. The goods were recovered by the Indians. And because the technology of writing was unknown to them, this demonstration suitably impressed the Tsenacomocoans while also going some way to ransoming the Englishman. Clearly, he was more valuable alive than dead.

As the progress of towns continued, Chawnzmit—or John Smith, to use the English pronunciation—began to master the Indians' language. A very well-traveled polyglot, he had already learned enough Algonquian to explain abstract concepts like the distance from Virginia to England, the function of a compass, the earth's spherical shape, and the paths of the stars. All the while, their meanderings were getting closer to the capital, Werowocomoco, where Wahunsonacock lived. The paramount chief would ultimately decide what to do with the prisoner. Smith found Wahunsonacock's court resplendent in all the glory befitting a paramount chief. The chamber was deep inside a longhouse, at the end of a twisting passage, and when Smith came to the last chamber he saw the man sitting upon his bench with very young wives on either side who were each flanked by a row of councillors, who were themselves backed by another row of women. All were dressed in finery ornamented with their jewelry and painted skin and downy white feathers in their hair. Smith was invited to join a ceremonial feast. Then came the speeches. Smith probably caught the odd word or phrase, although he could not follow the sense of the oratory.

Then commenced a strange ceremony in which as many as could touch Smith at the same time dragged him to a large stone and forced his head to lay upon it. They "made ready with their clubs to beat out his brains," which of course is the climactic moment at which Wahunsonacock's young daughter, Pocahontas—a mere child among the dignitaries, and flush with emotion—rushed forward and entreated her father for mercy. Wahunsonacock's stern face was unmoved, so Pocahontas ran to the prisoner, sat down, and took Smith's head in her lap. Finally, this lithe girl laid her own head upon the sunburned, bearded face of the old soldier, making herself a shield that the warriors with their clubs dared not strike.[42]

*Pocahontas Saves Captain John Smith*, part of the fresco frieze of the U.S. Capitol, painted by Constantino Bromidi circa 1877.

Most historians today think that Smith's life was never in danger. What he took for a ceremonial execution and Pocahontas's spontaneous rescue was really a scripted, symbolic adoption ceremony. The sequel confirms it. Two days later Smith was brought into another house and sat down before a fire. From behind a screen, Wahunsonacock appeared, dressed "more like a devil than a man" and accompanied by uncounted more painted "as black as himself." Smith again surmised he was about to be killed, but to his great relief Wahunsonacock said that "now they were friends." More than friends: Wahunsonacock made Smith a chief and bestowed upon him a territory called Capahowosick where the English could settle—a territory on the Middle Peninsula just "a few miles downstream" from Werowocomoco.

Smith was told he must move the English out of the Paspahegh district on the Lower Peninsula and onto this new ground. The English colony would become one of the many districts of Tsenacomoco, the same as Paspahegh or Kecoughtan or Powhatan. The English would not be killed. They would be ruled by Smith as weroance, who would pay allegiance to Wahunsonacock. They would trade, interact, join in hunts, join in warfare, join in ceremony, pay tribute, intermarry, which over the long years would splice the English into Tsenacomocoan families and villages until eventually they were wholly bound to Indian ways.

Smith had no choice. He was a prisoner among the savages. Understandably, his narrative says very little about what promises he made to the paramount chief. But later, among the English, he would never shake the suspicion that he had become a renegade. Some thought that his ambition was to deliver the colony into the hands of the Indians and set himself up as chief, so it is not surprising that he leaves his reply out of the story. But it seems almost impossible that Smith refused Wahunsonacock's proposal.[43] The conclusion of his initiation ceremony seems to confirm it. The greatest honor that Wahunsonacock could bestow—a symbolic rendering of Smith's status as a weroance and a token of Jamestown's absorption into Tsenacomoco—was a new name. Henceforth, the man they called Chawnzmit would be Wahunsonacock's son, Nantaquod.[44]

# CHAPTER THREE

## Nantaquod on the James

**The ground was crusted with frost.** Eyes peering from the James-town palisade squinted at the winter sunlight. From the leafless branches of the trees long icicles dangled. Perhaps forty men were still in the garrison, fewer than half of those whom Captain Newport had left when he sailed for England in early summer.[1] Renegades and deserters were living in the villages, where the Indians dined on "plenty of oysters, fish, flesh, wildfowl, and good bread." No house in England, John Smith wrote, "had better fires . . . than in the dry, warm, smoky houses" of Indian towns.[2] It must have been bitter for the sentry to look at the bleak parade ground of civilization, pocked as it was by low humps of dirt graves fringed now with hoarfrost. The bodies of Gosnold and Kendall rested under two of those heaps of frozen dirt. Wingfield, deposed, was confined to the pinnace. So far as those in Jamestown knew, Smith was dead or a renegade. Martin was perpetually sick. And, contrary to the Company's laws, President Ratcliffe installed Gabriel Archer on the council. An imposter president, an invalid, and an illegal councillor ruling two score dispirited survivors.

If not for the pinnace, their lifeline to England, they would be marooned, abandoned. But the boat was too small to carry all the survivors, depleted though they were. Nevertheless, President Ratcliffe gave the order to provision the pinnace for an ocean voyage.

Ratcliffe and whomever he favored would sail away, abandoning the weak and lowborn and unlucky to scratch out sustenance until Newport finally came with their resupply. Or they would starve. Or be killed. Or they would join the "naturals" in their villages. Just before Ratcliffe cast off, right after Christmas, a bitter-cold wind pinned the boat to its berth alongside the fort. No sailing ship could beat against the wintry blast to the mouth of the bay. The very rigging froze in the cold and wet.

A sentry still at his post saw an Indian approach the fort. He was admitted. He handed over a written note that was passed along until it reached Ratcliffe. The message was dumbfounding. John Smith was alive. He was thriving in Werowocomoco, the guest of the shadowy Indian king, Wahunsonacock. Flourishing, well served, Smith asked that Ratcliffe arrange for certain items—probably the usual assortment of hatchets and pots and trifles—be delivered to a designated spot in the woods.

Captain John Smith, alive!

Wingfield, Archer, and George Percy all left accounts of those last days of 1609, but none discuss the reaction triggered by this remarkable document. It would not take long for the rumor to spread to everyone, and their reactions split into two camps defined, no doubt, by those whom Ratcliffe favored and disfavored. Those whom the president was about to abandon would have considered the news another blessing from God. Smith would be their deliverance. But those ready to sail on the pinnace knew Smith would disrupt their plans. There was no gainsaying Smith's popularity with some of the men. He might prevent Ratcliffe from escaping in the boat. Worse yet, what if Wingfield had been right all along? What if Smith "intended to usurp the government, murther the Counceil, and make himself King"?[3] Make Jamestown into a sort of pirate stronghold? What better way to do that than ally himself with Wahunsonacock? Smith might have staged his capture. Certainly he was colluding with the savages. He had been fattening himself on Indian bread and meat, and he had been sleeping snug in an Indian town, more than likely with the warmth and comfort of a savage woman, all while the English froze in their meager fort. The eyes of the garrison waited for Ratcliffe's decision. The note asked for a ransom to be delivered. What could Ratcliffe do but comply? His own suspicions and his own discomfort could not justify abandoning Smith. The goods were delivered. They waited. Nothing happened, and Smith's failure to appear must have confirmed Ratcliffe in his suspicions. Day after day passed, some in the fort hoping for Smith, others hoping for the wind to change.

The second of January dawned a little warmer. It broke the bitter cold and wet that had hung the icicles from the bare branches of the trees. If the sentry who was peering over the pointed logs of the fort looked to his left, toward the river, he could see that the pinnace was stirring with activity. The sun touched the high rigging, and the tackle fastened to the highest mast was thawing already. The sailors were stirring to life, ready for the sunlight to climb down the mast and stand on deck, bright and warm. With the change of the tide and the sun higher in the sky, the ship might actually weigh anchor and slide toward the mouth of the bay. At that very moment a short man dressed in English fashion led a troop of a dozen Indian warriors across the causeway connecting Jamestown Island to Paspahegh territory. Perhaps the rays of sunlight had descended far enough down the trunks of the trees that it glinted off his helmet.

John Smith's behavior in the first few hours of his redemption lent credence to Ratcliffe's suspicions. He and his troop of Indians came into the fort. He spoke to the Indians in their language, a clumsy version, perhaps, but it was talk. The English soldiers on guard couldn't comprehend a word. Smith spoke to one of the Indians, someone named Rawhunt, on what appeared to be intimate terms. Rawhunt responded, addressing him respectfully and calling him by a new name, Nantaquod. Yet these were the very people who had shot full of arrows the two men who had gone into the woods with Smith: the gentleman Jehu Robinson and the carpenter Thomas Emry. Perhaps this very Rawhunt had taken part in the bloodthirsty torture of the laborer George Cassen, helping to cut off his fingers and disembowel him alive.

Smiling and happy, Smith brought the savages over to one of the cannons and offered to give it to them. In their ignorance they tried to lift it, but they might as well have tried to lift a boulder in the air. Of course they could not carry it off. Smith was laughing. But what could he mean by offering to the Indians the colony's best defense? Smith ordered that the cannon—a demiculverin—be loaded with stone, and apparently there were men willing to take the captain's orders. He fired the thunderous gun into the trees. The scattershot obliterated a massive tree branch, shattering the icicles and sending crystals and sawdust into a cloud. The Indians were gone before the cloud settled to the ground, nearly before the echo of the gun died away, fled into the woods, and John Smith was laughing when he sent some men to retrieve them with soothing gestures and trinkets.

As these diversions were going on, Ratcliffe was busily trying to unmoor the pinnace. Smith noticed the commotion; one of his loyalists must have explained what Ratcliffe was up to. Ratcliffe, realizing how precarious his own authority had become, hurried the preparations along. Sailors would have cast off had Smith not pointed the demiculverins at the boat. Flanked by his Indian allies and whichever English were loyal to him, Smith shouted across the little space of water. Belay, or he would sink the pinnace where it was. No one doubted him. He was not laughing. Ratcliffe gave the order to desist, and he came ashore in a sort of détente between those who were about to leave and those who were about to be abandoned.

Smith must not have realized the degree of Ratcliffe's enmity, for later in the day he let down his guard. Ratcliffe's men arrested Smith, and Ratcliffe charged him with the deaths of Robinson and Emry.

Whether through negligence or through collusion with the Indians, Smith's actions sentenced those two Englishmen to death. Forget the Company's rules. Ratcliffe conducted a summary trial and pronounced quick, Old Testament judgment: an eye for an eye. For the second time in a year, Smith was condemned to hang the following morning.[4]

## CAPTAIN JOHN SMITH

It is very tempting to call Smith the first true American: a self-made man elevated by his own merits and elected to office by virtue of talent and accomplishments, rather than by the privilege of his name and rank. "It is a happy thing to be borne to strength, wealth, and honour," Smith wrote near the end of his life, when he pondered his long experience and sought to pass its wisdom on, "but that which is got by prowess and magnanimity is the truest lustre . . ." "He did what millions who came after him dreamed of doing," wrote his recent biographers, Dorothy and Thomas Hoobler: seize "the opportunity to invent himself." According to this version, Smith "gave birth to the American dream." The Hooblers were influenced by what might be called a revision of Smith's reputation in American letters, which was energized by Philip L. Barbour's self-described "scientific" 1964 biography, *The Three Worlds of Captain John Smith*, a book that is still unrivaled and hardly contradicted today. David A. Price painted Smith (in his 2003 *Love and Hate in Jamestown: John Smith, Pocahontas, and the Start of a New Nation*) as exhibiting an "unassuming equality—an unusual attitude in his class-conscious homeland." A fit model for a meritocracy: Smith was a commoner with "a total lack of respect for his social betters—or anyone else who hadn't proven himself through his merits." A leader who preferred the colony to be settled by "sturdy men and women, not get-rich-quick dandies," Smith exemplifies the "formative stage in our national history," according to Alden T. Vaughan. J. A. Leo Lemay insisted that Smith was the

Captain John Smith. Detail
from John Smith's *Generall
Historie*, 1624.

first to "define what it meant to be an American and first claimed that American identity was distinctive and desirable." "Whatever else Captain John Smith may have been," Lemay insists, "he was and regarded himself as a self-made man."[5] There is much truth in those characterizations. Smith fit a new type of character in Western society, and that type reflects an ideological shift toward the individualism and meritocracy that dominates American culture. But when biographers lionize men like Smith, they obscure the truth that no one could be "self-made" in England in 1600. One might rise in society through one's own merit, but you could only be "made" by attaching yourself to the aristocracy, and Smith embraced it with his whole heart.

Smith was born in 1580 in Alford, Lincolnshire. His mother's family, the Rickards of Yorkshire, could boast and apparently did boast about "one marriage with a knight, and a tie with an Archbishop in Dublin." Although Smith's father was a yeoman, the son bragged that he was "anciently descended from the ancient Smiths of Crudley in Lancashire." He farmed several acres of his own land, and he leased more from the local Lincolnshire lord, named Willoughby, who condescended to notice his tenant. The tenant cherished his landlord's good opinion. He carefully instructed his oldest son to "honour and love" the aristocrat, and the young John Smith learned well.[6] Smith trots out various Lords Willoughby onto the stage in the second paragraph of his own autobiography. They march in order under two generations of splendid banners (barons, earls, the lord chamberlain of England).

Smith did not attend to his other lessons. He distinguished himself in grammar school by running away across the "fat and marshy land of eastern Lincolnshire." (He was caught and brought back.) Nor did he much like being apprenticed to a merchant. His restless nature revolted from the tedium of the countinghouse. When he was not yet a man, his father died and left him an estate worth seventy-seven pounds, a prosperous farm, and several acres of pasturage. Smith pressured his appointed guardian to dissolve the indenture that bound him to the paperwork of commerce. Swords were more interesting by far. By the time he was in his late teens, John Smith was billeted with other English in the Netherlands, a common soldier in one of several outfits loosely connected to Lord Willoughby. Peace in Europe brought him back to England. In 1599 he recrossed the channel to France, escorting Willoughby's younger son to Willoughby's older son. Having executed that charge, Smith ingratiated himself to the Humes, an influential family of the Scottish aristocracy. Armed with letters of introduction, he headed for Scotland in the hopes of becoming a courtier of King James, but his ship was wrecked, and he was cast ashore at Lindisfarne, where he relied on the kindness of locals, which was inspired either by the letters or his charm or both. The plan to be a courtier did not work out, but he was given enough charity to see him back, at age twenty, to Alford.[7]

Smith then retired, Thoreau-like, to live in the woods. Shaded under the fresh green leaves of spring, he studied Machiavelli's *Art of War*, Vannoccio Biringuccio's *Pyrotechnics*, and the stoical philosophy of Marcus Aurelius. Probably he read more, but in later years these were the three books he cared to mention, which suggests that they helped form his character. In the long days of summer in his twentieth year, he learned the finer points of horsemanship under the tutelage of a bellicose Italian-Greek rider, Theodore Paleologue, who also taught him to hate the Turks.[8]

Smith was a charming, sharp-minded young man, skilled highest of all in the art of pleasing those above him on the social scale. The woods belonged to Lord Willoughby. The deer he hunted were the lord's deer. The expensive books he read came from Willoughby's library. Willoughby paid for his tilting lessons. What Smith got from the arrangement is obvious. Elizabethan England obligated aspiring yeomen to splice themselves to the aristocrats with fibers of loyalty and self-interest. No man was an island. No one "made" himself. An aspiring young man had to situate himself in a complex web of connections: if a commoner was made, he had to be *made* by an aristocrat at the web's center. Ambitious young men had to sense the vibrations coming from that center, interpret the signs, determine what pleased the lord, and give it to him. Smith had a genius for cultivating such patronage. He sharpened the skill till it was keen as a knife's edge, and Willoughby was the whetting stone.

In a romantic gesture, and probably under the influence of Paleologue, Smith decided he must join the fight against the infidels. His *Iliad* and *Odyssey*, as Phillip Barbour called Smith's Turkish adventure, took him far outside the circle of Willoughby's influence. The comparison to Homer's Odysseus hardly exaggerates, or maybe Voltaire's Candide would better capture Smith's admixture of innocence and experience. On the boat across the channel, Smith was swindled out of his money and luggage. Striding down the gangplank, he carried nothing but the clothes on his back and his talent for being well liked by men of means. It was the pattern of his life, initiated by the Lindisfarne shipwreck: to start anew, stripped of everything, sustained by the kindness of strangers and restored to prosperity by his own deeds. He found passage east, through the Mediterranean Sea, but the papist pilgrims on board found his Protestantism odious, and they tossed him over the side. He swam ashore, talked his way onto a merchant ship bound for the East as far as Aleppo and Greece. Traders were sometimes pirates, and this crew took revenge on Catholics by plundering a Venetian trading ship. Smith put ashore with his share of loot: new luggage and enough money to "travel like a gentleman . . . for as long as five years."⁹

Smith toured Italy for a while, bumping into the Willoughby boys, still on their three-year grand tour, in Siena. He took in the sights of Rome, Naples, Florence, and Venice. He still burned to fight the Turks, so eventually he made his way into the Holy Roman Empire, where, through his connection to an English Jesuit, he presented himself for action. A series of petty nobles, all involved in raising troops, passed him along till he settled in a battalion raised by the Count of Modrusch in Vienna. When the count's troops attempted to rescue a city besieged by Turks, Smith contributed a key bit of new technology, an advanced method of signaling using codes and torches that he learned from reading *Pyrotechnics*. That and another bit of diversionary fireworks proved crucial to lifting the siege. As a reward, Smith was promoted to "captain" of 250 horsemen. During another siege, Smith invented bombs of pitch and fire that artillerists propelled over the walls of the city by giant slings. For the next several years, Modrusch's soldiers fought in Transylvania, sometimes in a cruel civil war between the Holy Roman emperor's general Giorgio Basta and the Transylvanian prince Zsigmond, sometimes against the invading Turks, sometimes against marauding bands of soldierly outlaws. The violence was as vicious, futile, and bloody as anything described in *Candide*. The land was laid waste.¹⁰

Christian forces, some seventeen thousand troops, besieged one Turk-held city in the summer of 1601 or 1602. While the sappers dug their trenches, soldiers on both sides of the walls grew fat and flabby for want of exercise. For diversion, a Turkish captain shouted a challenge from the city's ramparts proposing a duel on horseback, in full armor, the winner to take the head of the loser in trophy. Smith was chosen by lot to represent the Christians. The jousting lessons in Willoughby's woods paid off: at the first pass Smith's lance went right through the visor of the Turk's helmet, piercing his face and brain. True to the rules, Smith got off his own horse, drew his sword, and hacked what was left of the shattered trophy from its shoulders. Then another challenge: the dead Turk's friend wanted to win back the head to bury it with the body. Smith agreed. They fought. Smith dispatched him. A third challenge, this time issued by Smith, who must have been feeling invincible. No lances this time: battle-axes. At first Smith got the worst of it. He lost his axe, and as the Turkish side of the audience roared with delight, he had to shift and duck to stay alive. The dexterity of his horse gave him an opening, and he maneuvered the tip of his falchion, a curved sword, under the armor plates at the small of his opponent's back. He shoved it home, flesh swallowing blade.[11]

Although the duels mattered nothing to the siege, they divided John Smith's life in two. Six thousand cheering troops conducted him to their general, who bestowed gifts of horses and trophies to the value of three hundred ducats. Count Modrusch promoted him to major. But most important of all, Prince Zsigmond granted him the right to paint his shield, which hitherto bore the blankness of ignoble birth. The heads of three Turks would decorate the coat of arms of Captain John Smith, henceforth signifying that he was made "an English gentleman." That coat of arms divided the older Smith from his youth, and it divided him from that gigantic majority of people in England considered to be "common."[12] This elevation, his calling card into England's top 2 percent of families, colored his view of other people for the rest of his life.

Eventually the Christians' siege prevailed. Modrusch executed every male Turk who was old enough to fight and decorated the walls of the city with their heads. The display could hardly have been meant to terrorize his enemies, since he had killed them all. It must have pleased some impulse seated in his own heart. He was not alone. The savagery when Turk vanquished Christian or Christian vanquished

Turk is hardly to be comprehended by civilized society. The Christians captured a few Turk scouts, chopped off their heads, and tossed those spheroids "up and down before the trenches." The Turks caught some Christians, flayed them alive, and hung their skins like animal pelts on poles. It is worth mentioning, because it reminds us that the worst terrors of Virginia would not have shocked a man like Smith.[13]

The Christians lost one particular battle paid for dearly by the Turks: in Smith's own words, "neere 30000 lay; some headless, armlesse, all cut and mangled." Smith himself was wounded, and he "groan[ed] among the rest." Turkish pillagers swarmed over the battle-field to plunder the corpses. They would have dispatched Smith like the other half-dead Christians, but his painted shield told the gleaners that he was a gentleman, perhaps a knight, who might be ransomed.[14] Smith was not ransomed. A yeoman's son so far from home had no one to pay. So his captors sold him to a merchant who gave Smith to his beloved, Charatza Trabigzanda, a girl of Greek background living in Istanbul. Smith charmed the girl. She schemed to turn him Turk. For finish and polish, she sent him to her brother, a minor military official on the far side of the Black Sea, across the Sea of Azov, to the very edge where the Ottoman Empire bumped up against the wilderness. Just beyond that frontier, the terrifying Tatar nomads roamed. Trabigzanda's machinations backfired. Her brother, perhaps guessing she had sexual designs on the Christian, clamped a metal collar round Smith's neck, stripped him naked, threw a coarse woolen tunic over him, and made him slave of the slaves. Smith was abused at every turn. One day during threshing time, the master came out in the fields and raised his hand against Smith, who, armed with a threshing bat, gave in to his impulse to beat out the brains of his oppressor. He hid the body, stole its clothes, grabbed the horse, and took off into the Eurasian steppe. He came across a caravan trail, which he followed for a couple of weeks, till, on the far side of the wilderness, he reached an outpost of Christian civilization: a palisaded fort of Muscovy.

History loses sight of Smith for the next couple of years. Wing-field claimed that he saw Smith, an unemployed mercenary, looking for work in Ireland. An enterprising captain might finish an Irish campaign as a lord of confiscated lands, but if that was Smith's design, it did not pan out. By 1605 or 1606, Smith was back in England, where he fell in with the remnants of those who had organized Sir Walter Raleigh's ill-fated Roanoke expeditions. He befriended Bartholomew Gosnold. About this time Henry Hudson was sending Smith maps of the new world. It became known that this enterprising soldier was interested in trans-Atlantic schemes.[15] His old connection to the Willoughbys must have come into play. As Karen Ordahl Kupperman reminds us, Smith "always depended on the patronage of noblemen and women," and we have no reason to doubt that he exploited his connections to Willoughby's prominent Lincolnshire family.[16] Even after Turkey, that was his most important identifier among Englishmen. Willoughby's patronage gave Smith credibility, stature, substance. One can imagine, for instance, the Virginia Company's investors discussing him in 1606:

> "Who is this Captain Smith?"
> "He fought in the Low Countries, and against the Turks in
>     Transylvania."
> "He comes out of Lincolnshire."
> "Yes, one of Lord Willoughby's men."
> "Willoughby, is it?"
> "Indeed. Bertie sent him to France."

Smith's connection to the Willoughbys made him safe enough for the Jamestown council. But we cannot discredit his own merits: the man himself impressed everyone he met. Gosnold and Captain Newport would have approved the energy that drove him. Smith "loved action more than words." Experience—to do and to learn by doing—was his first guide. He hated sloth. His other traits were suited well to the work of colonization. He was used to deprivation. He "would rather want than borrow, or starve than not pay." He was generous. Courageous. His head swelled when a few underlings boasted that Smith sent no soldier into danger "where he would not lead them himself." He was, perhaps, even better defined by what he abhorred. When others were racing for gold, Smith "hated covetousness worse than death." The courtier who accepted the perquisites of office but refused the responsibilities felt his contempt, as did the officer who demanded obedience but evaded his duty; the councillor who supped richly when others sipped from a cup of porridge. Smith reserved his praise for those who did well what was required, whether the office was president or captain or carpenter or fisherman.[17]

These traits might lead people to think that Smith was democratic. There can be no doubt that he did help move English society in the direction of meritocracy. Having moved up in class himself, he approved of social mobility. And he helped other lowborn men of merit raise themselves. Anas Todkill, for instance, came to Virginia as John Martin's footman, but Smith quickly recognized his worth and trained him as a sailor, soldier, and crew chief among lumbermen, launching Todkill on a trajectory toward gentleman.[18] Smith imagined that America might develop without the stiffening effect of an upper crust. England did not allow the rich much room to maneuver. A gentleman could do little without losing dignity. He might manage his lands, lead soldiers, captain sailors, hold government or church office, but that was about it. Most types of work shamed a gentleman in the eyes of his peers. Such an attitude had no place in America, according to Smith. Gentlemen willing to break ground to plant crops, whose "tender fingers . . . oft blistered" from swinging an axe, ought to be lauded with praise as well as profit. Smith admired such a gentleman: only three or four in ten, he figured, were made of such stuff. He also admired the "common wood-hacker." He calculated that two willing laborers were worth ten shirkers in America.[19]

But that does not mean he thought nothing distinguished the gentleman from the "diggers up of roots." Smith was no leveler. Once he had secured his own coat of arms, he cherished the privilege it gave him. All his life he would insist on receiving these dignities. This point is subtle but important, for it prevents us from thinking of Smith as some sort of revolutionary. He maintained that meritorious individuals, distinguished from the common sort by industry, courage, boldness, generosity, perseverance, and resolution, must be admitted to the club.[20] And he scorned the esteem given to the undeserving gentry, who rested on their birthrights rather than shoulder the responsibilities of leadership that justified class privilege. But Smith insisted on the club. Not for anything would he have relinquished the three Turk heads painted on his shield. He viewed the world the way an officer who rose from the ranks views an army. Some men give orders. Others obey. To be fair, many of those who give the orders don't deserve their authority. But no foot soldier had the right to challenge them. Foot soldiers earned Smith's respect not by demanding to rise themselves but by doing their jobs competently and without complaint. In short, by taking orders from men like himself. Smith was imperious. He was arrogant. He could not keep his mouth shut. He laughed when men born to the manor should not laugh. He lacked discretion. He did not hide his contempt for a man. He made enemies easily. Edward Maria Wingfield was just one. Although Ratcliffe and Martin banded with him to overthrow Wingfield, that triumvirate could not last long.

When Smith issued from the woods on January 2, 1608, surrounded by his native escort and speaking the language of the

Indians—and when he pointed the cannon on the pinnace and usurped the president's authority—plenty of the survivors sided with Ratcliffe, Martin, and Archer. The divide is sometimes cast in class terms, but we really have no evidence one way or the other. Probably most of the gentlemen supported the president and his two councillors. But they probably had some commoners on their side as well, among them those who sailed the pinnace, who were promised escape. Similarly, we might guess that Smith earned the loyalty of a few gentlemen, and perhaps a higher proportion of commoners. We might guess the proportions approximated Smith's ratio of blameworthy settlers: six or seven out of ten followed Ratcliffe. That would mean about twelve or fifteen of Jamestown's forty supported Smith. Whatever the proportions, Ratcliffe had enough support to arrest Smith, try him, and sentence him to death.

There would be no delay to erect a gallows. Ratcliffe wanted to move fast. They would string Smith from a mere tree or some crossbeam in the fort or from the yardarm of the pinnace. For his last night alive, Smith was probably shoved belowdecks on that boat, where Ratcliffe's authority was secure. If so, he sat cheek by jowl with aged Wingfield, who, arrested by Smith, was still moldering. Wingfield was not one to gloat. It was all too sobering and humiliating, this ruination of his enterprise. When Wingfield told the story later, it was all about Ratcliffe's coup d'état and nothing at all of Smith's own comeuppance. We might guess that Wingfield shared the murk and gloom belowdecks with equanimity, something Smith could admire in the man.

The two prisoners would have heard a commotion of feet above. Shouts. Voices. A new note in the loud cries: not alarm or despair or resignation but rejoicing. Real joy and merriment. And when the irons were struck off Wingfield and the irons were struck off Smith, they would have come up to the dusky winter evening in wonderment. The river had been so long empty that men no longer even gazed with any hope across the waters, but there, filling up their sight, was a ship—Newport's ship—with its magnificent sails furling and its anchor cast out and crowds of encouraging people. Deliverance.

### THE FIRST SUPPLY

Captain Newport, newly arrived from London, found the colony on the verge of self-destruction. The greater part of the settlers had disappeared, either buried in the frosty earth or dissolved into the woods. Those who remained seemed ready to point guns at one another. The president had been deposed and imprisoned, one member of the council executed, and another ready to be dispatched the following morning. Newport took command. Ratcliffe's resolves were swept aside. There would be no execution. For the second time in a year, Newport pulled John Smith's neck from the hangman's noose and installed him on the council. There would be no more talk of sailing the pinnace to England. Archer was expelled from the council. Wingfield was released from bondage, although he still was barred from government. At the direction of the Company's directors back in London, Newport put Matthew Scrivener, a "very wise, understanding gentleman," on the council. Some semblance of order was restored, for both factions respected Newport's leadership. Five men now sat at council: Newport, Ratcliffe, Smith, Martin, and Scrivener. But in truth, so long as Newport was on the Chesapeake, he acted as chief executive.[21]

Sixty or so new settlers brought the colony back to its original numbers. Unfortunately, soon after their arrival, a sudden fire "consumed all [but three of] the buildings of the fort and the storehouse of ammunition and provision." No one was hurt, but most of the colonists were left destitute, stripped of all personal possessions. The Reverend Robert Hunt, one of the originals, lost his entire library.

Francis Perkins and his son, just off the boat, lost everything they owned except the clothes they were wearing and a mattress yet to be brought ashore. In the bitterest weeks of winter, the loss of food was critical, for the colony would not be able to produce its own for months. The river froze nearly all the way across: big fish were caught in the ice, and the industrious settlers were able to chop these out and fry them up in their own fat.[22]

But they needed food from the Indians. In February, when the ice broke up, Newport sailed round the point of the peninsula and up the York River in embassy to Werowocomoco. He took forty men, half of them gentlemen soldiers, along with Smith as interpreter and chargé d'affaires. Four or five hundred warriors greeted the English. Twenty painted concubines surrounded the paramount chief, who was full of laughter and hospitality. They exchanged boys: Wahunsonacock sent Namontack to live with the English and learn their language, and Newport left the teenager Thomas Savage to live in Werowocomoco. Wahunsonacock would not condescend to trade, but he was happy to exchange gifts, which suited Newport, who, following Company instructions, meant to "bewitch" the Indians "with his bounty." Newport pretended to accept gifts of corn and meat as a gesture of his own kindness rather than need. Wahunsonacock, Smith realized, was only too willing to take advantage of the strategy, getting all the useful goods—tools and such—for a few bushels of corn. Smith was disgusted. He had little respect for gestures of diplomacy and had come only to horse-trade. Taking little care to hide his contempt for an Indian policy drawn up in the comfort of a London boardroom, he finagled two or three hundred bushels from the chief for a "few blue beads."[23]

But the damage had already been done. Under Newport's direction, the English paid four times the amount Smith offered for Indian corn and meat. Newport countenanced private exchanges, and settlers' and sailors' trade flooded the region with European goods—copper, iron tools, beads, trifles. Hungry colonists and eager sailors paid more and more for less and less. Soon a pound of copper fetched what an ounce did before Newport's arrival.[24] The palisade became meaningless. Indians came and went every day, talking with whom they wanted, and settlers wandered beyond the fort without any talk of passports.

Worse yet was the main business that interested Newport: looking for gold. The spring of 1608 blossomed with these golden dreams, which had been seeded by Newport himself, who had brought home to England barrels full of ore the previous May. The refiners in England proved all those samples false, but Newport, having convinced himself that riches were to be mined in Virginia, staked his reputation on that commodity, and so all his heart went into finding it. The Company's directors were so convinced that they banned anyone but Newport from exploring the Chesapeake, lest some colonist discover gold on their own and pocket the treasure. Now Smith was angry. He quarreled openly with Martin, who had bought into Newport's scheme. So much of the colony's resources, Smith felt, were spent on a fool's errand when they needed to be clearing fields and planting crops and rebuilding the fort and staking weirs in the streams. What little stock was left in the ship of "beef, pork, oil, aqua vitae, fish, butter and cheese, [and] beer" was eaten up by sailors and gold diggers in the fourteen weeks that Newport dallied on the Chesapeake. Smith wished the mariner had put all that food ashore and sailed off in January. He grieved "to see all necessary business neglected to [freight] such a drunken ship with so much gilded dirt."[25]

Finally, Newport left, on April 10, 1608, his ship filled with more samples of ore and foolish hopes. Powhatan sent him twenty turkeys in a gesture of respect, which, by agreement, Newport reciprocated with a gift of twenty swords.[26] Wingfield sailed with him, that thorn removed at last from the colony's side. Ratcliffe's protégé, the ambitious Gabriel Archer, stripped of his seat on the council, went home as well, no doubt to be sure that the directors heard Ratcliffe's version of the colony's first, disastrous year. And Namontack, Wahunso-nacock's emissary, was on board, the Company's first native guest to London.

Newport was gone five months, from April to September, and Smith started undermining Ratcliffe the moment he left. It began with the *Phoenix*, a ship that had sailed from England with Newport in the First Supply, but had gone missing in a fog near the end of their journey. Contrary winds that Newport managed to escape drove the *Phoenix* off the Virginia coast. Unable to beat back toward the main-land, eventually she relented, and wintered in the Caribbean. Such was the industry of her captain, Francis Nelson, that their victuals were not diminished but augmented by the delay. Provisions obtained from native islanders were laid in store, and Nelson gave these freely to the Virginia settlement along with forty more settlers, an "honest dealing" that distinguished him from Newport in the eyes of two Smith devotees, Anas Todkill and Thomas Studley.[27]

Smith and Ratcliffe disagreed about what to load in the *Phoenix* for the return to England. Smith wanted to fill it with cedar, which would recoup at least part of the Company's investment and begin to demonstrate how Jamestown might eventually become a going concern. The colony could profit, slowly, if a steady stream of commod-ities might spring from Virginia, such as tar and pitch cooked from the pine trees, wainscoting cut from cedar, furs, and other mate-rials. Some cash crop would manifest years in the future. To develop such resources, the English needed to turn Jamestown into a proper plantation, and Smith and Scrivener organized work gangs to fell trees, repair of the palisade, rebuild the church, and reroof the storehouse. Fields were readied, as they were in the Indian villages, for the planting of corn.[28]

Meanwhile, Ratcliffe dreamt of gold and wanted to fill the *Phoenix* up with ore. He ordered Smith to take sixty men up beyond the falls to look for commodities in the stony upcountry toward the mountains. The expedition would take almost half of the population out of productive work, and Smith did not expect to find anything valuable, but the scheme played into his hands. He had his company "so well trained to their arms and orders" that "[w]ithin six days . . . they little feared with whom they should encounter." Well armed and properly disciplined, sixty European soldiers could roam Virginia with impunity. And they took their orders from John Smith, a personal corps du guard. Part of this company was made up of the gentlemen already familiar with arms and soldiering, but others were drawn from the commoners. Some hated the discipline. Some loved it.

Anas Todkill was one who loved it. He came to Virginia as John Martin's servant, perhaps a footman, the lowest of the low in Smith's view. Smith scorned this type of laborer as having no more initiative than the idling type of gentleman. A rough-hewn carpenter or smith was infinitely more useful than the groomed, liveried servant of an aristocrat. Such men could hardly be said to have *chosen* to come to Virginia. To what extent could someone bound in service refuse to accompany his master? He might have the legal right to refuse, but to what degree did economic necessity coerce "consent"? But Todkill broke the mold. Serving in Smith's company of soldiers released him from service to Martin. Who would not prefer to take orders from a man like Smith and carry a sword and musket than take orders from Martin and carry his luggage? It was probably the most meaningful act of self-determination in Todkill's life, and he proved to be a daring soldier and loyal subordinate. By 1608 the narratives stopped calling him a laborer. By 1612 he was listed as a soldier. By 1624 he was a gentleman. Smith's command transformed several laborers into soldiers, which elevated their dignity and knit them together by faith and loyalty.

The expedition beyond the falls never did get off the ground, but it gave Smith the clout he needed to defy Ratcliffe and Martin. Scrivener had allied himself with Smith, which split the council two against two. At least technically, Ratcliffe, the president, had the power to break ties. But Smith had his sixty soldiers. The real trouble started in early summer. Wahunsonacock sent another twenty turkeys to Jamestown with the expectation of getting another twenty swords. Smith took the turkeys but gave no weapons in recompense. The Indians staged any number of "ambuscadoes," apparently not harming anyone but surprising them "at work" and making off with "spades, shovels, swords, or tools" whenever they could. Following Company policy, which instructed them to "be anything [but] peace breakers," Ratcliffe and Martin required the settlers to suffer these affronts.[29]

But it "chanced" that some Indians attempted to ambush John Smith himself. The irascible captain would abide no affront to his own person. He "hunted up and down" Jamestown Island, sweeping it clean of Indians, whipping and beating any that he found. A posse of his loyalists captured seven Indians, whom "for their villainies [Smith] detained prisoners." He bound the men in the hold of the pinnace. In retaliation, the local Indians seized a couple of unsuspecting English roaming in their woods. These two were merely following general practice, allowed by Ratcliffe's lax rule and encouraged by the peace concluded between Newport and Wahunsonacock. But Smith exhibited little concern for the two English hostages: to him, they were caught because they were undisciplined. When a delegation of Indians appeared at the fort's gate demanding that he exchange hostages, Smith opened the gate and led a furious charge, "and in less than half an hour he so hamp'red their insolencies that they brought them his two men" without any reciprocation.

Smith proceeded to terrorize his prisoners. He dragged one man out of the boat's lower deck, leaving the other six to imagine his fate.

They heard the Englishman give commands. A volley of musket fire and the smell of powder. The hatch swung open again, flooding the dark with summer light and the silhouette of John Smith. He informed the remaining six that he had just executed their fellow, and then he dragged off his next victim. He showed this man a rack and explained how that device of torture would stretch a man. Then he pointed a file of muskets at him. This man, who happened to be a councillor from Paspahegh, broke down and confessed Wahunsonacock's grand scheme of betrayal. The chief meant to pretend he was their friend until Newport came back from England with Namontack safe and sound. Then the Tsenacomocoans would prepare a feast and so "enamor Captain Nuport and his men" that the Indians could "cut their throats."[30]

In truth, Smith had killed no one. The ruse was designed to get the Indians to "confess their intents," and he thought it succeeded. But just as likely the Paspahegh's confession was a ruse as well. Tortured psychologically, facing physical torture, men tend to confess what their tormentors want to hear, and John Smith certainly wanted to hear about Wahunsonacock's duplicity. It served his purposes. But Smith had not calculated on Pocahontas. She proved the peacemaker. She appeared at the fort, sent by her father to plead for mercy, and she gave certain gifts to demonstrate Wahunsonacock's goodwill. The powerful Opechancanough did the same, sending a token and asking that Smith release two of the prisoners, his particular friends. Smith accepted the gifts, quit terrorizing his prisoners, and kept them for another two days, treating them more humanely before he "sent them packing."[31]

Ratcliffe and Martin were furious but could do nothing, because the incident shifted power away from them. The *Phoenix* was laden with cedar, as Smith had wanted, not ore, and Martin climbed aboard, too, or was carried aboard, leaving the land that rendered him "always very sickly and unserviceable." His old servant, Anas Todkill, thought Virginia was well rid of him. In a year and a half Martin had ventured no farther than Paspahegh, seven miles upriver, and even then he was careful to return to Jamestown before nightfall "lest the dew should distemper him." In Todkill's narrative, one can hear the ex-servant's reserve of contempt for the master who claimed the honor of rank without earning it. With Martin gone, Smith said that the colony was now "free from mutinies" and that everyone was "in love with another."[32] Dry irony: what he meant was that he controlled the council and no one dared defy him. The president's second vote was used only to break a tie, so Scrivener and Smith together carried every vote, two to Ratcliffe's one. Smith could do what he wanted.

He did not want to take sixty men on a hike into the mountains. He fitted out the barge for a seven-week "discovery" of the upper Chesapeake, beyond the Potomac River, in clear defiance of the Company's order that only Captain Newport search the bay. Smith took only seven "gentlemen" and seven commoners: a fisherman, a fishmonger, a blacksmith, a tailor, a carpenter, a humble laborer, and Todkill, the gentleman's servant. Smith hoped that the headwaters of the bay would bring them to some narrow isthmus so that they might climb to the spine of a ridge and sight the South Sea. Short of that, they would reconnoiter bands of Indians on the frontier of Tsenacomoco and even beyond. They visited the Indians of the Eastern Shore. They sailed across the bay to the Western Shore and traveled thirty leagues farther inland to uninhabited woods thick with undergrowth and full of "wolves, bears, deer, and other wild beasts." They looked for the Massawomeks, a civilization rumored to be as advanced as the Aztecs of Mexico. The bay was still nine miles wide at this point and they seemed to be no closer to its headwaters.[33]

At first the gentlemen thought that "our captain," John Smith, "would make too much haste home" and that they would need to urge him on. Smith's fortitude surprised them. Then his perseverance alarmed them. At least six of the gentlemen were newly arrived. (The seventh, James Burne, appears in neither the original manifest nor in the list of settlers who arrived in the First Supply.) They were not used to the June climate or the deprivations suffered by explorers. They were tired of rowing. After about two weeks of eating soggy, spoiled rations, they would go no farther. Discontent became grumbling and finally erupted in "continual complaints." Smith must turn the boat around. By contrast, four of the seven commoners had been in Virginia over a year, while only two came in the ships of the First Supply, and one, the fishmonger Richard Keale, appears on neither manifest. None of these commoners raised a fuss. They were used to hard work and servitude. Or perhaps they were just devoted to Smith, as we know Todkill was.[34]

How Smith reacted demonstrates just how flexible he was. Like a Machiavellian cat, he could withdraw his imperious claws if the situation demanded. It was not just a matter of telling the men to shut up and row. On a boat of fourteen people, the discontent of seven armed men must be respected, and so Smith tried persuasion. He delivered an oration. Like Shakespeare's Henry V, he exhorted them to glory. Gentlemen, he began, remember the great English explorers who came before us! They did not flag. Ralph Lane's men in Roanoke "importuned him to proceed" so long as they had a dog to boil and sassafras to season it. "What a shame it would be for you," he said, with a month's provisions in the boat, "to force me return" to Jamestown. Besides, he lied to them, the worst of the journey was behind them! And whatever dangers and discomforts they suffered, hadn't their captain suffered them, too, taking "the worst part to myself"? "Regain therefore your old spirits," he implored them in his peroration, "for return I will not (if God please) till I have seen the

Massawomeks, found Patawomek, or the head of this water you conceit to be endless." This speech is the emotional climax of the tale. Rousing words indeed, but the hearts of the gentlemen were not moved, and the sequence ends in anticlimax. It did not turn out like Agincourt, with heaps of glory. Winds blew in their faces for the next two or three days, making progress up the bay impossible. And three or four of the gentlemen fell horribly sick. Smith agreed to ride home on the ebbing tides, but he wrangled a concession from the gentlemen: they would explore the Potomac River on the way home.

Nearly everything we know of Smith's explorations come from him. This most prolific of all the English explorers wrote three not-quite-distinct accounts of Jamestown's early years. The first, *A True Relation of such occurrences and accidents of Note as hath hapned in Virginia since the First Planting of that Collony, which is now resident in the South part thereof, till the last return from thence*, runs to thirty-seven pages in Haile's 1998 edition and has the virtue of immediacy. Smith wrote this "letter" when he was still in Virginia and the events were fresh. It tells the story from the Atlantic crossing in late 1606 through spring 1608, when he sent it to England. Not long after his return to England, Smith published a longer account, which incorporated contributions by several other "Diligent Observers that were Residents in Virginia." Included in that 1612 book was Smith's now-famous *Map of Virginia*, accompanied by his *Description of the Countrey, the Commodities, People, Government and Religion*, which also provides modern anthropologists with their richest source of information about the Chesapeake's Indians circa 1600. (An earlier map that Smith sketched in 1608 resembles English military maps of Ireland's coast, noting the havens and coastal towns of Tsenacomoco. Though used by the earliest settlers, that map disappeared from English history. But Spain's ambassador to England, Pedro de Zúñiga, obtained a copy through espionage and sent it to King Phillip III, who filed it away until the nineteenth-century American scholar and editor Alexander Brown rediscovered it in the Archivo General de Simancas near Valladolid, Spain.) Finally, in 1624, Smith reworked all of his material in a *General History of Virginia, New England, and the Summer Isles*. This is by far the most extensive account we have. In Haile's edition, the Jamestown parts of the *General History* (Books I, II, and III) total more than 130 pages.

As Edward Haile puts it, Smith "rewrote" his narratives "again and again and again," and what he did not write he edited from accounts submitted by his own devotees. His texts must always be interpreted with a fair degree of skepticism. As the heroic treatment of his character indicates, Smith was not humble, and (among other things) the *General History* was meant to enhance his own stature in the public eye and cement his place in history. Nevertheless, self-aggrandizement is not a slavishly consistent purpose. Smith honestly wanted to record everything he thought was significant, and so the *General History* allows for a multiplicity of interpretations. Not everything flatters the author. For example, the failure of Smith's speech on the Chesapeake reveals the limits of his powers. The gentlemen's right to petition authority gave them a measure of self-determination. Although the *General History* touts Smith's natural talents for leadership, the narrative still reveals that government in this small community was a matter of consensus building, at least among the gentlemen. The government's word was not law unless the "better sort" of settler acquiesced. If the actors in this exploring party had been reversed—if it had been the gentlemen who supported him and the commoners who refused to go any farther— Smith would probably have acted the tyrant.[35]

After about six weeks the weary bargemen oared up to the high bank along the Jamestown fort and found the settlement was in bad shape. Those who had arrived in January with Newport and in April in the *Phoenix* were passing their first summer in the swampy Virginia heat, and they suffered the inevitable seasoning. Among them was

Matthew Scrivener, Smith's ally on the council. The remnants of the original colonists were healthier but dispirited and ill-led by Ratcliffe, who, during Smith's absence, diverted them to the construction of a "pleasure" house "in the woods." Smith roused Scrivener long enough to depose the president, two months shy of his term's expiration. This part of the story was recorded by Smith's partisans, who minimize the drama, dispatching Ratcliffe in a subordinate clause. Todkill insisted that Smith acted to "appease" the "fury" of the settlers, who other-wise would have "strangely tormented [President Ratcliffe] with revenge." But no vote was taken. The popularity of this coup d'état was attested to by Smith's men only, and whatever popular support Smith may or may not have had in his power grab, we know that he generated his own discontents. No matter how Todkill phrased it, Smith was not promoted by universal acclamation. At least some people disliked and distrusted him. But Smith had the soldiers.[36]

Having deposed Ratcliffe, Smith felt he could renew his survey of the Chesapeake. After just three days in Jamestown he abandoned the sick and groaning garrison and got back on his barge. He took six gentleman and six soldiers: four men in each group were veterans of the first trip, which suggests that Smith still enjoyed a high degree of loyalty and confidence among a cadre of settlers. They sailed down the James River, pausing at the end of the peninsula to visit Kecoughtan, which was becoming one of the most familiar of the Indian towns. Prudently, they skipped over Wahunsonacock's river, the Pamunkey or York, and proceeded up the Rappahannock, searching for that elusive passage to the Pacific and, more importantly, making contact with each Indian district and mapping the towns.

Whether or not this was Smith's original intent, his discoveries had turned into embassies and intelligence gathering. By this time the adopted son of Wahunsonacock, the man dubbed Nantaquod, understood the Indians' way of life, he spoke their language with some proficiency, and he exploited such advantages. On his first trip up the Chesapeake, several Tsenacomoco districts resisted his overtures. Indians lay in ambush along the wooded banks along "a little bayed creek" approaching a town called Onawmanient. Three or four hundred warriors—or so it seemed to the English, although the number must be exaggerated—"painted, grimed, and disguised," tried to frighten the English with "shouting, yelling, and crying as so many spirits from hell could not have showed more terrible." Smith was not impressed. He ordered his men to shoot low so the Indians could see the shots skip across the surface of the water, and then to shoot high so they would hear the lead thudding into the trees. That show of strength was enough. The Indians lay down their arms, exchanged hostages, and "used" the English "kindly." The English found similar welcomes farther up the Potomac at Patawomek and Cecocawonee: initial hostility quickly followed by friendliness.³⁷ Smith had good reason to cultivate these friendships. The towns were too far from the James River to have yet shared in the English trade, so the value of European goods had not yet deflated. Iron hatchets, copper, and glass beads were still in high demand, and if Smith would part with them, swords would be higher yet.

The Indians had nothing against Smith, they told him. They staged this masquerade of enmity because Wahunsonacock had ordered them to oppose the English. The paramount chief had informants following Smith's progress on the Chesapeake, and he knew that these movements endangered the cohesion of Tsenacomoco. Smith was contracting friendships with chiefs on both sides of the Potomac, including several villages belonging not to Tsenacomoco but to the "Conoy chiefdom," an Algonquian polity of about six districts.³⁸ Wahunsonacock had good reason to fear that those districts would fill up with European weapons, and he must have pondered what might happen when they discovered that the English were not really his subordinates.

Smith's guide on the Potomac, his "old friend Mosco, was a lusty savage" sporting a full beard, a rarity among Native Americans. The English supposed him to be the son of French trader. Mosco explained the enmity between two of Tsenacomoco's districts: the Moraughtacunds on the north bank and the Rappahannocks on the south. It was a dispute typical among neighbors in a traditional society. At the heart of the matter were three women who had been kidnapped, and Mosco helped Smith broker an exchange of bows and arrows and women that settled a peace between the two districts.[39] Back in Werowocomoco, Powhatan was watching his empire dissolve. His own prestige, which had once been the guarantor of peace among all the districts of Tsenacomoco, was now competing with the growing stature of John Smith.

Smith had his own problems. Enmity in Jamestown ran deep. On the south bank of the Potomoc, the Onawmanients revealed to Smith that "discontents at James town" were in league with Wahunsonacock. In an ambiguous passage that still puzzles scholars, the *General History* claims certain settlers betrayed Smith because he "did cause them to stay in [Indian] country against their wills." James Horn thinks that the "discontents" were men in Ratcliffe's faction who hoped to use the Indians to murder Smith. Edward Haile thinks that Smith, unable to feed everyone in Jamestown, "forced" some settlers to live among the Indians against their will, and so they plotted his death.[40] Or maybe during the worst of disease and poor leadership, discontents fled Jamestown in the summer of 1608 as they had in the summer of 1607, and they freely gave Wahunsonacock intelligence on Smith. Not everyone took to Smith's discipline as willingly as Anas Todkill, and many found Ratcliffe's incompetence terrifying. Felling trees for Smith or building a house in the woods for Ratcliffe was all of a piece: a slave's life that ended in a quick miserable death. Without more evidence, we will never know for certain who among the English was collaborating with Wahunsonacock, but it's pretty certain that English were still turning renegade.

When Smith finally returned to Jamestown on September 7, the crisis of the summer was past. Many of the sick had died, and those who had not died had recovered. Though much spoiled by rain, a harvest had at least been "gathered." And the deposed president Ratcliffe was now a prisoner. While Smith was gone, Ratcliffe tried to regain his office, but Scrivener, recovered from his illness, accused him of mutiny and clapped him in irons. On September 10, Smith officially claimed the presidency. Though often before "importuned" to take over Ratcliffe's presidency, the *General History* explains, the captain hitherto had always refused. Now he was chosen "by the election of the council and request of the company." The "election" of the council means that Scrivener approved it. Every other councillor but Smith himself was dead or exiled or under arrest. But who was included in "the company" and how did they "request" Smith? The *General History* offers no details of a formal vote, so it was probably an equivocal, informal acclamation. The only legal candidates for president were Scrivener and Smith, so there is no reason to question this purported preference for the experienced Captain Smith, regardless of the enemies he had made since leaving England a year and a half earlier. Although there is no evidence one way or another, we might surmise that the "company" who asked Smith to take over the presidency—those with enough moral authority to influence proceedings—now included some commoners. Only gentlemen were invited to witness and thus legitimize the council's election of Wingfield in 1607. By contrast, the assent of commoners like Anas Todkill must have lent legitimacy to Smith's ascension.[41]

Smith immediately divided the colony into five "squadrons," and each squadron was trained in how to take a "watch." Under Ratcliffe, all sense of military order had dissolved. Sentries that had fallen into disuse. Settlers and Indians came and went as they pleased. Smith's regime swept such laxity away. Under the west bulwark a clearing became known as "Smithfield," and the captain drilled "the whole company [there] every Saturday." The Indians would gather to watch the maneuvers of well-commanded European troops. Everyone trained in arms, forming files that shot at targets in the trees. "More than a hundred savages would stand in an amazement" when the fusillade "would batter a tree."[42] But just at the moment Smith began to mold the colony in his own image, it was snatched from his hands.

꧁꧂

## CHAPTER FOUR

# Call of the Wild

**Sails again appeared in the bay,** the "Second Supply" of Jamestown, the third wave of settlers. Captain Newport brought seventy fresh colonists, including the first two English women in America since Roanoke, "Mistress Forrest and Anne Burras her maid." Twenty-seven gentlemen, fourteen tradesmen, twelve mere "laborers," two boys, and the anonymous "some others," who were probably commoners also, joined the few survivors of the first settlement and the remainder of the First Supply. Among the settlers were eight craftsmen from Poland and Germany whom the Company had recruited "to make pitch, tar, glass, mills, and soap-ashes." Whether these foreigners earned shares in the Company or were mere wage earners—and whether or not they had the same legal protections as Englishmen—is unclear, but it would not take long before they decided that the conditions in Jamestown violated the terms of their contract.

The Second Supply came ashore to a settlement meager in people, food, and buildings, but as well organized and drilled as a military garrison. The Company sent two officers, "ancient soldiers and valiant gentlemen," Captain Richard Waldo and Captain Peter Wynn, to augment the council. Peter Wynn, a tall, imposing, soldierly man with a dark complexion, was the "embodiment of his age," or at least one type of the Elizabethan soldier, already so familiar to Jamestown. He came from an aristocratic Welsh family that was sliding towards obscurity, and he tried to claw his way back by becoming a mercenary soldier, sometimes for and sometimes against England. In Ireland he saw—in fact, he had a hand in—scenes as bad as those Smith described in the Turkish wars: the slash-and-burn tactics of Mountjoy's final campaign against Ulster rebels. He had seen his share of garrison life, both in Ireland and the Netherlands, the latter in a prestigious position garnering five hundred guilders a month, a plum job secured on Mountjoy's recommendation. This service brought him into contact with Sir Thomas Gates, whose long association with the Virginia Company secured for Wynn passage on the Second Supply and a seat on the colonial council. Wynn probably considered Jamestown to be yet another in a long string of military postings. Valued as "an old hand and a steady one," the Company's directors appointed Wynn as "sergeant-major" of the fort, essentially making him the commander of the garrison.[1]

Although their arrival meant the end of his own authority, Smith gave credit where credit was due and admitted the military worth of both Wynn and Waldo. While Captain Waldo seems very quickly to have come under Smith's influence, the youngest councillor, Matthew Scrivener, who till then had been Smith's protégé, attached himself to the equally impressive Captain Wynn. Wynn, Scrivener, and Newport all strictly followed Company policy, which made three votes against Smith and Waldo.[2] Newport's semiannual consultations with the directors in London gave him a special privilege, and in the fall of 1608 his domination of the council gave him command again. He delivered to Smith a formal, written, and severe rebuke from the Company's directors for encouraging factions and for producing so little return on their investment. And he restored the colony's old policy of conciliating Wahunsonacock. Newport came bearing gifts for the chief: a scarlet cloak, a poster bed, and a crown.

The coronation of Wahunsonacock was an idea cooked up back in the committee rooms of London, among tables strewn with hand-drawn maps, surrounded by shelves filled with every book ever written about America. The directors were not naive. They had John Smith's handwritten letter, the *True Relation*, recounting his monthlong captivity. They had Newport's firsthand intelligence on the Tsenaco-mocoans and his measure of Wahunsonacock. And they had a live Indian, Wahunsonacock's representative, Namontack, dressed in animal skins, tattooed, tall, and strong-limbed as Algonquians tended to be compared to Europeans, standing right before them in the warmth of an English fireplace and speaking broken English. On paper, the coronation made perfect sense. It would concede Wahun-sonacock's authority over Tsenacomoco, but at the same time it would subordinate him to England and, by extension, subordinate his people.

Smith thought the whole thing was stupid. He grumbled while he and four others trudged twelve miles across the peninsula to deliver an invitation he knew would be refused. At the south bank of the York River, he hired paddlers to take the deputation in a canoe to the Tsenacomocoan capital. Smith called at Wahunsonacock's spacious house and asked if the paramount chief of the Tsenacomo-coans might come to the little fort at Jamestown to accept his crown. The chief, who surely knew that the delegation was coming, was not to be found at home. He might be back tomorrow. Pocahontas, full of her "wit and spirit," greeted Smith's delegation. It was a mere nine months since she had saved his life in this very place, but in the interim she had come of age. She was now the "nonpareil" of Tsena-comoco. Pocahontas would entertain them while they waited for her father to return. She sat them down on mats before a fire in a clearing.[3] Suddenly the woods erupted with "a hideous noise and shrieking." The five Englishmen jumped to their feet, unsheathed their swords, grabbed a few of the old men as shields, and faced what they thought would be their death at the hands of hundreds of warriors. But the other men, women, and children sitting round the fire assured them that no one was about to do them harm. And Pocahontas herself appeared and assured them that no one was about to attack. The English relaxed. They released the old men. They sat back down. All eyes turned again to the trees. "Presently," Smith recounts, "thirty young women came naked out of the woods."

The sight stunned the Englishmen. The women shrieked and shouted as they burst from the trees, their skin painted, each woman a different color, each wearing horns on her head. Giant antlers crowned the leader, and she brandished a bow and arrows, and the others each had some prop, a sword, a club, "another a pot stick . . . everyone with their several devices." They formed a circle. They danced and sang. Singly, they fell into "infernal passions" before joining the dance and song again. It was magnificent and provocative, and while, no doubt, the nakedness of the women was hardly shocking to the native audience—after all, the entire village was there, children included—neither can we doubt that the whole ritual had a sexual dimension. It was calculated to provoke male desire. The sight of so many naked women, painted, outlandishly horned, dancing, seized by frenzy—how could it not arouse the abstemious Englishmen? The dance went on for nearly an hour, the firelight throwing shadows of the women's limbs and horns across the faces of the audience. Then the dancers withdrew again into the woods, shrieking and shouting as they went.

Silence. John Smith might have guessed what would happen next, and perhaps three of his companions, Andrew Buckler, Edward Brinton, and Samuel Collier, did as well, for these four men had been in Virginia a long while. Smith of course had spent many nights in Indian villages, not just during his captivity, but during his previous embassies and during his discoveries. Probably the others had too. But the new councillor, Captain Waldo, was a novice. This was his introduction to Indian culture, and he would have been unprepared for the return of the dancers, no longer naked and horned but "reaccommodated" and solemn. A "nymph" led each man to a lodging, brought him inside, and crowded and pressed and offered her body. If the English showed the least resistance, the woman hung about him crying, "Love you not me?"

Smith's narrative fades to black. Although it assumes a moral high tone, it evades describing what happened next. Significantly, it does not positively declare that each Englishmen resisted his enchanting escort. Altogether, Smith's narratives—the *True Relation* of 1608, the *Proceedings* of 1612, and the *General History* of 1625—are prudishly quiet about sex. In this instance, the next thing the reader sees is the postcoital feast, another cornucopia of the senses, baskets of fruit, "fish and flesh in wooden platters," beans, peas, women serving, women again dancing. Deeper into the night, after the last of the food was eaten or cleared away, the "mirth being ended," each man, fattened and bewildered, was again taken up by a woman, who carried a firebrand through the dark street as she led him to his lodging.[4] Smith's tone follows the trend in European accounts of Indians in the first century of the encounter between these worlds. Very few European intellectuals could see Indians as anything but the devil's party.

There was one great exception to that rule. The third son of the late mayor of Bordeaux, Michel Eyquem de Montaigne inherited his father's château and its "large, complex estate with its extensive land-holdings." He did not need to work. His wealth came from the hard labor of peasants. So on his birthday, February 28, 1571, at the age of thirty-eight, he retired from politics to a little study off his library. Montaigne dedicated the second half of his life to books. He would read and think and write. Nine years later, he published the fruit of his meditations, *Essais*, which sowed the seeds of revolution.[5]

In 2003 the philosopher Ann Hartle described Montaigne as a "great-souled man without pride." *Great-souled* is an ancient term, coming first from Greek and then through the Latin term, *magna-nimitas*, whence our word *magnanimity*. According to Aristotle, excellence and virtue not only reside in the great-souled man but are concentrated there, magnified. Aristotle thought magnanimity must come with pride, because if the great-souled man down-played his virtue, he would be lying or at least engaging in false modesty. He must accept the honor he deserves. In this, as in so many things, Montaigne rewrote the rule. He possessed this "clas-sical greatness of soul" but alloyed to it "Christian humility," a sense that one's entire existence, and hence one's virtue, is an unmerited gift.[6]

This magnanimity without pride, a great yet humble soul, accounts for Montaigne's achievements. It helped him invent the literary genre we know as the essay, but more than that, Montaigne invented a new way of thinking about the world—new at least to Renaissance Europe. *To essay* means *to attempt*, to try to do something, to think through an issue with dispassionate logic. Most importantly, with ruthless humility one must recognize and try to transcend one's own prejudices. Montaigne's essays are like mental excursions or journeys, meditations on subjects that range from smells to drunken-ness; he wrote about prayers, cruelty, cowardice, thumbs, and Cato the Younger. They essays have the provisional tone of a trial run at something, an experiment, an unmapped attempt to get somewhere. Never is Montaigne doctrinaire, never the pedant. He tries out ideas, tries out new ways of thinking, tries to see things through someone else's eyes. He doubts his own preconceptions as he would doubt the most obvious fool. This was his genius: Montaigne recognized that his education, his class, his religion, his nation, and his personal proclivities had tracked habits of thought into his mind the way the wheels of wagons will track ruts in soft earth. The French aristocrat's habits of thought were so long trodden by previous generations and so dried up by the hot sun that they made deep, hardened grooves in the brain. The wagon train of ideas tended to roll in those ruts. Montaigne tried very hard to bump out of the grooves, so the wagon would follow not custom but reason. A generation later, when he helped invent the Scientific Revolution, Sir Francis Bacon, who had read Montaigne's *Essais* in the 1590s, called these bad habits of thought "idols," false effigies we bow down to. Honest observations of phenomena, logical interpretation of those observations, the courage to follow logic wherever it leads, even if the wagon carrying our thoughts move toward heresy—these are tenets of science even today.[7] Galileo used his new telescope to observe Jupiter's moons and the phases of Venus. He recorded his data in notebooks, reasoned from the evidence, and concluded that Copernicus was right: the earth orbits the sun. Accused by the Church of heresy, he recanted. He conceded that an immobile earth was the center of the universe. But tradition tells us that as he left the Inquisition chamber, where the instruments of torture were so persuasively laid out on the table, he could not help but mutter beneath his breath, "And yet it moves." No matter what the Church said and no matter even that Galileo himself recanted, the scientific truth was indisputable: the earth spins round the sun. Galileo could not disbelieve it. It was an expression of humility, not of pride, to follow evidence to its logical conclusion.[8] Montaigne's essays pioneered this skeptical way of thinking and applied it to human society. Stephen Greenblatt, the twentieth century's most prominent critic of the English Renaissance, described Montaigne as a leader among "thoughtful men and women [who] were asking the most basic questions about the social order, the oppressive force of custom, the nature of obedience, and the ineradicable longing for liberty."[9]

The French aristocrat learned to think this way from Native Americans. In 1562, eighteen years before the first edition of *Essais*,

French explorers brought a few Tupinambá Indians from the mouth
of the Amazon River to Paris. The nearly naked ambassadors met
twelve-year-old King Charles IX, whose face peeped out from under a
crust of stiff, embroidered finery. The Indians witnessed the pomp
and circumstance and the obsequious rituals of the French court.
They were puzzled. They asked questions.

Why would "tall men with long beards, strong and well-armed . . .
submit themselves to obey a beardless child"?

Their impertinence ranged a little wider: Why were some people
in France "full-gorged," while others were "hunger-starven and
bare with need and poverty"?

More radical yet: Why did the needy "endure such an injustice"
rather than strangle the fattened rich or "set fire on their houses"?

The king's attendants smiled, amused by the naiveté of their
savage guests. Inequality was so rutted into their brains that they
could not see wisdom. The Indians' incomprehension of French ways,
the courtiers imagined, indicated the savagery of the Tupinambá. It
was a symbol, like their nakedness, of their inferiority to the French.
People who eat their enemies, the courtiers smugly mused, could not
be expected to comprehend the structure of a complex, modern
society like France.[10]

The Tupinambá did eat their enemies. That made it hard for the
French to take their ideas about politics seriously. A few years earlier
a very popular and quaintly titled book appeared: *Veritable Historie and
Description of a country belonging to the wild, naked, savage, man-eating
people situated in the New World, America*. The slim text recounted the
exciting tale of a European soldier, Hans Stade, a German who was
employed as a gunner at a Portuguese garrison fort on the coast of
Brazil, near present-day São Paulo. One day Stade wandered beyond
the stone walls in pursuit of his tardy servant, an enslaved Indian,
when he was ambushed by several Tupinambá Indians, who shot him,
clubbed him, stripped him naked, and dragged him to the beach. The

Cannibals in the
sixteenth-century
European
imagination.

captors were from different villages, which presented a problem: Who
would get the prize? Some resolved that they must butcher Stade on
the beach, lest someone go without his morsel. But the "king" among
them settled the issue: they must bring their captive home in one piece
so their wives could see him alive. Then they would "brew drinks and
assemble together," make their feast, and, as Stade told the story back
home in Homberg, "eat me among them." Stade was not eaten. The
king decided he was too valuable to kill, so he lived among these
people for nearly a year, long enough to observe their ways in detail.
"When they first bring their enemies home," he explained, "the
women and children beat them." Then they are painted, adorned with
feathers, and treated well. A young woman is given to each prisoner,
and they have sex and live together till she becomes pregnant, which
was a sort of death warrant for the captive. Then the Tupinambá
invite their friends from neighboring villages, and they all dance
and drink liquor for days. They intricately decorate a killing club,
inscribing designs in a dust of eggshell on its barrel. They bind the
captive, build the roasting fire in front of his eyes, parade the
club before him, go through a few ritual verbal exchanges with the

prisoner, trash talk, and then "his brains are dashed out." The victim is skinned at the fire; the legs and arms are cut off and given to four women who dance around the village "raising great cries of joy." They make a broth of his entrails. They eat everything: "the brains in the head, the tongue, and whatever else is eatable." Stade's book helped to form the prejudices of Europeans, who slipped easily into the habit of thought that defined Native Americans as devils or devil-worshippers. Cannibalism became a symbol of irredeemability.[11]

But among the king of France's retainers, standing hardly more than an arm's length from the boy sovereign, was a young Michel de Montaigne. The questions that the Indians asked stuck in his brain, for they cut through the frippery of France with Socratic precision. Nor would he forget the supercilious smiles of the courtiers, the oh-so-superior attitude with which the civilized imagines himself better than the primitive. The scene haunted Montaigne for nearly twenty years. The Tupinambá pulled Montaigne's mind out of the rutted tracks so he could trace the trail of reason. So what if Indians do eat their enemies? Was that a true marker of moral depravity? The rough villages of America—Montaigne toyed with the idea—had more nobility in them than those who roistered under all the chandeliers in all the châteaus of France. Barefoot, half-naked, their spines unbent by the exigencies of modern life, their ears not yet assaulted by the din of cities, Amazonian savages stood up straight and tall and their broad shoulders expressed a natural human dignity. Why wear clothes? The primitive's nakedness proves that human skin can endure the elements as well as animals' skins. Witness the Irish, Montaigne suggested, or the ancient Gauls, who wore hardly anything against the northern cold. Not necessity but custom dresses civilized men and women, and then the clothed skin loses its natural durability.[12] The Tupinambá fashioned their morality like they fashioned their tools: simply, with the stuff that nature provided. Such simplicity steered them closer to the truth than morals hewed by all the sharpened swords of Christendom. Who could doubt it, when so-called civilized men tortured and killed whole towns over such arcana as the interpretation of the Eucharist? When the machinery of the Christian state manufactured such horrors as the Saint Bartholomew's Day Massacre, who could claim that every step that brought us further from our primitive origins brought us closer to God? Perhaps, Montaigne pondered, the savage retained a natural nobility that the artificialities of civilization disfigured and crippled, like the spine of a Paris beggar made crooked by years of poverty. Primitive societies were not far removed from nature, not much higher than the brute animals, but maybe—Montaigne was no longer playing with the idea—being closer to nature was better than being civilized. Isn't birdsong sweeter than the flute?

The Tupinambá represented a state of existence that the French, so far removed from their own tribal origins, had long since forgotten. Not since Roman swords forced civilization on the Gallic tribes had the French even imagined a casteless, primitive way of life. One and half millennia separated the modern Frenchman from his uncivilized ancestors, before writing and history and inequality and a thousand luxuries came with the Romans over the Alps. In the last fifteen centuries, had the French lost more than they had gained? In the lush Amazon and the frozen wastes of Canada lived people who reproved the depravity and inhumanity of Europe. Nature's "puritie" shone in the faces of the Tupinambá visitors, shaming France for the vanity and frivolity of its painted "enterprises." Primitives, Montaigne suggested, lived according to "the true and most profitable vertues." The more civilized a society became, the more "corrupted" were its tastes and pleasures. Europe, for example, divided its people into the very few rich and the multitudes of poor. It made no sense that many people hungered while a few feasted, that starving men should not raise a hand or weapon against the rich. It was unnatural. That grown men would bend their knee to a weakling child—it made no sense. An Indian from Brazil, whose brain was unscored by a thousand years of inequality, could see the matter clearly. The hungry and poor acquiesced in their fate because Europeans had long ago suppressed their natural selves.[13]

Montaigne's view of Americans was romanticized. He never went to Brazil. Besides his brief interview with those Tupinambá ambassadors, which he admitted was marred by poor translators, all he knew he had read from books. He was not speaking after long, careful, scientific observation of Native Americans. He was testing out ideas. And the central idea of his essay "Of Cannibals" is that the Indian life reminded Montaigne of the "golden age" fabled by poetry and philosophy. That term derives from Greek and Roman notions of history, which held that humanity began in a near-perfect era, and with each generation we slipped gradually into the corrupted here and now. Hesiod and Pindar both described the golden age as more primitive than contemporary Greek society. In the 1590s, Edmund Spenser's *Faerie Queene* described the golden age as a time when people were contented with what they needed and did not covet more; the very earth offered up her produce; people loved truth and hated fraud; there was no need for war, and "peace universal reign'd amongst men and beasts." Spenser invoked this mythic image to cast in greater relief "the harsh, corrupt reality of Elizabethan England." As one literary scholar puts it, Elizabethan writers fused the Greek and Roman concept of a golden age with the Christian notion of Eden's paradise before the Fall.[14]

Montaigne thought that America brought that paradise close to hand. The natives of America, he wrote, "hath no kinde of traffike, no knowledge of Letters, no intelligence of numbers." They wore no clothes. They did not improve the lands and had "no use of wine, corne," or metal. (As Tsenacomoco demonstrates, Montaigne's description paints Indians as far more primitive than they actually were.) The Indians' deprivations, Montaigne theorized, were a virtue, for neither had they magistrates or political inequalities. None were rich, but none were poor. They inherited nothing and didn't worry about passing things on. They had no occupation but idleness. They had no use for contracts. "The very words that import lying, falsehood, treason, dissimulations, covetousnes, envie, detraction, and pardon, were never heard of amongst them." Far better than Plato's commonwealth, Montaigne suggested, was this world without government.[15]

"Of Cannibals" might have romanticized Native American life, but it demonstrates how some Europeans might be attracted to traditional societies like the Algonquian districts on the Chesapeake. Montaigne invented the notion that before people developed governments, before they even developed what we might call "societies," they lived in a nearly "natural" condition. The Tupinambá seemed to prove by real-life example what the Greeks could only imagine. Neither Montaigne nor any European yet conceived of what would come to be called humanity's "state of nature," but "Of Cannibals" has the idea in embryo. In the Americas, Montaigne thought, people lived in close accordance with their nature. The concept of an ancient state of nature might have come from a romanticized view of America, but that thought was a herald of dawn, an early ray of light on the tops of trees before the full sunrise of Enlightenment.

## LOVE, AMERICAN-STYLE

John Smith understood at least this much: the allure of Pocahontas threatened traditional English ways. Sex is the most important understudied aspect of colonial Virginia. What we know comes mostly from analogy: what happened elsewhere probably happened on the Chesapeake. For example, Algonquian youths in Massachusetts, the historian James Axtell explains, "took to sexual exploration early in their teens and found nothing shameful about their bodies or their amorous potential." Feeding that curiosity was the lack of privacy in Indian lodges: children could watch and in darkness listen to their parents having sex. Indians generally "placed no great value on premarital chastity," and their notions of fidelity after marriage were too liberal for Englishmen. Even the "praying Indians," those few who converted to Christianity, retained their old habits, and with some comic effect Axtell discussed the Puritans' attempts to clean up Indians' behavior. With no sense of irony, English ministers blithely insisted that they were teaching Indians to be ashamed of "what nature is ashamed of"—that is, sex.[16] Very few Indians were persuaded. They had a better sense of what was natural sexual behavior. In fact, Europeans converted to Algonquian mores far more frequently than Indians adopted puritanical habits. Perhaps not so many Puritans converted. Axtell notes that the "English population" disdained "such 'mongrel' matches." But "French readiness to marry Indians stood in marked contrast to the ethnocentric disdain" of New England's Puritans. As Axtell points out, all three civilizations mingling in North America—indigenous, French, and English—tried to convert the others to their way of life. The English failed horribly. Practically no one saw Puritan ways as superior to their own. The French enjoyed reasonable success, as many Indians and significant numbers of English converted to Catholicism and swore allegiance to France. History tends to forget that "the Indians, in the face of incredible odds, managed to convert several hundred English and French colonists" to the supposedly "primitive" way of life. The "ineluctable pride, social warmth, and cultural integrity" of the Indians' traditional society accounted for the phenomenon that so baffled Massachusetts' Puritans. In the mid-eighteenth century, Cadwallader Colden observed that it was practically impossible to persuade Europeans captured by Indians to return to civilization. "No intreaties, nor Tears of their Friends and Relations" could induce them to give up their new way of life. And those few who did return to white society "in a little Time grew tired of our Manner of living, and run away again to the Indians." Even Benjamin Franklin remarked upon it:

> When an Indian Child has been brought up among us, taught our language and habituated to our Customs, yet if he goes to see his relations and make one Indian Ramble with them, there is no perswading him ever to return . . . [But] when white persons of either sex have been taken prisoners young by the Indians, and lived a while among them, tho' ransomed by their Friends, and treated with all imaginable tenderness to prevail with them to stay among the English, yet in a Short time they become disgusted with our manner of life . . . and take the first good Opportunity of escaping into the Woods, from whence there is no reclaiming them.

Franklin was thinking like Montaigne, with the humility of the scientist not afraid to follow the evidence where it led. The woods sang a siren song.

Part of the problem of understanding this phenomenon is that we hear about it mostly from those who resisted. It was the people who did not respond to that siren song who told its story. For example, as Richard White explains, the histories and narratives of French/ Algonquian encounters in the Great Lakes Region tended to be written by the Jesuits. Such intellectuals provided the standards by which Europe measured Algonquian culture. The Jesuits simply did not have the tools to understand Indian morality. They were using a yardstick to measure sound. Indian women especially were misconstrued. Through the lens of Jesuit morality, they looked like "a disorderly and lewd set of Europeans." But French commoners, the rugged men who pioneered and traded with the Indians, had no problem discarding the Jesuits' prejudicial way of judging sexual behavior.

They enthusiastically embraced the "entirely different social logic" of the Indians, including the "virtually complete sexual freedom" of unmarried Algonquian women.[17] Sex was like a gateway drug, and there is no reason to believe that what happened in the eighteenth century did not happen in the seventeenth, just as what happened in the North more than likely happened in the South. In fact, what evidence we have gives us every reason to believe that Jamestown's settlers, especially commoners, were "escaping into the Woods" in high proportions, and that young women were the lure. One sermonizer in London in 1609, while recruiting for the colony, preached the special dangers of sex with Indians: English settlers must "keepe them to themselves." They must not "marry nor give in marriage to the heathen" lest God "may breake the neck of all good successe of this voyage." This degree of anxiety must have been triggered by what was perceived in London as all-too-common practice in Virginia.[18]

As Martin Quitt has, I think, rightly observed, the Tsenacomocoans constantly tried to seduce the English with lavish feasts and attractive women. The goal was assimilation.[19] Race mattered little to the Indians, who willingly absorbed foreigners. By the fall of 1608, they had already absorbed many of the English settlers, and Wahunsonacock had good reason to think that he might still be able to convert John Smith. Although Smith's summer exploits on the upper reaches of the bay argued against it, Pocahontas might yet be able to convert John Smith. Jamestown might yet become just another chief's town in the patchwork quilt that made up Wahunsonacock's nation.

### THE WEROANCE OF JAMESTOWN

Sly as John Smith was, he probably recognized this sexual strategy when he woke up the next morning on his palette in an Indian lodge. The fantastic images of the women dancing in the firelight were fresh in his mind as the new day dawned. The other Englishmen, roused either from their single beds or untangling themselves from the limbs of Indian women, rose with the sun. Were Smith's arms tangled round Pocahontas? She was only about thirteen years old at the time, but that did not matter to Tsenacomocoans. Menstruation was all that divided a girl from adulthood, and we know for a fact that Pocahontas was a woman by the age of fourteen, for she was married then to a warrior named Kocoum.[20] She might have matured by the fall of 1608, which would have allowed her to indulge in the same sexual freedom of all unmarried Powhatan women. The special affection between Smith and Pocahontas was well known, and the English settlement took it for granted that they were lovers. Every time the comely girl visited Jamestown, which was often, Smith's delight for her company was on open display. Smith might insist he had no dishonest or indiscreet intentions, but still he fed the rumors. At stake, of course, was more than the slight embarrassment a councillor might incur from the public exposure of his sexual exploits. For suspicious minds, Smith having sex with Pocahontas, the favorite daughter of Wahunsonacock, confirmed that he intended to make himself chief of the English and turn Jamestown into a constituent district of Tsenacomoco. To dispute such rumors, Smith's supporters pointed out that if Smith wanted to marry Pocahontas, he would already have done so, "for there was none that could have hind'red his determination." And anyway, Smith's apologists reasoned, Pocahontas was no heir. Rountree concurs with that point: Algonquian chiefdoms were matrilineal, so none of Wahunsonacock's children would inherit the paramount chiefdom. But that thinking ignores the basic fact that Wahunsonacock installed his own sons as weroances in important towns. Smith's marriage to Pocahontas could facilitate and symbolize if not enact Jamestown's absorption into Tsenacomoco, just as Wahunsonacock's coronation was supposed to subordinate him to King James. Jamestown's absorption would be further demonstrated if Smith, a.k.a. Nantaqoud, Wahunsonacock's appointed weroance, moved the colony to Capahoasic, the territory reserved for it on the Middle Peninsula.[21]

Whatever happened between Smith and Pocahontas that night, Wahunsonacock was disappointed when he finally came into town. Smith delivered his message: Would the paramount chief come to Jamestown, he asked, to receive a crown bestowed by King James of England?

"I am also a king," Wahunsonacock replied, "and this is my land." Smith, if not Captain Newport, expected such an answer. Newport "is to come to me," Wahunsonacock continued, "nor I to him nor yet to your fort, neither will I bite at such a bait."

After some further "courtesies," Smith brought this answer back to Newport.[22]

So Newport came to Werowocomoco and laid gifts before the chief: "basin and ewer, bed and furniture set up." A "scarlet cloak and apparel" were proffered, which Wahusonacock warily eyed until Namontack, who was now familiar with English culture, assured him they were safe to don. "But a foul trouble there was," Newport discovered, "to make him kneel to receive his crown." The *Proceedings* claim that Wahunsonacock knew nothing of the "majesty nor the meaning of a crown nor bending of the knee," but the symbolism of that action must have been obvious enough. Wahunsonacock needed no English token to prove his authority in Tsenacomoco. He stood firm, refusing to bend. In a farcical ceremony, Newport tried to fix the crown on the chief's head. Most Algonquians towered over the malnourished English, and one must imagine that Newport looked up to the Indian. The one-armed sea captain pressed on Wahunsonacock's shoulder, leaning hard, until in a brief moment "he a little stooped," and at that precise moment, like a seasoned mariner trimming sails to new wind, the Englishman swept up the crown and clamped the offensive article on the old man's head. The whole thing was Kafkaesque. Newport had his symbolism, and it would fill out a very fine report to be submitted to headquarters, but it did nothing to actually subordinate Tsenacomoco to the king of England. Smith had no patience for nonsense. Forget crowns and beds and trinkets. The reality was that Jamestown stood on Tsenacomocoan ground, and the fledgling colony would starve without Indian corn. The question was how to get it. The grace of gifts would not work. Only awing Wahunsonacock with might of arms would work.[23]

Newport ignored Smith's advice and proceeded again to the falls of the James River and beyond, going farther than he even had before in the search not of food but a profitable mine. He had with him "William Callicut, a refiner, fitted for that purpose," all the councillors except Smith, and three-fifths of the whole colony, 120 men, on a five-day tramp through the woods.[24] Captain Wynn found the foot hills salubrious. This veteran of plantations in two Irish provinces, captain of the soldiery in the Netherlands, mercenary in the Turkish wars, and now garrison commander praised the "high ground and fertile," full of "delicate springs of sweet water" and free of the pestilent mists of Jamestown Island. When they met the Monacans, their Siouan language sounded to the English like the speech of Wynn's fellow Welshmen.[25] The expedition proved a waste of time, energy, and resources, as Smith knew it would. The Monacans were not hostile but neither were they friendly. The English army marched forty miles above the falls and forty miles back, returning to their barges and boats sick, tired, and carrying a few unpromising barrels full of dirt and rock. Their provisions were consumed by the time they made it back to the falls, and they turned to the Indians of the Powhatan district for their dinner. But the Powhatans had hid their corn in the woods. Scrivener was sent to Werowocomoco, but he found Wahunsonacock "more ready to fight than trade." It was now clear that Newport's gifts had not worked, and the English believed that Wahunsonacock's plan was to starve them out of the Chesapeake. Only through the offices of Namontack were the English able to wrangle even a few "hogsheads of corn." By necessity and even before Newport was decently gone, Smith began stealing corn from Indians. He set men ashore on the Chickahominy with muskets cocked and lines of smoke trailing up from their matchlocks. He demanded bushels of corn and baskets of fish and fowl. The Indians surrendered their food. The English and Indians "parted good friends," Smith's story goes. What that meant is that the Chickahominy properly understood their relation to the English: they must "trade" their food at whatever price Smith set.[26]

From Newport's point of view the Second Supply was a mixed success. He delivered seventy new colonists to Virginia, including the first two women, and several expert tradesmen, the glassmakers from Germany. He crowned Wahunsonacock and gave him a new bed and a new coat. He reprimanded Smith for his hawkish policies. His expedition yielded some samples of something that might be silver. If he had not found the gold mine he hoped for, neither had he unequivocally ruled out the promise of one. He carried new samples of ore home for further testing. And through Smith's industry, the ship's hold was also full of samples of American-made "pitch, tar, glass, frankincense, soap-ashes . . . clapboard and wainscot." While Newport was on his expedition, Smith had put his own men to good use.[27]

From Smith's point of view, the Second Supply was a disaster. Newport's mission to Werowocomoco and his expedition above the falls had eaten up precious supplies better left in Jamestown's storehouse. Discipline went out the window. The sailors and the settlers themselves renewed the black market, flooding Indian villages with European goods. The "damnable and private trade" between sailors and soldiers on one hand and "savages" on the other deprived the colony of "things that were necessary." Dissensions again flared to the point that Smith suspected Newport and Ratcliffe were conniving to depose him. Many settlers, it seemed, would sooner starve than see

Smith continue his methods of squeezing corn from the Indians. And starvation was again a possibility now that Newport had deposited seventy more mouths to feed.[28]

As Newport was leaving, Smith handed him a letter, a time bomb set to explode in London.

❦

For about eight months Smith was the effective dictator of the colony. It was the most oppressive period in the colony's history. It was also the safest. Fewer English died in that period than in any similar stretch of months. Smith fed the colony by stealing from the Indians. By mid-December, winter had already arrived with its famine. The ground, hard frozen, was dusted with snow, and Smith had two hundred mouths to feed and little food stored, so he took the barges across the river to a Nansemond village. Wahunsonacock had banned trade with the English, so Smith was obliged to order a volley of musketry, which scattered the Indians into the woods. He proceeded to methodically burn the vacated village. The first house shot up in flames and smoke, giving the Nansemonds visions of becoming landless refugees. So they delivered up half of their winter store, a hundred bushels of corn. They promised that in the coming spring they would plant fields for Jamestown and give up the harvest when Smith asked for it. Tribute: this was something new, a tectonic shift in Chesapeake politics. Smith detached Nansemond from Tsenacomoco. No longer would that district, at the extreme southeast of the coalition, give its allegiance to Wahunsonacock and the other Tsenacomocoans. John Smith became their paramount chief.[29]

Jamestown had become an existential threat to Wahunsonacock. He spread the word across the districts: Have nothing to do with John Smith. Give him no feasts. Trade no food. Smith went upriver, where the population was denser, to the towns of Chawopo and Weanock. He found "the people were fled," their villages ghost towns, their victuals hidden. On the Appomattox River, the same thing. Smith returned with empty boats to Jamestown, where word came to the fort from the great chief himself: if Smith wanted any Indian corn, he must come to Werowocomoco to get it from his king. Wahunsonacock wanted "a grindstone, fifty swords," a few guns, copper, and beads. He also wanted a cock and hen. Before contact with the English, the Tsenacomocoans kept no fowl—no domesticated animals at all except hunting dogs. They were adopting English weapons and English husbandry. The most curious request of all: Wahunsonacock wanted carpenters to build an English-style house.

In retrospect, we can see what Wahunsonacock was up to, for the carpenters Smith was willing to send were Germans, who had been scheming to escape the English. Somehow, Wahunsonacock knew they wanted out of Jamestown, and he provided their passport. The excuse of building a house not only facilitated their escape but gave them an excuse to take all manner of tools with them. Smith was hugely suspicious of Wahunsonacock, but he trusted the Germans so much that he sent four of those craftsmen, including an "Adam" and a "Francis," along with the boy Thomas Savage, who now spoke the Algonquian language fluently. Later, when he learned of the Germans' treachery, Smith attributed it to Indian "plenty" and English "want." Wahunsonacock had food; the English did not. More than likely, a dose of garrison despair was involved as well. The settlers of the Second Supply found Jamestown as disillusioning as their predecessors had.[30]

As the Germans traveled overland with their tools, Smith sailed the pinnace and two barges with forty-six armed men downriver, round the point, and up the York, descending on Wahunsonacock with a substantial guard of soldiers.[31] The council was opposed to this maneuver. Smith's hostility flouted Company policy, and Scrivener and Captain Wynn "did their best to hinder" the expedition. Smith thought that they went so far as to plot his ruin by passing information to Wahunsonacock.[32] The most useful piece of intelligence, of course, was that Smith's death would lead to a friendlier regime in Jamestown. Wahunsonacock certainly knew that factions divided Jamestown and that he could play one off against the other. The split between Newport and Smith was obvious to anyone with eyes in his head, and Wahunsonacock knew that Newport would never have authorized setting fire to villages. And wasn't it clear as day that Newport, though often absent, was Smith's chief? Whether the council did or did not feed information to the Indians, Wahunsonacock had his sources of intelligence. Plenty of Indians visited the fort. Plenty were visited in their villages by talkative and friendly Englishmen. And there was the witting or unwitting whinging of those English who had already gone renegade. Wahunsonacock understood what Smith was up to. The English chief was acting like an Indian, like a rival trying to poach districts from Tsenacomoco.

After the first day of sailing, Smith and his forty-six men swept down on the town of Warraskoyack, which was between Jamestown and the tip of the peninsula. The Indians there were friendly, either from habits of intercourse with their neighbors or because they knew what had happened across the river in Nansemond. Playing host to such a crowd of hungry soldiers would have challenged even larger villages, but the Warraskoyacks did their best. They fed the English. Smith asked for and received two Indians to guide Michael Sicklemore on a search for any survivors of the Roanoke colony to the south. The village took in Smith's page, Samuel Collier, presumably to teach him the language as Thomas Savage had learned it. Most importantly, the weroance of Warraskoyack took Smith into his confidence.

"Captain Smith," he said, "you shall find [Wahunsonacock] to treat you kindly, but trust him not; and be sure he have no opportunity to seize on your arms, for he hath sent for you only to cut your throats."[33]

Smith was already on his guard. But the fact that the weroance of Warraskoyack informed on the chief of Tsenacomoco demonstrates how power already was shifting on the James River, how loose Wahunsonacock's grip was on the fringes of Tsenacomoco. Smith now counted two of Wahunsonacock's districts as his dependants. The next day, he added a third: Kecoughtan at the point of the peninsula. "Extreme wind, rain, frost, and snow" prevented the barges from rounding the point, and Smith was obliged to wait out the weather, which lasted a full week, in Kecoughtan. His little army was happy enough. The Kecoughtans offered up feasts of "good oysters, fish, flesh, wildfowl, and good bread." If any of the young women of the town found the soldiers attractive, we must assume the customary sexual freedoms were enjoyed, although the *General History* is characteristically reticent. Bitter as were the snow and frost, in these smoky warm houses no one missed their English hearths. It is no mean feat to feed forty-six Englishmen for a week, and the Kecoughtans must have considered the expense an investment. They were buying a privileged connection to the most powerful district in Tsenacomoco, which was governed by a weroance so confident and haughty that he was on his way to confront the paramount chief himself.[34]

Eventually, the sun broke through the weather. Once more to the waters, which were cold but calm, and the boats reached Werowocomoco on the twelfth of January. But the late freeze left a half mile of ice between Smith and shore. It was no grand arrival, no procession such as Captain Newport's embassy a few months earlier. Along shore was a margin of thawing oozy mud, and Smith and a guard of either eight or eighteen men—the accounts differ—waded through it, carrying their arms. They were met with hospitality. Houses were open to them to sleep the night. They dried off. They were fed "plenty of bread, turkeys, and venison." And the next day Wahunsonacock came to speak with Smith.

The negotiations began cautiously, with an unfriendly question.

"When are you leaving?" Wahunsonacock asked.

He hadn't much corn, but, if pressed by Smith's need, he might part with forty baskets for forty swords.

Smith asked "how it chanced he became so forgetful." Hadn't Wahunsonacock sent for Smith? Weren't those warriors standing to the side the very messengers who had brought the invitation?

Wahunsonacock laughed merrily. So they were. Let him and Smith get down to business, then. Corn this season was worth more than copper, for the harvest was poor and the winter already colder than normal. The Tsenacomocoans would take payment only in guns and swords.

Smith answered shrewdly. The English neglected to plant their own corn and store up their own turkeys and venison because Wahunsonacock had promised that Tsenacomoco would "supply [their] wants." And now Smith found that Wahunsonacock had forbidden his people to trade with the English at all. "As for swords and guns," Smith countered, he had none to spare. And then, in a polite, barely oblique threat, he mentioned that if Smith used those weapons, he could procure as much food as he wanted. The incident in Nansemond was proof enough, and it hovered off the edges of their conversation unmentioned yet by either. "Yet steal or wrong you I will not," Smith concluded more mildly, "nor dissolve that friendship we have mutually promised." Unless Wahunsonacock refused to give him food.

That formulation of their relationship—that the two men were equals who had made promises to each other—irked Wahunsonacock. "Many inform me," Wahunsonacock said, in reference to his intelligence network, that Smith came "not for trade but to invade my people and possess my country." Of course, that was exactly what the English planned to do, and apparently plenty of the renegades had confessed England's real intentions. Wahunsonacock challenged Smith to prove his friendship by ordering his men to lay down their arms. Negotiations dragged—a little corn for a little copper—till the next day, when Wahunsonacock picked up the same theme, this time getting straight to the point. What business did Smith have shooting guns in Nansemond, burning a house, and threatening the whole village? The Tsenacomocoan people had no desire to hide from the English. Wasn't it "better to eat good meat, lie well, sleep quietly with my women and children, laugh and be merry with you, have copper, hatchets, or what I want, being your friend?" Neither the Nansemonds nor Wahunsonacock himself wanted to "lie cold in the woods," eating "acorns, roots, and such trash," all the while hunted by the English until at every broken twig his "tired men" cry out, "There cometh Captain Smith!" Wahunsonacock was ready to trade, if Smith would only lay down his arms in friendship. "I never use any weroance so kindly as yourself," he told Smith, "yet from you I receive the least kindness of any." No other chief refuses "to do what I desire, but only you." Bearing arms in the presence of the paramount chief was equivalent to denying his authority. Was Smith his subordinate or not? Was he Captain Newport's subordinate or not? Smith did whatever he wanted to do, the chief complained, no matter what Wahunsonacock said and regardless of what Newport said.

"I live not here as your subject, but as your friend . . . ," Smith said haughtily. As friends, they made mutual promises, which was quite a different matter from taking orders. Even so, the next day, if Wahunsonacock demanded it, Smith conceded that he personally would "leave my arms, and trust to your promise."

Both men knew the emptiness of that gesture. The ice was breaking. The boats were approaching shore with the full strength of Smith's army. Smith himself might lay down his arms with perfect impunity, so long as the firepower of his troops were within ear shot. But the two chiefs parted for the day politely. Wahunsonacock left Smith with "two or three women," who, in what we must presume is euphemism, spent their time "talking with the captain." With Smith thus preoccupied, Wahunsonacock left town with his "luggage, women, and children." His warriors surrounded the house. Smith, roused from his revels, snatched up his shield and brandished his pistol. Stepping out of the house, he found himself surrounded by grim warriors. Boldly, he made toward his corps du guarde, daring anyone to get in his way. He fired a warning shot, and "these naked devils" tumbled over each other in their haste to flee.

Wahunsonacock sent a messenger. All this was a misunderstanding. The corn was ready to be loaded on the boats. Let the two parties resume their talks. Smith supervised the loading: warriors laid down their weapons and under the smoking matches of the musket men, they waded through the mud to the boats, which were "left on the ooze by the ebb." Smith was obliged to wait for the next tide, so he returned to the house and resumed his "mirth," but his "talking" with the women was again disturbed. Pocahontas, the paramount chief's "dearest jewel and daughter," came through the dark and "irksome woods" to warn her friend, Captain Smith. Soon enough, she said, her father would send a feast, and once Smith laid aside his weapons to eat, they would set upon him. The girl was in tears. Leave at once, she urged. Smith refused to go, but wanted to reward her with some gift. Pocahontas refused. A gift would tip off her father, and he would kill her for the betrayal. Then she snuck out of the house and disappeared once more into the trees.

Less than an hour later, eight or ten Indians, "goodly well proportioned fellows, as grim as devils," arrived with "platters of venison and other victuals." The English were vigilant, matches lit for their muskets. The Indians told the Englishmen to put out their matches, for the smoke made them ill. Lay down their guns. Eat. Smith would not. Indians and Englishmen stared at each other. More Indians came, poking their heads into the house to see what was up. Then even more Indians. The English never put down the guns till the tide had turned. They left Werowocomoco with "ten quarters" or eighty bushels of corn. The Germans stayed to finish building Wahunso-nacock's English house, and Edward Brynton, one of the soldiers, stayed to shoot fowl for the chief.

Smith went farther up the York River to meet with Wahunso-nacock's younger brother, Opechancanough, who was second in line to inherit leadership of Tsenacomoco. It was Opechancanough who had captured Smith almost exactly a year earlier and dragged him along a circuit of villages and towns before finally depositing the captive with his older brother at Werowocomoco. After Wahunso-nacock's ambush was foiled only by Pocahontas's warning, it seems strange that Smith would travel to Pamunkey to trade with the chief's heir. But he could have been attempting two things here. First, he might have been probing politics on the York River to see if he could exploit a rift between chiefs, in much the same way that Wahunso-nacock seemed to be playing one faction in Jamestown against another. If Opechancanough proved perfectly loyal to his brother's commands, then Smith might use the encounter to further demon-strate his power to every Indian on the Chesapeake: with his guns and armor, he could force any Tsenacomocoan district to deliver corn, even those of the two most powerful chiefs.

Events in Pamunkey mirrored those in Werowocomoco. Smith found himself yet again huddled inside a house, surrounded by hundreds of Indians, all with their bows ready and arrows nocked. Smith grabbed Opechancanough by his hair and pressed a loaded pistol to his chest. Smith knew enough Algonquian to shout out: "Shoot he that dare!"

Bowstrings were relaxed. Weapons were laid on the ground.

In the cold bare sunlight of this January morning, Smith presented his ultimatum to Opechancanough. This was the back-bone of his Indian policy. "If you shoot but one arrow to shed one drop of blood of any of my men," he told the Indians, "or steal the least of these beads or copper . . . I will not cease revenge, if once I begin, so long as I can hear where to find one of your nation." But if they would freight his ship with food, and accept his goods in exchange, "your king shall be free and be my friend, for I am not come to hurt him or any of you." For the next five or six days, Indians came in from as far as twelve miles away to bring food. Smith called it "trade," but it was simple extortion. The Indians, "who wanted [corn] themselves," gave up their insufficient store only because the English "threat'ned their ruin and the razing of their houses, boats, and weirs and canoes."[35]

Smith and his band of soldiers terrorized the river for another two and a half weeks, touching as many as thirty-one different towns and villages. Opechancanough's son, Wecuttanow, offered them venison at one town, which Smith and a few others ate. Wecuttanow disappeared; the English guests turned violently sick. They did not die. They expelled what they assumed was poison either by vomiting or diarrhea, and a day or so later they recovered. Farther up river, they spied Wecuttanow again, who, surrounded by "forty or fifty of his chief companions . . . proudly braved it" right in front of the English. Smith marched right up to the "stout young fellow" and thrashed him "like a dog." Then he walked away, "scorning to do him any worse mischief." The townsmen quickly brought food to be rid of the English.[36]

In Youghtanund and Mattapanient, two districts at the highest navigable reaches of the York River, under the immediate surveillance of Wahunsonacock and his brothers, Smith seems to have reversed his policy of terror. The English could have taken whatever they wanted, leaving a few hatchets and pots and beads in payment, but the villages had little to give. The Indian women and children wept openly, knowing what Smith had done in the towns downriver. But Smith recognized the "cruelty" they were about to inflict, and he was "moved with compassion." That his boats and the pinnace were laden by this time with 479 bushels of corn and almost 200 pounds of deer suet might have urged this Christian charity. Besides, treating the periphery of Tsenacomoco as kindly as he served cruelty at the center might undermine Wahunsonacock's prestige and authority. Divisions among the districts would serve the English, because some districts would court them as allies.[37]

Smith's violence actually derived from a high respect for the Tsenacomocoans. He appreciated better than anyone in London—who had only read about Indians in books or seen the odd "savage" paraded in European courts like a freak—that superior English technology was counterbalanced by what later generations of pioneers would call "woodcraft." The English did not even know how to gather and cook the foods that lay everywhere at their feet, how to catch the fish, which roots to dig up, where the deer could be found. For all their superior weapons, Smith knew, the English might still lose a war to the Indians. The Tsenacomocoans could not challenge an armored column of soldiers face-to-face. But in ambush, in a war of attrition, an isolated garrison like Jamestown could be overmatched. Smith's reputation for violence, the swiftness with which he resorted to arms, was meant to avoid even greater bloodshed. The best policy in his mind was to demonstrate to the Indians that the English *could* burn their houses with impunity, and that they *could* steal all the corn in their granaries if they wanted to, and they *could* seize their fishing weirs. Only demonstrations of such power would foreclose the need to exercise it. Essentially, that was how Wahunsonacock himself had become paramount chief. It was how Smith would carve out in this world a place for the fledgling English colony. He would offer violence until the Indians acknowledged that the president of Jamestown was a paramount chief. Certain districts needed to pay Smith, not Wahunsonacock, tribute in corn and meat. And all Tsenacomocoans had to realize that any hurt they inflicted on one of the Smith's men would rebound tenfold upon their own village or town.

The spring of 1609 saw the fulfillment of Smith's Indian policy. His reputation for violence had spread so thoroughly among Tsenacomoco that he could soften. He could show mercy. An incident in February demonstrates this pattern: first savage violence, then, after capitulation, mercy. In walking back from the glass factory to the fort one day, Smith happened to bump into Wowinchopunck, the chief of Paspahegh. Paspahegh was Jamestown's closest neighbor; Jamestown Island had once been Paspahegh's foraging and hunting ground. So, while individual Paspaheghs certainly were very friendly with individual Englishmen, the district's official attitude to the English was uneasy and cold if not unfriendly. That this chief happened to be by himself so close to Jamestown is odd but unexplained.

The two chiefs—of Paspahegh and of Jamestown—instantly grappled with each other. As if they were in a melodramatic movie, they tumbled into the river, where they continued to struggle until Smith was able to draw his falchion. Threatening to cut off Wowinchopunck's head, Smith took the Indian prisoner, dragged him back to Jamestown, and clapped him in irons. Smith sent word to Wahunsonacock: he would release the Paspahegh chief if Wahunsonacock would send back to Jamestown the renegade Germans. Wahunsonacock refused. Then Wowinchopunck's own "wives, children, and people" came to Jamestown begging for his life, leaving gifts of tribute. Smith refused mercy. Somehow, fettered as he was, Wowinchopunck made his escape—perhaps through the help of sympathetic Englishmen. Smith was infuriated. He attacked a Paspahegh village. He killed six or seven warriors, took that same number prisoner, "burnt their houses, took their boats with all their fishing weirs, and planted some of them at Jamestown for his own use." Smith "was resolved" to revenge himself upon "all them who had injured him."

But the Paspaheghs gave up. They sent their best orator, a man named Ocanindge, to plead their case. How could John Smith take

Map of Virginia
drawn by John Smith,
1612.

offense at Wowinchopunck's escape? Don't "the fishes swim, the
fowls fly, and the very beasts strive to escape the snare and live?"
Isn't it proper and right that human prisoners do the same? "Then
blame not him [for] being a man." If Wowinchopunck injured
Smith, "he was compelled to it." Philosophy was well and good, but,
more importantly, Ocanindge made the necessary obeisance: Paspahegh would pay tribute to Jamestown. When their crops ripened, a
portion would be delivered to John Smith. Englishmen could visit
Paspaheghan villages. They could live in Indians' houses, if Jamestown could not provide for them. "Upon these terms," the *General
History* reports, "the president promised them peace."[38]

Smith imprisoned two Paspaheghs, Kemps and Tussore, as "the
most exact villains in all the country." After some time, as English
supplies dwindled and feeding these prisoners became an issue, they
were released from custody. But by then they had become so accli-
mated or fascinated by English ways that they wanted to stay on
Jamestown Island. The admiration went two ways, and many of the
settlers befriended the two Indians. Jamestown's manufactured goods
certainly impressed Kemps and Tussore. But these Paspaheghs had
superior knowledge that impressed the English. They understood

how to live on this land. The Englishmen's efforts at sowing crops were comically clumsy, and the two natives lent a hand themselves. Although it was women's work in their own minds, they stooped to show the ignorant Englishmen "how to order and plant [their] fields," and under their direction thirty or forty acres of Jamestown Island were given over to that purpose.[39]

Smith's personal stature began to rival Wahunsonacock's, which put people who lived in districts close to Jamestown, like Paspahegh and Kecoughtan, in a delicate diplomatic situation. They owed tribute and allegiance to Wahunsonacock, but now, "for love or fear," they became close allies with Jamestown. Not only Jamestown's "bordering neighbors" but "all those countries" on the Chesapeake, reports the *General History*, feared Smith more than they feared Wahunsonacock. Nearly every district on the whole Chesapeake, Smith bragged, "would have done anything he would have them [do]." Nor is that far from the truth. Villages on the lower York dreaded to see him but dreaded more to cross him. Wahunsonacock moved his capital inland several miles, away from the water and the range of ships' cannons. The towns and villages on the periphery of Tsenacomoco—the Potomac River, the fall line, the Eastern Shore, and even those closer to the center on the Rappahannock—paid lip service to their duties to Wahunsonacock while trading freely with John Smith. By spring, English settlers could walk through most of Tsenacomoco without fear of harassment. Troubling an Englishman would mean swift and terrible retribution. The chiefs of various districts even began to extradite to Jamestown any of their own people who offended the English or stole their goods. John Smith had set his lands in order. All but Jamestown.[40]

## "HE THAT WILL NOT WORK SHALL NOT EAT"

The Germans, for instance, betrayed Smith the moment they he left them in Werowocomoco. While Smith and his retinue were terrorizing the York River, Adam and Francis—"two stout Dutchmen," as Smith described them—surrendered their weapons to Wahunsonacock and went back to Jamestown for more. They told Captain Wynn, commander of the fort, that Smith had taken their weapons for use by his guard and that he had sent them back for replacements. Wynn issued them new weapons. Then Adam and Francis induced "six or seven" others—not just Germans but Englishmen—to join their "confederacy," and by hook or crook they smuggled "a great many swords, pike-heads, [muskets], shot powder, and such like" out of the fort. As soon as they were out of sight of the fort, they delivered these goods to Indians, who stole them away to Wahunsonacock. The haul was significant: fifty swords, eight muskets, eight pikes, and, somehow, three hundred hatchets.[41]

While Smith was away, guns and tools were continually smuggled out of the fort. Eventually, four or five Englishmen made the ultimate, portentous decision to escape the garrison and, like the Germans, take refuge with Wahunsonacock. They had to cross the peninsula on Indian roads, then find passage on a canoe across the York River to Werowocomoco, where the Germans had prepared a welcome. In the midst of their hike they came upon Raleigh Crashaw and Robert Ford, fully armed gentlemen tramping the road in the opposite direction. They were part of Smith's crew dispatched by the captain to report to Jamestown about his expedition's progress. The "confederates" hastily made up some plausible story for why they were headed away from the fort. That their story could be believed indicates just how normal such roaming was, even as late as January 1609. Englishmen moved freely for miles throughout the peninsula without passports, apparently on their own authority. Even so, these would-be deserters thought it prudent to accompany Smith's officers back to the garrison, where they bided their time.[42]

Smith shut down the black market that had thrived until January 1609. Wingfield and Ratcliffe had not been able to curb it, nor had Wahunsonacock, and when Captain Newport was on the Chesapeake, he seemed to wink at his sailors as they welcomed Indians on board and lined the ships with Indian furs and other goods. Indians, settlers, and sailors conducted clandestine transactions almost every day. Indians came to Jamestown, and English wandered into the villages. These transactions encouraged theft of Company property: stores were raided by sailors and settlers alike, who bartered away precious supplies. But the English traded their personal property as well. Everyone in the Second Supply, for instance, knew that trifles in England were rare commodities in Virginia, so even the humblest laborer had treasures to trade. When Smith took his army to Kecoughtan and Werowocomoco and to thirty other villages and towns on the York River, Smith was determined to stifle this traffic. Just as Wahunsonacock commanded his own people to stop doing business with Jamestown, Smith demanded the English do the same. All trade must go through him.

When Smith went to Werowocomoco with his guard of forty-six soldiers, he imposed a strict rule of trade. Every individual in the expedition had to surrender his personal trade items to a common pool. These were added to the Company's supply under Smith's control, and Smith alone could negotiate exchange with the Indians. No private deals would undercut Smith's negotiations. The Company's supplies of hatchets and copper bought food that would feed the whole colony, while the private stores of trifles yielded a second supply of provisions. Smith assured the expeditionary soldiers that only they, who had faced the dangers together and suffered the deprivations of winter weather in open boats and contributed their own private items to the common pool, could draw from this second fund of food. When they returned to Jamestown, Smith's guard of forty-six were privileged men. Each was privileged to draw "a month's provision extraordinary" from the Company store.[43]

Smith found that Jamestown had deteriorated to a sorry state in the few weeks that he was gone. Councillors Waldo and Scrivener had drowned in a boating accident, and while Captain Wynn, officer of the garrison, exercised some authority, to Smith's mind the bulk of the settlers had idled away while he and his forty-six men toiled for food. Smith gathered the entire settlement together, and the ragged crew shuffled into place to hear the president.

"Countrymen," he began, "our late miseries" must persuade them to change behavior. Some of them, he conceded, "deserved both honor and reward," but most of them had been shirkers. In the past, the council had protected them whenever they defied Smith's orders. Now the council was no more. "Power," Smith explained, "resteth wholly in myself." And then Smith delivered the famous decree: "he that will not work shall not eat." No longer would "a hundred and fifty idle loiterers" consume the food gotten by "the labours of thirty or forty honest and industrious men."

Everyone knew whom he meant. The forty-six soldiers, freshly back from their expedition on the icy river, flush with their "reward" of a month's provisions, stood apart from the others, if not literally, then certainly figuratively. They were Smith's favorites, a new aristocracy.

On this episode rests Smith's reputation as the first American. His decree, summed up by the dictum that the idle would not eat, is typically interpreted as a leveling of society, a cutting down of aristocrats in favor of men who work. Historians tend to blame two things for Jamestown's stubborn refusal to do the hard work—the clearing and plowing and planting and hunting and fishing—required to ensure its own survival: gold fever and an aristocratic aversion to manual labor. Both are blamed on the gentlemen. The national lessons are often repeated: America rewards hard work and weeds out the idle, as if the place itself reintroduced natural selection to a European society encrusted with artificial hierarchies of privilege. Some consider Smith's decree the first shot in a revolution, not yet heard round the world, but the true opening of the American Revolution. On Jamestown Island, on or about February 1609, human character changed. Merit slayed the blue bloods. Appealing as that view is, it misinterprets what really happened that day in Jamestown. Meritocracy was not established. Democracy did not vanquish aristocracy. John Smith was a tyrant.

"Though you presume the authority here is but a shadow," Smith reminded the hundred fifty or so disfavored settlers, "and that I dare not touch the lives of any," they must remember that the council had the power of life and death.

And Smith was the council. He had the Company's constitution read aloud to the assembled settlers to confirm this fact.

No power remained, Smith said frankly, "to curb my authority." Everyone had better follow orders, for "he that offendeth let him assuredly expect his due punishment."[44]

This threat was not aimed at the gentlemen, nor were the majority of laborers nodding in solidarity with John Smith, thinking that now their hard work would finally get them their due. Roughly equal measures of gentry, craftsmen, and laborers made up the 150 idlers. Both gentlemen and commoners turned soldiers made up Smith's favored forty-six. Smith was not dividing working commoners from idle gentlemen. *Work* was a euphemism for doing what Smith told you to do. *Idleness* meant disobeying orders. The only people cheered by this new regime were those men who enjoyed Smith's favor, especially the hardened veterans of his several expeditions.

Smith divided everyone into work crews of ten or fifteen, depending on the assigned task. Reportedly, they worked about six hours a day before knocking off for "pastime and merry exercises." The first order of business was to secure all Company stores, for

Smith's regime, like Wahunsonacock's, depended on the bestowal or withholding of rewards. Smith must have relied on his most loyal men, such as Anas Todkill, to guard the Company's food and its store of potential trade goods, like swords, pikes, muskets, hoes, and hatchets. He tried to shut down the casual intercourse between English and Indian. To some degree he was closing the barn door after the horse had been stolen. By early 1609 "the most part of our tools and a good part of our arms" already had been "conveyed to the savages." But he did succeed in making it almost impossible to smuggle one of the remaining swords out to the black market. A guardhouse was built and garrisoned on the neck of land connecting Jamestown Island to the Lower Peninsula, and no one was supposed to pass in either direction without permission. These changes, of course, chafed against the long habit of liberty.[45]

Smith's leadership also accounts for improvements long neglected. Workers dug a well, bringing "sweet water" into the fort. It seems almost incomprehensible that leadership had been so incompetent as to have failed to perform this simple task till the spring of 1609. Smith had twenty houses built. Fields were planted under the direction of Kemps and Tussore. Three sows produced more than sixty pigs, which were transported to a river island aptly named "Hog Island," which became a convenient larder. Another "blockhouse and garrison" was built on Hog Island to give Jamestown advance "notice of any shipping" approaching Jamestown. Despite Smith's belief that in its early years all colonial energy should be directed at self-preservation and expansion, he dutifully experimented with potential paying commodities. He established efficient work camps that filled dozens and dozens of barrels, which waited for the next ship to take them back to England: pitch and tar distilled from pine trees; soap-ash . . . Even the glass factory was producing samples.[46]

With better luck, perhaps Smith's regime eventually would have won over the bulk of colonists. Maybe his favored forty-six would have expanded at least to a majority as more people profited from his despotism. But hunger again pricked dissension into crisis. The "greatest number" of the colonists opposed Smith through his entire reign. Around late March or early April, those guarding the casks of corn discovered that half the supply had rotted and that the other half was eaten by "thousands of rats." These vermin, carried over on the ships, multiplied in the hospitable environment of the New World. The crisis of starvation came upon Jamestown suddenly, not gradually.[47]

Smith drew upon his client districts for immediate relief. Each day Indians brought a hundred "squirrels, turkeys, deer, and other wild beasts." The English fancied this an "expression of their loves," but that is the euphemism for tribute. This steady diet of meat kept Smith's men alive, but it did not take long—just sixteen days—before the region had been hunted out. This was the hungry time for Indians as well, when winter stores were depleted and spring seedlings had barely broken ground. A season of forage: like the Indians, English had to live off the land. But the environs of Jamestown Island could not feed over two hundred souls. Smith divided them up. Between sixty and eighty were sent downriver under Ensign William Laxon to live off oysters. Lieutenant George Percy, the youngest son of the Earl of Northumberland, took another twenty men downriver to Point Comfort, near Kecoughtan at the peninsula's tip. They were to live off fish. And Francis West, brother to Lord De La Warr, took another twenty up the James River to the falls. But this strategy did not solve the problem of hunger. West's men found only "berries and acorns," hardly sufficient to keep them alive. Percy's men managed to stay alive for six weeks, probably through the intervention of Kecoughtan Indians, because they caught no fish. The *General History* reports disgustedly that "in six weeks they would not agree to cast out the net," which surely must have been an exaggeration. Whether they dipped the net or not, they caught no fish, and Percy proved an unpopular leader. His detachment ended under suspicious circumstances: a pouch of gunpowder hanging from Percy's belt caught fire and exploded. He was not killed, but the burn incapacitated him.[48]

Although the meager remains in Jamestown's storehouse had been procured "by the hazard and endeavors" of those few who accompanied Smith's expedition back in January, the president realized he had to suspend his policy of favoring that minority. All were given an equal share of the remnant corn. Things were not yet desperate in Jamestown. They caught a lot of sturgeon, which they dried, pounded, mixed with "wholesome herbs," and cooked. They had so much of it they were feeding their dogs the scraps. One of the settlers who had lived among the Indians learned how to gather tuckahoe, that potato-like root growing in marshes. They were not prospering but at least they were surviving by living off the land.

But the same problem plagued the fort as before: most of the settlers hated Smith's government. Such willfulness made no sense to Smith himself. It seemed that three-quarters of the garrison would rather "have starved or eaten each other" than done what they were told to do. Not quite, because it was clear the settlers entertained several other strategies for survival. Some would barter with the Indians till Jamestown was stripped bare of all tools and weapons. Others wanted to sail back to England. Some wanted to maroon themselves among the Indians. In particular, one settler named William Dyer maligned Smith with a thousand whispers. We know nothing about this man. No one by that profession or name appears in the manifests of the first settlers nor in either of the resupplies. One of the chief complaints, apparently, was the favored status Smith bestowed on his forty-six picked men. Dyer's disgruntlement blossomed until others took it up themselves and openly complained about Smith's tyranny.

The president cried enough. He seized this Dyer, "whom he worthily punished." Then he summoned the settlers for yet another speech.

"Fellow soldiers," he began. Months earlier it had been "countrymen"; now it was "soldiers." Smith dropped any pretense that Jamestown was a proper settlement, a plantation. It was a garrison. The settlers were conscripts. If anyone was thinking of running away to the Indians, he had better forget about Wahunsonacock, Smith told them. No rescue would come from him. And those who pined for English food and scorned to eat the roots and forage because they were "savage trash" unfit to grace their stomachs must forget about sailing the pinnace to meet the fishing fleet in Newfoundland. Smith would hang the next "runner" he found. Nor would Smith tolerate disobedience of any kind. Three months earlier Smith had decreed that he who would not work would not eat. Now the law was more severe: he who would not work would suffer punishment. Anyone who spoke against Smith's regime would suffer punishment. As for the complaint that Smith was distributing more food to his favorites, the president insisted that he had never taken from the store more than a single man's portion. And now he himself, the president, would dig tuckahoe, and he would help fish for sturgeon and dry and pound it, and any man who did not forage food as Smith did would be "set beyond the river," marooned, "banished from the fort as a drone," where he might starve for all Smith cared.[49]

That particular threat was not much of a deterrent. As a matter of fact, Smith was obliged to billet many of the settlers among the neighboring Indians, probably at nearby villages of the Paspahegh and Kecoughtans. The Indians could not object: they knew that Smith had "such a commanding power" that they didn't dare withhold their hospitality. The English lucky enough to be so billeted found themselves so well treated, the food so good, the lodging so comfortable, their escape from Smith's authority so sweet, that several chose to abandon Jamestown forever. They would sooner turn Indian than stick with the garrison.[50]

But a true escape from Jamestown meant slipping deeper into Tsenacomoco, getting beyond the circuit of Smith's threatening power, into territory where people feared Wahunsonacock more than they feared Smith. A certain group of men—we do not know how many but probably no more than a few—decided the best course was to do just that, and they figured if they could find their old friends Kemps and Tussore, those Indians would help them escape. They could give the English introductions to the chief of some distant village. Maybe directions to find those English who had already escaped to the Middle Peninsula.[51]

It is unfortunate that we do not know who these deserters were, not even their names, let alone any bit of information to give them some substance. Without a scrap of individuating personality, for four centuries they have been imprisoned by the scant historical record, which was written by Smith and his cronies. "Discontents," "idlers," "counterfeit" Christians, and "counterfeit" subjects are the words we know them by. Edward Wright Haile is the rare historian uncorrupted by this prejudice. "Who can blame them?" he asks. "Failure of supply is a failure of leadership," and Jamestown was a colossal failure. Sympathy requires imagination, and few historians have imagined Virginia seen through the eyes of these would-be maroons. Perhaps some evening or some morning they slipped out of the village, probably soon after the soldiers' latest round of surveillance. Into the woods, following some Indian road, heading inland to the next village and then the next, unsure of what they would face, knowing little more than broken phrases of the language, searching for Kemps and Tussore. They knew the roads and villages closest to Jamestown, but it would not have taken too long before they were in unfamiliar territory. It would have been swifter to take a dugout canoe upriver on the rising tide. The terrain and villages along the water's edge would have been familiar to many of the settlers. But the open water was dangerously exposed to view. One of the barges rowed by a troop of soldiers or even the pinnace with its mounted cannon might materialize suddenly. More than likely these fugitives tramped through the shady paths paralleling the shoreline. "Many others" in Jamestown knew what they were up to, wished them success, and hoped one day to follow in their footsteps. These fellow travelers watched Smith to see what he would do.

The escapees found Kemps and Tussore in some town, probably not yet beyond the Chickahominy River, which cuts into the Lower Peninsula. It was still Paspahegh territory, well within the reach of Smith's vengeance. They applied for aid. Could their old friends convey them to some village beyond Smith's ken? The refugees brought what tools and weapons they could carry with them and offered them to the Indians as a token of gratitude. To their horror, these refugees found that their friends, the once-captive Indians, had come entirely under Smith's influence. Kemps and Tussore seized the English, who were quickly surrounded by a guard of warriors and delivered back to John Smith. Their sympathizers in Jamestown watched grimly as these would-be renegades were marched back into the garrison under guard and most likely in chains. All knew what was coming: swift sentence by the president, followed by swift punishment, probably a severe beating. They were made an example. This was a military camp, and Smith would tolerate no desertion.[52]

Smith realized that the deserters living under Wahunsonacock's protection were a constant lure for other discontents. A "soldier" named William Bentley, for example, had by this time successfully escaped the fort and joined the German deserters who were living somewhere on the Middle Peninsula. Smith recruited a Swiss craftsman, William Volday, to act as emissary: he was to find the deserters, carrying "pardons and promises" from the president, and negotiate their return to Jamestown. But Volday proved a "double villain," and when he found Bentley and the Germans living happily among the Indians—stooping, in the words of the Smith loyalists, to the "lewd conditions" of Indian life—he joined them.[53]

Smith's grip was slipping. The settlers were distributed widely up and down the James River, most of them beyond Smith's immediate surveillance and power. The deserters on the Middle Peninsula had so many sympathizers among the remaining settlers that a plot developed to deliver the garrison into Wahunsonacock's hands, overthrow Smith, and allow "the most part of our company" to join the Indians. The Indian chief would secretly invade the Lower Peninsula, and the conspirators presumably would throw open the gates of the fort or otherwise ease his attack. It seems to have been the laborers who concocted this scheme, for it was two of their ranks who revealed the plot to Smith. The "Christian hearts" of Thomas Dawse and Thomas Mallard, who had come in the Second Supply, could not betray their countrymen to the pagan Indians. Secretly, they confessed to Smith what was afoot. Smith turned these informers into spies. Keep their part in the conspiracy, Smith ordered them, and gather intelligence on the plot's development. When Wahunsonacock came to the Lower Peninsula, Smith would be ready. An ambush would crush the attackers, defeating and perhaps killing the great paramount chief. Jamestown would be fully secure, and Smith's prestige would spread across the entire Chesapeake watershed.[54]

These forebodings did not develop into a crisis. They didn't have time enough. They were forestalled by the arrival of a Company ship, the *Mary and John*, captained by Samuel Argall. He was scouting a northern route from England that bypassed the West Indies, and though becalmed for a couple of weeks the *Mary and John* had taken just over two months to cross the Atlantic, about a month quicker than the southerly route. Arriving at Jamestown on July 23, 1609,

Argall meant to "truck" with the colony, fill his hold with sturgeon, and head straight back to England to deliver his information about his northerly route as soon as possible.

Smith delayed that mission. He confiscated the ship's provisions. Then he seized the ship. It is not clear if Argall disagreed with these necessities. Having believed reports about Virginia's plenty, Argall was shocked to discover destitution. True, most of the settlers were alive and in apparently good health. But eighty had been living off oysters for weeks downriver from Jamestown. "Many" of the others were in Indian towns, in Argall's view "living upon [the] alms" of savages. Perhaps most shocking of all, Smith had outlawed private property. All goods went into the common store of "natural and primary community." The conditions appalled him. It seemed a failure of leadership. But that would soon change. As Argall informed John Smith, perhaps just a week or so behind him was a fleet of seven ships, settlers who would quadruple the population, horses, livestock, supplies, women and children—a veritable English town packed into the decks of the vessels. Most important of all: a new charter, a new council, and a new governor. John Smith's days were numbered.[55]

## CHAPTER FIVE

꧁ ꧂

# *Maroons*

**Captain Newport completed the Second Supply** when he sailed
into London in January 1609. He could not have been looking forward
to meeting with Thomas Smythe, the de facto chief executive officer
of the London branch of the Virginia Company. Newport had promised gold mines and an overland passage to the South Sea, like that in
Panama, and the Company had outfitted the Second Supply to secure
both. All that Newport brought back was disappointment and "some
petty commodities." Seventeen tons of iron ore, which the Company
sold at four pounds per ton. Soap-ash. Wainscoting. Some pitch and
tar. Nothing near enough to pay the cost of the expedition.[1]

At least once every three months, the two or three dozen earls
and knights and lords and merchants who formed the London council
would meet in Thomas Smythe's house to conduct the Company's
business. Newport's return forced the council to reassess Jamestown. It had no dearth of information. The council in Virginia sent
official reports. Individuals sent letters. Returnees gave verbal testimony in London: the lawyer and secretary Gabriel Archer; William
Brewster, gentleman; Robert Tindall, sailor and cartographer.
Lieutenant George Percy, brother to the ninth Lord Northumberland, and the deposed President Wingfield each had their *Discourse*;
John Smith sent his *True Relation*; every faction clamored to be
heard by the Company's directors. Newport carried two Indians

to London: Namontack for a second time, along with Wahunso-nacock's brother-in-law, Machumps. Newport himself, who hovered above the factional din, carried special weight with the Virginia Company's directors in London.[2] But here he was, back a third time, with none of his promised gold and, most ominously, a sealed letter from the president he left in charge, John Smith.

Smith wrote in response to the rebuke that the directors had sent to him with the Second Supply. If they had expected their employee to cower, the directors found out quick enough that deference was not much part of Smith's character. His letter spurned courtesy. It spared no one's feelings. The London council had been foolish, the letter told them, for bankrolling Newport's expedition. Newport and "120 of the best men he could chuse" sailed as far as they could up the James and then went overland, carrying in four pieces a special boat to be put down in a lake on the far side of the mountains. They might as well have burned the boat and carried its ashes in bags: it would have done them as much good and would have been less cumbersome. All Newport had to show for the gigantic undertaking was a map of about thirty miles of previously uncharted ground. Smith alone could have mapped the same for a pound of copper. The Company's rebuke had mentioned two thousand pounds' worth of supplies. Smith told them those were mostly peddled to the Indians by corrupt sailors. If the Company sent even more, as they claimed, they must ask Newport where the provisions had gone, for Smith never saw more than twenty pounds' worth of victuals.

One can imagine the looks that flew back and forth across the boardroom table. Impertinent though Smith was, those earls and merchants and government ministers who had sunk considerable money into the business sat up and listened. Smith might be a loose cannon, but he had the sound of a man who knew his business. His harangue went on: London must not demand commodities from Jamestown, like pitch, tar, glass, and soap-ash, when the "poor" settlers could "scarce get necessaries" to survive and were living "hand to mouth." Wait "till more necessary things be provided" before the Company demanded profits from Virginia. As for Ratcliffe, Smith had sent the president packing before the settlers "should cut his throat." Never return him to Virginia, Smith warned: Ratcliffe and his crew would "keep us always in factions."[3] When they sent the next wave of settlers, Smith advised, forget about the highest and lowest orders. Don't recruit gentlemen and leave the unskilled laborers in England. Jamestown needed skilled "carpenters, husbandmen, gardeners, fishermen, blacksmiths, masons." For good measure, Smith tacked on "diggers-up of trees' roots," which was a practical consideration, since foraging in the woods proved crucial to survival. Send thirty such men to Virginia, Smith urged the directors, and keep in London "a thousand of such as we have." Gentlemen and wage laborers would starve before they could be "made good for anything." Dumbest of all was the Company's policy of placating the Indians and tolerating depredations. The coronation of Wahunsonacock was beyond stupid. On whose advice, Smith wondered, were the directors of the Company so misguided as to give to Wahunsonacock a bed and a crown?[4]

This letter was sobering. It confirmed suspicions that had been growing among some councillors since the previous November, when the Company began to plot the Third Supply. Smith's letter urged the Council toward decisive change. An extraordinary meeting was arranged at the Earl of Exeter's house, where all evidence was sifted: Smith's letter, Newport's debriefing, testimony from Ratcliffe and Archer, as well as, no doubt, a dozen other bits of information lost to history. This "solemne" gathering transformed the colony. On Smith's advice, the Company completely shifted its strategy. But it did not follow his request for a mere thirty skilled craftsmen. "We always thought at first we would send people there little by little," Thomas Egerton, the lord chancellor, said after that meeting. "[N]ow we see that the proper thing is to fortify ourselves all at once." They wanted to send eight hundred settlers to Virginia in March along with the victuals and tools to supply them, which would cost tens of thousands of pounds. The directors devised a new investment scheme, a new Indian policy, and a new type of government. Sir Edwin Sandys, a close associate of King James, drafted the necessary document. He incorporated a few articles from the First Charter, but by and large this Second Charter (as it is known to us today) rewrote Virginia's constitution.[5]

## THE FIRST AMERICAN DREAM

Two of the oldest men attending Exeter's meeting were Thomas Harriot and Richard Hakluyt. They brought to the table the wisdom learned from England's first transatlantic plantation, Sir Walter Raleigh's failed colony at Roanoke. Harriot actually went to the New World and was Europe's leading expert on Algonquian Indians, while Hakluyt, England's most learned cosmographer, had drafted England's first American policy. Their activity in the Company gave Virginia's First Charter some continuity with earlier efforts. Their very presence should have shamed the proceedings in 1609, but there is no evidence that anyone saw any great discontinuity between the policies enacted in 1609 and the spirit of liberation that Harriot and Hakluyt represented. They themselves did not protest the results. Not even Hakluyt seems to have realized what would happen when profit became the main engine of empire. In retrospect, we can regard these two men as monuments to the high hopes and noble, if naive, aspirations of England's first endeavors in America. Those eminences stand in high moral contrast to the new way of thinking about Native Americans and their land. Although it was not yet mentioned or even contemplated, the cataclysm of North American slavery might be traced to this meeting of corporate shareholders, when the Virginia Company pivoted England's role in world politics.

Thirty-five years before Jamestown, two little English ships cruised the coast of Spanish Panama looking for loot. Crews of determined sailors raided towns, hoping with some swift stroke to find a mayor's or a merchant's storehouse of gold. They skirmished. They extorted villages. Brandishing swords and pistols, they robbed coastal vessels. They exchanged gunfire with shore batteries. But all their work had little effect. By Christmas the whole Panamanian seaboard was alert, and still the English had no plunder. Letters and rumors spread the pirate's name, still unknown in England, across the Spanish Main. To be well known and feared bloated the egotism in this proud man, but infamy was bad for business. The alarm had been sounded. Treasures were moved from the coast. No Spaniard in Panama or sailing the Caribbean could be taken unawares by Francis Drake.

The British Empire did not yet exist. England had not yet even a toehold on the vast territories of the western hemisphere and no interest in "planting"—that is, settling any part of the New World. It was not always so. Just after Columbus discovered America, it seemed the English would compete with Spain. In 1497, Henry VII of England commissioned an expedition organized by Columbus's fellow Genoan, Giovanni Caboto, or John Cabot, who revealed to Europe the continent of North America. When Henry VIII, the greatest Tudor king of England, married Catherine of Aragon, the daughter of Spain's Ferdinand and Isabella, who were Columbus's patrons, England's role in the New World might have seemed ordained. But while the churches and palaces of Spain were encrusted with barnacles of American silver, England's king was preoccupied with plundering his own monasteries, splitting the English church from Rome, and divorcing Catherine. England spent decades in civil strife, sorting out its lines of succession and its religious loyalties. Meanwhile, Spain spent the seventeenth century sharpening her skill at colonization the way one hones the edge of knife, carving up half a hemisphere, perfecting how to subdue native peoples, learning what infrastructure to build and when, determining how to find and extract or grow the marketable commodities, how to construct the best ships for transatlantic transport, and charting the best sea routes to the New World.

Columbus established a permanent Spanish colony on Hispaniola in 1493. He first touched the coast of Panama on his fourth and last voyage in 1502, seventy years before English ships sailed those waters. By 1510, Spaniards began their conquest of Panama. In 1513, Balboa, crossing the isthmus, saw the Pacific Ocean. In 1520, Magellan found a sea route into that ocean around the southern tip of the continent. Pizarro garroted the Incan emperor Atahualpa, in 1533 and immediately set about the business of fleecing Peru of gold and silver. When the Incan riches were looted, Spain used American, then African, slaves to work the mines. They shipped the lucre of this foul industry up the Pacific coast to Panama. Trains of fifty to a hundred mules plunged into the jungle, carrying the treasure to Venta Cruz, a depot just over the continental divide, where the treasure was loaded onto river boats and floated down to Nombre de Dios, the Atlantic seaport where, finally, it was loaded onto great ships that carried the bars of silver and gold in convoys to Spain. French pirates started raiding the Caribbean shipping almost right away, so by the time the English tried to get in on the action it took ingenuity as well as daring to pry this loot from the Spanish.

Francis Drake had plenty of both. The age suited him. He exemplifies that entrepreneurial energy unleashed by Queen Elizabeth's new, partially meritocratic society—energy that had lain dormant for generations under rigid hierarchies. Capitalism was walking on the lanky, jointy, and clumsy limbs of its adolescence, running wild all over the globe, round the Horn of Africa, across the mysterious Atlantic, and finally round South America's treacherous wave-raising windy cape into the Pacific. Those historians of class conflict, Marx and Engels, thought that these oceanic explorers triggered the modernization of Europe. Capitalism "sprouted from the ruins of feudal society" only when ships opened up trade routes—and markets—between societies hitherto isolated from each other.[6] One does not need to be a Marxist to agree that these bold mariners had to come before factory owners. Before new commodities and new means of producing commodities could be invented, the explorers had to open markets. The masters of ships were the pioneers of a meritocratic, post-feudal society that rewarded ingenuity, innovation, risk, and industry. Such men did not generally come from the manorial estates. Landed aristocrats luxuriated and their peasants toiled according to roles assigned to them ages ago. Their habits chained them to the land. Sea captains were another breed, and they came from the ranks of merchants and yeomen farmers, men who might be made wealthy by their own initiative.

Drake grew up in a two-room "longhouse": a typical sixteenth-century English farmhouse with a central chimney flanked on either side by a single room with a loft. One side of the chimney belonged to the animals, while the other belonged to the farm's people. Francis spent his young life in this fifteen-by-fifteen-foot square, or in the loft above it, or in the fields and lands surrounding the Drake family's couple of hundred acres. They were not peasants. They were yeoman farmers, prosperous by the standards of the day, gaining in each generation. Francis's father, Edmund Drake, was an educated man, an ordained a minister. Nevertheless, the Drake family ate a peasant's plain, hearty diet of bread, "peas and beans, greens, parsnips, turnips, carrots, and beets . . . milk, butter, cheese . . . chicken and eggs . . . apples, plums, and berries." Beer was another staple, and the local variety was an oat beer that outsiders found undrinkable.[7] Had Drake been born in 1440 instead of 1540, the smell of soil and cows would have saturated his hair and clothes his entire life. But their fields were near Plymouth, and Francis could smell the salt air of the sea. Edmund Drake sent Francis to Plymouth to train in the house of a kinsman, William Hawkins, a prominent merchant in that seafaring town.

In 1562, William's son, John Hawkins, sailed four ships from Plymouth to Sierra Leone, where he took a cargo of "blacks, stealing some from Portuguese traders, capturing others on his own, and finally taking a Portuguese vessel to carry the slaves that could not be crammed into his own holds."[8] Then they sailed for the Spanish West Indies. Spain forbade its colonies from trading with the English, and so the proffering of slaves was highly irregular and purchases were often accompanied by violence. There was a good bit of extortion in this early version of what American schoolchildren call the "triangular trade." Plymouth merchants emptied their cargoes of English textiles in the Canaries and Africa, often doing so illegally. In Africa, they filled their holds with slaves, bargained for illegally or simply snatched from villages within raiding distance of the coast. They smuggled this human cargo into the Spanish West Indies, where they filled their ships once again with whatever loot they could procure or steal from Spanish colonists. Highly innovative, high-risk, and high-reward. In a word, entrepreneurial.

Drake's first true pirate cruise made enough money in Panamanian waters to finance his second cruise in 1572. The small *Pascha* (forty tons) and the tiny *Swan* (twenty-five tons) menaced the Atlantic coast, making the ambivalent gestures regarding trade (tin, pewter, and cloth) that were necessary to pretend that any thieving they did was not piracy but a defense of open markets. The Spanish refused their commerce. Drake forced them to "trade" at gunpoint. He raided the main seaport, Nombre de Dios but found it was the wrong season for plucking treasure. Even so, the locals defended it valiantly, and Drake lost several men and had to be carried himself, bleeding, back to the pinnaces.

The incident demonstrates Drake's character, which was not far from Hollywood's idea of a Caribbean swashbuckler. Neither short nor tall, he was somewhat stocky and fair-haired, altogether an average-looking Englishman. But he had the air of "forceful" authority and a reputation for firm command. He was "feared and obeyed by his men," according to a Spanish witness, a gentleman prisoner who observed him closely. "Alert, restless, well-spoken, ambitious, vainglorious," the Spaniard wrote, "but generous and liberal; not a cruel man."[9] Drake was prone to gallantry. He could be mild and generous to prisoners, but on at least one cruise he carried a kidnapped woman to his sea cabin. He had little ideology: like a good entrepreneur he was governed by profit. His personal bravery was both a virtue and a defect. It proved his valor to his men, but it robbed him of discretion. He smiled carelessly at the enemy's sword and musket, as if addicted to the excitement of the melee, where treasure and death were equal chances. Or not quite equal. He did try to stack the odds in his favor by a bold stroke or ambush. But he loathed the clerkish work of meticulous planning, so he hacked at details like a machete cutting a path from tangled vines. Sometimes his improvisations seemed providential. Luck hovered over him like a guardian angel. But some of his capricious decisions were self-defeating and got himself and his men into fixes. The smaller his crew, the more effective his leadership. He captained a hundred desperadoes gallantly. He admiraled a naval fleet like a pirate would, with too keen an eye to his own affairs and too little attention to the state's. He never knew if the queen was going to be pleased or mad about his latest exploit.

In 1572, when Drake captured a coasting vessel off Panama, he would rifle the cargo, put the Spanish ashore, and pump the slaves for intelligence. They told him stories about people living in the dense jungles and rugged mountains of the country. Bands of escaped slaves, whole towns full of Africans, were hiding in the rugged Panamanian interior. They were a nation of outlaws living within a stone's throw of the Spanish colonies, yet in near-total isolation from those outposts of civilization. Even as Drake learned about these *Symerons*, or "wild men," the *Symerons* heard rumors about him. Drake's name was "most precious and honoured" among them because he harassed the Spanish, and no one hated the Spanish more than Panama's *Symerons*.[10]

They had very good reason. Spain's treatment of Native Americans was amazingly cruel. Back in 1492, Columbus brought a few natives to Spain, baptized them in Guadalupe, and paraded them around Seville, which helped stir up interest in his second voyage to the Americas, seventeen ships ferrying more than a thousand men and farm animals. So the slaughter of Americans began.[11] The cruelties performed by Spanish settlers defy the comprehension of anyone with a belief in humanity. With gunpowder and metal and armor, the Spanish could do whatever they wanted to the natives, despite the imbalance in numbers. Civilization was an ocean away. No hand in Hispaniola would stop them, certainly not the admiral and governor, Christopher Columbus. Soldiers roamed the countryside slaughtering, raping, maiming people with no apparent motive other than to satisfy some sadistic pleasure. Some babies they fed to fierce war dogs in front of their mothers. Others they took by the ankles and swung round to bash their heads against rocks. Soldiers tested the sharpness of their swords by disemboweling their prisoners. Columbus ordered that natives who provided too little gold should have their hands chopped off. These details come to us from Bartolemé de las Casas's *Short Account of the Destruction of the Indies*. His father was with Columbus on the second voyage, and Bartolemé himself came to Hispaniola in 1502. He reported, for example, that he had seen the Spanish tie "native leaders and nobles . . . to a kind of griddle consisting of sticks resting on pitchforks driven into the ground and then grill them over a slow fire, with the result that they howled in agony and despair as they died a lingering death." He witnessed several chiefs tortured in just this manner.[12]

Naturally enough, the Indians "took to the hills to get away from the brutal and ruthless cruelty that was being inflicted on them."[13] In the Spanish reckoning, this was theft. Runaways were hunted by

Spanish atrocities in the New World. Here soldiers are murdering women and children and feeding the bodies to their dogs.

mastiffs, dragged back, and condemned by kangaroo courts before suffering their inevitable and often fatal flogging. Within a generation, sadism, disease, overwork, and starvation depopulated the once-thriving indigenous communities of Hispaniola. Tens of thousands died in a year. Cubans and Bahamians were enslaved to replace the dead of Hispaniola, but these did not suffice, and within a quarter century the Spanish had "effectively liquidated . . . the Caribbean's millions of native people."[14] As early as 1510 they began importing Africans.

This pattern was repeated all over the New World. As quickly as the Spanish and Portuguese erected the horrifying apparatuses of their slave societies, slaves sought refuge in the hinterlands. Escape was the purest form of resistance. By the mid-1500s, bands of fugitives were living just beyond the borders of every colony: Peru, Honduras, Venezuela, Brazil, Cuba, Santo Domingo, Panama.[15] They hid in the inhospitable hinterlands: mountains or swamps or jungles where pursuit was dangerous and uncertain. These bands, called maroons, might operate as brigands, raiding plantations for supplies, or they might attempt total self-sufficiency in their isolated territories. Their design was to never return to "civilization."

In 1525 slaves first escaped Spanish settlements in Panama and took off for the dense forest, from which they occasionally raided plantations for supplies. They were hunted down and killed. But the cruelties of slavery insured a perpetual cycle of revolt, flight, and recapture. For twenty-five years, various groups of slaves repeated the pattern of escape, freedom, recapture, death. In 1549 a man named Felipillo led a more successful flight of escapees, who managed to build a village and re-create what the historian Ruth Pike, drawing on contemporary Spanish accounts, calls the "African way of life" they had left behind, although truly that must have been a creole culture derived from several places in Africa. They lived free for two years, periodically harassing the Spanish, until the village was discovered, attacked, and burned, and Felipillo was captured and executed. Several in his community avoided recapture, rebuilt the village, and became the seed of the most successful maroon community in Spanish America.[16] Within a few years about eight hundred *cimarróns* or *Symerons*—escaped slaves melded with the remnants of Panamanian indigenes—congregated under the leadership of a "strong good-looking man" named Bayano, a "king" obeyed and feared by his followers. As many as three thousand slaves escaped into the "long chains of high and jagged mountains" of the interior, where they built and fortified their villages and "lived a free life based on African tribal customs." At the height of his powers, Bayano ruled over at least forty lesser chiefs, a paramount chiefdom like Wahunsonacock's.[17]

Drake first made contact with the *Symerons* in September 1572. Twelve black men came down out of the mountains to ally their people with Drake. The *Symerons* joined the pirates in their island hideout, showed the English how to build houses out of palmettos, and helped construct a European-style fort. The *Symerons* were armed with bows and four types of arrows. The heaviest were large-game arrows with heads of iron sharpened to a knife's edge and weighing one and a half pounds, which made "so large and deep a wound ... as can hardly be beleeved of him that hath not seen it." Lighter arrows were for birds. For killing men, they had arrows longer than those made famous by Scottish bowmen and tipped with iron, wood, or even fish bones.[18]

Sir Francis Drake.

Through late autumn, the *Symerons* kept the English supplied with fresh meat from wild hogs and pheasants and fresh vegetables that they rooted out of the woods. But gradually their failure to steal any big treasure demoralized the English. One of Drake's own brothers, John, died in an impetuous raid on a frigate that the Spanish ably repulsed. Then their health flagged. In January 1573 a mysterious "calenture" infected half the men, and the English were carried off, one by one, until the survivors were tempted to despair. Among those stricken was another Drake, young Joseph, who died in his brother's arms.[19] On top of this came the news that the powerful Spanish naval fleet, which would convoy the treasure ships, had arrived in Nombre de Dios. Such a powerful force seemed to dash their last hope for plunder. Twenty-eight were dead. Only thirty or forty English were left, and none wanted to continue risking their lives for the trifles they took from the few boats they succeeded in seizing. Drake knew he had to try some bold stroke. If fighting the way pirates fought was not working, why not try the ways of *Symerons*?

On Shrove Tuesday, February 3, 1573, a company of forty-eight men—eighteen Englishmen and thirty Africans—headed into the wilderness. The English carried their own weapons, while the

*Symerons* carried provisions, which they augmented by hunting wild pig and otter. Along the way they gathered wild mammeas, guavas, oranges, lemons, and something they called "pinos." Every evening, the *Symerons* built sturdy, watertight houses out of palmetto boughs and plantain leaves. On the third day they stepped out of the trees into a town of fifty or sixty houses arranged on three pleasant streets, where the *Symerons* lived "very civilly and cleanely," bathing in the river, wearing clothes "very fine and fitly made." These families grew crops and raised fowl and animals, and as marvelous as this sight was to the English, the Africans told them of another town—a veritable city—where their king lived with seventeen hundred "fighting men."[20]

The next day the pirates and *Symerons* resumed their march into the trackless woods. Four blacks scouted the way about a mile ahead of the main group, breaking boughs to mark the route; then came twelve *Symerons* warriors; then the English with two *Symerons* captains keeping them quiet; and finally a rear guard of another twelve maroons. They were climbing, and the high trees provided shade, and the undergrowth thinned out, so that the march was easy and cooler than an English summer day. At about ten in the morning on the eleventh of February, they came upon an open space cleared of trees and dotted with shelters that the *Symerons* had built for travelers. Maroons from "diverse places in those waste Countries" frequented the spot.[21] A *Symeron* leader named Pedro took Drake by the hand and led him to a tall, broad tree growing from the very spine of the ridge. Steps had been carved in its trunk. Up high in the branches a platform could accommodate a dozen men, and Pedro took his guest up this height. A breeze was blowing. A few clouds hung in the blue sky, too few to obscure the view. To the north, Drake could see the Atlantic Ocean whence they had come, miles off in the distance but spreading to the curved horizon—an impressive view, but something that could be seen, after all, from the heights of Drake's hometown on the Devon coast. But when he turned around he witnessed what few white men ever had, what he called the "South Atlantick" and some called the "South Sea": the Pacific Ocean. The poet John Keats described the feeling when a Spanish explorer with eagle's eyes stared at the Pacific, and his men in wild surmise stood silent upon that peak in Darien. So were the English awed.

After a minute Drake regained his composure. If it pleased "Almighty God of his goodnesse," he whispered, give him "life and leave to saile once in an English Ship in that sea."

One of his lieutenants, John Oxnam, stood by his side and replied that unless Drake "beat him from his Company," Oxnam "would follow him by Gods grace."[22]

Whether by God's leave or not, Drake got his treasure. They ambushed one of those caravans carrying bars of silver overland from the Pacific to the Atlantic. The *Symerons* cared for none of it: they wanted only iron, which Drake gave them gladly. Drake got to launch his famous career. The notoriety of this cruise brought the attention of the Earl of Essex, who tapped Drake for his invasion of Ireland, which eventually brought him to the attention of the queen, who granted permission, kept secret for reasons of diplomacy, to raid Spain's ports and shipping in that magnificent sea that he first spied from a maroon tree house. With his loot from Panama, Drake built the 150-ton *Golden Hind*, sailed through the Strait of Magellan and round the world, and returned to England a national hero and "one of the richest men in the country."[23] He bought Buckland Abbey, was knighted and granted a coat of arms by Queen Elizabeth. Of all riches and awards, Englishmen regarded this recognition—a coat of arms—higher than any other. Two silver stars and a silver wave adorned Drake's shield, and the helm was crowned with a ship in full sail.

Drake earned these honors by his own ingenuity, industry, and considerable personal risk. He was self-made in that sense. But, like John Smith in later years, he was not really "made" until he was granted his coat of arms. Then he entered the ranks of privilege. One might imagine the ancient, feudal, aristocratic system, which was so intent on one's ancestry and contemptuous of any commoner, as the root and bole of England. Meritocratic capitalism was a vine twining round the trunk of that tree. Over the centuries, the vine thickened and strengthened until it choked the tree, which withered, hollow in the end and held erect only by the vine. But such a transfer of strength was three hundred years away, and in Elizabethan England capitalism was yet a thin vine. Plenty of true bloods scorned upstarts, even upstarts as popular as Francis Drake. Lords and earls snubbed him. Lord Sussex declared that it was no "great accomplishment" to be a pirate. Lord Burghley "rejected [Drake's] gift of ten bars of gold, saying that he could not in good conscience receive stolen goods." Drake would never shake off his start as "a private man of mean quality," as one government document put it.[24] If contemporaries did not, we must give Drake his due. His alliance with the *Symerons* inspired the British Empire.

### LEADERS OF THE FREE WORLD

In 1568, four years before young Drake's cruise to Panama, a sixteen-year-old orphan at Westminster school in London, Richard Hakluyt, walked across a section of London to visit his patron and cousin, a lawyer in the Middle Temple, who shared his name.[25] The lawyer lived just a stroll away from the "creaky medieval monastery" that was Westminster school. The two Richard Hakluyts sat comfortably and chatted earnestly in the library of this house near the Thames River.[26] The younger Hakluyt happened to observe a few geographic books open on the table along with a map of the world. The older Hakluyt, eager to share his own enthusiasm, pointed out "all the known Seas, Gulfs, Bayes, Straights, Capes, Rivers, Empires, King-domes, Dukedomcs, and Territories of each part . . ." And then he conjured up divine aura in the form of Psalm 107:23–24: "they which go downe to the sea in ships, and occupy by the great waters, they see the works of the Lord, and his wonders in the deepe."[27] Sunlight opened on young Hakluyt's mind. It was a revelation and direction. For seven years he studied the stories of mariners till he became one of England's first professors of cosmography and the greatest of the age. His uncle was himself a "clearinghouse for information" coming from overseas, a sort of spy-informant for William Cecil, Lord Burghley, the architect of many of Queen Elizabeth's foreign policies.[28] With his cousin's contacts, by the late 1570s the younger Hakluyt could boast that he had grown "familiarly acquainted with the Chiefest Captaines at sea, the greatest Merchants, and the best Mariners of our nation," whom he interviewed at the ends of their journeys, recording and publishing their narratives.[29]

These labors served the program of an influential cadre of Queen Elizabeth's advisors and courtiers who were trying to lure the queen's gaze across the Atlantic: men like Drake, Sir Humphrey Gilbert, Sir Walter Raleigh, Sir Philip Sidney, and secretary of state Sir Francis Walsingham. When Drake came back from his Panamanian cruise, Hakluyt interviewed either him or members of his crew, and then, while Drake departed on his then-secret mission to sail into the Pacific Ocean and raid Spanish colonies, Hakluyt wrote a short paper advocating that England take an audacious and spectacular first step into the Americas: seize the Strait of Magellan, the Western gateway to the Indies, and plant a colony there. The main impediment to the project was manpower: Who would consent to live down in the inhospitable climate near the southern cape of America, and who could possibly thrive there?

Hakluyt's answer was Drake's *Symerons* of Panama. They detested "the prowde governance of the Spanyards," which was a qualifying consideration, and Hakluyt reasoned that those people could "easely be transported by Drake or others of our nation to the Straights, and there may be planted by hundreds or thowsands." Hakluyt reasoned that they would gladly adapt to the inhospitable habitat, so different from the tropical mountains of Panama, as long as the migration guaranteed their freedom. More than anything, the *Symerons* loved liberty. "[B]y our nation made free from the tyrannous Spanyard," the Symerons "shall easily be induced to live subject to the gentle government of the English." As fanciful as this scheme might sound, in 1580 it seemed plausible to the best English experts.[30]

The boosters of plantation thought that settling America was a moral imperative. An entire generation in England had grown up reading *Foxe's Book of Martyrs*, which luridly chronicled the tortures inflicted upon Protestants by papists, especially under Bloody Mary. In 1572—the same year Drake raided Catholic Panama—French Catholics slaughtered Protestants on Saint Bartholomew's Day. Huguenot survivors poured out of France. In the late 1570s, "London was abuzz with news of the tortures Englishmen were suffering" in Spain at the hands of the Inquisition: their property confiscated, their bodies confined to the galleys. Protestant provinces in the Netherlands, in near perpetual revolt against the heavy-handed rule of their Catholic monarchs, looked perpetually to England for succor, men, and arms. Revolts by the native Catholics in Ireland threatened civilization in that kingdom. It seemed to men like Richard Hakluyt that England was the Protestant citadel that must check the resurgent Catholicism from tipping the world backward in time to barbaric tyranny.[31] The history of Catholics in America proved that barbarism. *Crimes against humanity* and *genocide* were not yet terms in the political lexicon, but they capture the English view of Spanish conduct. In 1583, Bartolomé de las Casas's exposé of colonial crimes finally was translated into English, and it left "an enduring influence on the Protestant nation." Everywhere in England men were talking about the barbarism with which the Catholics killed "many millions of me[n]."

In this context, Drake's allegiance with the *symerons* took on a significance it did not have just ten years earlier. The English imagined "themselves as liberators . . . allied with blacks against whites," to quote Edmund Morgan's assessment of English thought in the 1580s, and that became the theme of English history. Virtue and piety make nations prosper, Sir Walter Raleigh explained in his copious *Historie of the World*, while vice and deformity make them wretched. Raleigh praised Elizabeth's successor, King James, for preserving "the liberty of England," while Philip III of Spain was in thrall to "Romish Tyrants." The contemporary account of Drake's circumnavigation pioneered this new national identity in "England's developing imperial imagination." According to Drake's *World Encompassed*, the "handsome, friendly, apparently harmless native people" of America, "in bondage to dark spiritual forces and threatened by sinister [Catholic] European powers," would flock to the "brave, kind, and pious" English.[32]

While Drake was still circumnavigating the globe, the flanks of the *Golden Hind* fattening with treasure, one of his ships turned around, returned to England, and reported his progress to Hakluyt. Hakluyt sensed the touch of destiny. "There is a time for all men," he wrote. The Spanish and their archaic system were waning. A new era dawned. "[T]he time approacheth and nowe is," Hakluyt wrote, that England should plant its flag "in part of America."[33] These words prefaced Hakluyt's 1582 book, *Divers Voyages Touching the Discovery of America and the Islands Adjacent*, which compiled the latest intelligence on the New World. Secretary of State Walsingham, who had been interested in Hakluyt's ideas for several years and already had sent a Portuguese pilot, Simon Fernandes, to scout the American coast, read it, and put Hakluyt on the payroll, so to speak, with a well-paid prebendal stall in the Bristol cathedral.[34] According to Sir Philip Sidney, to whom Hakluyt had dedicated *Divers Voyages*, the cosmographer "served for a very good trumpet" for the expedition that followed. Unfortunately, the flagship of that expedition foundered in the mid-Atlantic, and all souls drowned. Sir Walter Raleigh eagerly snatched up the torch, and by July of 1584, Hakluyt was in London consulting Raleigh at Durham House, his mansion on the Thames River, a recent gift of the queen. From August to September, Hakluyt was holed away writing up a report for Raleigh, which adverted to a likely landing place at Roanoke. The report was dispassionate. Reasonable. All the more persuasive coming from the professor rather than the courtier, Sir Walter Raleigh. Hakluyt squared his rationale for a new American policy neatly onto several sheaves of paper, which Raleigh arranged for him to hand to Queen Elizabeth, a treatise he called *A particular discourse concerning the great necessity and manifold commodities that are like to grow to this Realm of England by the Western disoveries lately attempted*. It is known today as *The Discourse on Western Planting*.[35]

Hakluyt's *Discourse* was bold. English soldiers who fought the Spanish in the Netherlands would sail to Panama to ally themselves with maroons, Native Americans, and others "desirous of libertie and feedome." Word would spread like wildfire to all of Spain's dominions. Elizabeth's reputation for "humanitie, curtesie, and freedome" would induce the "naturall people" in the Americas, by which Hakluyt meant the Indians, to rally with the English. Under Elizabeth's banner these slaves would all revolt against Spain, "who governe the Indies with all pride and tyranie." The liberated communities would willingly "yelde themselves to [Queen Elizabeth's] governmement" because Elizabeth's "noble navie" and "people moste valiaunte" would defend them against Spanish retribution.[36] American maroons, after all, whispered the same desperate prayer heard from the lips of unfortunate European captives enslaved on Turkish or Moroccan galleys: "*Liberta!*" England would hear their prayer.[37] To Hakluyt, racial distinctions were inconsequential. All people had a natural right to freedom. The *Discourse* predicted that African maroons would assimilate into common polity with English settlers, living side by side as equal, if subaltern, subjects of the crown. At a stroke, England might deprive Spain of its empire.[38]

## CONSENT OF THE GOVERNED

At about the same time that Hakluyt presented his *Discourse* to the queen, Arthur Barlowe captained one of the two ships that Sir Walter Raleigh sent to Roanoke to scout locations for a garrison of soldiers that would follow the next year. When the ships dropped anchor, "fortie or fiftie men, very handsome, and goodly people," rowed across Pamlico Sound to greet them. The Indians displayed the kind of simplicity that Barlowe could read about in Montaigne's *Essais*. The Indians were fascinated by the strangeness of the English. The tips of their fingers touched the white skin of the Europeans, probing with great wonder and polite civility. Their eyes ranged up and down Barlowe's ship, marveling at the masts as tall as trees and at the web of rigging and the vast size of the vessel, for they had never stood upon its like. The Indians were taken by surprise. They were intellectually, emotionally, and politically unprepared for this encounter. As we have seen, it was not as if they had never heard of Europeans. Stories circulated. Probably everyone living on the Carolina sounds had seen some European objects—an iron hatchet, a knife, or a copper pot. But few had seen a European ship with their own eyes, and fewer yet had stood on deck and touched the skin of the men who had sailed the ship across the water. Barlowe appeared out of the blue, so to speak, a shock. Or so Barlowe imagined it.

For Barlowe also the encounter was significant, but it did not come as a shock. He had seen Indians in the West Indies, where he watered and victualed his ships, and probably bartered with them. Besides, the captains of English ships had read their Hakluyt. And yet, Barlowe's report smacks of romance as much as reality. "Wee found the people," he told Sir Walter Raleigh, "most gentle, loving, and faithfull, void of all guile, and treason." Perhaps influenced by Montaigne, he decided that they were a window that opened upon the fabled "golden age."[39] Barlowe ate at the hearths of Roanoke houses. He slept on reed mats. There's a good chance he had sex with a young Indian woman, or he turned down the offer. (Barlowe, like most English travelers, was shy about discussing such matters.) He was actually there, and yet he still looked at the Indians on Roanoke Island through Montaigne's rose-tinted lens.

They were not perfectly golden. Peace did not reign in Roanoke. Barlowe knew that the various bands of Indians constantly warred with one another, just as Montaigne knew that the Tupinambá ate their enemies. People were sometimes killed and often injured. But Barlowe was a soldier from European wars. He probably fought in Ireland. Compared to the efficient, dehumanizing brutality of European warfare, Indian battles had an aura of innocence, as if the combatants were children playing with sticks and stones. Violence diminished Barlowe's paradise, but hardly so. Roanoke Island and its environs were "a most pleasant, and fertile ground, replenished with goodly Cedars, and divers other sweete woods." One needn't work for food. Deer, rabbits, and other beasts were there for the taking. "[T]he goodliest and best fishe in the world" surrounded the island "in greatest abboundance." Fecundity and bounty were his main themes. "The earth," Barlowe observed, "bringeth foorth all things in aboundance, as in the first creation, without toile or labour." Historians often dismiss such descriptions as mere propaganda meant to attract settlers. But in some places Barlowe paints a very realistic portrait. If one eye belonged to the romantic or poet, the other eye belonged to the businessman. He calculated profits to be made in this Garden of Eden by harvesting grapes and flax "and many other notable commodities." Besides, Barlowe was reporting to his boss, not writing for recruits. He truly believed what Montaigne articulated so well: *savage* meant simple, pure, very close to a state of nature. In other words, Barlowe really believed that one might see in the faces of the Indians the expression of innocent humanity before the Fall had condemned men to work for their food: only "in the sweate of thy face," as the King James Bible of 1611 told good Englishmen, "shalt thou eate bread."[40] The serpent lurking just beyond the margin of the garden was, of course, the Spanish, which the English might beat away with their swords.

Wanchese, an Indian who grew up on the quiet waters of Pamlico Sound, and Manteo, who came from Croatoan Island, one of the barrier islands that protected those quiet waters from the ocean, sailed back to England, and Barlowe deposited them at Durham House. Thomas Harriot, one of Raleigh's scholars, had been with Barlowe, and on the return voyage and then at Durham House he learned the Algonquian language, sketched out a dictionary, and taught the Indians to speak English. He and Manteo communicated well enough for Harriot to learn the recent history of the Croatoan and Roanoke Islands, and the subtleties of tribal alliances and broken faith.[41]

For his part, Raleigh had no illusions about prelapsarian man. He exhibited the Indians to guests, who viewed them as curiosities, exotics, "white Moors" in the words of one visitor from Germany, who concluded that they "made a most childish and silly figure." Raleigh, too, saw them as childish and ready to grow up. He dressed them as English gentlemen, in "brown taffeta." He brought them to Parliament, a living representation of England's potential subjects in America. The point was to demonstrate how pliable Native Americans were, how susceptible to Anglicizing. Raleigh showed Wanchese and Manteo to a succession of potential investors. The Indians probably were presented at court, where, just as the Tupinambá had done in the French court a quarter century earlier, they observed the elaborate rituals of deference paid to Queen Elizabeth. If so, they were probably less dumbfounded than Montaigne's cannibals had been. Costume and ritual enriched Algonquian life, just as they did in English court and church. Nor were Indians unused to female power: Manteo's own mother, after all, was chief of the Croatoans, and their society was matrilineal.[42] Queen Elizabeth was impressed. The seed of empire finally germinated in the flinty soil of her mind. Parliament granted Sir Walter Raleigh a patent to plant North America. Sir Francis Drake assembled his expeditionary force of ships and soldiers. If we looked for a single year to mark the start of the British Empire, 1585 would be the best candidate.[43]

Drake would attack Spain's Atlantic shipping, ransack its colonies, and stir up slave revolts, while Raleigh's settlement at Roanoke would provide a permanent naval base that would protect, refit, and resupply English ships.[44] Raleigh sent Ralph Lane in five ships with six hundred men, sailors, soldiers, carpenters, smiths, lumbermen, geologists, and coopers to build a fort at Roanoke. That was almost a feint, a mere jab, while Drake was supposed to deliver the roundhouse hook: twenty-five ships and several smaller shallow-keeled boats, thousands of soldiers, and an immense supply of ordnance. That would coldcock colonial Spain, knocking over a hundred years of conquest.

Harriot went to Roanoke to continue his study of the Indians and to interpret for Ralph Lane. To his surprise, Wanchese shucked off his English clothes at the first opportunity and returned to his primitive way of life. He warned the local chief, Wingina, that the English were after territory, and the notion of a benign English-Algonquian alliance was further strained when Wingina came to his bitter end. Under a flag of truce, Lane attacked Wingina and his entourage. Most of his retainers fell in the first sudden blow, and Wingina went to the ground as if killed, but he suddenly sprang up and sprinted into the woods. A pistol shot hit him in the buttocks, and one of Lane's more enterprising lieutenants, an Irishman named Edward Nugent, plunged into the woods after him and emerged, eventually, with Wingina's severed head dangling from his fist.[45] But still Harriot had faith. On his return to England, Harriot prepared his own report about Virginia, with chapters called "Of Rootes" and "Of Fruites." The final, longest section was a dissertation on "the nature and manners of the people." These pages gave the English their most authoritative and compelling account of Americans, and it represents our best notion of what Richard Hakluyt and the Virginia Company's directors first thought their settlers would find on the Chesapeake.

"They are a people clothed with loose mantles made of Deere skins," Harriot began, and "aprons of the same rounde about their middles; all els naked . . ." Not possessing any "edge tooles or weapons of yron or steele," the English have nothing to fear of them. Quite the contrary: the Indians "have cause both to feare and [love us]."[46] Harriot admired the Roanokes in nearly the same terms that Montaigne admired his cannibals. Their government was so rudimentary as to be nearly nonexistent: each small town had its "Wiróans" (*weroance* in the Tsenacomocoan dialect farther north). Above these were a "chiefe Lorde" who might control as few as two or as many as eighteen towns. Government was a matter of personal relations: each person knew his chief. They had no writing, no history, but they had a crude sort of theology populated with anthropomorphic gods. Above all, they seem to be "simple" people. No matter their wit and ingenuity, the word *simple* comes up again and again. They were so awed, Harriot surmised, by manufactured goods like lanterns, fireworks, "gunnes, bookes, writing and reading, spring clocks that goe of themselves, and manie other thinges that wee had," that they imagined the English were gods. But here is where Harriot's mind veered off in the old grooves of prejudicial thinking. The Roanokes were, it seemed to Harriot, highly susceptible to being converted to

Christianity, if only his skill with their language were sufficient to teach them. Although they had "no such tooles, nor any such craftes, sciences and artes" as did the English, they seemed to be "very ingenious," Harriot thought, and "they shewe excellencie of wit." In other words, they could be Anglicized.[47]

Their susceptibility to become English subjects was a figment of Harriot's imagination, spun from his own unreflecting sense of England's superiority. What is important here is not so much how accurately or inaccurately Harriot painted his Indians but what his colors tell us about the lens through which he peered at them. Harriot's text admired the primitives, but it stops well short of suggesting that their ways were superior to English ways. He did not, as Montaigne did, suggest that civilized man ought to learn from primitives how to reform civilization, how to cut through the encrustation of artificiality and better harmonize European customs and government to human nature. Harriot concluded that if the English were careful to use "good government," if they avoided the mistakes that the Spanish made, the Indians "may in short time be brought to ciuility." Implicit in that conclusion is the unchallenged premise that one *should* prefer civilization—at least Protestant, English civilization.

Whether or not Drake shared this view, he put it into action. As impressive as his flotilla was when the pennants of twenty-five ships crowded breezy English harbors, they were taking on a hemisphere. They had to contend with a far-flung archipelago of fortified islands, several rich and entrenched mainland colonies, a citadel of American forests—all the while dodging Spain's navy. Even if the Spanish were unprepared, a colossus tends to stand in place, and Drake did not have enough weight to topple the Spanish behemoth. But Drake and his ships might be a fulcrum if they could only get Spain's slaves to serve as the lever.

Drake sailed in July 1585 with the queen's overt blessing, and Elizabeth herself invested two ships, the *Elizabeth Bonaventure* and the *Aide*, valued at ten thousand pounds, and another ten thousand pounds of "Readie money" for ordnance, gunpowder, victuals, and other supplies, a good third of the capital needed to assemble his fleet.[48] Thus Elizabeth stamped her imprimatur upon the venture—the good adventure, as the name of her ship predicted. War was big business and required investors. Drake himself, aristocrats, and merchants supplied the rest of the venture capital, either in the form of ships, supplies, or "Readie money," lured by returns that could come back in multiples as high as ten to one. Thousands of volunteer soldiers and sailors wagered their lives. Sailors and soldiers were recruited "without any imprest or gage from her Majestie or any body els." (By contrast, Raleigh used his power of impressment to force several sailors to sail to Roanoke against their will.)[49] The sailors put themselves under the authority of each ship's captain. The soldiers went under the discipline of their officers, who were commanded by Francis Walsingham's adopted son, Christopher Carleill, who was "Generall by land." Everyone, even General Carleill, pledged to follow the command of Sir Francis Drake. Foot soldiers and sailors were not paid wages. In an arrangement that foreshadowed the Virginia Company's contracts with its settlers, Drake's recruits were promised a share of "that bountifull masse of treasure" that Drake said they would steal from the Spanish.[50] The Spanish thought that Drake meant to establish an English and maroon colony near the tip of South America to control the Strait of Magellan, but he really aimed to take over Panama, the more reliable overland gate to the Pacific. Once Panama was secure, he would deliver hundreds of maroons to the naval depot that Raleigh was setting up in North America. Drake and Raleigh both imagined English would replace Spanish rule, only the new dominion would look very much like utopia. For starters, there would be no slavery.

As Edmund Morgan aptly explains, Drake's experience in Panama taught him the value of African Americans, and his relations with them was "untroubled by racial prejudice . . . the Cimarrons of the south [and] the good Indians of the north, would enjoy gentle government, civility, Christianity, superior technology, and abundance."[51]

Drake's armada sacked the town of Santiago in the Cape Verde Islands. Then the prows of these vessels pointed "ouer the great Ocean and [made] our course continually west ward for the west Indies." Nineteen days later they reached Guadalupe. On the island of Dominica they encountered their first Native Americans, whom the Spanish had not yet colonized. The island was densely wooded and inhabited, they estimated, by fifty thousand "savages." Most of the Englishmen in the expedition had never before seen an Indian. They were surprised to find that the inhabitants were "personable and handsome strong men." To be sure, they were naked and (so the English thought) they were cannibals, but neither of these facts prevented the English from enjoying their commerce. The Indians shared oranges, potatoes, cassava bread, and fruits of all types, and "help[ed] our folkes to fill and carie on their bare shoulders fresh water from the riuer to our ships boats, and fetching from their houses, great store of Tobacco." But the natives did not welcome English rule. Spanish depravity had made them wary of all Europeans. The equanimity with which the English reported this fact demonstrates how willing they were to see the world as Indians perceived it. In their own moral figuring, this imaginative dexterity distinguished them from the sinister Spanish.[52]

On the first of January, Drake landed a thousand men on Hispaniola. In February they captured Cartagena, in present-day Colombia. April saw them in Cuba. In May they harassed Florida. They anchored off present-day North Carolina's Outer Banks in June, where they conferred and collaborated with the Roanoke colonists. And by July of 1586, one year later, Drake was back in England.[53] From the Spanish

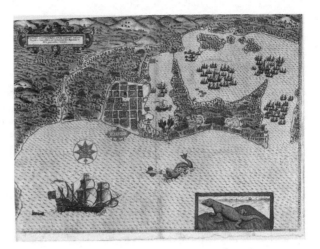

Drake's fleet taking
Cartagena.

perspective, Drake's cruise was horribly destructive, and they complained bitterly about how he had disrupted the slave system. When Drake arrived in Santo Domingo, a hundred-fifty slaves "deserted from the galleys." One witness said the Spanish themselves struck open the irons that imprisoned the galley slaves, thinking they would help fight the English. Without their chains, the Spanish were surprised to discover, these galley slaves "rose against us and did more looting than the English." The English took the galley slaves with them when they left Hispaniola, as well as "[m]any negroes belonging to private persons." All of these joined Drake "of their own free will." In March, Tristan de Orive warned Spain's other colonies that Drake "carries presents for the negroes, of whom he expects to make use." Another report indicated that at least fifty slaves from Santo Domingo had joined Drake.

The pattern followed in Cartagena. The Spanish "loosed" their galley slaves "from their irons" to help defend the city, but the slaves did "more damage . . . than" the English did. The slaves had seen the Spanish bury their valuables, so they knew right where to dig. Just as Drake had planned, African plantation slaves and Moorish galley slaves deserted to the English. And Cartagena's maroon community living in "the bush," as the governor of Cartagena, Pedro Fernández del Busto, put it, joined Drake's attack. When the English finally left Cartagena on April 10, "[t]hey carried with them some of the galley-slaves and negroes who deserted to them." In some cases, the Spanish slave owners tried to ransom their property, but "the English would not give them up except when the slaves themselves desired to go."[54]

Yet, from Drake's perspective, the cruise tottered on the edge of financial disaster. The Spanish treasure convoy had slipped past them in the Atlantic. They did capture Santo Domingo relatively intact and occupied the town, while its residents fled to the country-side. English soldiers ransacked private homes. The churches and monasteries gave up their splendid finery. In the storehouses they found "plenty of wyne, oyle, sugar, gynger, hydes, etc." But the English found no treasure troves, no storage house full of gold and silver bullion, no ships in the harbor packed full of America's natural resources. There was not enough to pay Drake's investors, not by a long margin. Drake demanded a million ducats to ransom the town. He might have well have asked them to deliver the moon. The citizens offered twenty thousand. Drake replied he would sooner sell the city for a lady's ring. Eventually the Spanish convinced him that he could get no more blood from this turnip, and Drake gave back the remaining, unburned, finer portion of the city for twenty-five thousand ducats. After five weeks, the English boarded their ships and left, taking the "bells of the churches, artillery from the fort, and ships, and other smaller things of every sort," leaving behind not even "the copper coin that circulates in this city."[55] Some men might "maruell greatly that such a famous & goodly builded Citie so wel inhabited of gallant people, very brauely apparelled . . . should afoord no greater riches," the official narrative admitted, but they must bear in mind the inhumanity of the Spanish colonies. "[T]he Indian people," the narrative explained, "which were the naturals of this whole Island of HISPANIOLA . . . were many yeares since cleane consumed by the tyrannie of the Spaniards." As a consequence of this genocide, no one was left "to worke in the Mines." This explanation carried "political value" in 1588. If the investors made less money than they expected, the English nation must take some satisfaction that Drake delivered a blow to Spanish tyranny.[56] An odd incident early in the fighting for Santo Domingo illustrates just how important it was for the English to imagine themselves as liberators. Under a flag of truce, a Spaniard rode toward the English for a parlay, and Drake for some reason sent out a "Nigro boie to talk with him." The Spaniard might have been insulted that he was forced to negotiate with a freed slave, or it might have been something the boy said that infuriated him, but whatever his motive the mounted soldier drove his staff through the boy's body, killing him. At the next parlay, Drake demanded that the soldier be executed. The Spaniards delayed. Drake hanged two Franciscan friars to demonstrate his earnestness. Finally, the offending Spanish soldier was offered up and hanged. The life of a young black boy was compensated by three dead white papists, an algebra that was a point of honor in English propaganda.[57]

Drake got only a little more money out of Cartagena, which had been forewarned. Private families stashed their movable wealth or carried it with them into the interior. Gold and silver from the churches were carried out of town. The governor, Pedro Fernández del Busto, dug trenches round the city and arrayed his 2,500 soldiers in various key places. Nearly eighty English were killed taking these defenses, but in victory Drake found himself possessing no more than Cartagena's bare buildings. Drake again tried ransom, demanding four hundred thousand ducats. He started burning houses, beginning with the poorest quarters. The Spanish paid nothing. He burned more neighborhoods. Eventually, the citizens coughed up 110,000 ducats, the largest portion of the ransom being two hundred silver bars belonging to King Phillip. This amount, the equivalent of about twenty-seven thousand pounds, recovered more than half the cost of outfitting the fleet. But it was nowhere near the fabulous profits that everyone expected. The English also liberated about five hundred slaves: about three hundred Indians, mostly women, and two hundred "negroes, Turks, and Moors." The Spanish marveled that the English would take no ransom for the slaves, despite the fact that such menial workers "are not useful" in England.[58] The English prided themselves on their fair dealing with these slaves, which was the main indicator of their moral superiority over the Spanish. This moral purpose raised the whole enterprise above the common thievery of Caribbean pirates. That theme weaves its way through *A Summarie and True Discourse of Sir Frauncis Drake's West Indian Voyage*. When the English gave up the city, great sections lay in ruins, the smell of charred rubble wafting through the streets. The Catholic shrines had been desecrated. Hundreds of slaves had been liberated and had joined the English. It would take years for the colony to recover.

But the grand scheme for toppling an empire was dashed. In Cartagena, Drake learned that the *Symerons* of Panama had made peace with their late enemies and overlords. The maroons promised to leave the Spanish alone, and the Spanish would leave them their own territory in the jungles of the interior. Live and let live. Drake's entire strategy hinged on conquering Panama, and conquering Panama hinged on the eagerness of the maroons to trade Spain's dominion for England's. Drake had barrels upon barrels of matériel down in the holds of his ships, tons of European clothing and weapons and iron with which to treat with the *Symerons*. Drake did not despair of someday turning the maroons against their traditional foes, but this cruise would not do it. Panama and its gate to the Pacific would have to wait "for another occasion."[59]

Drake had to contend with another disaster. Somewhere, perhaps in the Cape Verde islands, a "verie burning and pestilent ague" infected the fleet, and by the time they sacked Cartagena, the disease had spread. Very few who caught it escaped with their lives, and some of those few were deranged in their wits. The night airs seemed to feed the infections; the English were tossing corpses overboard every day. The Spanish estimated that eight or nine English died from this tropical fever every day of their six weeks' occupation of Cartagena. The "inconuenience of continuall mortality" also argued against a "stroke for the treasure" in Panama. With so many dead, injured, and sick, the English were reduced to about seven hundred effective soldiers, and everyone in the English expeditionary force, from the captains on down to the rank-and-file foot soldiers, were worried about their pay. General Carleill consulted his captains about whether they should continue on to Panama, where they had originally hoped to find the fabulous treasures that would give "full recompense" for their "tedious trauailes." The captains consulted with their soldiers, while similar questions were put to the captains of the ships, who consulted with the sailors. Sobered by Cartagena, they weighed their expectations against the dangers. On February 27 the captains wrote up their opinion in a set of resolutions.[60]

The resolutions pay remarkable attention to the conditions and opinions of the "poore men," the sailors and soldiers, who had spent "their apparell and such other little provisions as their small meanes might have given them leave to prepare." These men had joined Drake of their free will, putting themselves under his authority and the authority of his captains. In return, Drake promised them riches. But the sacking of three strategic cities—Santiago, Santo Domingo, and Cartagena—exploded that promise, and with so many of their company already dead, it was clear that an attack on Panama would yield little more recompense. The essence of the resolutions pointed out to Drake that he had broken his side of the bargain, and no amount of work by the sailors or soldiers was likely to change that fact. In short, they knew they would not be paid.[61]

They knew when they joined the expedition that rewards might not materialize. No one disputed that fact, and the resolutions fall well short of declaring that Drake's authority was dissolved. Everyone had taken an oath of obedience. "It is farre from our thoughts," they insisted, "either to refuse, or so much as to seeme to be wearie of any thing, which for the present shalbe further required or directed . . . from our Generall." Nevertheless, the resolutions indicate that, although he was the expedition's supreme commander, Drake did not wield the authority of a typical general. Authority had been established, literally, by a contract, which defined reciprocal obligations, reciprocal expectations. Drake's command was not all that different from a pirate captain's, which always depended on the consent of those he governed. Drake's sailors and soldiers had formally agreed to be commanded by their captains, told where to go, what to do, when to fight, when to sheath their swords, when to rob a house, and when not to. Deviation, they knew, might be punished even by death. Sir Francis Drake had full executive power and judicial authority. He hanged at least one soldier, an Irishman, for killing his corporal. In Santo Domingo, he threw some thirty or forty soldiers into jail for "contempt and disobedyence" to their captains, a direct violation of "there oathe." Yet, always in the minds of Drake and the minds of his captains was the voluntary nature of that subjection. Lurking always behind their orders were the reciprocal obligations of authority. The soldiers and sailors felt they had "discharged the parts of honest men," while the loot gotten from the three conquered cities "being all put together, are found farre short to satisfie that expectation which by the generality of the enterprisers was first conceived."

In the end, the capital investors made a decent profit: fifteen shillings for each pound wagered, or a profit of 75 percent. That seems well enough, but it pales in comparison to Drake's original prospectus, which promised to net as much as two million ducats. For their share, the "poore men" split between themselves one third of the net profit for the whole voyage, which amounted to approximately seventeen thousand pounds. Given that more than a thousand survivors had to split this portion, the individual soldier made a modest wage for his hazards and labor. Technically, Drake had not violated his end of the bargain, but with so little to show for so many sick, dead, and dying, he could hardly govern on that technicality. In Cartagena, he realized, he needed to renew the consent of the governed.[62]

The governed wanted to go home. Take the meager ransom for Cartagena, forget about Panama, cut their losses, and "returne towards our gracious Soveraigne and Country." Drake accepted their counsel. The ships sailed out of Cartagena's harbor in mid-April. To catch the trade winds home, they had to retrace their route through the West Indies—which was just as well, because they carried with them hundreds of liberated slaves whom they intended to settle in Roanoke as free subjects of the English crown. They passed by Cuba, threatening but not attacking that well-prepared colony. They sacked Saint Augustine in Florida. They tried to sack the Spanish outpost at Santa Elena in present-day South Carolina, but the winds and currents prevented it. Finally in June, as they skirted the coast farther north, hundreds of miles beyond the last outpost of European civilization, they spotted smoke from a signal fire: Roanoke.

Drake found that the remnant of Raleigh's colony was eager to abandon the settlement.[63] Ralph Lane and his hundred men were little better than maroons. The natives had not consented to English rule. In fact, Lane's boneheaded dealings had stirred up their enmity, and English dominion stretched only as far as their small ordnance, a falconet, could shoot. Twentieth-century archaeologists found a small cannonball about 1,100 feet from the remains of the Roanoke fort, so we can presume the English ruled at least that much territory, maybe the forty acres that fell within the effective sweep of the four falconets.[64] Lane's men were hungry, weakened, and discouraged, and every day they looked for rescue to come over the ocean. On the

eighth of June, 1586, relief finally came. More than twenty ships and
a host of smaller craft, a veritable city—Drake's fleet—sailed into view
of the barrier islands. Captain Edward Stafford stoked a fire, which
sent a signal of smoke snaking into the sky. Drake had what any colony
needed: tools, furniture, all pilfered from the Spanish cities he
had looted. Weapons. Ordnance. Powder. Provisions. Hardware
even down to door hinges and locks stolen from Cartagena. Ships.
He would give Lane as much shipping as he needed. But Lane
wanted none of it. We do not have to imagine how the English,
besieged in the fort at Roanoke, felt when the first boat tied up at
their slipway. Ecstatic. Weary but ecstatic. They hastily packed what
they needed to bring back: besides personal belongings, they had
plenty of samples of American resources, including ores. Notes. Maps.
Sketches of the plants, animals, and Indians, all quickly packed into
chests or barrels and stowed on the small landing craft. On the way
out to sea, one of these boats ran aground on the sandbar. Stuck tight,
the waves quickly began swamping the vessel, and Drake's sailors
tossed chests and barrels overboard mercilessly till the lightened
boat floated. Along with samples of resources painstakingly
collected went the richer portion of Harriot's journals and sketches,
a treasure trove for the historian and anthropologist lost for all time.
It symbolized the folly of Ralph Lane's expedition. A year's enterprise was reduced to an unmanned fort on Roanoke Island and three
English stragglers who could not be found when the boats departed.

How these three came to be elsewhere when Lane and his
hundred men took to the ships is unexplained by any of the journals.
It is tempting to think they hid, having made some furtive connection to one of the Indian villages. Lane handled his own men roughly
enough for some to desert. But this is mere speculation. However it
happened to come about, these three were truly abandoned, and have
remained lost to history. David Beers Quinn, whose opinion on the
matter is more informed than anyone else's, thinks they probably lived

their lives out among the Chawanoacs.[65] He very well may be right. Whatever the case, they were the first of Roanoke's lost settlers. The fate of the more famous group—the men, women, and children who were left behind the next year, who disappeared mysteriously, who are still today the subject of so much sleuthing and speculation—will be taken up in chapter 8.

What of the freed slaves? The hundreds of Africans and Native Americans liberated from slavery by Sir Francis Drake? They were in the twenty-some-odd English ships when Drake left the West Indies and sailed through the Florida Straits. Their numbers increased when the English occupied Spanish Florida. Drake had made promises to them, and there is no reason to think he failed to deliver. In any case, he did not carry them to England. He must have put them ashore somewhere between Santa Helena in South Carolina and Roanoke in North Carolina. Remarkably, they vanish from the historical record, and that record is actually pretty extensive. Once Drake sat down with Lane to plot out evacuation of Roanoke, no one mentions them again. That fact itself should amaze us. Where did they go? How did they live? How did they govern themselves? No one knows, and few seem to have cared. Historians and archaeologists and amateur genealogists who even today eagerly try to solve the mystery of a hundred or so English settlers lost at Roanoke the next year seem unconcerned that the greatest portion of the English settlement, hundreds upon hundreds of liberated slaves, have just disappeared. Perhaps that suited them. True maroons, after all, wanted to escape so-called civilization and were content to be left alone. One of the few historians interested enough to even speculate about their fate is Karen Ordahl Kupperman, who thinks they might have "live[d] on and melt[ed] into the native population."[66] No matter what they chose to do, the first people England permanently settled in North America included these escaped slaves, the maroons of Roanoke.

# CHAPTER SIX

᙭

# *The American Adventure*

**Time passed: a dozen years** of inactivity. On March 24, 1603, Queen Elizabeth died, ending the Tudor line. The Stuart line began the same day when King James VI of Scotland ascended the English throne. At this propitious moment, Richard Hakluyt brought the flame of empire to kindling again. The old cosmographer visited the aging knight Sir Walter Raleigh, who still held a monopoly on Virginia. They probably met in Durham House, Raleigh's London mansion, which had been headquarters for North American activities for so many years. Hakluyt, who had been a frequent contributor to the Durham House salons, posed a delicate question: Would Raleigh surrender his patent on planting North America? Hakluyt did not ask on his own behalf. A man of his slight means could not finance even a single ship. He spoke for a group of merchants similar to those at the heart of the East India Company. In all truth, Raleigh was sick of North America. His fifth and last attempt to find his lost colonists, Samuel Mace's 1602 journey, never came within fifty miles of Roanoke. Virginia had worn out his purse and patience. Some estimates put Raleigh's losses at more than forty thousand pounds. Besides this waning interest, Raleigh's mercurial nature sometimes could be uncommonly selfless, and in this case he resigned his dream of ruling a Virginia territory far bigger than any earl's or duke's fiefdom in England, reserving for himself only "the fifth part" of any "gold and silver ore" the new adventurers might find.[1]

Hakluyt contributed his expertise to Jamestown's First Charter, and the benevolent Indian policy should probably be attributed to his influence. While the Virginia Company, as a joint-stock company modeled on earlier trading corporations, was undoubtedly driven by the profit motive, it still retained that habit of thought, first laid down by Hakluyt, that made the English imagine themselves as purveyors of liberty.

By 1609 the Virginia Company had sent three separate groups of settlers to America. Newport's three ships had delivered the first colonists in late April 1607, and he returned with the First Supply—provisions and more than seventy new settlers—in January 1608 only to find the president deposed and more than half the original colonists gone, either dead or defected to the Indians. Newport returned with the Second Supply nine months later, just after John Smith deposed the second president. The Company had outfitted his expedition to find gold and the South Sea; had presented gifts to Wahunsonacock; had tolerated thefts and black market sales of its property, and still Jamestown had generated almost no revenue.

Two years of pouring money into the morass sank Hakluyt's dream for an empire of liberty. The terms of the Second Charter were so contrary to the ideals that inspired Francis Drake to liberate hundreds of slaves from Spanish America, contrary even to the somewhat equivocally sanguine notions of the First Charter, that it is hard to believe that Richard Hakluyt and Thomas Harriot could have been party to it. And yet they were. It seems that no one at the time quite realized how significantly the Second Charter shifted England away from its original ideals. While the Company still paid a degree of lip service to the evils of Spanish colonization, it instructed its employees to begin using Spain's methods. Protestantism, once the mark of liberty in comparison to tyrannical Catholicism, became the triumphalist justification for kidnapping, murder, and slavery.

The Second Charter split the Virginia Company in two, so the London branch became its own "body politick or corporate," known then and now as the London Company. King James gave it full dominion over the land two hundred miles north and two hundred miles south of Jamestown, and the interior territory "west and northwest" to the Pacific Ocean. That turned out to be half a continent, although in 1609 the Company would have preferred that the Appalachian Mountains looked out upon the Pacific Ocean. James also allowed it to sell shares widely across England. To fund its Third Supply of Jamestown, the London Company organized what would be called today a media blitz. They drafted a letter laying out the scheme, and Sir Humphrey Weld, the Lord Mayor of London and one of the nobler investors in the Company, sent it to all of the trade organizations, sometimes delivering it by his own hand and exhorting the tradesmen in person. Grocers discussed the adventure in their "company" meeting. Clothworkers were talking about it. Fletchers buzzed. Embroiderers offered their shillings. Fifty-seven different companies of tradesmen were lured into the scheme, investing their money communally—bricklayers, plumbers, founders, paint strainers, cordwainers, woolmen. The wealthier in each trade's company dumped in pots of money, enough for full shares, while humbler folk contributed their drams. London's fishmongers met on April 24, 1609 to discuss Jamestown, and John Wolverston added his two pounds to the five shares (or sixty-two pounds, ten shillings) ventured by another fishmonger, Mr. Richard Poyntell. Altogether, the treasurer of the fishmongers collected £783 at that meeting, enough to buy about sixty-two shares in the London Company. Each contribution was carefully listed, and those few fishmongers who

NOVA BRITANNIA.
OFFERING MOST
Excellent fruites by Planting in
VIRGINIA.
Exciting all such as be well affected
to further the same.

LONDON
Printed for SAMVEL MACHAM, and are to be sold at
his Shop in Pauls Church-yard, at the
Signe of the Bul-head.
1 6 0 9.

Robert Johnson's 1609 pamphlet promoted by the Virginia Company.

were too poor to invest or unpersuaded by the hoopla had their refusals recorded also.

All London caught the investment fever. "The people are mad about this affair," the alarmed Spanish ambassador complained to Madrid; "shameless," he added for moral emphasis. Besides the hundreds who invested through their trade organizations, more than six hundred people bought shares for themselves: eight earls, twelve more lords, a battalion of knights, lawyers enough to fill several courtrooms, rafts of gentlemen, fifty members of King James's first Parliament. Hundreds of obscurer men about whom we know nothing but their names enrolled their money. Each share in the London Company cost twelve and a half pounds—about one-third of yeoman family's entire wealth in the 1590s—so anyone who could buy an individual share was a man of some means. Each of these "adventurers" was listed in the Company books and given a share, which entitled him to a proportionate share of the adventure's proceeds.[2]

The Third Supply required more than money. The London Company wanted to recruit eight hundred people to sail to Jamestown, so it spread pamphlets, broadsides, letters, circulars, and sermons. The archbishop of York complained to the Earl of Somerset that so many tracts had appeared touting Virginia—"divine, human, historical, political, or call them as you please"—that he could read no more. The *Nova Britannia*, a semiofficial pamphlet about Virginia—it was dedicated to Company director, Thomas Smythe—is probably the single most important document in this campaign. It opens by dropping the name of the famous Captain Newport, a kind of celebrity endorsement that was calculated to reassure potential settlers that the whole enterprise was on the up-and-up. The pamphlet went on to "entreat all well affected subjects, some in their persons, others in their purses, cheerfully to adventure, and jointly take in hand this high and acceptable work." It appealed to religious zeal: the "savage and blind" Indians might see the light of Jesus. On this point we hear the faint echo of Hakluyt's hopes for Roanoke: Was it not infinitely better for the Indians to be "bought and ransomed, not by storms of raging cruelties" as the Spanish used—"rapier's point and musket shot"—but by "fair and loving means suiting to our English natures"? (That particular appeal was contradicted by the Second Charter, which was still being drafted.) More in tune with the true nature of the Third Supply, the pamphlets invoke a pugnacious sense of national identity: "Where is our [English] force and ancient vigor?" the pamphlet asked. Weren't they better than the French, who were exploring the northern parts of America? Weren't they as good as their fathers were in Queen Elizabeth's time? Yes! "Our plant is firmly rooted . . . [and] our branches fair and much desire to spread themselves abroad."

At the end of those branches, the tree of state had grown "superfluous twigs" that needed pruning. Wasn't it in the national interest to transport the "rankness and multitude of increase in our people"? Now that the long war with Spain was over, undesirables multiplied like vermin in the city streets. The Lord Mayor of London's circular urged "the necessity" of "enticing" the poor, who "infested their streets" with "plague and famine." "Swarms of idle persons," people without trades or any "means of labor," who descend into "lewd and naughty practices," must be enticed to emigrate. "Swarming" idlers appear in different tracts, a common talking point that suggests how well the London headquarters coordinated the campaign. Preaching in April, the Reverend William Symonds put a more positive spin on the metaphor, suggesting that the superfluous poor were a "swarme [of] . . . young bees in a hive in June." Overcrowded England needed the "old strong bees [to] thrust the weeker, as younger bees, to swarme and hive themselves elsewhere": Virginia, whose climate and plenty of "Fish and Fowle" made it better than the "Olde Mistresse" England. Besides, the *Nova Britannia* reasoned, better to cross the sea than the threshold of prison, where many idlers would otherwise end up. Even so, no one would be thrust out of the old hive against their will. The Company was not yet employing the kind of involuntary transportation that in later years would rid England of undesirables and supply her colonies with labor. In 1609 the Company still wanted its swarms of worker bees to volunteer.

The blitz called for men from "every trade and profession." The *Nova Britannia* recruited "carpenters, shipwrights, masons, sawyers, brickmakers, bricklayers, plowmen, sowers, planters, fishermen, coopers, smiths, mettlemen, tailors, turners, and such like." Every trade but John Smith's diggers-up of roots. Another broadside added vintners, hunters, bakers, weavers, architects, and shoemakers. By the end of 1609, the Company published a precise "Table of such as are required to this Plantation." It recruited 132 men in an expanded list of thirty-four different professions: druggists, gunfounders, ironmen (for a smelting furnace), mineral men, sugarcane planters, brewers, bakers, coopers, salters, surgeons, fowlers, joiners, sturgeon dressers, etc. The Company expressly banned four types of people: monopolists, Catholics, atheists, and bad magistrates. Most significantly, it recruited "women, who have any occupation, who wish to go out in this voyage for colonizing the country with people." Jamestown, finally, would grow beyond an isolated military garrison. It would be an English town. Settlers would be given "houses to live in, vegetable-gardens and orchards, and also food and clothing, at the expense of the Company."[3]

## STEPHEN HOPKINS

One of the recruits was Stephen Hopkins, a twenty-eight-year-old farmer, husband, and father from the south of England. Almost everything we know about his life before he joined the Virginia Company comes from the dusty dry bones of church records, lawsuits, and wills. The meat of life has melted away, as it has for most people of common birth. Hopkins came from Upper Clatford in Hampshire, an attractive village with its main road running along the banks of the slow flowing river Anton, surrounded by fertile fields and shaded by linden trees and willows. His father tilled three fields, one of wheat, one of barley, and one a "summer" field. The family had lived in this village for generations, but something prompted Stephen's parents, John and Elizabeth, to pull up roots and move ten miles to the "bustling" cathedral town of Winchester, where they prospered. Their home had six rooms, including the kitchen. Stephen, the third of four children, was about six years old when England mobilized to face Spain's Armada. Fear of invasion penetrated every home in the south of England, and Winchester was only about fifteen miles from the coast. John Hopkins was an archer in the local militia, and the soldier's helmet and armor hung at the ready in the kitchen of their home. The Spanish threat passed in 1588, but the armor still hung there when John died five years later. Stephen was twelve years old. An inventory detailed about thirty-seven pounds of property: table boards, cupboards, several beds, feather mattresses, pillows and "five Holland pillowcases," wooden chests, plenty of linens, table cloths, and napkins.[4]

Stephen seems to have grown into the quiet grooves laid down by his father. He knew how to read and write. Evidence later in his life suggests that when he was growing up he displayed an acumen for letters. But by and large those young years are blank. He probably married around 1603, at twenty-two, to a woman named Mary, and they were living not in Winchester but the village of Hursley when their first child was born in 1605. Two children followed in the next three years. They might have settled in Hursley, because Mary's father owned a hundred acres and the Star Inn, a thriving establishment in the village. But Stephen might have had connections there also. Nearly sixty years earlier, Thomas Sternhold, a "gentleman of the bedchamber" to Henry VIII, was buried in Hursley. He wrote a psalter that was taken up and expanded by an Oxford minister named John Hopkins. Eventually it became the standard text for the English church for several centuries. The last names could be mere coincidence, but it is also possible that Stephen was part of a lesser branch of this scholar's family.

Up until 1608, Hopkins seemed to be doing very well, but in that year he lost his lease on the manorial lands he had been farming, perhaps because of some transgression. This financial uncertainty might have propelled Hopkins to go to Virginia. Hopkins's biographer also surmises that he was the clerk of Reverend Richard Bucke, an Oxford graduate who had been recruited to be the new minister for the colony, replacing the dead Robert Hunt. If Hopkins was related to the famous psalterist, perhaps he hoped to advance in the labyrinth of lower church offices. Whatever lured him to join up, when he took his share in the Virginia Company, it was as a minister's clerk, whose chief duty was to read the psalter. This might have given him some slight distinction, but Hopkins was still on the low side of England's great divide. He was a commoner, not a gentleman. Later events place Hopkins in the very center this story, as important in his own right as John Smith, but he is also valuable as an example of type. The little we know about him is far more than we know about most of the commoners in the Third Supply, so we can use him to represent that wide and various class of people.[5]

The Company's broadsides directed volunteers to apply to Thomas Smythe in London's Philpot Lane, where "they will be entered as Adventurers in this aforesaid voyage to Virginia."[6] Smythe was the Company's "treasurer," a position that combined chief executive and financial officers into one. Laborers lined up at the house, as well as skilled craftsmen, gentlemen, and knights. Everything there was nautical. The spacious house served as a sort of weigh station for the captains of ships involved in Smythe's many enterprises: Russia, Turkey, India. (Richard Hakluyt was still briefing these mariners before their trips and debriefing them on return.) Upstairs was a gallery displaying "the strange interesting trophies of the voyages North, East, South, and West." The house full of bustling people and exotic items must have impressed upon volunteers the enormity of Smythe's range, his competence, the full scope of power, and the enormous amount of money behind the Virginia enterprise.[7]

Historians have been strangely incurious about what exactly was transacted at Smythe's house. In their defense, the paucity of evidence prevents us from definitively answering some questions. But it should not prevent us from asking: What did a man like Stephen Hopkins agree to when he became an adventurer? Indeed, what did anyone—not only the tradesmen and laborers but the knights and lawyers and gentlemen who consented to sail with the Third Supply—agree to? We are relatively sure that each volunteer, high or low, received one share for contributing their body to the endeavor. Man, woman, or child made no difference: Smythe entered the names of these volunteers on the Company's ledger as if they had invested twelve and a half pounds. Some were given extra shares. Because skilled craftsmen were vital to the settlement, Smythe might assign them more than one share. Gentlemen were automatically given a second share. According to the actual charter, one might earn extra shares through "special service, hazard, exploit, or merit" after getting to Virginia. Some personal property that each settler carried onto the boat became the property of the Company, but it was compensated for with proportionate shares or, we must presume, the return of goods—new clothes and the like—as needed, for it is unlikely that many commoners contributed property worth as much as twelve and a half pounds. For several years, while the settlement established itself, settlers were allowed very little private property. When the dividends came, all would receive a part that was proportionate to their contributions. "Implements, furniture, cattle, horses," tools and weapons, even clothes, the Company would supply it all.[8] Smythe pointed out to each settler "what they will receive for this voyage," the exact number of shares in exchange for their person, money, and property. Their names would be entered into company records for however many shares, which would earn them a due proportion of "all the products and profits that may result from their labor." The Company planned to discharge those debts through "a share in the division of the land." Some of the propaganda spoke of five hundred acres for each share, while others promised one hundred. In any case, acreage would be delivered up only after some period of time: seven years or some shorter interval if the Company so decided. So long as one's name was in the Company's ledger as a shareholder, he or she was guaranteed their portion of the Company's accumulated assets. That much was spelled out in the Charter.[9]

Smythe by himself or three of the Company's council administered to each volunteer an "oath of sovereignty," just as under the First Charter. This required the settlers to swear that their highest loyalty went to the English crown, not to the pope.[10] So far as formalities go, that seems to have been it: the entering of names and shares into the ledger and the oath of sovereignty. No formal contracts were written up—not in the sense that we understand, with paragraph after paragraph of complex terms, mutual obligations spelled out, and blank lines at the end for the settler's and Thomas Smythe's signatures. Nevertheless, it is clear that each party imagined that they entered into a set of mutual obligations by mutual consent. The political term was not yet invented, but the Second Charter was a "social contract."[11]

Every "adventurer" should "enjoy all singular grants, privileges, liberties, benefits, profits, commodities and immunities, advantages, and emoluments." The word *adventurer* was England's first label for what we today would call a "venture" capitalist, someone who contributes to the capital of a company by buying shares. They need not have anything to do with the business of running the company. They need not suffer the trials of actual work. Risks are borne by their money. What we think of today as an "adventure"—some feat of action, derring-do, and danger—was originally just a metaphoric comparison to a financial gamble. One ventured his own life the way an adventurer risked money, in some uncertain gambit that might pay off big. What is particularly unique about the Second Charter is that it made the metaphorical meaning literal. Those who risked their own bodies—even the "superfluous twigs" of London—became shareholders, with the same privileges enjoyed by wealthy armchair investors.[12]

In theory, the least shareholder could vote in assembly. A simple majority in an assembly of these shareholders could make changes to the council's members—more likely for deaths or resignations than expulsions. Replacements were to be drawn from the ranks of the shareholders themselves, so a shoemaker could contend for office against a duke. The lowly, homeless vagrant lured from the slimy back lanes of London and newly dressed in Company duds had the right to vote for councillors. A majority of adventurers could "disfranchise" any shareholder for "good cause," but the Second Charter stipulates no other way of denying full rights to each adventurer, no matter whether he invested his money or his person. The considerable authority that King James gave to the Company, though vested in the treasurer and council, resided in the adventurers themselves. No one recognized it yet, but this was nascent democracy: once King James launched the London Company, government rested upon the authority of the governed. At least in theory.[13]

The Second Charter gave the council the power to write into law whatever in its "good discretion" it thought "fittest." New "ordinances, constitutions, directions, and instructions" would be devised to ensure that the settlers "live[d] together, in . . . Christian peace and civil quietness, each with other." Because the council's authority resided in the shareholders, the Second Charter seemed to give ordinary people a far greater right of self-determination than anything bestowed on the typical Englishman. If all citizens of England enjoyed certain rights and privileges, the ordinary Englishman did not vote for members of Parliament, had no say in the laws that governed him, and certainly never *chose to be English*. By contrast, those who joined the Company did so through a deliberate act of consent. They bound themselves to that government, just as the Second Charter bound that government to them.

But even as the Second Charter wrote such radical rights into law, the Company contrived to deny them to the common adventurer who risked only his life. There is no evidence that the common volunteer who swore his oath of sovereignty at Thomas Smythe's house ever even saw the Second Charter or knew what rights it gave him. (The final version of the charter was not even made official until *after* the settlers sailed from London; it was hurried overland to catch the fleet at Plymouth.) One recruitment letter suggests that only those who invested twenty-five pounds—the cost of two shares— would be "free" to "all priviledges and liberties." The Company's leadership told the Lord Mayor of London that one had to purchase two shares of stock to become an "assistant" of the council, and in practice it seems that only those who bought *four* shares could be admitted to the council itself. Most assuredly, such practices protected the Company from mere laborers who might want to exercise the prerogatives given to every shareholder. More than likely, it also excluded middle-class yeomen, like Stephen Hopkins, who could not scrape up the cash to buy extra shares. Despite the radical language lurking in the Second Charter, the Company established a caste system that privileged the wealthy over the poor and middle-class. Only gentlemen were given full "freedom" of the Company.[14]

## WILLIAM STRACHEY

Shakespeare's England was what the *Economist* calls an "inheritance" society, in which family is more important than personal merit, and "marrying an heir is a surer route to riches than starting [a business]."[15] About 2 percent of England's population enjoyed the privilege of the aristocracy over the other 98 percent. The division between the two groups was as forbidding as a high stone wall. On one side a gentleman in his fine clothes might quietly walk the gardens of fruit trees and shaded arbors and flower beds and consume all those things of beauty that derive from leisure. On the other side of the wall, the crowded hurly-burly of commerce and industry and labor jostled in the muddy lanes where carts and horses and foot traffic crisscrossed. Laws and customs prevented the peasant farmer, say, or the sailor from hunting deer or bearing a sword. But while the wall protecting the 2 percent was tall and solid, it had gates. A few extraordinary men, like Francis Drake and John Smith, might earn their way into the aristocracy, usually through feats of arms. More often, the successful merchant or the rich yeoman farmer bought his coat of arms and joined the garden party. Traffic went the other way also. The dandy gentleman covered in debts might be roughly shoved out of the club.

The College of Arms, which derived their authority directly from the monarch, kept the ranks of the aristocracy nearly constant. The people in the 2 percent were officially recognized "eminent persons." That meant their "race and blood or at least their vertues doo make [them] noble and knowne." More often than not, their "eminence" consisted only of the prestige bestowed by a coat of arms inherited from the previous generation. Within the top 2 percent there was another strict hierarchy of rank: in descending order, "nobility, knights, esquires and 'last of all they that are simplie called gentlemen.'" Nevertheless, the greatest divide in England's society, the one that mattered most, was between this 2 percent and the rest of the population. A coat of arms granted all manner of distinction and privilege.

Times were beginning to change. Merit was clawing its way into feudal society. Steadily and inevitably, England's economic climate was shifting. Capitalism already was promoting "skill over nepotism," to use Thomas Piketty's pithy phrase.[16] But the pace was glacial. Such "made" men as Francis Drake still proved the general rule: England drew most of its governors, generals, admirals, diplomats, bishops, and professors nearly exclusively from those who had been born into the aristocracy. And for at least another hundred if not two hundred years after Jamestown, the single most defining social fact for any Englishman or Englishwoman was the realm's "distinctive and all-pervasive system of social inequality."[17] Altogether, families with coats of arms owned half of England's land and 65 percent of its wealth. By way of comparison, in the United States today, the richest 1 percent of Americans, made notorious by such social movements as Occupy Wall Street, owns about 37 percent of the nation's wealth.[18]

Some commoners, either townsmen working in one or several industries or successful yeomen who worked their own farms, were richer than the poorer aristocrats, even if society regarded them as inferior. Geography contributed to this anomaly. Proximity to London facilitated the accumulation of wealth and sophistication, while the remote northern reaches of the kingdom were relatively poor and at least in popular perceptions somewhat wild and untamed and unlearned. Many a southern commoner could boast many times the wealth of a northern knight living in his drafty, ill-lit manor house and collecting paltry rents from infertile land. At the absolute bottom of privilege, a family with as little as fifty acres and an annual income hovering just below £250 could maintain its gentility. At the top of this class, peers might own twenty thousand acres producing as much as ten thousand pounds year. Poverty would eventually disqualify a family, and those who fell out of the ranks of the aristocracy were replaced by eager nouveaux riches. For example, in Lancashire between 1600 and 1642, 278 families fell out of the aristocracy, thirty-five because they fell on such hard times that they had to sell their lands, but most for "less dramatic failures to maintain their social position." That was well over a third of the aristocratic families of the county. Meanwhile, 210 families rose from obscurity onto the heralds' rolls: "some were wealthy townsmen establishing them-selves on estates, but the majority were prosperous yeomen who crossed the indefinable but crucial threshold of recognition as gentlemen." Yorkshire saw similar upward and downward mobility, suggesting that such was the case everywhere in England.[19]

All men of rank had to own land. Even those townsmen who bought their way into the aristocracy were obliged to purchase landed estates. And so this part of English society could be described as sharing a "collective consciousness." The beliefs of the aristocracy were the beliefs of landed wealth, their opinions were the opinions of the rural rich, and they demanded and mostly received deference from everyone else. It was a gigantic club, a fraternity committed to preserving privilege and believing its privilege served the national interest. They assiduously excluded others from their culture of idle-ness, country sport, and its incredibly arcane set of regalia and symbols, from style to dress to that ultimate marker of status, the coat of arms itself.

"Argent on a cross," was how the College of Heralds described the coat of arms conferred on William Strachey's father on July 4, 1587, "ingrayled betweene foure Eagles Gules a flowredeluce & foure cinquefoyles Gould." Above this shield was "his Creast or Cognisince vpon ye healme a wreath of his Colours Argent & Gules a lyon rampant ermyn crowned & susteyning a Crosse formy fitched Gould Mantler Gules Doubled Argent." A silver cross, its edges saw-toothed, dividing the shield into four spaces; red eagles; a spotted lion. Strachey was no soldier. He would never use this shield in battle. His "eminence" consisted of a modest fortune, which he inherited from this father, who was a yeoman farmer and businessman.

The history of the Strachey family was pretty typical of the lower aristocracy. The first William Strachey, the father of the man who bought the coat of arms, was a draper and sheep farmer.[20] The "younger son of a younger son," Strachey used his own industry and wits to compound the family fortune. Eventually he bought a brewery, stables, and wharf in Westminster near London. Nearer to his home-town of Saffron Walden, he accumulated thirteen houses and three hundred acres of farmland. He might have bought his way into the gentry, but Saffron Walden exuded an anti-aristocratic mentality to which he ascribed. For generations the locals had enjoyed near autonomy from feudalism. Since 1548 a corporation of "assistants," hereditary officers, ran the town. Twenty-three of the twenty-four assistants were commoners: yeomen farmers, manufacturers, and merchants. There was more than a whiff of Puritanism perfuming the air around Walden, and the excesses of the trueborn, leisured gentleman stank like sin to a pious burgher.[21]

The second William Strachey was made of less stern stuff. He grew up wealthy. He went to Walden's grammar school, which borrowed its curriculum from Eton and hired its headmaster from Cambridge. He studied at the Inns of Court in London. He married Mary Cooke, daughter of a wealthy family of London merchants who already had bought their way into the society of Kent and were, by this time, entrenched members of the gentry. If the father shunned aristocratic pride, his son embraced it. Soon after the first William died, the second William purchased a coat of arms.[22]

The third William Strachey, with whom we are concerned, was fifteen years old at that time. He loved the glitter of rank over the dull austerity of his grandfather's industry. Shunning business, he sought a life of letters. In February 1588 he enrolled in Emmanuel College at Cambridge, which plugged him into a dense web of elite connections. One of Strachey's best friends was Francis Michell, whose father was the steward of Windsor Castle and a member of Parliament. Michell, brilliant and ambitious, enrolled at the prestigious Gray's Inn in London, and Strachey followed early in the 1590s. The Inns of Court were the Elizabethan age's version of law schools. But Strachey did not plan to follow the law. He found the society of the inn, the contacts he made, and the peripheral life of the school more congenial to his temperament than case precedent and moot court proceedings.[23]

London offered brothels, card games, tavern drinking and brawling, theater, and bear baiting, and Strachey seems to have tasted many of these delights. "All manner of sinnes" he committed in "all manner of wayes." Those autobiographical lines are as vague as they were remorseful, and we're led to infer that he was the "roaring" type of student, "a young gallant," in the words of his biographer, "sowing his youthful wild oats with the city." At least he did not roister to his own ruin. His excesses were just barely excessive. William was allowed thirty pounds a year to sow those oats, and even if he exceeded that sum and borrowed against his expectations, he never indulged so extravagantly as to suffer his father's strict disapproval.[24]

He was meeting the right people. Under Queen Elizabeth, Gray's Inn was the most powerful of the four Inns of Court, and it served as the center of life not only for students but also for its graduates, a combination of professional guild, residential complex, and exclusive social club.[25] Its buildings stood on the north side of Holborn, a suburb

of the city of London, less than a mile from the Thames and a walk
of perhaps two miles to the brewery that the Stracheys owned in
Westminster. Its quadrangles of apartments, situated with gardens
laid out by Sir Francis Bacon, with elms and hedges and other plants
along the walkways, gave pleasant views of fields, and the monastic
quietude was accessed through country roads flanked by hedges on
the way to Kentish Town. Londoners strolling the parks of Gray's Inn
found a wonderful respite from the bustle of the city. "For centuries,"
the school's historian writes, "Gray's Inn has been esteemed a most
agreeable residence, and not only barristers and students of the law,
but divines and literary men have been tempted to live here by the
quietness of the spot."[26]

Elizabethan politics and culture met within these grounds, a
confluence of these two great streams, to which might be added a
third realm of learning: science. The Inn's most famous pensioner,
Francis Bacon, embodied all three. In the 1590s, when Strachey was
a student at Gray's Inn, Bacon's anti-Spanish political tracts were
turning him into a major political figure. Bacon was out of favor with
Queen Elizabeth, but he worked within the compass of the Earl of
Essex's political circle and was prowling for a government post
with a decent salary. Either as amusement or to grease the complex
machinery of patronage, Bacon was writing "revels" for performance
at Gray's Inn. The height of those performances came in 1594, when
in addition to Bacon's compositions Shakespeare's *Comedy of Errors*
was performed at Gray's Inn. Attending the festivities were "a most
honourable Presence of Great and Noble Personages": five earls,
including Essex and Southampton; nine lords; Sir Robert Cecil;
as well as "a great number of Knights, Ladies, and very worshipful
Personages."[27] The place was an incubator of movements, political,
literary, and expeditionary. Sir Walter Raleigh plotted Roanoke under
the trees of Gray's Inn, and several of the attendees at these revels
would later invest their money and energy in the Virginia Company.

Strachey was one of the many young students "whose purpose in being at the Inns had little to do with the ostensible purpose of the institution." He meant to obtain "the social cachet so avidly sought by the rising gentry."[28] Sir Walter Raleigh, Francis Bacon, the Earls of Essex and Southampton—Strachey's social cachet was the milieu of American adventurers.

Strachey was a clever up-and-comer. In the summer of 1795, at the age of twenty-three, he married higher into the aristocracy. And he was inside London's literary circle. He was well acquainted with Shakespeare, who by this time was something of a celebrity. Shakespeare gently mocked his friend in *Twelfth Night*, when Malvolio refers to "the Lady of the Strachy" who "married the yeoman." The dig was probably meant in good fun, and it came with a wink. After all, Shakespeare was a climber too. His own father had married up in society, and the playwright himself bought the family's coat of arms about the same time Strachey married. In any case, the in-laws liked Strachey well enough, and the couple's residences in the coming years were always among his Surrey relatives, never in Saffron Walden.[29]

Nevertheless, the Strachey fortune was slipping away. When his father died in 1596, Strachey discovered that the estate, though managed well enough, had diminished. The will perpetuated annual allowances for William's closest siblings and several half sisters from his father's second marriage. William's stepmother took a large share of the property around Walden. The brewery in Westminster produced a steady income, but his sister's dowry encumbered it.[30] The businesses needed reviving, but Strachey was not the man for that job. He was a gentleman. Gentlemen did not pursue the grind of business. It is not that Strachey was a failure—not by contemporary standards. His peers encouraged indolence, for only he "who can live idly and without manual labor ... shall be taken for a gentleman."[31] A gentleman might be very busy, even industrious, but he did not think of his work as a living. He did not work to sustain his estate. The estate should sustain him and his activities. Some gentlemen might go into government service. Some might take an officer's commission in Ireland or the Netherlands. The unfortunates might need something akin to a salary, a "living," such as a priest in some prosperous parish. Many did nothing, which was perfectly respectable.

Strachey at least did something. This was England's golden age of letters, "when every other man," Virginia Woolf once mused, seemed "capable of a song or sonnet."[32] The lively, raucous stage produced the plays not only of Shakespeare but George Chapman, Ben Jonson, Thomas Nashe, Thomas Middleton, Thomas Kyd, Christopher Marlowe, John Webster, John Fletcher, and Francis Beaumont. Poets like John Donne and Edmund Spenser are the pride of the English canon. Strachey coveted their life and tried to achieve it. He befriended Donne, and like Donne he circulated his poems in manuscript among London's literary set. Unlike Donne, no one cared to preserve Strachey's verse. Strachey hung out with the playwright Ben Jonson and the other young men who followed him, the Tribe of Ben, an informal club of litterateurs who met once a month at the Mermaid Tavern. But Strachey never wrote a play. By 1605, at the age of thirty-three, his greatest boast was a sonnet that Jonson stuck on the front of his tragedy, *Sejanus*.[33] Strachey invested in the Blackfriars Theatre and lost more money. To avoid bankruptcy, he went to Turkey as the English ambassador's secretary, and though that episode ended poorly, it established his name among England's entrepreneurial merchants.

When the London Company advertised the Third Supply of Jamestown, Strachey saw a chance to launch himself into the higher echelons of gentlemen, knights, and peers who operated the national government. And he would make back the family's fortune. He recognized that a litterateur who had studied at the Inns of Court would prove valuable to the Company. Like scores of other gentlemen on the downward slide, Strachey scraped together enough money to buy two shares in the Company, then he made his way to the Smythe house in Philpot Lane.

## THE COMPANY CONTRACT

Thomas Smythe's interview with William Strachey must have been considerably different from his talk with Stephen Hopkins. Strachey's two shares made him an "assistant" to the London council, which entitled him to full "freedom" of the Company. He and other gentlemen like him were vested in a way the unskilled laborer never was, and Smythe would have treated him accordingly. As a gentleman, Strachey would have been informally or perhaps even formally recruited into the apparatus of the new regime. His later alliance with that governor suggests that Smythe spoke to him with a high degree of confidence. It is very likely that Strachey read a draft of the Second Charter and understood perfectly that the Company needed to rely on the "better sort" of its settlers to sustain the new government, which the Company expected to be unpopular with the "common sort."

The London council was empowered to appoint governors, officers, and any ministers it deemed necessary to administer Virginia. Most ominously, those officers were granted "full and absolute power and authority to correct, punish, pardon, govern, and rule." Officially, a settler hewing Virginia logs into lumber still enjoyed his rights as freeborn English, the same as if he were plowing in Surrey or making shoes in Kent. He could not be seized up arbitrarily and thrown in prison. But English courts were far away, and in Jamestown the governor would be Leviathan: in addition to executive, he was prosecutor, judge, and jury, and legislature. "In case of necessity," the governor himself was empowered to issue new ordinances, constitutions, directions, and instructions. "As near as conveniently may be," these "ordinances and proceedings" were supposed to be "agreeable" to English law and practice. But what settler could insist that this or that decision by the governor disagreed with English law? Virginia's governor could put to death and bury whomever he wanted before any complaints would be heard in London. The Second Charter replaced the uncertain, fractious, and consequently weak authority of the Jamestown council with a dictator. The recruitment pamphlets don't mention this crucial fact, and it seems unlikely that Thomas Smythe explained it to commoners whom he enrolled in his ledger. Probably he emphasized the acreage each adventurer would own at the end of seven years and skipped over the governor's arbitrary power to kill people.[34]

With so much power vested in the governor, it was most important to appoint the right man. The council selected an old Devonshire soldier, Sir Thomas Gates, to occupy this terrible office. In some ways he was an obvious choice. His career began back in 1585, with Sir Francis Drake's army when it sacked Cartagena. He saw the corpses of diseased men tossed over the sides of the ships. His captain was among those men who petitioned Drake to give up the plan to attack Panama and head for home. He saw hundreds of maroons taken aboard. Lying at anchor off the shallows of the Outer Banks, Gates saw the maroons put ashore. He saw the remnants of the first Roanoke colony, led by Ralph Lane, abandon the low-lying, marshy shore. Back in England, he published a narrative of that adventure, dedicating it to Robert Devereux, the Earl of Essex. Gates was with Essex's army when it sacked Spain's port of Cádiz in 1596, and the earl knighted him for his service there. He was among the original planners of Jamestown, buying four shares in the Company in 1606, and King James appointed him as one of the few incorporators (along with Richard Hakluyt) named in the First Charter. In fact, the Company might have intended for him to have sailed on the *Susan Constant* with the original settlers. Had he gone, he would have been a councillor and probably would have rivaled Wingfield for the presidency. But Gates turned up instead as part of garrison in South Holland fighting the Spanish. In 1609, he was granted a leave of absence from that service, and he came back to England in plenty of time to command the Third Supply, the grandiose expansion of the colony. He would be governor until an even more eminent member of the Company, Thomas West, the Baron De La Warr, arrived in the Fourth Supply.[35]

A soldier through and through, Gates would not put up with the hesitant obedience of discontents nor the disobedience of malingerers. Nor would anyone mistake his orders: he was not the type to equivocate. In command, he was like John Smith: confident, decisive, impatient, a man of action. Like Smith, he inspired a corps of guards to fierce loyalty. The Company instructed Gates (in Article 9 of his orders) to organize a personal cadre of soldiers that would follow him around, protect his body, and overawe the other settlers. Gates and his guard were given carte blanche. Do whatever you have to do to keep order, Article 8 told him, and forget about the "niceness" of the law.[36]

The entire settlement was to be organized along the lines that John Smith had pioneered. For defense against the Spanish and against the Indians, every man would be drilled regularly in the militia. So far as regular industry went, each settler would be part of a crew of ten or twenty people. Each group had its assigned task and was to be supervised by an overseer. The overseers would file weekly work reports detailing what the work gang had accomplished and what they had failed to do. The settlers were to be allowed three hours of leisure each summer day and two in winter. Otherwise, the daylight hours belonged to the Company. Meals would be taken in "messes" of five or six people. The fare, Gates was told, must be nutritious and plentiful: anything less would undermine discipline. Discipline was the watchword—garrison discipline.

Men like William Strachey were probably let in on these plans. The common settler did not know what he was in for. The farm hands, tradesmen, and laborers expected to find something better in Virginia than what they had left behind. They were ready for hard work and certain temporary deprivations. Those went without saying. But they also expected to enjoy the same liberties they had had in England. At a bare minimum, they expected the customary command over their own bodies. Work in gangs, overseers, meals in messes, militia drills, the harsh command of captains were such things one might expect as a soldier conscripted to duty in Ireland. Nothing in the existing record suggests that the settlers knew they were to be virtual slaves for seven years. The London council kept that secret. And the council knew that once the settlers discovered the true nature of the colony, they were bound to be disillusioned. Some would want out. The council told Gates how to deal with such cases of buyer's remorse. Ships would be coming and going with regular frequency, but no one was to leave Jamestown without Gates's personal, express written permission. The settlers could not opt out. Every communication, even personal letters to relatives back home in England, must be approved by the Company. Complaints about their treatment, pleas to friends and family for rescue, appeals to the English judicial system, would be discovered and destroyed.[37]

An apparatus of administration, discipline, and surveillance descended from Gates. Jamestown would still have councillors: George Somers, who would take charge of all ships in Virginia; John Smith, who was demoted to the command of the outpost near Kecoughtan; Ratcliffe and Martin, who, against Smith's express wishes, were returning to Virginia; Wynn, Waldo, and Scrivener, who were written into Article 4 because the London council did not yet know they were dead; and two new adventurers, Captain Wood and a Mr. Fleetwood. These councillors would be given "preferrements," but they were advisors only. Neither individually nor together could they challenge Gates. To be admitted to the council they had to swear that Gates and only Gates had "full authority." He could proclaim any "lawes or ordinances" he wanted. Gates would have more authority than a general has over his troops or a jailer over his prisoners.

It seems not to have occurred to the London council that in a remote location, where communication took at least half a year, despots might not be benevolent. It is likely that the councillors felt that only such strict discipline could provide for the general welfare of the whole colony—that the interests of the settlers themselves would be best served by a dictator. But from the point of view of the aristocracy, common settlers could not be expected to understand what was in their best interests, so the governor's powers must not be revealed until they safely arrived in Jamestown, when Gates would assemble the company, old colonists and new, and read his commission aloud. As Thomas Smythe secured the consent of his recruits in Philpot Lane, men like William Strachey, who would oversee the work gangs, understood the terms of their contract. Men who would populate the work gangs, like Stephen Hopkins, did not.

The fleet gathered on the river Thames at Woolwich, a bustling hub of docks and warehouses just south of London. Thomas Smythe regularly organized convoys through the Mediterranean Sea to Turkey and across the Baltic to Russia, so much of the preparation was familiar work for him. The biggest ship in the fleet, the *Sea Venture*, was three hundred tons; then the *Diamond*, *Falcon*, *Blessing*, *Unity*, *Lion*, and a small pinnace, their masts and yards and rigging crowding the sky. Holds were filled with ballast: flint and scrap iron and stones. Gravel was spread on these to even the surface, which provided a floor for the lowest layer of barrels and chests. The standard provisions all came aboard easily enough: "butter, biscuit, meal, oatmeal, aquavitae, oil, bacon," as well as lemon juice and dried fruit to ward off scurvy. These were for the long transit. A stallion, fifteen mares, cows, bulls, goats, pigs—their noise and stink were packed along-side their human counterparts. In their makeshift sty, pigs grunted an arm's reach away from common folk staking out their corners. Most settlers' "cabins" were no more than mattresses thrown on sea chests or on the gun deck itself. Families might nail up a cloth partition for privacy. The better sort—the gentlemen—had it a little better. Boards were knocked into place for the makeshift cabins.

Excitement, anticipation, apprehension, surely, from those who had never before sailed on open water. Hope for their future: Why else would they have consented to go? So it must have felt exhila-rating to be part of this grand enterprise, to stand on the deck and watch the banks of the Thames sliding by, to leave the river's delta and find themselves in the open sea, the open winds pulling the smell of salt air in streamers off the whitecaps, battalions of fat clouds marching against a field of blue. At dinnertime, the smell of food. The hungry were satisfied: already they were eating meals served out of Company stores. Plenty of people crowded the deck taking the fresh air. They had good weather for five days straight as they sailed down the coast. The first leg was long enough for friendships to form among strangers and for petty annoyances to begin to tally. All the complex-ities that bind people together were being woven. And with several hundred passengers distributed among the ships, there must have been a wide variety of emotions. Some were plagued with seasickness and probably thought of little else. Some would have felt the rush of adventure. All felt extraordinary. The sea journey was beyond nearly every settler's previous experience. Knowing they had signed on for seven years, and that at the end they would own acreage in Virginia, many must have felt they watched the shores of England for the last time in their lives. Even those who left behind a miserable life of poverty must have felt some twinge of melancholy. The known world slid away. The unknown waited over the ocean.

All the settlers would have been familiar, to some degree, with *plantations*. Enterprises of this sort, which transported groups of settlers in numbers large enough to make whole new communities, had been ferrying across the waters for years. But those went no farther than Ireland. That land might be exotic enough to a gentleman from Essex or a Hampshire farmer, but Englishmen had been to Ireland by the tens of thousands and returned home again. Their settlements, established in lands that war and famine had depopulated, tried to replicate English town, farm, and estate life. In the English imagination, the plantations were supposed turn Ireland into a province of 'west England.' "[38] Everyone in England must have known someone who had been to Ireland, a cousin or the innkeeper whose shingle hung on High Street.

Probably none of the common settlers had a cousin who had been to Virginia and back. All they knew were the reports in the propaganda, the sermons, the circulars, and rumors. Jumbled together on the boats, they eagerly listened to tales from the first eyewitnesses they met: the sailors who had been to Virginia before. Some yarns might have been encouraging. But sailors had seen the starved survivors of Jamestown's first summer, when more than a hundred settlers had been reduced to thirty-eight. They had seen the miserable conditions of the fort, the dissensions, the desertions, and they told tales that would have troubled the most optimistic heart. Second thoughts must have begun to take root in some people. What had they gotten themselves into?

The fleet sailed into Plymouth, Drake's old city, yet there is no record of anyone jumping ship there. Two more ships, the *Swallow* and the *Virginia*, a pinnace, joined the fleet. For nearly two weeks the settlers did nothing while the fleet "laid in some necessaries" and took on those settlers whom the Plymouth branch of the Virginia Company had recruited. Stephen Hopkins might have embarked there. The *Swallow*, captained by Samuel Archer, loaded six mares and two stallions, among other "necessaries." They moored in this harbor for nearly two weeks while the spaces below deck grew less sanitary every day. At every meal they ate up supplies that might have been used in Virginia. Most of the settlers must have been restless. But no one snuck away. A nervous hopefulness probably still dominated the atmosphere. They seemed to be in good hands. The competence of the Company was manifest in the fleet itself, which was an immense gathering of resources and manpower. The settlers had all come aboard willingly. They had consented to this enterprise. No one yet had an inkling of the secret clauses to their contract, the instructions given to Sir Thomas Gates. Indeed, they did not even see Gates until they sojourned in Plymouth. When the ships left Woolwich, he was still detained in London awaiting the king's final approval of the Second Charter.

Once those papers were sealed and delivered, Gates hurried down to Plymouth by overland carriage and joined the ships there. Nor had the admiral, George Somers, sailed with the settlers from the Thames River. He lived in Lyme Regis, a picturesque town on the sea between London and Plymouth. He might have actually watched the flock of sails glide by on May 18 or 19, his summons that it was time to travel the coast road to the Devon seaport. Gates and Somers both came aboard the *Sea Venture*, the largest ship, which had space for the most comfortable cabins, a mark of distinction both men seemed to have relished. There was some jealousy between the governor and the admiral, some question as to who took precedence over the other, which erupted in a quarrel that was open enough to be noted by settlers.[39]

They put out to sea finally on June 2, but even this was a false start, as contrary winds forced them to find haven in Falmouth down in Cornwall, closer to the very toe of England. Later that first week in June they were finally at sea. The skies were fair. Those taking the fresh air on deck could watch England gradually sink into the sea. Then all was water.

For weeks and weeks a trailing breeze carried the fleet swiftly over the long, low-rolling waves. They enjoyed the friendliest breeze they could hope for. Day after day in perfect consort the ships sailed together, and nights were so clear that when morning came the sails of every vessel were still clustered in formation, each seen by the others. But not all was well. Disease touched two of the ships, and thirty-two corpses were dropped into the sea. Nor were the passengers comfortable. Men and women used to the close quarters of London would have found the crowded lower deck awkward and frustrating. The cannons were all on the upper deck in the open air to provide more room below. Still, everyone but the highest-ranking officers—such as Gates, Somers, and Newport—would have been cramped between decks, where sea chests and mattresses and cages of chickens competed with each other. Chamber pots sloshing with urine and feces. Curtains might have been tacked up to divide the space into little semiprivate rectangles, but the result after a week at sea must have been a squalid stench. Luckily, with all the fine weather, the passengers could take the open air in shifts. Not all at once—that would interfere with the sailing of the ship—but everyone would have gotten their daily dose of fresh air and clear blue skies or the fantastic starry dome at night.

On July 23, 1609, Captain Newport, who had been reckoning their direction and speed every hour, said they were no more than a week from sighting Cape Henry at the mouth of the Chesapeake. It was a remarkable crossing, and it would prove that one ship might circulate between Virginia and England three times in a year.[40] But the luck ended. That night the atmosphere changed. Clouds loomed over the ships. The stars were blotted out. In the pitch-darkness the wind was "singing and whistling most unusually." Foreboding worried the faces of veteran sailors who had sailed the western Atlantic.

Newport and Somers reckoned the chaos building in the chop of the seas. Wind came out of the northeast, and winds from that direction were trouble. The sailors knew it. The captain and the admiral knew it. There was no equivalent in the Old World. It was a phenomenon of the wild Atlantic: a hurricane.[41]

CHAPTER SEVEN

*Lost*

**It was on a Monday,** Saint James's Day, the twenty-fourth of July, 1609, that the storm swallowed the Third Supply. The best piece of William Strachey's writing is the three-thousand-word account of the storm in his *True Reportory*. It's far more compelling than the other eyewitness account, Jourdain Sylvester's *A Discovery of the Bermudas, Otherwise Called the Isle of Devils.* Strachey was wider-traveled than all of the settlers and probably more than some of the sailors. He had sailed the length of the Mediterranean Sea. He had seen storms on the open water. He sailed through tempests off the Barbary Coast of Africa, and, belowdecks in a Cretan ship, he weathered a northwest gale in "the black gulf of the Adriatic." And yet, he confessed, "all that I had ever suffered gathered together might not hold comparison with this." Nothing "characterized" the strangeness "of the New World" as well as hurricanes, not even the exotic Indians themselves. "Sailing ships," writes the Renaissance scholar Peter Hulme, "were absolutely helpless." The "cyclonic form" of these Atlantic storms "defeated any possible nautical strategy."

Europeans struggled to make sense of them. Words failed them. "What shall I say?" Strachey asked in his narrative. How could he describe the storm to his English readers? Nothing in their own experience could convey the "fury and rage" of these Atlantic "winds and seas," nor the despair of the voyagers. If he had had the strength of fifty voices, Strachey complained, he could not convey the anguish in the "outcries" of the settlers. He lacked the words to capture the "languishing" and "wasting" of their spirit. Neither the English language nor fifty other Old World tongues, he explained, had the words to describe it. Europe had no word at all that could properly label the phenomenon. They needed a foreign word. Arawaks told the Spanish, and the Spanish told the English, so that in 1555 the term first appeared in an English text: "These tempests of the ayer," wrote Richard Eden, "they call *Furicanes*." Sir Walter Raleigh called the storm a "hurlecano."[1]

Mediterranean storms had their place in the English imagination. They called them "tempests," and tempests made sense. The Bible laid down their meaning in the story of Saint Paul's shipwreck on Malta around 60 C.E. An angel explained to Paul that the storm was an instrument in God's hand, and Paul explained to the mariners, passengers, and prisoners that it was God who ran the ship onto a reef. "The forepart stucke fast," the 1611 King James Bible reads, "and remained vnmouable, but the hinder part was broken with the violence of the waues." And then, fulfilling a prophesy given to Paul, God rescued all 276 people aboard. Some swam ashore. Some floated "on boords, and some on broken pieces of the ship . . ." Why God might send any particular storm might not be clear, but none doubted that each Mediterranean tempest was a part of His design. God used tempests to scold people and prick them to righteousness. The storms' sound and fury signified.[2]

Atlantic storms signified nothing. As late as 1638, even after the English had established colonies on five Caribbean islands (Antigua, Barbados, Montserrat, Nevis, and St. Christopher) and a generation of settlers had lived in Virginia and Massachusetts, after various English communities had suffered several cyclonic storms, hurricanes were still beyond the frontiers of English comprehension. They sank ships, flooded towns, tore roofs off houses. Sometimes hurricanes erased whole communities, wiping them off the land. Unless God hated the English, the biblical interpretation did not seem to apply. The chaotic, indiscriminate, destructive violence of these storms did not square with events ordained by God. These storms belonged to the forsaken parts of the globe: "where God is least known and honoured . . . this *Hurri Cano* is frequent." One seventeenth-century pamphleteer wrote that in the waters of the western Atlantic "there the Devill hath most power and domination." There lived "many Heathens, *Indians*, and barbarous Nations unconverted." In other words, hurricanes bred in the dark, wild places outside the Gospel-lit world familiar to Europeans. Civilized nations had nothing like them. Savage storms came out of the wilderness.[3]

The terror of drowning was intensified by this suspicion that the *Sea Venture* was in the grip of something weird and wild, a rough beast bred in the Atlantic and more ferocious and tenacious than anything known in Christendom. It seemed they were abandoned by God. The very heavens, Strachey reported, "look'd so black upon us." "Prayers might well be in the heart and lips," but they did not lift to heaven. "[O]ur clamors drowned." How could prayers rise above such wild howling winds? Sixty years later, English balladeers were still thinking of "hurrycanes" in these terms: "So hideous was the Noise," go the lyrics of a song, "that one might well / Fancy himself to be with Souls in Hell." Faith, like the ship itself, "had split," leaving the ship's master unsure "which way into Heaven" to steer his soul: "Starboard or Larbord," he didn't know.[4] Lost.

Perhaps the first European mariner to feel existentially *lost* was none other than Christopher Columbus. In a sad end to his long decline and disgrace, Columbus's fourth voyage ended in shipwreck. Just ten years after his discovery of the New World, at fifty-one the admiral was feeling very old. He was sick. Gout swelled his limbs with pain and shackled him to his bed. Despite all the loot that Queen Isabella and King Ferdinand gained from the New World, Columbus did not "possess a roof in Spain that [he could] call his own."⁵ But the admiral held fast to his messianic view of history. Hadn't God reserved for him a key role in bringing round the end times? If only he could find the elusive waterway through all the western lands, he could finally open Cathay, which would hasten Spain's hegemony over the world, which would hasten the biblical apocalypse. It was his fixed idea, his North Star, and Columbus stared at it till his reason wandered.⁶

Queen Isabella, herself in her fifties and not long from death, smiled on him a final time. In 1502, four superannuated ships, one of them serendipitously called *Bermuda*, made a quick crossing, touching at Hispaniola, weathering a hurricane in the slight haven of an estuary. The little squadron continued to the unexplored mainland, giving Europeans a first glimpse of a "rich, civilized and industrious" people who manufactured copper hatchets and wove clothing out of cotton.⁷ Columbus discovered Panama.⁸ But the vessels, only two now, were "rotten, worm-eaten, and full of holes."⁹ Water seeped in. Sailors worked the pumps in endless shifts and bailed with kettles. Simple arithmetic foretold the end: water was gaining faster than it was removed. When they sighted Jamaica, Columbus gave the order to run the ships up on the beach.

They came aground a crossbow's shot from shore. Water filled the lower parts, up to the decks, where the 150 survivors lived in makeshift cabins. Most of their supplies were ruined. The verdant jungle beaconed with relief, but Columbus permitted no one to go ashore. According to his son, Fernando, the admiral feared that the Europeans, "who were by nature disobedient," would "scatter across the island," steal food from the Indians, rape the women, and kill the children.¹⁰ But in truth Columbus was more worried that his men would mutiny, abandon him, and melt into the tribes. Go native. A faction of discontents grew up around the brothers Francisco and Diego

Porras, one the captain of the *Bermuda* and the other the expedition's accountant. Nearly fifty men demanded to know if Columbus had connived to "keep us all marooned here." *Marooned* is the modern English translation; the 1571 Italian word in Fernando's account was *perduti*: lost.[11]

*Lost* itself is a complex term. There is the literal sense of losing track of one's heading, either on unfamiliar streets or losing your bearings in the wild. And there's the metaphoric, religious meaning. In William Tyndale's 1526 translation of the Bible, Jesus came to Earth to tend "the loost shepe of the housse of israhel." Allegorically, people who turned away from God were "lost," on the way to perdition not paradise. By forgetting God, they had been forsaken by God. That was how Columbus felt. The Porras brothers did mutiny, and they and all their men abandoned Columbus and took refuge in the Indian villages. It broke the admiral. Dispirited and sick, he imagined he was forgotten by his beloved queen and forsaken by God. Had he a priest to consecrate the bread and wine, to bring Christ among the castaways under the penetrating, merciless Jamaican sun, he would have been relieved. But there was no priest. The shore of the savage island was a godforsaken place. Columbus feared that when he died, unshriven, "in this foreign land," his very soul "would be forgotten."[12]

Columbus, a natural tyrant, inspired dissension, which had been brewing from the moment the ships left Spain. His sailors and officers endured his depotism, storms, and shipwreck. They endured six months of imprisonment on the ships, the shore of Jamaica barely a stone's throw away, obeying Columbus all the while, till desperation made them bold. Staying on the ships seemed to lead toward a slow and bitter death. The fact of the shipwreck itself, of being marooned and cast away on a wild island inhabited only by what one considered to be savages, dissolved normal hierarchies. Being *lost* freed Columbus's men from the obligations normally obtained. On the deck of the

*Bermuda*, Francisco Porras shouted to the other sailors, "I am going to Castile with anyone who will follow me." According to Fernando Colón (Columbus's son), some of the men "began to shout loudly, 'We want to go with him, we want to go with him.'" They would never escape Jamaica, they reasoned, "unless they set about securing [rescue] for themselves." These discontents "signed up" with Porras. *Signed up* here is surely metaphoric, because the event seems to have been too slapdash to involve contracts and signatures. But the phrase does indicate the dissolution of another contract, this one more formal, in which the sailors *did* formally sign on to or agree to the terms of the expedition, which placed them under Columbus's authority in the first place. Being *lost* dissolved that obligation. Porras and his supporters commandeered ten large canoes that Columbus had acquired from the Indians ("purchased," his son insisted) and left Columbus with a few loyalists, mostly soldiers, and those who were too sick to join Porras in the canoes. "If all had been healthy," Fernando bitterly complained, "not even twenty would have stayed with the admiral."[13]

Columbus's marooning on Jamaica was prelude and prototype for Atlantic castaways. For the next hundred years the essential elements of this story were told over and over again. Out of these tales, like shipworms burrowing into the solid oak of old traditions, two things in particular ate away at old patterns of political thought. Firstly, soldiers, settlers, sailors all signed on to the ships, entering into a contract that bound the captains and the sailors by reciprocal obligations. Secondly, native societies and wilderness often proved attractive and congenial to unhappy voyagers. These two facts awakened minds to the concepts of liberty and equality. As Europeans stood on so many desolated American shores with the waves of this or that reef pounding and prying apart the frames of their foundered ships, when they stripped off their salt-soaked clothes, the hot sun dried all bodies the same. All were equal. And liberty was the island, where they might wander at will. Being *lost* was the chrysalis of metamorphosis.

❧

A series of volcanos in the mid-Atlantic left several caldera, circular ridges that, from the air, look vaguely crater-shaped, and these constitute the Bermudan Islands. Strachey's description in the *True Reportory* is generally accurate, and since it is the conception of the place held by the castaways, it justifies a somewhat long quotation:

> The Bermudas be broken islands, five hundred of them in manner of an archipelagus (at least if you may call them all islands that lie how little soever into the sea and by themselves) of small compass, some larger yet than other, as time and the sea hath won from them and eaten his passage through, and all now lying in the figure of a croissant within the circuit of six or seven leagues at the most [roughly twenty-four miles] . . .[14]

This croissant-shaped string of islands lies in the open sea on a diagonal, southwest to northeast. The tail at the southwest end is formed by the widest of the extinct volcanic craters. Only the part of the crater's ridge is above water, largely encircling what is called today the "Great Sound," a very large bay protected from Atlantic storms. Eventually the British used slaves and convicts to build a gigantic dockyard here. The largest cruise lines berth there today along with ferries, innumerable pleasure craft, as well as Bermuda's commercial shipping. At the other end of the croissant, three smaller sounds are cradled by semicircular islands. These are broad and quiet waters that could shelter the largest fleets of early sixteenth-century shipping. "The argosies of Venice," Strachey wrote, without much exaggeration, "may ride there with water enough, and safe landlock'd."

Map of Bermuda drawn by Sir George Somers in 1609.

The trick was finding the channels into these harbors: "It is impossible," Strachey remarked, "without great and perfect knowledge and search first made of [the shoals] to bring in a bauble boat so much as of ten ton without apparent ruin."[15] A series of submerged reefs spread well out into the ocean on the northwest side of the islands, a faint reflection of the ridges of land, clearly visible from the sky but mostly invisible from the sea. During the last ice age, when the sea level was much lower, these reefs broke the surface and were covered in lush forests of green. Now they are crusted by meadows of coral, the rich, multicolored habitat of marine life. Especially at night, mariners cannot see these reefs until they grind suddenly and cruelly into the hulls of their ships. Because of these reefs, Bermudan shipwrecks were slow and torturous. The ships did not sink. The rocks pierced hulls under the waterlines, filling belowdecks with water, but they also held the hulks in place, half full of water, half above their waterlines, till the waves pounded them to pieces. On the southeast side of the islands, the reefs tuck much closer in to land, barely a cannon's shot away. The *Sea Venture* approached from this side. Waterlogged and nearly unsteerable, driven by the winds of the hurricane, their only chance was to crash into a reef, to be borne up out of the sea by the vise grip of coral. They nearly missed it.

Relieved as they were when George Somers cried "Land!" from the poop deck, weary as the sailors were after three nights of pumping and bailing and sailing in the towering waves, they had work yet to do. The island would not come to them. The winds had lessened. The sea calmed. The rain slowed or stopped altogether. But the ship was still full of water and still taking on more faster than the pumps' jets could discharge. Sailors scrambled aloft. Sails unfurled, those great canvases fluttering down, flooding with wind. Hope spread. The sluggish ship turned toward the shore. The sailors wrestled the sluggish whip staff, turning the ship against its own inertia. Those aloft could see the reefs protecting the island. Seething lines of surf indicated where the razor rocks were beneath the surface. Even if they could discern a channel through those reefs, they could never maneuver the *Sea Venture* through it and into a sheltered haven. The best they could do was get it as close as possible to "run her ashore." The boatswain threw out his sounding line: first thirteen fathoms, then seven, then four fathoms. Just twenty-four feet of water.

Then the shock of a sudden stop. The waves kept sliding by while the ship stood still, wedged between "two massive coral heads," submerged sentries of what looked on the surface like a "V-shaped opening in the reef." Immobility made feet feel, dizzyingly, for their purchase on the deck. Behind the stern were the rough waters of the stormy Atlantic. Ahead, past the reef, were calm waters, and then the land. Archaeologists in the 1980s found the "scant remains" of the wreck thirty feet deep and a half mile southeast of the point that is now Fort St. Catherine, on the northern tip of the Bermuda archipelago. If the *Sea Venture* had been a mile farther north, it would have missed Bermuda entirely and drifted out to sea, sinking in the deep. They survivors peered at a slight crescent shape of beach facing east, toward them, not even a half circle but enough to help enclose a sort of bay, "Gates his Bay," as Thomas Gates named it. Today it is still Gates' Bay. That beach was their salvation.[16]

The sailors went about their business. The first cohort to be ferried ashore probably included Gates, Somers, and the passengers of highest prominence, among them William Strachey. The women-and-children-first ethic so strong with us today did not develop until the nineteenth century. Besides caste privilege, prudence dictated that guns and swords lead such a landing.[17] The longboat had a capacity of about thirty people and the skiff another ten, so, accounting for the men pulling the oars, it would have taken perhaps five trips to ferry everyone ashore—all one hundred fifty people—"ere night" fell on the island. A half mile of rowing across the now-placid water. The voyagers climbed over the gunwales and dropped into water up to their thighs. They stumbled the last stretch toward shore. Their sea legs, acquired during the seven-week voyage and the three-day storm, struggled to ascend the beach from the buoyant water. Legs weak with exhaustion discovered that they had forgotten how to walk. Salt water dripping off their clothes, people probably flung themselves prone on the sand, where their dizzy heads might safely adjust to the not-heaving of the earth. Some if not most must have fallen dead asleep. The sound of oars working in their oarlocks, sailors going back to the wreck for the next batch of settlers, faded in the distance. The swooping, soothing creel of sea birds. Sleep.

Woodward suggests that the castaways built a great fire just above the high-water mark on the beach, then moved inland till they found a suitable campground, where they built another great fire. But we don't really know. Most of what happened in those first hours and first days is speculation.[18] It must have felt like waking from a long nightmare to have come out of the incessant moving, howling, dark, rain-sodden terror of the hurricane and the open sea, to find oneself on sunny solid ground. Their consciousnesses had to adjust to not being drowned. The wind that had whistled monstrously through the ship's rigging and tackle now fluttered the fronds of palm trees. The waters of that cove were so quiet that their ears could barely make out the voice of the sea. Somewhere human voices were shouting out orders. Probably this unhoped-for rescue was intoxicating. Surely, they felt gratitude. A year later, writing at a desk in Virginia, William Strachey said that they made it ashore "by the mercy of God." Silvester Jourdain used the same words: God's "most gracious and merciful providence." Not long after everyone was ashore, Reverend Richard Bucke conducted a service offering the proper prayers of thanks to God. Some attempts were made to reduce the experience to familiar terms. But divine providence did not explain all. Jourdain also said that the appearance of Bermuda was random chance, blind fortune "in so great a misfortune." The whispers of the sailors infiltrated the prayers, unsettling the formulaic praise of God. They might not have drowned, the sailors pointed out, but they were landed on the notorious Devil's Islands.

"Above any other place in the world," the sailors despaired, these islands were "feared and avoided of all sea travelers alive." "Every navigator and mariner," Jourdain reported, avoided the islands like they were Homer's "Scylla and Charybdis, or as they would shun the Devil himself." The castaways had been hurled beyond the realm of normal experience, safe from the storm but thrown into a place that defied comprehension, that existed outside the scope of civilization. The islands might have been charted, but they were on no one's sea route. The few ships that sailed the Atlantic gave the islands as wide a berth as possible. Bermuda's submerged reefs were notorious. Like a siren song, the tropical islands beckoned to weary transatlantic voyagers, and the wrecks of those who had been seduced proved ample warning to living sailors. The ghosts of other shipwrecks haunted these waters. The *Sea Venture* voyagers could hope for no rescue. No Europeans would visit these islands to fill their water casks or replenish their supplies of fruit and meat. They were utterly alone.[19]

The two experienced sea captains, Newport and Somers, understood their chances of survival. The *Sea Venture* was not the first wreck on Bermuda's shoals. The archipelago had been discovered just thirteen years after Columbus discovered America. The Spanish ship, *La Garza*, was returning to Spain from Americas in 1505, captained by Juan de Bermúdez, when she sighted the low-lying ridges in the mid-Atlantic. Bermúdez did not stop to explore, but he noted the location and spread the word, so that six years later, when Peter Martyr d'Anghiera produced his famous map of the Atlantic world, he immortalized the Spanish captain by naming the islands "Bermuda." Four years later Gonzalo Fernández de Oviedo y Valdés passed within a cannon shot, observed that the islands seemed to be uninhabited, and tried to land six hogs upon it to provision later settlers or visitors. They were prevented by contrary winds, but eventually some Spanish sailors succeeded, because the island was awash in swine by the end of the century. By the mid-sixteenth century, the islands had become a "navigational reference" for the Spanish ships sailing home from the Americas.[20]

The first known wreck was the *Santa Maria de Portugalete*, a treasure ship that Hernán Cortés had filled with "two million ducats" of gold stolen from the Aztecs. It sank on a reef in 1533, and a few survivors must have made it ashore, because fires were noticed three years later by a passing vessel. The castaways were never rescued, and it seems they died on the islands, because another Spanish ship in 1538, damaged by a storm, sequestered in the islands while it made repairs. For nearly a month its captain surveyed the islands, and no one was ever found. In the 1540s a Portuguese slaver grounded on shoals almost ten miles from dry land. They made it ashore, and for two months the thirty survivors cannibalized the ship and built a new vessel, all the while living on the turtles and birds and plants they could hunt and forage on the islands. They succeeded in launching the boat and sailing it to Santo Domingo, where they told their harrowing tale of adventure. In 1550 two castaways of a wreck began a two-year stay on the islands before they were rescued.

Four ships of a Spanish flotilla went down near Bermuda in 1563, including the five-hundred-ton admiral of the fleet, carrying Don Juan Menéndez de Avilés and another 1,250 people, all lost. In 1582 a dispatch ship went down, and survivors made it ashore, where they lived for two years until another dispatch ship was wrecked on the western reefs. The maroons helped the survivors of the second wreck make it to Bermuda, and together they built a ship big enough to carry them back to Santo Domingo. Ships wrecked in 1588, 1591, 1593, 1596; hardly three or four years went by without a Spanish or Portuguese merchant or French pirate ship wrecking at Bermuda, and half the time some survivors made it to shore, sometimes waiting for rescue, and sometimes out of salvage and native cedar the castaways built their own escape boats. In 1594, French castaways salvaged the carpenter's tools and rigging from their wreck. They built their own rescue ship. Having no pitch, they were obliged to seal the planking with a mixture of crushed lime and grease from turtle meat. Just six years before the *Sea Venture* wrecked, a Spanish galleon was damaged in a storm and driven onto a reef. Captain Diego Ramírez sent a crew ashore in one of the ship's boats, but as they approached shore, the sailors heard the screaming of the legendary devils thought to populate the islands. They turned back, frightened, and sent a black sailor to investigate. This intrepid mariner made it ashore, where he discovered the devils' songs were actually the caws of immense flocks of seabirds. Ramírez stayed at the islands for several weeks, his carpenter repairing the ship with native lumber, and his crew subsisting on Bermuda's fauna. The captain and the ship's master used the time to circumnavigate Bermuda in one of the boats and sketch the first chart of the islands and their encircling reefs. Two years later, in 1605, his map did not help a two-hundred-ton carrack carrying Honduran "gold, pearls, rosewood, [and] dye." It ran onto the reefs and sank, losing its cargo but staying fixed in the rocks long enough for the crew to escape ashore. The scant record of these adventures demonstrates the ingenuity born of necessity.[21]

In some of the narratives the experience of shipwreck wipes the slate clean of authority, leaving each suvivor to decide how to associate with their fellows. Sometimes the principle of democracy—majority rule—peeps from the stories. Shocked by being wrecked; immersed in the struggle from reef to shore; washed clean, so to speak, of old habits of servitude; having been baptized anew by the salt water, after they struggle ashore and begin the work of salvage, castaways seemed to naturally resort to voting. In 1556 a French pirate ship and its prize, a Spanish carrack filled with treasure, sailed too close to Bermuda's reefs. The carrack crashed on the rocks, and the

French abandoned the boat and its Spanish crew of forty-five erstwhile prisoners. The Spaniards built a couple of makeshift rafts out of barrels and planks from the ship's quarterdeck and floated on the tide to Bermuda. For months these castaways survived on the abundant food while the carpenter directed them in building a small boat out of the native cedars and salvage from the wreck. As the boat was shaping up, the master, carpenter, and pilot determined that taking all forty-five people and the stores of food might make the thing founder in high seas. So they secretly recruited a dozen sailors and planned to slip away, betraying the other thirty castaways. But the plan was found out, and the thirty quickly got the upper hand over the other fifteen. Like so many other maroons before, they were immediately faced with a critical decision: What to do with their betrayers? Acting now as judge and jury, the thirty took a vote, and in the first act of improvised government in the islands of Bermuda, the majority voted to pardon the dozen sailors and condemn the three ringleaders. Forty-two souls departed in the tiny boat, packed to the gunwales with dried fish, turtle meat, bird meat, and casks of water. After three weeks of dangerous sailing, they made it safely back to the Caribbean islands.[22]

Maybe that's why we're so fascinated by shipwrecks and castaways. Readers "latched onto" *Robinson Crusoe* in the eighteenth century "for the same reason teenagers flocked to James Cameron's *Titanic* in the summer of 1997." According to the literary scholar Steven Mentz, both tales dramatize the tension between "our hopes for an ordered universe" and the "disorienting" effects of "the most powerful nonhuman actor in world history," the "inhospitable sea." Mentz, who has made a detailed study of shipwreck tales, both fictional and real, has concluded that they often follow a three-part psychological pattern: shock, immersion, and salvage. As a ship breaks apart, as the deck disappears underfoot, after the body is thrown away, cold seawater shocks the voyager. The slap of water insults his sense of a rightly ordered world. Then comes immersion: into the sea, that most inhuman, alien territory. "All forms of order," even gravity, are put "in suspension." Cultural values float away like so much wreckage. Differences of rank and title, privilege and inferiority, become flotsam, like the material debris detaching itself from the wreck and drifting away. Shakespeare dramatized this leveling of artificial distinctions when his boatswain commands Gonzalo and the king's retinue. Strachey's narrative noted that the three-day storm erased distinctions. No man was above another as gentlemen stripped down to their shirts and worked the pumps or plugged leaks or bailed water like the lowliest servant or laborer.

Shipwreck detaches castaways from these previous marks of distinction. Each survivor floats alone in the briny deep, metaphorically and sometimes literally. But this suspension cannot last. Eventually the surf coughs up the refugee, feet find sand, and survivors stagger onto the beach. The desert island is truly terra incognita. Psychologically, survivors are disoriented. Metaphysically, they are lost. They blink the saltwater from their eyes and look at each other anew. They begin the work of drying out, of salvage, of clothing themselves. As they never have before, they choose what garments to wear. The drapery of the Old World that carry the old markers of class and status? Or will the castaways dress themselves in something better suited to the desert island? Even if they clothe themselves in old values, the castaways *choose* those values that before were merely given or inherited. This is the radical, psychological result of shipwreck. Getting wet—at least metaphorically—allows people to "think through changing views of humanity and the natural world."[23]

## SALVAGE

Whether or not he understood that democracy lurked on the shore of shipwrecks, Thomas Gates immediately began asserting his authority. His first order of business was salvage. As the first day dawned over the waters of the cove, the beach would have begun to liven in activity. The boats were carrying every last provision that could be salvaged from the ship: the sea chests belonging to individuals; weapons, tools, charts; the Company's matériel and papers and the ensigns of command. Pigs. Chickens. Rowing from shore to wreck, then back again to shore, went on for days until the ship was emptied of everything not ruined by seawater. And then they cannibalized the ship itself: the sails, the tackle and cordage, the wooden superstructures, were pried apart and reduced to lumber, then the planks of the decks themselves and the iron fittings were removed. Piles onshore grew steadily, hour by hour, day by day. Gates selected the men of his guard and gave them arms, and the chosen men began to watch the piles in shifts.

Competing with what we might call the norms of authority was the settlers' sense of wonder. The sailors who had seen more of the world might not have been so affected, but as that first day dawned on Bermuda, the settlers, both gentlemen and commoners, awoke to a most "strange" and "enchanted place," as Jourdain described it. A true wilderness, inhabited by no one. If the ferocity and duration and cyclonic winds of the storm exceeded anything their imaginations could tame, if they felt they had escaped the jaws of a savage sea, then to be castaway on this exotic shore must have been wondrous. They blinked at these exotic tropical trees. The smell of fecund vegetation filled their nostrils. Flocks of birds reeled in the sky. The name Devil's Island seemed, perhaps, a misnomer. On what magical place had the sea coughed them up?[24]

But work prevailed. Stomachs growled with a three-day hunger. Faces so long in the dark first welcomed the warmth of the sun and then shrank from it into the shade. Their skin and clothes dried to a crust of salt and sand. According to Sylvester Jourdain, who was a minor and largely unsuccessful merchant from the same hometown as Admiral Somers, every man fended for himself on that first morning, searching the island for food. A young woman named Elizabeth Persons had come on the voyage as the servant of a gentlewoman, Mistress Horton. In this extremity of hunger and exhaustion, after passing through the storm and wreck, did Elizabeth Persons, at the dawn of day, look first to her mistress's needs or to her own? We don't know. Several families were among the settlers, and fathers and mothers surely attended to their children. John Rolfe was onshore with his wife, who was pregnant. William Strachey was not one of these: he left his family behind and intended to return to them once his fortune was mended. Hopkins's family was not there, either: he planned for them to join him in Virginia once he was well situated. One hundred and fifty-three people survived. About thirty-five were sailors—from old Admiral Somers and one-armed Captain Newport down to the merest ship's hand. Many of these at least retained some semblance of the ship's order. About 115 or 120 people stood outside the ship's line of command. Most of their individual searches for food met with little success. Luckily, Sir George Somers, the seasoned mariner, knew what to do in a shipwreck, and in half an hour he and some of his sailors caught enough "fishes . . . very fat and sweet" to feed everyone for a day.[25]

Governor Gates was issuing orders. Some settlers did what they were told. Others did not. Two men ignored him all together. Namontack and Machumps, Algonquian Indians sent to England by Wahunsonacock, stepped off the bright, sunlit beach and disappeared into the gloom of the forest. Neither William Strachey nor Silvester Jourdain noticed. In fact, neither writer even noted that the Indians were on the *Sea Venture* in the first place, as if they did not count—were literally uncounted—in the manifest. But some of the castaways must have watched the vegetation close behind them like a door. It made one think. In the background they could hear Governor Gates issuing his orders, an irrelevant cackling to the Indians.

The salvage operation was organizing on the beach. Someone was building a pen for the pigs. Someone was piling the salvage from the wreck. Someone was guarding the Company's property. Somers and sailors were fishing in the lagoons. Stones were gathered and arranged in circles, and great fires were stoked with wood that someone gathered. Some people were following orders. The beach and the ground immediately behind buzzed with activity. Chaos and confusion were gradually assembling into organization. And yet, more than a few eyes lingered on that spot where Machumps and Namontack had disappeared and pondered the example of the Indians. They had simply opted out.

### DISSENSION BEGINS

At least once nearly every day, the rain poured down in buckets out of a black sky. Lightning flashed in the darkness, and thunder echoed off the sea. But blue sky always followed. The days were warm. At first the castaways took shelter under the palm trees along the beach, tall and branchless but tufted at their tops with leaves so broad that "a man may well defend his whole body under one of them, from the greatest storm rain that falls," William Strachey wrote. Within days they had erected huts. These might have been built just a hundred yards or so from the beach on a flat area high off the water, an apron of land backed by a high hill. None of the narratives describe what their huts looked like, but we have some idea of their shape and construction. The National Museum of Bermuda uses paintings by the Bermudian artist Christopher Grimes to illustrate what the maroon encampment might have looked like, and those illustrations represent our best guess. These are squared frames of small timbers, joined, probably, by cordage. Few walls. The huts were open to the circulating air, although some sides are thatched, like the peaked roofs, with palmetto fronds. Such huts provided little privacy but plenty of shelter from the rain and sun. Makeshift though they were, they perfectly suited Bermuda's warm climate.

The Bermuda cedar and the palmetto tree provided their basic materials. The cedars in the "high and sweet-smelling woods" could be turned to lumber. Not true cedars, these trees are junipers that can grow to a height of fifty feet. The trunks of mature trees, which might be hundreds of years old, can measure four feet wide. The islands were virtually covered in forests of Bermuda cedar, and the English quickly learned that the wood from these giants was pliant enough to be worked easily, but sturdy enough to construct furniture, houses, and ships. The other main building resource, the Bermuda palmetto, had fibrous leaves ideal not only for roofs but for weaving baskets and hats and splicing into rope—a most useful resource for any castaway.[26]

Among the *Sea Venture* passengers were four carpenters, but the raising of their crude dwellings did not really require their skills. Given the proper tools, any commoner could fell a small tree, sketch out a frame, and thatch a rough roof, and they had plenty of axes, hammers, nails, and saws for any reasonably skilled man to build his shelter. A farmer like Stephen Hopkins would have had no trouble. Probably these houses were erected with little to no organization. Several families were among the colonists, and it seems natural that each head of household would build a shelter for his own family. Men unattached to families probably followed that lead, congregating in small, ad hoc groups of bachelors.

Neither Strachey nor Jourdain discussed the details, which leaves us with several important unanswered questions. For example, how did the gentlemen secure their shelters? If a farmer could easily build a hut, this was the kind of work no gentleman in England would ever undertake. Did their common deliverance from the storm engender, at least for a little while, a spirit of generosity? Did the leveling evident during the storm, when gentlemen stripped to their shirts and bailed water, extend to the first days on the island? If so, the gentlemen would have been somewhat humbled, having to follow the lead of the men who had the proper skills, men who were otherwise their inferiors. Or did the gentlemen have their huts built for them? Either way, huts were probably built in close proximity to each other, and in very little time an expedient little village blossomed just above the beach at the northern tip of what is now St. George's Island, thatched roofs like so many flowers blooming in the newly cleared meadow.

Some work must have been organized. Admiral Somers "daily hunted and fished for our whole company" in the first days. He must have supervised men into work parties—more than likely sailors already under his direct command—to supplement the provisions that survived in barrels, casks, and chests from the ship. His men hunted wild pigs. Very quickly Somers began charting the shores of the islands and mapping the reefs that defended them. No doubt this task took several weeks, and it required a crew of sailors. Discipline among the mariners remained: they still took their orders from the admiral. Somers might rule a vacant kingdom, the battered wreck of the *Sea Venture*, but he felt responsibility for the welfare of the desperate community, and he acted accordingly.

The ill-will between commanders widened. Gates felt that Somers was treading on his authority. (Strachey tried to dispel rumors of this rivalry; ironically, they have been preserved through the centuries largely Strachey's insistent but unconvincing denials in the *True Reportory*.) Gates and Somers had quarreled back in Plymouth. The very fact that the governor sailed in the admiral's ship when eight other vessels might accommodate him suggests Gates's jealousy. Common sense and practice dictated that the Second Charter's two chief officers, the governor and admiral—along with double copies of the charter itself and the governor's special instructions—should not sail in one ship. Somers, being the naval commander, had the prior claim to the best cabin in the fleet's flagship. Gates should have sailed on another ship, but he perceived an affront to the dignity of his own high office, and he insisted on sharing the prestige of a cabin in the *Sea Venture*. The antipathy of these two men, trifling as it might have been in Plymouth, grew like a native weed in Bermuda.[27]

While Somers was on the water, Governor Gates consolidated his command on land. Fulfilling one of the Company's instructions, he formed a corps du guard made up largely of gentlemen, which took charge of all of the Company's food, tools, and arms piled onshore. Strachey was part of that guard, and he quickly ingratiated himself to the governor. Backed by these soldiers, Gates commandeered the ship's longboat, which he decided to refit for an ocean voyage. Using the hatches from the *Sea Venture* for planks, he set the carpenters to work closing the open boat with a deck so tight "that no water could go in her." But Gates could not command the sailors. He was obliged to recruit them. He found the master's mate, Henry Ravens, "easily" persuaded to pilot it. This "bark of aviso" would sail to the garrison at Jamestown. Gates was especially worried about his authority in Virginia and hoped to mitigate the delay of his own arrival. If the other ships survived the hurricane, more than four hundred new settlers would arrive without their leader and without papers defining the shape of the new government. No doubt Gates was thinking of men like John Smith when he predicted that "the younger and ambitious spirits" at Jamestown might invent their own government. Gates dictated a letter, which Strachey, now acting as his secretary, copied out. Captain Peter Wynn, Gates instructed, should act as lieutenant governor of the colony until such time as Gates himself came to Virginia. To aid Wynn, or perhaps to dilute his power, Gates appointed six new councillors, "gentlemen of quality and knowledge," named in his orders but lost to history. (Possibly if not probably, John Smith was among those names, because the Virginia Company still valued his unique talents, and the new regime was supposed to give Smith command of the outpost at Point Comfort. Nevertheless, the choice of Peter Wynn for lieutenant governor, even in an interim command, suggests how eager both the Company and Gates were to remove Smith from the presidency.) Wynn was to immediately dispatch a letter to England reporting the wreck of the *Sea Venture* and the situation of her survivors. And, of course, the colonists in Jamestown were told to send a rescue mission to Bermuda.

Somers did not outright oppose this scheme, but he expected its failure. His sailors planted a large garden of "muskmelons, peas, onions, radish, lettuce, and many English seeds and kitchen herbs." Somers was pragmatic and realistic, and had long knowledge of Atlantic waters. If Ravens and the refitted longboat made it to Jamestown, they would be rescued long before the reaping of this garden. The settlers could interpret the meaning of Somers's vegetables: the admiral did not have much faith that help would come from Virginia. Virginia might not be in their future at all. The admiral expected that they would be marooned for a long time. Within ten days the seeds Somers sowed in the rich soil sent sprouts peeping toward the sun.[28]

Seeds of another kind were settling into the soil of the settlers' minds. While the carpenters worked on the longboat, a sailor named Robert Waters took a shovel and walloped another mariner, Edward Samuell, "under the lift of the ear." Waters apparently struck out impulsively, perhaps as he and Samuell were digging post holes for shelters. The improvisational weapon proved as lethal as a pirate's sword, and Samuell died quickly. It does not seem to have been a fair fight. No one seemed to think that Waters used the shovel in self-defense. But most of the sailors sympathized with him anyway, which suggests there might have been some history of provocation. The sailors thought that something mitigated Waters's crime. He killed the man, sure enough, but it was not murder.

Admiral Somers was still away surveying the reefs, so Gates took charge of the situation. The veteran soldier had no regard for the vagaries of maritime justice, especially its mercies. Killing Samuell was inexcusable. No provocation could mitigate the act. The governor decided that it was a clear case of murder. This was the first real test of Gates's authority, and the seasoned military commander did not shrink from exercising the powers invested in him by the Company. Robert Waters was taken up by the corps du guard and bound, and in a trice Gates pronounced sentence: Waters "was appointed to be hanged the next day." The speed of the trial, condemnation, and execution cannot but suggest that Gates wanted the matter thoroughly resolved before Somers had a chance to intervene.[29]

No doubt every settler watched the precipitous actions of their governor with fascination and dread. They knew that their contract bound them to live under Gates, but not until the summary treatment of Waters was the full consequence of that contract revealed to them. The convict was tied "with many ropes" to a tree, where he sat or stood awake all night awaiting the fateful dawn. Gates must have smelled the tension rising in the camp, which disapproved of his precipitousness, because he assigned five or six armed men to guard the prisoner. It seems hardly likely that each and every one of Gates's appointed guards should fall asleep in the night; nevertheless, that's what they told the governor the next morning when Waters's unbound ropes were lying on the ground. A vigilante's knife had cut them.

Gates seems to have been genuinely astounded that everyone did not agree with him. How could the sailors feel no "horror" at Waters' "sin" and no shame for the "unmanliness of the murther"? How could his own guard have been so negligent? Surely someone must have heard the vigilantes at their work. Why had no one sounded the alarm? Why indeed. Gates learned then how precarious his authority was on a desert island. In open defiance of the governor, the sailors "conveyed" Waters "into the woods." Each night they smuggled food to the man, who could peek at the campfires from the trees.[30]

Strachey's phrase *into the woods* suggests how quickly the English transformed the geography of Bermuda. Within a week or so, Bermuda was divided into civilized territory, consisting of the beach and its vicinity, which already had been tamed, and the terra incognita of the wild woods. Surrounding the little makeshift village was a border, and to cross that line was to step into wilderness, where the Indians had disappeared. The English sensed that norms of authority did not exist beyond that line. By escaping "into the woods" one literally became an outlaw: outside the geographic territory governed by law. In September 1609, only three people lived out there: Namontack, Machumps, and Robert Waters. Waters was barely on its edge, close enough to the castaways' camp to communicate with it each night. He hadn't the woodcraft of the Indians, so he had to rely on camp provisions rather than what the thickets provided. This was Robin Hood's Sherwood Forest, close to civilization but a geographic blank, where the outlaw's piratical justice prevailed.

When Admiral Somers returned to camp, the sailors hastened to tell him their side of the story. No matter the appearance of the crime—that Waters administered an unprovoked deathblow. When he considered all of the circumstances, the admiral would see that Waters was not guilty of murder. The sailors explained their own bold defiance of Gates's orders. They could not in good conscience allow a fellow sailor to be condemned and hanged by his judgment. Somers listened, considered, and agreed with his sailors. Gates was wrong to condemn the man. He would speak to the governor to clear the matter up. This interview between Somers and Gates would determine the nature of power among the castaways. Strachey's narrative gives but half a sentence: Somers's "mediation" got Gates to reverse his sentence, but only "upon many conditions." The conditions are not enumerated, but they helped Gates save face and retain at least a de jure claim to sovereignty over all of the castaways, sailors and landsmen alike. But in the end Waters was set free and returned to the bosom of his mates, and a de facto limit to Gates' authority was established: he was not in charge of sailors.[31]

## NEW TERMS OF AGREEMENT

After about three weeks, the longboat was ready. Ravens eased her out into water of Gates his Bay on August 28, 1609. Although the boat drew no more than twenty inches below the water's surface, it still had to feel its way past the reefs. For days Ravens took wrong turns and had to ease the craft back out of dead ends. Finally he went out the same way the *Sea Venture* had tried to come in, and the little crew set sail for Virginia in early September. Gates put William Strachey in charge of a company to maintain a signal fire. Strachey and his men were rowed across the quiet waters of what is now called St. George's Harbour to St. David's Island, hiked through the thickets, and climbed to the high bluff that is Bermuda's easternmost point. A tall plume of smoke from his fire would show mariners where to round the point and approach Gates' Bay. Like the refitting of the longboat, this fiery vigil required crews of organized and compliant labor. The fire itself had to be maintained for weeks on end. Fuel had to be cut. Huts built. Food and water procured. It was a significant undertaking, and it kept Strachey out of the main camp for a couple of months. Consequently, he did not witness several of the incidents he narrated. He was busy at his own watch. The high cliff was hairy with vegetation, but Strachey could see the calm waters lapping at rocks below. Farther out to sea, lines of white water formed and dissolved and re-formed on the breakers offshore, not too far out, showing where the reefs were. Beyond that white water, nothing but the flat ocean changing its colors from turquoise to deep blue as the sunlight played with clouds. They stared at the empty ocean in shifts, day after night after day.

Life for Stephen Hopkins and the others back on St. George's Island settled into routine. Food was passed out of the store according to Gates's orders. Everyone had a roof to protect him or her from the sudden downpours, which lasted through October. All had enough leisure to roam, venturing into the woods to discover for themselves just what the island had to offer. They began to adapt to the island. Great stands of cedar trees, "fairer than" those in Virginia, sprouted berries the size of currants, which the maroons crushed and filtered into a very "pleasant drink." In addition to thatch, the wild palms—the sailors told the settlers they were *Symerons*—produced a fruit, the palmetto, which when roasted tasted "like fried melons." Soaking the palmettos in water turned them into a vegetable with the consistency of cabbage. The gentlemen found this too foul to eat, but the commoners, whose stomachs had fewer scruples, "murder[ed] thousands of them." If the palms gave them the flux, they learned they could bind up their bowels with "a round blue berry" like sloe that grew on trees deep in the woods. They harvested prickly pear. Fish swarmed Gates his Bay. The settlers made a "flat bottom gondola of cedar," a little thing that must have resembled the dugout canoes of the Chesapeake, which they could pole or paddle out into the deeper water of the bay, where they hooked "angelfish, salmon, peal, bonitos, stingray, cavally, snappers, hogfish, sharks, dogfish, pilchards, mullets, and rockfish." They found "crabs, oysters, and whelks" near shore, and under "the broken rocks" they found "crayfishes oftentimes greater than any of our best English lobsters." Every cove had its fish; every creek its snails. Birds were everywhere. "Sparrows fat and plump" and a kind of robin came right into their cabins. The variety astounded them: "white and gray heronshews, bitterns, teal, snites, crows, and hawks."

People could pluck what they wanted whenever they hungered. Yet the procurement and distribution of some foods was centralized. The commodities from England were in finite supply, and they must have become something of luxury items to be husbanded and given out in measures. The hunting, slaughter, dressing, and serving of meat was well organized. They ate communally. Gates divided everyone into two dozen "messes" of six or seven people, who ate together as a unit. Two tortoises, which tasted neither of "fish nor flesh," provided a "reasonabl[y] toothsome" meal, enough for a day's dinner served out to all messes. Six hogs could do the same. The castaways had their own domesticated English swine, which survived the wreck, and these were left to wander freely in and out of camp. Their wild cousins sniffed them out fairly quickly and, on occasion, a boar followed a domesticated sow back into camp. The sailors knew how to snag them. One seaman lay down among the English sows waiting till the boar came groveling near them. The sailor "rubbed the side gently of the boar," coaxing the animal to lay down, docile and tame; then the man slipped a rope over its hind leg, hobbling him for later eating. The sailors also had a "ship dog" that helped them hunt. It would clamp its teeth on the boar "and hold whilest the huntsmen made in." The islands had thousands of these wild swine—enough to feed the castaways for a long time. They caught between thirty and fifty a week all through September and October, keeping the pigs in sties and "franking" them, or fattening them with berries, till slaughter.[32]

Bermuda proved to be no devil's island. It was a paradise, without the serpent. This wilderness hid not a single "venomous thing as toad or snake, or any creeping beast hurtful." The worst they came across were some spiders, which they were glad to see, because English lore made spiders into "signs of great store of gold."[33] Gradually, the castaways began to appreciate Bermuda. They began to dread the day when boats might come from Virginia to ferry them off the islands.

Gates kept their signal fires burning for two months, but no sails appeared on the blue water. So the governor assembled all of the settlers. In all likelihood, he explained, they would not be rescued by Jamestown. They must assume that Ravens did not survive the voyage. (As it turned out, Ravens and his crew were never seen again, at least not by any English, either in Bermuda or Virginia.) If they were not to live out their days on these desert islands, Gates explained, they must construct the means of their own deliverance out of salvage and native timber. They must build a ship. Gates's ship was going to be about fifty feet long, twelve or thirteen feet wide, a sleek, swift vessel. That was big enough to carry many but not all of the survivors. "Compelled by the tyranny of necessity," he told them, he would have to leave some people on Bermuda. But he would not "forsake them so, as given up like savages." He would leave them tools and provisions enough "to defend them from want and wretchedness," even if it meant depriving the pinnace of needed supplies. Those who were left behind, Gates explained, should expect to be stranded for at least a year, for none could tell how long the "many hazards accompanying the sea" would delay their rescue. The castaways would be divided, some chosen to leave and some to stay.[34] This speech had the air of a new negotiation, as if the shipwreck had rendered obsolete the agreement first made in London. To the ears of the settlers, this sounded like a new contract—albeit informal and necessarily provisional. The implication of Gates's speech was undeniable: *if you build this pinnace, here's what I'll do when the pinnace is finished.*

Work on the pinnace significantly changed life on the island. The task was so huge that it required almost all hands divided into groups of workers, who were commanded by overseers. The camp of castaways began to approximate the shape of society dictated by the Second Charter, which reflected the Company's fundamental distinction between gentlemen and commoners. Consent to Gates's new enterprise probably came informally, no more than silent acquiescence, but men did shuffle into line, shouldering the tasks assigned them, accepting the leadership as appointed by the governor. Strachey was probably put in charge of a crew, just as Hopkins took his assigned place as a worker. Gangs began felling cedar trees on St. George's

Island, hauling logs, shaping spars with the adze, sawing logs for planking. Nearly all of the work of a seventeenth-century shipyard could be accomplished with simple hand tools, like the chisel and adze, and fairly basic carpentry skills that many mariners and farmers might be expected to have and that many unskilled workers might quickly acquire when sequestered on a desert island. To make a spar, for instance, one began by felling a likely tree, stripping the bark with a special tool, and proceeding to hack it down to size with an adze. The adze man first shaved the log into a square; then the square was shaped into an octagon and the faceted corners were shaved into narrower and narrower edges until the spar was nearly round and the correct diameters, tapering as demanded by the rigging. It's almost all adze work, and any shipyard worker would grow proficient pretty quickly if he didn't already have the skill. With time enough, a labor force, and trees, all that was needed was a shipwright to direct the work.[35]

It was no coincidence that among the castaways was one Richard Furbusher, an accomplished shipwright who practiced his art in the yards of Limehouse, on the Thames River near London. In the seventeenth century, shipwrights were naval architects, engineers, expert craftsmen, and managers of work crews all rolled into one. He had no blueprints. The plans resided in his head. Long experience drafted the complex details onto his brain. Building a ship was more craft than science: the engineering came from tradition, generations of ingenuity tested only by trial and error. Furbusher found a likely spot for a "building bay," a makeshift shipyard, probably facing the protected waters of St. George's Harbor. He knew how to lay the keel, what shape it must have, the proper curve of the ribs, the ratios, the angles. The *Deliverance*, as the new pinnace would be called, was just about sixty feet long. The size of a smallish brontosaurus. Under Furbusher's supervising eye, the butchered carcass of the *Sea Venture* melded with the fresh-cut wood of the Bermudan forest, and the rib cage of this sauropod, propped by angled stilts, began taking shape. With so many workers at hand, in less than a year Gates might see his pinnace assembled, rigged, caulked, tarred, and then launched into the bay. By the end of August a kind of wharf and stocks were built to prop the boat's ribs. The skeleton took shape, a great hollow thing almost twenty feet wide.[36]

### INTO THE WILDERNESS

As autumn progressed, the settlers began to understand the regime they would live under in Virginia. And the sailors could corroborate that the division of labor in Bermuda resembled what they had seen in Virginia. The sailors repeated their tales of garrison life in Jamestown; of work gangs; of settlers being driven like conscripts under the discipline of officers; of deprivations, desertions, and deaths. Poor provisions. Poor houses. No reliable source of freshwater. Surrounded by wilderness. Surrounded by savages. The people who had survived all that were marooned in Virginia just as surely as they themselves were marooned here in Bermuda. Promises of land in five years, in seven years. Hogwash! None would live so long. Mines of gold and silver! They were chasing ghosts. No one was going to get rich, quick or slow, in Virginia. Make no mistake, the sailors insisted: anyone who went to Jamestown was truly "lost to friends and country." Their families would never see them again. They would never again see their native land.

The castaways' own handiwork, the forty-foot keel laid in "Furbusher's Building Bay," and the hulking monstrosity, made half of salvaged oak and half of Bermudan cedar, took on a new and ominous meaning. The settlers realized that they labored against their own interests. If the boat ever swam, it would carry them to long days of "wretchedness and labor" in Jamestown. With her rakes forward and aft, the boat's full length would run to almost seventy feet. Her ribs, gigantic, open to the sky, were larger than Gates had first imagined, big enough for two decks with four and a half feet between them and a "great cabin" with a windowed gallery. The rudder was massive: five feet by six. No one would have to be left behind in Bermuda. Gates might make everyone go to Virginia.

The settlers began to think they were giving up paradise for hell. In Bermuda fish were abundant, birds' eggs might be gathered from innumerable nests, and wild pigs were in high supply and easily caught. They had all they needed. Here they might spend many of their hours "at ease and pleasure." Why not just stay? The "common sort," the backs and arms and sinews of the work gangs—those settlers with little more claim upon privilege than the lowly sailors—began to circulate such thoughts among themselves. But the arguments reached the ears of "the better sort," too—the gentlemen who stood to lose money if Jamestown failed—and even some of these were beginning to be persuaded of the propriety of cutting their losses on this adventure.[37]

As this talk prospered, work flagged. Each day Gates sent the whole "ill-qualified parcel of people"—which is to say those whose skills were not needed for the finer work at the Furbusher's shipyard—into the woods to fell trees, carry the timber to the waterside, and saw it into rough form. Reluctantly these gangs moved about their tasks like tortoises dragged to the task. Then they started shirking altogether. Gates went into the woods to see what the matter was. He lent a hand at chopping down trees, trying to lead by example. His own hands filled with calluses. No task, he wanted to demonstrate, was beneath anyone's dignity. All must work hard and all must pull together. His example had some salutary effect on some of the people, but in the end, most were not moved. Dignity was not the issue. The settlers believed that each plank they hammered into place was another board of their own coffins. By one contrivance or another they shifted out from under Gates's orders.

Six men in particular—Christopher Carter, Francis Pearepoint, William Brian, William Martin, Richard Knowles, and John Want—formed a conspiracy. Slowing work was not enough, because sooner or later the ship would be finished. Instead they should make a clean break "from the society of the colony," shifting themselves and their families and their belongings to another island, where they would make their own "habitation and settlement" apart from the Company's camp. When they had started work on the pinnace, Gates promised to leave tools and clothes and food on the island with those who were left behind. Why not decide themselves to be left behind and claim those items now? Like Machumps and Namontack, they would disappear into the woods. They would become true maroons, conforming to the word's original sense, living like the *Symerons* of Panama who escaped Spanish slavery. It was a simple choice, and, facing what seemed a certain death, they figured they had to take responsibility for their own lives.[38]

The conspirators whispered in the ear of the blacksmith, hoping he would join them. They probed one of the carpenters, Nicholas Bennit: his skill and tools would ensure their success. A carpenter for building shelters; a smith to fix or forge whatever tools they needed. Imagine it! They would carve their village of cabins right out of the wild woods. Foraging and fishing and hunting would provide all their food. They would form their own colony. The carpenter needed little convincing. He, too, was ready to abandon the Company's camp. The sailors who instigated the scheme could be counted on for support. They could advise Want and the others where to go, and convey the renegades across the water with provisions and tools before Gates or any of his loyalists caught wind of what they were up to. A lot of people were in on the plan. Stephen Hopkins almost certainly joined the conspiracy. Strachey estimated that most of the commoners and some of the gentlemen were party to it, which suggests that at least several dozen and perhaps more than sixty or seventy men, women, and children knew of the scheme, sympathized with it, and hoped to join it at some point.

But word spread to one person too many. Someone revealed the plot to a gentleman who seemed a likely sympathizer but was not. This informant went to Gates and revealed all he knew. Gates, who misunderstood the conspiracy, thought of it as mutiny. The shock and chaos and confusion of the shipwreck, he thought—the very irregularity of all the confusing activity in the early days—had diminished in peoples' minds a proper regard for his authority. The castaways had gotten a taste of what Gates sneeringly called "liberty." In the early days after the shipwreck, their time had been their own. With plenty of food to eat and a roof to keep off the rain, they got it into their heads that they might decide for themselves how to spend their hours, and many were spending them on idleness and the "fullness of sensuality." The pinnace required the first real imposition of authority on the settlers, and they took to that task with little sense of duty. They dragged their feet. They grumbled. Gates had tolerated their reluctance, which had, apparently, made the settlers mistake his powers. Now he must sketch those powers in definite lines.

Gates summoned certain settlers to give testimony. If anyone had entertained misapprehensions about his authority, they did so no longer. He interrogated settlers until he was satisfied that he knew who the plot's ringleaders were. He put six men in irons: Want, Carter, Pearepoint, Brian, Martin, and Knowles. The shape of their plan molded itself in his mind. They meant to maroon themselves on one of the islands and settle there, outside the circuit of his own governance. So be it. Their punishment would fit their crime. If they wanted to be renegades, Gates would oblige them. He would cast them outside of civilization, hurl them into the wilderness. But they must take nothing with them: no food, no tools, nothing. He banished them from St. George's Island. The six men were rowed across the water to one of the hundreds of other islands and stranded there.

Their island would be a prison. No one would be able to sneak them provisions at night, as the sailors had for Waters. No one could cross the wide water without a boat, and surely now Gates would keep a tight grip on all craft. They would be alone, without an ax or knife or fishing line. These were common Englishmen, not Indians. They didn't have the knowledge or the skill to manufacture from shells and plants all they needed for tools and weapons and shelter. The silence of the wilderness loomed toward them. They were alone. After some interval—several days at least—Gates sent the boat to check on the six maroons. The conspirators "missed comfort," Strachey reports wrily, playing for a laugh. Perhaps they did laugh back in London in 1610, but today such jokes fall flat. Probably the six men were starving. Bermuda had plenty of food, but they had little means to pluck it. They could neither fish nor hunt. They could forage berries and, perhaps, eat some raw shellfish. Maybe they could find some eggs, if any birds were nesting. Their only drinking water was the rain. They could make no fire. They had nothing but their hands to build a shelter, nothing but fingernails to tear the fibers of the palmetto. No blade or ax to hew brush and branches. They felt forsaken. Strachey wrote, again with comic intent, that the prisoners regretted "that their complement was not more full." They craved the companionship of their fellow beings. They were broken. Their attempt at self-determination was ruined, and they acknowledged they must be ruled by Governor Gates. They sent "many humble petitions" to the governor "full of their seeming sorrow and repentance and earnest vows to redeem the former trespass."[39]

Gates was satisfied. This was contrition. The hungry, ragged prisoners were fully shamed and discredited. Gates's authority was acknowledged. Now he could play the magnanimous autocrat, which would demonstrate his powers all the more. The governor was "at all times sorry," Strachey wrote without a hint of irony, to punish the

offender who was truly contrite, and so he "was easily content to reac-
knowledge" the maroons. The six renegades were rowed back to
St. George's Island, their thinned, gaunt faces, wretched condition,
and broken spirits a caution to all who might be tempted to imagine
that their labor belonged to themselves. A caution it was. No one
could mistake the nature of the Company's government now, least of
all Stephen Hopkins, who was very troubled by these events. Gates
had absolute authority over the castaways. They were trapped.

## CHAPTER EIGHT

# The First Frontier

**Through late spring and early summer 1609,** while the London Company was busy preparing the ships and supplies and recruiting the five hundred settlers of the Third Supply, John Smith was stabilizing the colony's position in Virginia. The town of Kecoughtan, as we have seen, had been detached from Wahunsonacock's rule. The Paspaheghs, just to the north of Jamestown, were Smith's vassals. The powerful, warlike Nansemonds on the far side of the river now paid tribute to Smith, who frightened them more than Wahunsonacock. The Chickahominy, who had never been fully under Wahunsonacock's command, were now awed by English power, and they kept the peace, if they did not pay tribute outright. Up and down the James River, Smith planted his men in Indian villages. This strategy satisfied the immediate need to feed the settlers, which Smith could not do at the fort. But it also solidified his status as a paramount chief in his own right. In essence, Smith made himself a powerful rival to Wahunsonacock, winning towns to his own chiefdom using the same means that Wahunsonacock used to acquire them in the first place: arms and the threat of arms.

Wahunsonacock had been ready to pounce, aided by Jamestown deserters living, probably, in Indian villages on the York River. Those deserters told the paramount chief that Smith had gone rogue and set himself up as a sort of pirate king in defiance of English policy and law. John Smith wanted more than the James River. He wanted to make "all those countries" on the Chesapeake fear him more than they feared Wahunsonacock.

The means to do so had fallen into his lap when the English ship *Mary and John* arrived in Virginia in midsummer. This was not a full-fledged resupply of the colony. Its captain, Samuel Argall, had come to fill his barrels with salted and dried sturgeon for sale in England. But Smith seized the ship and its fresh supply of food. More importantly, Argall had fresh fighting men and a broadside that could destroy any village or town within cannon-shot of deep water. So long as Smith had that ship, Wahunsonacock could not touch him. Wahunsonacock, on the advice of his defectors, moved his capital inland, beyond the long reach of these cannons. He knew that his only chance to defeat Smith came in the intervals between the visits of oceangoing ships, and, for the time being, the *Mary and John* closed that window. He conceded the James River to Smith's rule.

Culture in all of Tsenacomoco was evolving with lightning speed. While the English on the James River melded with their Indian vassals, the Indians on the next river over, the York or Pamunkey, melded with Jamestown's deserters, who delivered English tools and weapons into the hands of the "savages." Indians learned how to shoot muskets, while at least some of the deserters plotted the overthrow and massacre of Jamestown. Flooded with European goods and infiltrated with Europeans themselves, culture on the Pamunkey was no longer purely Indian. Wahunsonacock, wearing now a scarlet coat of English manufacture, adapted himself to English weapons and tried to interpret the subtleties of English politics. But if the Pamunkey River was no longer purely Indian, neither was Jamestown purely English. Smith, encrusted though he was with English arms, blended his men into the Indian towns on the James River and inserted himself into the fissures of Algonquian alliances. Neither English nor native, the James and the Pamunkey Rivers had become a sort of middle ground.

## MIDDLE GROUND

In relation to the colonization of the Americas, Richard White developed the notion of a *middle ground* in his 1991 book of that title. White and a generation of scholars who followed him have revolutionized our understanding of European occupation, settlement, and ultimate usurpation of native lands, because they focus less on political and military history and more on the lives of ordinary people who actually encountered each other in the frontier zones. *Frontier* here carries its political sense—the territory far from central governments where the edges of civilizations confront one another. White studied the intersection of Indian and French civilizations in the region known as the *pays d'en haut*, or Upper Country of French Canada, where Indian refugees fleeing the Iroquois mingled with French trappers, traders, and pioneers. The *pays d'en haut* belonged really to no civilization. It developed its own ways. According to White, the Frenchmen (it was mostly men) who actually lived in the *pays d'en haut* tended to have much more in common with the Indians they lived among than was ever acknowledged by the old narratives of colonization, which were written by elites "far from the site of actual contact." The people "who actually lived among the Indians" knew that the idea, promoted by the "intellectual and statesmen" writing the narratives, that Indians were "literally *sauvages*, or wild men," was false. Yet, until White's book, modern histories of the region relied almost exclusively on those ill-informed narratives. Take sex, for example. The sexual license enjoyed by unmarried Indian women had no equivalent in Europe, and so the French elite who wrote the books called them prostitutes. French frontiersmen, who tended to come of the peasantry, knew better, and gladly accommodated themselves to the women's sexual behavior. What shocked French orthodoxy seemed natural to frontiersmen. Similarly, the French pioneer found the diffused authority of Indian government congenial and had little trouble shedding the "system-atizing mode of French officials." What happened in the middle ground was not exactly European, Indian, or even a compromise in the conventional sense, where people meet each other halfway. In the middle ground, according to White, "diverse peoples adjust their difference through what amounts to a process of creative, and often expedient, misunderstandings." In short, the middle ground was a place where "whites could neither dictate to Indians nor ignore them." A new political and social culture, shared by the Europeans and the Indians, grew up in these regions.[1]

White's concept of the middle ground resurrected the frontier thesis of American history, an idea first voiced by an obscure historian from Wisconsin who, at the age of thirty-two, delivered a lecture at the 1893 Chicago World's Fair. The scene was not staged for a revolution in intellectual history. The young Frederick Jackson Turner read his essay at the end of a tedious line of five historical treatises. As John Mack Faragher described the scene a hundred years later, "it was already rather late" in the day when "Turner took his turn at the podium." He had been preceded by a sleepy narrative titled "Early Lead Mining in Illinois and Wisconsin." The "exhausted historians" in the audience might be forgiven, Faragher noted with some humanity, if they "had already begun to nod off." Turner began to read. He was a talented speaker, with a "deep, melodious voice," and few scholars are more passionate about their subject than Turner was about his. But the yawns overwhelmed the performance. When Turner looked out at the faces, his eager eyes met "bored indiffer-ence." No one was provoked. No one disputed. No one even asked a question.[2]

Turner published the essay the following year, and then he began a promotional campaign that adapted the strategies of P. T. Barnum to the decorum of academia. What really turned the tide was Turner's willingness, even eagerness, to address educated, nonexpert audiences:

"alumni audiences, teachers' groups, Chautauqua institutes, and civic societies." In the context of the great stock market collapse and bank failures of the 1893, Turner's ideas seemed to explain to Americans what made them distinctive, where their unique character came from, and why their way of life was in crisis at the close of the nineteenth century.[3]

In 1890, Turner explained, the superintendent of the census declared that the Census Office could no longer distinguish a line indicating "a frontier of settlement" in the United States. Though unnoticed by nearly everyone but Turner, the statement marked the end of the era that had forged America's key institutions, constitutional forms, and cultural beliefs and practices. Americans were a unique breed, Turner insisted, because of the frontier. Ever since colonial times, Americans had to adapt "to the changes involved in crossing a continent, in winning a wilderness," and transforming "the primitive economic and political conditions of the frontier into the complexity of city life." Turner described the process in a particularly poetic and mythic passage that enthralled scholars and laymen alike:

> The wilderness masters the colonist. It finds him a European in dress, industries, tools, modes of travel, and thought. It takes him from the railroad car and puts him in the birch canoe. It strips off the garments of civilization and arrays him in the hunting shirt and the moccasin. It puts him in the log cabin of the Cherokee and Iroquois and runs an Indian palisade around him. Before long he has gone to planting Indian corn and plowing with a sharp stick; he shouts the war cry and takes the scalp in orthodox Indian fashion. In short, at the frontier the environment is at first too strong for the man. He must accept the conditions which it furnishes, or perish, and so he fits himself into the Indian clearings and follows the Indian trails. Little by little he transforms the wilderness, but

the outcome is not the old Europe . . . The fact is, that here is
a new product that is American.

Turner's brushstroke is too broad to bear up under the detailed
scrutiny of most historians. And he trades on the notion, somewhat
naive even in 1893, that there is an identifiable "American" character
that one might narrowly and confidently define. But myth is always
susceptible to debunking by a million pricks of historical evidence,
even when it is true. Few historians today enthusiastically accept the
details of Turner's histories. His own pages have been problematized
to near disintegration. He describes the frontier as "the meeting point
between savagery and civilization," a characterization of the middle
ground that would embarrass a historian like Richard White. More
than fifty years of careful study by historians and anthropologists
have disabused us of these self-satisfying stereotypes. But his frontier thesis still undergirds one of the great origin myths to which this
book subscribes.[4]

Our first "frontier" was the Atlantic coastal areas up to and just
beyond the fall line. By August of 1609, that describes the extent of
John Smith's control of the James River. Smith had men quartering
in Indian towns and villages up and down the river, eating Indian
food, sleeping in Indian houses, folding themselves into the rhythms
of native life. Sixty were living somewhere "down the river" where
they were expected "to live upon oysters." Eighty or so stayed in the
garrison at Jamestown Island, drawing clean water now from their
well and eating a diet mostly of corn and any other food—"squirrels,
turkey, deer, and other wild beasts"—that came to the fort as tribute.
Smith had dispatched Francis West, the younger brother of Lord De
La Warr, and about twenty men to live at the falls near the town of
Powhatan, Wahunsonacock's birthplace. He had sent George Percy,
the younger brother of the Earl of Northumberland, with twenty
men down near the Indian town at Kecoughtan at the tip of the

peninsula. The English established a lookout there at a place they called Point Comfort. The *Mary and John* rode in the good anchorage there, guarding the river. No one could enter or leave the James without Smith's knowledge or permission.[5]

However, if Jamestown was no longer a proper English garrison such as one might find in the Netherlands or Ireland, neither had the "systemizing mode" of English authority dissolved yet into democracy. The best way to describe the James River is as an English paramount chiefdom. The Indians thought of it in those terms. Such an attitude was encouraged by Smith's own assimilation of Indian ways and symbolized by the name Wahunsonacock gave him, Nantaquod, when he formally made Smith into a weroance. Smith spoke to the Nansemonds and the Paspaheghs in their language. He learned Indian woodcraft. The first houses in Jamestown, built in the English fashion, had been like ovens in the summer heat, but the English learned quick enough from the Indians to clad their homes in cooler bark shingles, and the interiors were broken up with woven mats in the Indian fashion. "All the bordering neighbors" to Jamestown were under Smith's command, "and many of the rest" of the towns on the James River and others around the Chesapeake, had been made allies by either fear of Smith's arms or eagerness for his trade and "would have done anything" Smith told them to do. The presence of Indians was everywhere. Indian food, Indian furs, Indians themselves. Although Smith kept a stricter discipline about Indians loitering in Jamestown's fort, and although he kept a stricter, military-style discipline among the English themselves, he did not discourage the general intercourse between the peoples. The peace that Smith enforced on the James River encouraged rather than discouraged informal, black-market exchanges between European and Indian. With so many of his men quartering in Indian villages, things could hardly have been otherwise. And then there were the inevitable sexual entanglements that developed between English men and Indian women.[6]

Detail from John Smith's *Map of Virginia*,
1612, showing the James River (called
"Powhatan Flu") up to "The Fales" and the
town of Powhatan.

The James River had become an amalgam of cultures, a place
where a hundred mistakes and misinterpretations and accommodations were made every day, a stone-age chiefdom protected by
modern arms and led by a short, bearded warrior from across the sea.
Edward Maria Wingfield's prediction had come true: John Smith
had "usurp[ed] the government . . . and [made] himself king."[7] Smith
did not murder the councillors, as Wingfield had said he would, but
one councillor had been executed, and Smith deposed and exiled
two presidents. He did not call himself a king, but he ruled the James
River with less restraint than King James ruled England. He was
judge and jury, while his most loyal retainers were bailiff and jailer.
Those loyalists numbered about 40 to 50 men, and with these at his
back Smith tyrannized the other 150 or 160 settlers who had not
already died or run away to the Indians. They were scared of Smith,
and rightly so. He would execute them or maroon them in the
wilderness if they did not heed his orders.[8]

    And yet, discipline hardly reigned. Percy's men, as we have
seen, were supposed to snare enough fish near Point Comfort to at
least feed themselves, but not for six weeks could they "agree once to

cast out the net." Discontent grew. Percy was unpopular with his men, and he suffered the consequences. A musketeer in those days carried his powder in single wooden cartridges on a leather bandoleer, while he slung from his hip a large pouch of powder from which these cartridges might be refilled. The muskets themselves were matchlocks, which means that they fired when the trigger mechanism touched a lit fuse to the flash pan. A musketeer expecting action kept a live fuse twined in his fingers, ready to be placed in the trigger mechanism. With so much powder dangling about and lit fuses in every soldier's fingers, accidents were certainly possible. But the very possibility of an accident also could cover a deliberate attempt to maim or assassinate an unpopular officer. Whether in a true accident or one contrived by his men, Percy was "burnt sore with gunpowder" and forced to return to Jamestown.[9]

In early August one of Percy's soldiers at Port Comfort saw four ships sail into the bay and sounded the alarm. Smith presumed it was an assault by the Spanish. He deployed both English and Indian fighters to meet the challenge. This was the first time in history that English soldiers and native warriors allied themselves, and it demonstrates the extent of Smith's command over the James River. Soldiers' muskets were loaded, and fuses were lit and dangled from fingers. The English had three hundred muskets, but able-bodied, loyal men numbered fewer than two-thirds of that number, and many of those were attending the twenty-four cannons. Smith had hundreds of idle muskets.[10] The absence of any positive evidence suggests that he probably did not turn his Indian dependents into musketeers: he could not yet trust them that far. More than likely, bows and arrows hewn from native wood stood ready to help repulse a Spanish landing. With or without firearms, hundreds of Indians were poised to fight John Smith's enemies.

Smith's reputation for boldness suggests that he stood on the fort's bastions overlooking the swift-running water, looking for the

Spanish on the incoming tide. To get a good sight at the enemy, he would have been half-exposed above the palisade. He was confident. His men were ready. He welcomed this test of his command. His lieutenants sensed this intensity, his readiness to meet battle, and that sense communicated to those among the English who remained loyal to him. That was part of Smith's genius for leadership. No sign of fear. Possessing absolute physical courage, Smith was never cautious, always decisive.[11] But as the ships came up the river, Smith finally realized the truth. He gave the order to stand down, and the order would have spread through the fort and up the river. There would be no battle. Smith was bitterly disappointed. These were English ships.

Smith's intemperate letter sent back to London with the return of the Second Supply had asked for only a few dozen craftsmen. Here were four ships full of new settlers. "Happy had we been," Smith's account reads, "had they never arrived." It would have been better, he thought, had the London Company "forever abandoned" Jamestown and left Smith and his men "to our fortunes." Marooned. Cut loose from the "constitutions" enabled by the Company's charter, Smith knew he could accomplish something truly great. In August 1609 he was at the height of his powers. He might have had fewer than two hundred Englishmen, while Tsenacomoco had more than fifteen thousand Indians. But already he had detached the James River from Wahunsonacock's dominions. With more time and the *Mary and John* at his disposal, he might have conquered a nation.

### FRONTIER COUP D'ÉTAT

The hurricane that sank the *Sea Venture* damaged all of the other eight ships in the Third Supply. The *Blessing*, with "twenty women and children" on her manifest, was whipped by the "tail of the West Indian hurricane," but after forty-four hours of struggle the clouds broke. Blue sky returned. They could see clear to the horizon, and the ocean was empty. Not another sail in sight. For five or six days, they cleaned up the mess, repaired the damage, and hoped all the while that others had survived. Then they caught sight of the *Lion*, then the *Falcon* and the *Unity*. The *Unity* was badly beaten. Sixty out of seventy settlers were injured, sick, or otherwise incapacitated; "all her seamen were down" except the master, Mr. Pett, and his boy. The *Blessing* lent them some mariners, and in early August the four ships made it into Chesapeake Bay. Battered though they were, they sailed past Point Comfort, making straight for Jamestown and relief, their first landfall since they had left England. Two or three hundred people came ashore.[12]

The sight of Jamestown must have encouraged them. A bricked well punctured the open ground. Smoke from a forge and smithy snaked into the blue sky. The familiar smell of woodsmoke and leather and sweaty men and fresh-cut timber. The fort was in good repair. Each corner had its platform with cannon and artillerymen. All of this industry spoke well of the discipline that John Smith imposed on the colony. The survivors of the ocean voyage had every right to feel they had been rescued. They had every right to expect a hearty welcome. Handshakes should have congratulated them for surviving the trials of the crossing. Hearty food should have been passed around with eager questions about news from home. The settlers came ashore with all the indiscipline and relief of people who had survived disaster, and this disarray of refugees spread through the fort. What luggage they had was waterlogged and strewn across the parade ground. The buzz of their own excitement and relief and the noise of just getting them ashore was like a fair day in a village. But they found a grim welcome.

The survivors of the hurricane were imposing themselves on reluctant hosts. They could sense the unwelcome atmosphere. And something about Jamestown was not quite English. There was the palisade, for instance, a sight not seen in England since the Norman invasion more than five hundred years earlier. And there were the natives. As they came up the river to Jamestown, the new settlers could watch "troops" of Indians run along the shore "from place to place," some getting into "the tops of trees" to mark the progress of the ships.[13] Some of these natives would have sported articles of English clothing, a jerkin over the chest or a plumed hat or some other token of European civilization. It would not have taken long for newly arrived travelers from England to realize that there was some sort of collaboration going on, a mingling of the English and the "savages." It must not have taken long to sense that they had sailed into "middle ground." They would not have understood it as such. But in a dozen subtle ways Jamestown was not exactly English.

Two men stepped forward to represent the Third Supply, Gabriel Archer of the *Blessing* and John Martin of the *Falcon*. The survivors of the hurricane watched them confer with a short, energetic young man who had the swagger of command. His name must have circulated quickly among the new arrivals, for John Smith was notorious to the sailors. It was clear to any who witnessed this meeting that something was amiss. There was no cordiality in the greeting, no fellow feeling, from either side. Backed by his own lieutenants and perhaps by Captain Argall of the *Mary and John*, John Smith faced down Archer and Martin, who were seconded by the other "captains of the passengers," so designated by Company orders: Captain George Webb, Captain James Davis, and "divers gentlemen of good means and parentage" among the newcomers. The new settlers were getting their first inkling of trouble in Jamestown. Their arrival portended a struggle for power.

Smith was appalled by the return of Archer and Martin, whom he had virtually exiled from Jamestown. Do not let Archer come back to Virginia, Smith's letter had warned the Company's directors, for he would "keep us always in factions." Martin, Smith thought, was less

conniving than cowardly, and incompetent as well, but Smith felt no
need to malign him in the letter. Newport he defamed. And Smith
saved his greatest contempt for John Ratcliffe, the deposed president.
Smith called him "a poor counterfeited imposture," so unfit for leadership that Smith "sent . . . him home, lest the company should cut
his throat."[14] And yet, as Smith was soon told, the Company had sent
Ratcliffe back, too, as captain of the *Diamond*, the second-largest and
still missing vessel. They presumed that the *Diamond* had sunk, but
still Smith smarted from the slap in the face. Ratcliffe! Smith must
have felt his letter to the Company had backfired. The directors had
sided with the incompetents. And the bad news kept coming. The
Company had abolished Jamestown's council, dissolved the presidency,
and had obtained from the king a second charter, a new commission.
Smith was to be cast aside. Virginia was to be ruled by a governor.

*Who was this governor?* Smith wanted to know.

Lord De La Warr.

*And where was he?*

In England, still organizing the Fourth Supply. Until he arrived,
Jamestown would be ruled by the lieutenant governor, Sir Thomas
Gates.

*Where was this Sir Thomas Gates?*

On the *Sea Venture*, still lost at sea, along with Admiral Somers
and the Vice Admiral Newport.

*Could Archer produce this supposed Second Charter?*

All copies went down with the *Sea Venture*.[15]

Well then: until the Second Charter arrived, Smith announced,
the First Charter must remain in force. That kept power vested in the
president. But even under the old charter, Smith's term was supposed
to expire in a month, and the office would devolve upon John Martin,
the only living councillor then in Jamestown. On his shoulders would
rest responsibility for the livelihood of hundreds of settlers, including

the new arrivals, for whom there was little provender. Martin would have to contend with the formidable Wahunsonacock. Still, it was best, Smith explained. Martin's presidency would be the only legal course.

The prospect unsettled Martin, who was well aware of his own "insufficiency."

Perceiving Martin's fears, Smith made a bold gambit: he resigned his commission a month early. Before the entire company, Smith let it be known that henceforth John Martin would be president for a term of thirteen months. The new settlers must have wondered what was going on. John Smith's own faction must have been shocked and somewhat terrified. John Martin president? They might as well sketch out their own graves in the turf. It was plainly evident even to Martin himself how "little" the old colonists respected the new president. President Martin took but three hours to hand the office back to John Smith. Unless the Second Charter arrived sooner, Smith was president for another year.

Then the *Swallow*, "with her mainmast overboard," and the *Diamond*, similarly crippled and beaten, appeared in the bay. Once again, exhausted and hungry settlers descended on Jamestown, which had become a camp of refugees. In about a week's time the English population on the James River had roughly tripled to nearly six hundred people. There was not enough food: what little came in the ships was mostly spoiled by salt water. Nor did the garrison have the space to house so many. Worst of all, standing at the head of this new flood of destitutes was Smith's old nemesis, John Ratcliffe.

The struggle for power started all over again. Although the outcome would affect them significantly, the commoners did not participate. They watched from the sidelines as the "many unruly gallants," the gentlemen, threw their support behind one leader or another. "Today the old commission must rule," Smith's *General History* tells us, "tomorrow the new, the next day neither." As Archer told the story, "all the respected gentlemen of worth in Virginia" rallied behind him and Ratcliffe. They refused John Smith and elected in his stead Thomas West, Lord De La Warr's younger brother. Ratcliffe's backers "subjected" themselves only to West, who would reign until they "heard news from [their] council in England." George Percy added the prestige of Northumberland's name to Ratcliffe's faction, which increasingly looked like the aristocratic party. But that's probably too simplistic, because Smith had aroused plenty of enmity among the commoners. Strengthened by Ratcliffe's arrival on the *Diamond*, that discontent turned into open opposition to Smith, and opposition was manifest in this extralegal action. West's election amounted to a "frontier *coup d'état*," to use the words of the eminent historian Alden Vaughan. Neither the First nor the Second Charter sanctioned West's election to the presidency. Archer conceded that this power grab would be "blazoned a mutiny" by Smith's supporters, and he took great pains to justify it by emphasizing that Jamestown's gentlemen sanctioned the transfer of power.[16]

About six hundred Europeans, nearly all of them English, were living in Jamestown in August 1609—not quite marooned but not far from it. They didn't have enough roofs, not by half, to shelter them all. They didn't have enough food to get through the winter. How long before they would have starved was uncertain, but supplies were so short as to constitute a crisis. Decisive leadership was needed. The captains of the Third Supply all knew that the Company meant to replace President Smith with Lieutenant Governor Gates, but they did not have the new charter legalizing the change, nor did they have Gates. Smith, with some justice, convinced himself that no one else could save the colony. The James River Indians did not owe their allegiance to Jamestown: they owed it to John Smith, their paramount chief. If the English dumped Smith, they also tossed away their dominion over the James River. Some Indian towns might retain their alliance with the English, but more likely they would revert to their positions in Tsenacomoco. The balance of power would swing back toward Wahunsonacock, who could reunite the entire native community against the poorly provisioned English garrison.

Neither of Jamestown's legal constitutions could solve this riddle of leadership, and London was too far away to help. In a year or so, Lord De La Warr would arrive and restore legitimate government. Until then they had to shift for themselves. In essence, the settlers must improvise a government: that was their first order of business. Almost instinctively, Ratcliffe's faction selected its leader by election, which implicitly recognized the right of self-determination. But Ratcliffe extended that right only to "the respected gentlemen of worth." This brought Jamestown closer to majority rule than England, where only one in fifty were gentlemen. But even in Jamestown, though the proportion of gentlemen was much higher, they were still a minority. The commoners must have watched Ratcliffe's election of West with little enthusiasm. They had signed on to this adventure of their own free will, consenting to relinquish their legal status in England for a new status under the Company's charter in Virginia. As we have seen, they probably did not realize how much of their liberty they had surrendered to the Company, for the Company did not publish or publicize the Second Charter. But in August 1609, in the muddy, squalid fortress under a humid cloud of mosquitoes, they knew that they had consented to *something*. When that something had to be replaced, Ratcliffe did not consult them. An electorate of gentlemen decided to replace everyone's contract with the Company with a new contract, just as binding but without everyone's consent. No commoner participated in the formation of West's government. Some among them must have felt their rights were usurped. Most certainly, Smith's loyalists, who had joined the adventure under the provisions of the First Charter, felt the sting of tyranny.

But if they did not have a say in the formation of West's election, even the common settlers could vote with their feet. They could accept Francis West or follow John Smith. West appealed to the more conservative sensibility or the merely timid. If Francis West's election were extralegal, there could be little doubt that when Thomas West, Governor Lord De La Warr, arrived in Jamestown, he would approve it retroactively. Choosing Smith was more radical. For some (as we have seen), it expressed a preference for being abandoned by the Company altogether. Some of Smith's followers were probably emboldened by a practical consideration: settlers who had suffered the trials of Virginia probably thought that Smith gave them the best chance of surviving till the Fourth Supply arrived. Could West keep them alive so long? Each faction had its share of followers. We are relatively certain that a large number of the gentlemen, especially those who arrived in the Third Supply, supported West. The sailors sided with Smith, as even Archer concedes.[17] These facts seem to support the notion that the colony was divided according to class, and we might expect that those who benefited from England's caste system would tend toward conservatism, while the lion's share of Smith's followers, survivors from the original landing and the First and Second Supplies, had the frontiersman's respect for meritocracy. That interpretation would certainly contribute to Smith's reputation as the enemy of aristocratic privilege. But as we have seen, Smith was no democrat. Tempting as it is, and even if the preponderance of gentlemen took the conservative view and if most of the radicals were of low birth, no solid evidence suggests that a class consciousness was involved. The English system of inequality does not seem to have been on trial. What we do know—and this is important enough in itself—is that everyone had to make a choice. Their original contract with the Virginia Company was meaningless, obviated by the extremity of their situation. Of their free will they must choose government by West or by Smith.

For the next three weeks both West and Smith acted as if he were the legitimate ruler of the colony. Archer claims that he and the gentlemen electors "refused to be governed" by Smith and "only subjected ourselves to Master West." Smith claimed that he ordered Francis West upriver "to plant at the Falls" with 120 men and one of the ships. He ordered Martin to lead a similar number of men across the river to Nansemond territory, where they were to plant another settlement. He allowed each plantation "their due proportions of all provisions," meager as they were, out of Jamestown's store. West and Martin either consented to these orders or fancied they went on West's authority, for both men left the garrison with their contingent of settlers. The main body of men from the Third Supply accompanied West upriver, including most of the "land" captains, perhaps even including Ratcliffe and Archer. These men were bent on another expedition into the hinterland with the quixotic hope of finding gold or an overland route to the Pacific Ocean. These two plantations—up at the falls and down near Nansemond—relieved the crowding on Jamestown Island, and they also dispersed Smith's enemies, leaving the main fort in relatively secure hands.[18]

Soon after West established himself at the falls, Smith went up to check on him. He took only five men as his guard, despite knowing "how greedy [Ratcliffe and Archer] were of his blood." Such cavalier gestures were characteristic of the man: he faced danger against all odds, and he expected this very boldness to cow his enemies. It had worked in Transylvania when he beheaded three Turks; it worked when as a slave on the shores of the Black Sea he bludgeoned his master and rode off into the wasteland; and it worked when he grabbed Opechancanough and put a gun to his head, daring the hostile Indians to make a move against him. Smith's audacity moved Wahunsonacock to make him a weroance and give him a new name. Now he thought it would work on West or on West's men. Following the tides, the trip upriver to the falls took a couple of days, and midway in the journey Smith met a boat coming downriver. Inexplicably, Francis West was returning to Jamestown. Abandoning his post so soon? Smith was disgusted and hastened to get to the new fort, which was now apparently captained by Ratcliffe and Archer.[19]

West's company was erecting its plantation on Dewey's Island, a low-lying spot that Smith knew would flood with the periodic swelling of the river. Besides that, it was "environed with many intolerable inconveniences," problems perhaps not evident to the greenhorn's eye but clear enough to a seasoned frontiersman like John Smith. After surveying the possibilities, Smith decided the settlement had to move, and in the following days he opened a remarkable diplomatic mission with the Indians. Smith sent Wahunsonacock an offer to buy the nearest town, Powhatan, Wahunsonacock's birthplace, for a "proportion of copper." Wahunsonacock's son, Parahunt, or Tanxpowhatan, "the Little Powhatan," was chief of the town. A young man who had arrived in the *Unity*, Henry Spelman, thought that he himself was part of the payment that Smith offered. More likely, Smith arranged for Spelman to live with the Indians, just as Newport had exchanged the boy, Thomas Savage, for Namontack.[20] Smith's offer did not have to travel far. Wahusonacock had moved his capital to the inland town of Orapax, only a dozen miles from the falls. The town of Powhatan was strategic for Tsenacomoco, a fortress guarding against the Monacans of the foothills. Ringed by a wooden palisade, it was similar in construction though not in shape to Jamestown's triangular wall. About forty or fifty men—all potential warriors—lived there.[21] As the capital of a district, Powhatan would have been surrounded by productive fields and a populous scattering of villages, each administered by chiefs answerable to Parahunt. That Wahunsonacock would even entertain the thought of "selling" the town suggests how weak his influence was on the James River. Probably, Smith took this opportunity to formalize his de facto suzerainty over the district, an offer to pay Wahunsonacock for territory Smith already had more or less conquered by threat of arms. This gesture, Smith might have thought, would conciliate the old paramount chief. The other terms of the agreement suggest that Smith wanted to formalize English dominion in the district—normalize it in terms familiar to the Indians. As part of the deal, every Indian household in the district would pay to Smith "a bushel of corn" and "a proportion of *pocones*," a root plant that was the source of a red dye. This "yearly tribute to King James" would formalize the district's detachment from Tsenacomoco and its attachment to Jamestown. For his part, Smith promised that the Powhatan district would continue to be a first defense against the Monacans. This particular part of the agreement might have great appeal to the Indians: the English people, not Algonquians, would have to absorb the brunt of Siouan attacks from the foothills. It is not clear whether Smith meant for the English and Indians to live together in the palisaded town, or if he expected the Indians to abandon it before the English garrison moved in. And it is unclear what was to become of Parahunt. Would he remain chief of the district, distributing tribute now to the English rather than to his father? Or would he move north into territory on the York River that his father still controlled? These confusions about the district's status are not unexpected: the "middle ground" is a constant flux of negotiation, misunderstanding, renegotiations, and accommodations. However these issues were settled, settled they were, and Wahunso-nacock seems to have agreed to Smith's proposal, probably happy to get any compensation for a district already lost to him.[22]

These matters were so "well managed with discretion" that Smith persuaded several of West's men to come over to his own faction. Captains Wood, Webb, Moone, and FitzJames, and "Master William Powell, Master Partridge, Master White, and divers others" now recognized Smith's merits and realized that Archer's and Ratcliffe's opposition was motivated by "malice." Nevertheless, most of West's men thought the pact with the Indians confirmed rumors of Smith's ambitions. They refused to move into Powhatan. Probably they feared that exposing themselves to the Indians would deliver them into Smith's power. They "contemn[ed]" Smith and "his kind care, and authority." Smith would not tolerate such open defiance, and, despite being outnumbered twenty to one, he and his little guard attempted to arrest "all the chieftains" of what he called "mutinies." It did not go well. Smith found himself "forced" to "retire." Smith, Archer, Ratcliffe, settlers, and sailors stood at the edge of civil war, when no power but the strength of arms would determine who ruled the James River: no royal charter, no company rules, no election. Smith escaped the fort and fled in one of the boats, which he used to row out into the river where a ship was moored. Surrounded by water, he was safe. The sailors were for Smith, and most of the encampment's supplies were still aboard the vessel. And, despite being horribly outnumbered among Englishmen, Smith still had the upper hand. He had the Indians.

## THE DECLINE AND FALL OF JOHN SMITH

Meanwhile, John Martin botched his mission in Nansemond. According to George Percy, the English sent a couple of messengers to the "King of Nancemonde to barter with him for an island," where Martin wanted to plant his settlement. Martin sent a couple of messengers to offer a few "copper hatche[t]s and other commodities." The Indians had no desire to sell: the island was filled with temples that interred the remains of their dead. Percy reports that the Nansemonds "sacrificed" the English messengers and "scraped [the brains] out of their heads with mussel shells." It seems very unlikely that this was the first provocation. The Nansemonds were scared of John Smith. The Nansemond chief probably held the messengers at his capital, entertaining and detaining them.

In retaliation, Martin "beat the savages out of the island, burned their houses, ransacked their temples, took down the corpse[s] of their dead kings from off their tombs, and carried away their pearls, copper, and bracelets." Percy, who was as incompetent as Martin, did not comprehend the blunder. His narrative recalls the incident with braggadocio. The English also managed to capture the king's son and another Indian, whom they bound with cords, but one of these prisoners was "accidentally" shot in the chest, according to Percy. Shocked into action, the wounded Indian broke his cords, dove into the river, and swam to safety and to sound the alarm.[23] The Nansemonds swarmed the island, killing several of Martin's men. Both Martin and Percy retreated to Jamestown, forfeiting "a thousand bushels of corn." They sent a message to Smith pleading for permission to take thirty of his seasoned soldiers from Jamestown. Smith granted the request, but Martin so mismanaged these men that "they did just nothing," according to Smith, before retreating to Jamestown. How many English were killed is not known. Martin lost the regular tributes of food paid by the Nansemonds, lost the chance to plant another settlement, lost the entire Nansemond district, and roused a new enemy. And yet he and Percy bragged about stealing a handful of pearls and desecrating Indian graves as though they had accomplished some feat.[24]

West's men ruined the Powhatan district in the same way. According to the terms of their agreement, the English were supposed to be "protectors" of the Powhatans, but it turned out they were "worse enemies than the Monacans themselves." West's men stole stored corn and tore up gardens, and when the Indians got in the way, they were beaten. English ruffians broke into the Indian houses, kidnapped people, and kept them prisoner in the new English garrison. The Indians told Smith that they "had endured" these insults because of their obligations to him. They dared not fight back lest they enflame Smith's own wrath. They came now to their paramount chief for justice. Why hadn't Smith punished these criminals, they wanted to know, and if he would not do it, would he at least allow the Powhatans to do it themselves?

Smith claims he was in daily contact with the Indians of the Powhatan district, accepting their "contributions" of food and listening to their complaints. Whether these conferences were on ship or ashore in one of the Indian villages, they were noticed by the Englishmen in the garrison, who determined that Smith was colluding with the Indians. The old accusations resurrected. Smith wanted to set up his own kingdom on the Chesapeake, a state made up of Indians and Europeans united under his command. He was no Company man. He did not give his loyalty, as he should have, to his own countrymen above all else. He would even use Indians to get the upper hand on Archer's and Ratcliffe's faction. What happened next lends weight to these accusations. Smith started to sail down the river back to Jamestown. "No sooner was the ship under sail" than the Indians turned hostile on the garrison. They killed whites they caught outside the fort "straggling abroad in the woods" and stole their weapons and clothes. A force of Indians—Smith claims it was but a dozen warriors—boldly "assaulted those hundred and twenty at their fort . . . and so affrighted" the English that the kidnapped Indians who had been imprisoned inside were able to slip free. To the men at the falls, it looked as if Smith had orchestrated the whole thing. Henry Spelman, the youth who lived with the Indians and learned their language, thought Smith was responsible for the attack. So did George Percy, who thought that Smith had "incensed and animated the savages against Captain West and his company." Even worse, Smith revealed to the Indians that "our men had no more powder left them than would serve for one volley of shot." Smith's own narrative hardly dispels this impression: it might not admit that Smith gave his permission for the attack, but neither does it claim that he withheld it. The implication is clear: Parahunt, "the Little Powhatan," in charge of the district, was following Smith's orders.[25]

Many of the men at West's fort had been in Virginia but a week or so, and they must have felt lost in the wilderness. They buried their dead and, surrounded by hostile Indians, they contemplated their own bloody end. Smith's boat ran aground on a sandbar, which delayed his removal from the area and allowed him to summon a deputation from the fort. After this dramatic reversal, the garrison was eager to come to "a parley" on the boat. They were so terrified of the Indians, the *General History* reports, that they "submitted themselves upon any terms to [Smith's] mercy." Smith offered what he considered very forgiving provisos. They must deliver up the half dozen or so leaders of their mutiny. As Smith had first commanded them, they must abandon their open-air fort and lodge themselves in the "dry houses" of Powhatan, fortified behind its formidable palisade. They must give back to the Indians the things they had stolen. The English promptly complied with each of these terms, betraying their leaders to Smith, whom he stuffed belowdecks on the ship and clapped in irons. "Thus all were friends" again, Smith happily reported, English and Algonquian.[26]

So matters remained for some time, with the English sleeping in Indian houses, well fed and safe behind the palisade walls of Powhatan, planting a late crop in two hundred acres of cleared fields, establishing a true plantation. Then Francis West went back upriver and disrupted Smith's peace. West immediately protested the imprisonment of the garrison's leaders. Their rebelliousness, West told Smith, was only zealotry for West's honor. They had refused to follow Smith's orders because they thought to do so would contradict West's own instructions. They could not with justice be condemned for mutiny. Smith acquiesced. The prisoners were released. Their arms were restored. They rejoined the garrison, now lodged in Powhatan, and immediately resumed fomenting discontent. The Indian town was a trap, they whispered in everyone's ears, until they persuaded the garrison to return "to the open air at West's Fort." Smith was back at square one. In frustration and defeat, Smith washed his hands of them. If they fouled their relations with the Indians, they must pay the consequences—as Martin had paid in Nansemond. He headed back downriver.

The big ship had already gone back to Jamestown, so Smith was returning in the small boat. At some point on the two-day journey, Smith fell asleep. By necessity he was exposed to the elements. He had little reason to worry about his person: he was confident of the loyalty of all the men in the boat. Presumably the guard of five loyalists who accompanied him upriver were with him coming down. Who else was in the boat we don't know, but while Smith slept someone "fired his powder bag" in the same way that Percy's had been fired at Point Comfort. Smith woke to find himself "frying . . . in his clothes." Frantic, he jumped overboard into the water. He was so horribly burned that he couldn't swim and was "near drowned" by the time his men hauled him back into the boat. It was a grave wound. Skin about "nine or ten inches square" was torn from his thigh and groin. The boat still had "near an hundred miles" to go to reach Jamestown. There was no surgeon. Smith's guard dressed his wound as best they could. They kept him alive at least until they delivered the delirious president, "near bereft of his senses," to the old fort.[27]

The *General History* called this incident an accident. So agreed Smith's undisputed, definitive biographer, Philip Barbour. His version, written in 1964, suggests that "somehow a spark from the matches for their muskets or from a tobacco pipe lighted on Smith's powder bag." Till recently that seemed to be the settled opinion of historians. Alden Vaughan, the eminent historian at Columbia University, agreed with Barbour's assessment in his own 1975 monograph, and in 1992, University of Delaware expert J. A. Leo Lemay repeated the presumption in his own book on Smith. But James Horn, who is today the distinguished historian with the Jamestown Rediscovery Foundation, does not accept that interpretation. "The terrible injury," he wrote in 2005, twenty years after Lemay, "was no accident but a deliberate attempt to kill" the president. Smith himself knew only what he was told, because he was asleep when it happened and delirious for days after. It stretches credulity to think that just at this most crucial moment of the struggle for power, the random hand of chance took hold of events. The similarity between Smith's injury and Percy's lends weight to Horn's interpretation. Powder bag fires seem to have played the same role in seventeenth-century warfare that fragmentation grenades played in Vietnam. If anyone *were* to attempt to kill a superior officer, sparking his powder bag was about the only way he could get away with it.[28]

There was nothing equivocal about the next attempt on Smith's life. While the invalid still raved in delirium, an assassin ducked into the sickroom and aimed his weapon. But "his heart did fail him that should have given fire to that merciless pistol."[29] As so often happens in the *General History*, the phrase suggests more than it asserts. Who was the assassin? Barbour thought it was either William Dyer or Thomas Coe, taking orders from West's faction. They hated Smith enough to do it. The president had had them punished for conspiring with Wahunsonacock. Whoever the assassin was, when confronted with the immobilized wreck of the once formidable John Smith, his conscience intervened. No matter what he thought of Smith's sins and tyranny, to kill him in cold blood was too much. Besides, as anyone could see, Smith would never recover well enough to compete for power in Jamestown. The assassin lowered his pistols and slipped away again. Who witnessed the attempt is unclear: Was it the raving Smith himself or one of his loyalists? It seems odd that the would-be killer was not named. Perhaps it was someone from the Third Supply, a new arrival whom Smith did not recognize. But the *General History*, which was so circumspect about the powder bag, was unequivocal in this: Archer and Ratcliffe "plotted to have murdered [Smith] in his bed."[30]

The wound was grievous. Some historians speculate that it castrated Smith. All agree that it incapacitated him. He was unfit for duty and nowhere near the task of opposing the phalanx of captains who were disposing of him. Guarded now assiduously by his loyalists and watched warily by his enemies, Smith's cot was carried on board and stowed in a cabin on a ship bound for England. Ratcliffe, Archer, and Martin drew up a "comprehensive list of his abuses in office," a report for the Company directors that would arrive with the convalescent. Smith would "scarcely" be able to "clear him selfe from great imputation of blame," Ratcliffe predicted to the Earl of Salisbury.[31]

The list of Smith's crimes were mostly trumped-up. Behind them was the great suspicion that Smith meant to make himself a king in Virginia. "He had the savages in such subjection," the suspicions ran, and with that power "he would have made himself a king by marrying Pocahontas, Powhatan's daughter." A marriage in late 1609 seems unlikely, but it was hardly out of the question. As we have already seen, although she was young, Pocahontas's age was not an impediment. By Algonquian custom she was ready for marriage. In Werowocomoco she had danced provocatively for the English captain's delectation and had tried to lure him to bed. Maybe she succeeded, maybe not. We have no reason to suppose that she was less sexually active than the typical young Indian. She married an Indian sometime the following year, in 1610, so it is not unreasonable to think she was considered an adult in 1609. Nor would Smith's fight with her father prevent a union. As proven by later events, a marriage between Pocahontas and an Englishman could produce a rapprochement between the two biggest powers on the Chesapeake. Wahunsonacock might reasonably imagine that making John Smith his son-in-law would pull the James River districts back under his dominion. Englishmen had good reason to fear that Smith might marry Pocahontas.[32]

At any rate, Ratcliffe's faction suspected Smith of plotting to do this, and that suspicion tells us much about the colony Smith had constructed in Virginia. To the English, especially to those just arriving in the Third Supply, the colony looked very strange. Normal English law and custom did not apply. It was more like an outlaw kingdom, Robin Hood's Sherwood Forest in the ballads and plays, than like an English town. Smith had his merry men: by September 1609 it had grown to a hundred soldiers "well-trained" in the savages' "language, and habitations."[33] Smith had succeeded by learning from the "savage." He himself spoke their language. He studied their techniques of forage, hunting, and planting. He did not become an Indian, as some had feared. He was not Nantaquod. But neither was he a conventional English captain anymore. He could summon legions of Indian warriors and command them with nearly the same authority as he commanded his own soldiers. Many of his men lived with the Indians for some part of their tenure in Virginia. For all intents and purposes, Smith was the weroance of all the districts on the James River, and while those districts were still either Indian or English, none were purely so. In Percy's words, he aimed "at a sovereign rule," without any check on his authority.[34] Smith's Jamestown was a renegade regime, an outlaw territory on the frontier.

When Smith lost power to the men of Third Supply, the colony possessed "three ships, seven boats, commodities ready to trade [in Europe], the harvest newly gathered [from fields Smith had had planted], ten weeks' provision in the store." They had "nets for fishing, tools of all sorts to work, apparel to supply [their] wants, six mares and a horse, five or six hundred swine, as many hens and chickens, some goats, some sheep." The importance of domesticated animals, which were new to the Algonquians, cannot be overstated: the presence of chickens on the Chesapeake was as revolutionary as matchlock muskets, armor, and cannon. Not that the cannons were insignificant. Smith's polity was the most powerful force on the Chesapeake: "twenty-four pieces of ordnance, three hundred muskets, snaphances, and firelocks, shot, powder, and match sufficient, [cuirasses], pikes, swords" and more helmets than they had men to wear them. Jamestown's palisade was complete and well maintained. Sixty houses were well roofed. The Paspahegh, Kecoughtan, Nansemond, and Powhatan districts were dependencies, and probably others were as well. These peoples paid tribute in corn and game. The "reign of Romulus" in Rome was but a thousand houses. In addition to Jamestown's sixty, Smith ruled unnumbered hundreds of Indian houses on the James River. About two hundred Europeans lived on the Bay before the great influx from the Third Supply, and under Smith's presidency hardly anyone had died, the one long stretch of health in the first four years of that marshy, unhealthy settlement. Even proud Venice, the *General History* pointed out, "was at first but a [marsh] inhabited by poor fishermen." Smith was nearly dead and carried on a litter to a ship. He returned to England a virtual prisoner. But to his followers, he was the epic hero, the genitor of empire.[35]

Under the surface of this encomium, which sums up Smith's command in the *General History*, lurks tyranny. According to Smith's estimate, hardly any of those Englishmen whom the Company sent to Virginia brought with them the skills or, more importantly, the mentality required to live on a frontier. Most were "poor gentlemen, tradesmen, serving men, libertine, and suchlike, ten times more fit to spoil a commonwealth than either begin one or but help to maintain one." Those listed as laborers in the manifests were mostly "footmen" and other attendees to the gentleman "adventurers." They were not used to real work. According to Smith, "neither fear of God nor the law, nor shame, nor displeasure of their friends could rule them" in Virginia. If they were to bend to frontier life, someone had to crack the whip, stab, poison, imprison them, or impose some other punishment: whatever the president decided. Smith cracked his whip. Many of his men defected to the Indians. Others stayed in Jamestown, quieted by fear but disgruntled. In the end, more English loathed his rogue rule than were attracted to it. Ratcliffe, Archer, and West had a significant majority on their side.

But it was Smith himself who put a limit to his authority. While he lay wounded in Jamestown his "old soldiers" spoke candidly with him. If he would just consent, they would seize Archer, Ratcliffe, Martin, and West and execute them summarily by decapitation. The same fate faced anyone else foolhardy enough to oppose Smith's rule. Had Smith given the word, no doubt they could have done it. Though outnumbered, Smith's men were bolder and better soldiers than any in the opposing faction. But this end was too dark. Smith understood that his day was over. He would not allow the slaughter.

The outlaw kingdom, Smith's "commonwealth in Virginia," ended in anticlimax. He survived the burn, horrible though it was. It was about the tenth of September, 1609, when he was carried aboard one of the ships. He "appointed a guard for himself, and lay back, awaiting the departure of the fleet." A few weeks later the ships left Jamestown, carrying the bitter, defeated John Smith back to England, along with a letter from the triumvirate full of indictments against him. These came to nothing. Smith healed, publishing his *Proceedings* and his *Map of Virginia* in 1612. He sailed three more times for America, beginning in 1614, mapped and named the area we now know as "New England," was captured by and escaped from pirates in the Azores. Eventually, his adventures ended, and he retired to write his books. Virginia was one chapter in his eventful life.[36]

## CHAPTER NINE

※

# *Trouble Times*

**Bermudan days became dull routine.** The "ringing of a bell" summoned the settlers to a meeting spot, where Reverend Bucke led them in prayers. The name of each settler was read off, and if anyone failed to answer this roll call he was "duly punished." Then off to work, either building the ship or some other assigned duty. All day long the settlers were subject to the commands of an overseer. Their time was not their own. They worked until another ringing of the bell marked the day's end. Even then they were not set free. They must gather for another roll call and compulsory prayers. No matter one's private conscience: all solemnities came out of the Anglican *Book of Common Prayer*. All must participate. Mumblers, malingerers, and malcontents were punished. Strachey's *True Reportory* records these details approvingly as examples of the well-ordered nature of Governor Gates's regime.

Even in a labor camp, inmates might carve out time and space for private life, and such moments of humanity peek out here and there in the narrative. Unmarried men and women found time to court. Strachey recorded several marriages, the first one in October. In November, one of the sailors, the *Sea Venture*'s cook, Thomas Powell, and Elizabeth Parsons, who began the trip as maidservant to Mistress Horton, were married. Pigs were still plentiful and fat, so the unions might have been celebrated with roast pork. When a third couple was married on Christmas Eve, the swine, though numerous, were thinner, because berries were out of season. But Bermuda compensated for the loss. By late November "a kind of web-footed fowl" that they had not seen in summer suddenly appeared, a "sea mew" or gull, thousands breeding on two or three little islands in the harbor. These birds spend most of their life on the ocean, feasting on squid, shrimp, and other small fish, and come to the islands only to breed and brood. Naturalists would later name them the Bermuda petrel or cahow, a species endemic to the Bermuda islands, where, without any natural predators, they flourished by the hundreds of thousands. But the hogs that the Spanish put on the big islands in the 1500s burrowed into their nesting grounds, eating eggs and chicks. By the early 1600s, the cahows survived only on the smaller islands not yet invaded by European swine, still flourishing in those sanctuaries in massive numbers. It was probably the "strange hollow and harsh howling" of these nocturnal birds that the Spanish mistook for the evil cries of devils, which contributed to the islands' aura of taboo. The English found them heaven-sent. Settlers rowed or poled rafts over to one of these islets in the dead of night, where the cahows were so docile that all they needed to do to catch them was stand still and hoot and holler. Attracted to the noise, the birds settled themselves at the feet, on the head—on the very arms—of the hunter, who could weigh them in his hand, select the best, "and let the others alone." In an hour they snagged two dozen. They were good eating: "well-relished fowl [as] fat and full as a partridge." The English harvested a "great store" of their white-shelled eggs the size of hens' eggs.[1]

As the weeks went by, full comprehension of their predicament settled upon them. They were truly lost. England thought they had sunk. No one was looking for them. No ships—English, French, or Spanish—were likely to happen by Bermuda. Strachey had been called back from St. David's Island. The signal fires were left to burn out. No trail of smoke etched their mark on the sky. They knew then that they could depend on no one but themselves. They were beyond the frontiers of civilization, confronting a wilderness.

## "DEMOCRACY PRESENTS ITSELF"

In 1954, Stanley Elkins and Eric McKitrick, a pair of scholars writing for *Political Science Quarterly*, imagined what happens when a fairly homogenous people settling a remote territory experiences "a lack of, or a failure of, a traditional, ready-made structure of leadership." If leaders cannot solve the "basic problems" of existence, how do settlers cope? This would cause a "time of troubles," they said, a situation that was repeated so often in the history of the frontier that we might consider it a natural stage in westward migration. A group travels over the Appalachian Mountains, for instance; their leaders prove inadequate to the demands of rugged life; and so far from civilization rescue is unavailable. The frontier settlers must provide for themselves. In their old environments, before they migrated to the frontier, these people might have had no political power. But their experience on the frontier persuades them that they have the "personal competence" to make public decisions. Frontier settlements, Elkins and McKitrick argued, incubated democratic practices. "Democracy presents itself," they explained, "less as a bright possibility than as a brutal necessity." If the people do not start governing themselves, they'll die.[2]

Elkins and McKitrick tried to reconstruct the sociological experience of settling a frontier. To some extent, this was an exercise in speculation, because we don't have much evidence of the psychological experience of ordinary people. But solid research can help one speculate with some conviction. Elkins pioneered this method in his study of American slavery, which applied what psychologists told us about the mental and emotional effect of Nazi concentration camps to the slave labor camps of the American South. The result was a somewhat reductive notion of slave psychology, what came to be called the "Sambo" model: that slavery imposed such a sense of dependency on its victims that it debilitated the freedman's capacity for self-determination, a disability that clung to black communities through generations of putative freedom even into in the 1950s. Though admired when it was first published, and although it influenced some liberal public policies in the 1960s, Elkins's conclusions were challenged, as one might expect, by later researchers who found its portrait of slaves too simplistic and reductive. For example, John W. Blassingame's *Slave Community: Plantation Life in the Antebellum South* showed how slaves carved out for themselves a remarkably independent culture that resisted the very forces of infantilization that Elkins discussed. Yet Blassingame borrowed Elkins's method: an imaginative reconstruction of the psychological experience of a people based on what evidence he had at hand (largely slave narratives). Speculative though it is, without this kind of judicious analysis, our notions of historical causation are clothed only in what scraps of text the whimsy of chance happens to preserve. The full warp and weave, the real substance of history, is lost, worm-eaten, or dissolved by the mildew of time.

A "thousand times over," Elkins and McKitrick concluded, isolated settlements on these frontiers thrust ordinary men with no training or experience into roles of public trust and responsibility.[3] Curiously, Elkins and McKitrick never looked at the first frontier, England's adventure in Virginia, although surely the model applies: a more or less homogenous community removed to a place of near-total isolation, a failure of leadership, trouble times, and the mortal need for ordinary people to exercise self-determination.

Admiral Somers might not have thought that Gates's regime was a total failure of leadership. Nevertheless, when it was clear to him that rescue was not coming from Jamestown, he decided to take matters into his own hands. Somers abandoned the camp near Gates' Bay and established his own on another island. There he would begin construction on a second, smaller pinnace at his own "building bay." Although Strachey's narrative admits the autonomy of Somers' group of castaways, it insists on the governor's primacy. Gates "granted" to Somers "all things suitable to his desire and to the furthering of the work." Gates sent twenty of "the ablest and stoutest of the company" along with the appropriate "tools and instruments" to Somers's new camp. The men most skilled in hewing and squaring timber went as well, along with two carpenters, marching down to the southwest end of St. George's Island and ferrying themselves across a narrow channel of quiet waters to the northern tip of what the admiral, who had mapped the archipelago, was now calling the "main" island. So Strachey tells the story.[4]

But Strachey deliberately obscured the rift between Somers and Gates, always downplaying the limits of the governor's command, emphasizing—really overemphasizing—Somers's willingness to play the role of subordinate. No matter what spin Strachey put on the situation, Somers's removal from St. George's Island demonstrates how completely separate their commands were. Jourdain, for example, speaks of "Sir Thomas Gates' men" and "Sir George Somers' men" as distinct groups of people. Gates ruled on one island, while Somers commanded another. Significantly, Somers put about half a mile of water between himself and the governor. There would be no spying and no meddling or intimidation by the governor's corps du guard. (No archaeologist has ever found the location of Somers's camp, but most experts guess it was near the present location of Grotto Bay, now the site of a posh beach resort.) The stout and able men whom Gates theoretically dispatched to Somers's building bay were probably seamen who had already demonstrated their contempt for Gates's authority and abhorred the labor camp, ruled as it was by the muster bell morning and night.

The mentality of the sailors must have been different even from those settlers who had developed second thoughts about the whole adventure. The sailors had expected to be back in England by this time. If there had been no hurricane, they already would have dropped off the settlers and returned to Plymouth or London, their pockets full of pay. They should be sitting before a snug fire in their own homes and enjoying the profits from the Indian furs they had procured on Virginia's black market. Here they were, five months into the expedition, stranded and subject to the tyrannical orders of a soldier. Even allowing for the interventions of Atlantic mischance and misfortune, no seaman ever imagined he could be "duly punished" for failing to pray with enthusiasm enough to please the Reverend Bucke or for giving a smart answer back to one of Governor Gates's appointed lieutenants. No sailor ever suspected he could be treated like a mere settler. The admiral's camp on the Main Island restored something closer to what a sailor might expect after a shipwreck. They lived under maritime custom, glad to be bossed around by no one but their own admiral.[5]

The sailors' relocation to the Main Island was bound to affect the psychology of the other castaways, who still suffered the morning and evening bells, who still worked like slaves for the Company, who ate in messes like soldiers and were counted each morning and evening like prisoners. They were discouraged when Gates marooned Want, Carter, Pearepoint, Brian, Martin, and Knowles. They might have been terrorized into docility, but their reasons for complaint did not go away. Within this atmosphere of disillusionment and dissension on the frontier, democracy presented itself to the mind of Stephen Hopkins.

Like Elkins and McKitrick, we have to speculate a fair bit to reconstruct the perspective of the common settlers, because both of the eyewitness narratives were written by elites who served the interests of the Company. Jourdain's brief *Discovery of the Bermudas* never even mentions dissension among the castaways. The Company "allowed his narrative to be printed" in 1610 because it

The title page of Samuel Purchas's *Hakluytus Posthumus, or Purchas his Pilgrimes*, the 1625 volume that first published Strachey's *True Reportory*. Sir Francis Drake is pictured in the right-hand column, the middle of the second row from the bottom.

was good advertising. Had it frankly discussed what really happened on the Third Supply, it never would have made it into print.[6] By contrast, Strachey's *True Reportory* circulated only in manuscript until its first printing more than a dozen years later. Such narrow distribution allowed him to include a wealth of unsavory details that informed England's elites without alarming the public imagination. Everything we know about the several challenges to Gates's authority all come from the *True Reportory*, the purpose of which was to praise Gates, disparage those who opposed him, and demonstrate the need for despotic government. Strachey thought despotism was the proper response to the ungovernable tendencies of most commoners. Historians who attempt to see these events through the eyes of the common settler, let alone sympathize with their point of view, is forced to rely on the details Strachey chose to preserve, and they must strip away any coloring we can attribute to the author's hostility.

In Strachey's hands, for example, events in Bermuda unfold as a series of morality tales about the "devilish disquiets" exhibited by the "major part of the common sort" and a few weak-minded men from the "better sort." Strachey concedes the "adamantive power" of Hopkins's oratory. But he attributes this to an abuse of scripture and the receptivity of his audience. The shipwreck, Strachey mused, induced the commoners to indulge their natural tendencies toward "idleness" and the "fullness of sensuality." To succumb to such temptations was in the nature of commoners, just as the mark of the gentleman's civility was his power of forbearance, his ability to resist the savage impulse to grab at pleasures. In early seventeenth-century literature, the sensual acts that made people like Strachey very nervous were sex and drink. Debauchery in either dissipated the body and spirit. Some Renaissance sages thought that the effulgence of semen leaked the finite store of one's vigor. Shakespeare, for instance, suggested in his Sonnet 129 that "lust in action" was an "expense of spirit in a waste of shame." The Bard borrowed from an aphorism popular in the day: that one's sovereignty over the self seeps away with each ejaculation, like coins trickling from a spendthrift's purse.[7]

This logic is circular: the "common sort" are prone to sensuality because they lack self-sovereignty. They cannot control their savage instincts. If society allowed them to make their own decisions, they would self-indulge till they self-destruct. The widespread sexual diseases in the seventeenth century as well as the manifest dangers of abusing alcohol—the toothless, listless, homeless drunks haunting the streets of London—bore out such prejudices. Profligacy in sex and drink were almost inevitably self-destructive, and so commoners must be governed by their betters, who will impose discipline.

Bermuda did not offer much opportunity for the effulgence of semen. No naked painted women danced in the flickering light and shadow of a campfire, crooning, "Love you not me?" Unless settlers masturbated with profligacy or enjoyed the "unnatural" sexual acts they called sodomy, it is difficult to credit Strachey's accusation of "sensuality." He seems to use that charge out of mere habit. Nor could the castaways get drunk. Whatever kegs of aqua vitae were salvaged from the *Sea Venture* were kept under guard by Gates. Strachey's accusation of sensuality derive from the prejudices of class. In the ordered shelves of the rich man's mind, London's laborers occupied a box not too far from America's Indians. Accusing the "common sort" of sensuality was saying little more than that, like "savages," they acted according to their nature.

Strachey's accusation of idleness is even harder to credit. Mere survival takes a lot of hard work, even in a place like Bermuda. Hopkins and his coconspirators were not seeking a life of luxuriant leisure. Not even Strachey, who knew firsthand how much labor the primitive life required, could have believed as much. What accounts for the ubiquity of this charge? In Strachey's *True Reportory*, as in so many of the other Jamestown narratives, all written by Company men, being "idle" meant refusing to do the work that the Company told the settlers to do. Idlers resist orders. It was not that they did no work; the problem was that the work they performed did not profit the Company.

"Idleness" and "sensuality," then, were not about profligacy and laziness. They were about sovereignty. They were political crimes, because they usurped the government's authority—in this case, the Company's authority—over the settler's body. Any attempt to evade this authority, to usurp the power of command for themselves, demonstrated their depravity. And so "consent" was a dirty word to Strachey. If the poor settlers had been allowed to choose their governors, nothing would ever have gotten done. No industry at all. Society would have dissolved. Everyone would have become savage and starved. They would have died in Bermuda, Strachey's narrative asserts, had the expedition not been blessed with a "governor" willing to exercise the "authority" needed to "suppress" the will of the majority.

Stephen Hopkins struts upon the stage for fewer than six hundred words in the *True Reportory*, which gives Strachey enough space to make him out as a villain. But laced into his villainy are several details that, examined from a different angle, turn him into a tragic hero. For instance, Strachey admits that this farmer-cum-psalterer had an "adamantive power" to recruit people to his conspiracy. Strachey attributes this skill to sophistry and the weak wills of his audience. But in making his case, Strachey actually records the outlines of Hopkins' reasoning and perhaps even some of his exact words. Brief and prejudiced as the account is, the story of Hopkins's mutiny is by far the clearest window we have into the perspective of the common settlers, their disillusionment with the Company, and their aspirations for self-determination.[8] That story almost perfectly exhibits the pattern of Elkins and McKitrick's trouble times on the frontier.

Strachey says that Hopkins's plans were exposed on January 24, 1610, but we know that the conspiracy had been developing for some time before then. Indirectly, it began in early autumn, when Governor Gates marooned the first six conspirators. Gates meant to terrorize anyone who hoped to avoid transportation to Virginia by escaping into the woods. While the punishment of these six men succeeded in suppressing open defiance, it also must have broadened "disquiet" with the regime. The sailors' escape to the Main Island removed dozens of those disgruntled castaways from Gates's camp, which must have increased the proportion of Company loyalists. But the example of Somers's rival camp revived hopes for escape.

Perhaps what is most remarkable about Stephen Hopkins is how very unremarkable he was. He seems to have been a fairly typical commoner, a bit better educated than most, clearly endowed with a keen intelligence, but no Oxford graduate, no fellow at the Inns of Court. He was a husband and father and farmer who did not own his own lands. He had fallen on hard times. He must have had more than usual courage to risk the voyage to Virginia, however promising it seemed. Yet, all in all, his life in England was unremarkable. Bermuda transformed him. A remarkable confluence of events gave him an advantage that all the scholars and statesmen and political theorists of the English Renaissance could not equal. He had embarked on this voyage under a literal contract, in which he surrendered several liberties to obtain several benefits from the Virginia Company. He had suffered the horrible storm. Just when he thought all was lost and that he would drown, the ship had wrecked on a reef. He went through the psychological trials of shipwreck and immersion. He stumbled ashore, waterlogged and dazed, on a second Eden. And then he suffered the misgovernment of a tyrant. He watched the first attempts at salvage, and he disapproved. All of these experiences helped him to formulate a theory of natural law that would become the basis of modern democratic governments.

Sometime between the removal of the sailors in November and the exposure of his plans at the end of January, Hopkins's theory was propelled into active conspiracy. The trigger might have come in early January, when the days were shorter and the shadows longer. Bermuda could not quite be described as cold, not like an English winter, but when the winds came out of the north or northwest, as they often did, cold air blew, hail pelted the island, and even the quiet waters fronting Furbusher's building bay bestirred themselves. On the second day in January, a storm sent the surf high up on the beach and foaming round the half-built pinnace. Much of the vessel's frame had been joined, but the joints themselves were not yet reinforced, and the whole structure leaned on a wooden scaffold. The waves swirled round the braces holding up the boat's capacious rib cage. The workers must have been knee-deep or even waist-deep in the foam, scrambling to shore up these supports. Gates and the minority who shared his hopes were lucky that the waves did not wreck the whole thing. Unlucky for everyone else, who wanted to stay in Bermuda. In the following days, those reluctant workers were forced to bend their backs to a new task: hauling stone from the hills down to the building bay to lay down a breakwater, peaked like the prow of a ship, to protect the boat from other storms. This miserable hard labor rankled and annoyed.[9]

Stephen Hopkins began whispering to his fellow travelers. It was true that each of the settlers had signed a contract with the Company, which committed them to live and labor in Virginia for a period of years. The Company had undertaken to transport them across the ocean, feed, clothe, and house them. One contemporary estimate, rough as it might be, put the value of each settler's transportation to Virginia and their clothes and tools and food at twenty pounds.[10] The Company, essentially, promised to deliver to each settler goods and services equal to that value. At the end of the contracted period, each man would be given his proportional share of the Company's profits as well as a generous grant of acreage in the New World—far more land than any of commoners could ever expect to own in England. The people listening to Hopkins were familiar with such schemes. The Virginia plan did not sound all that different from plantations in Ireland, in which an eminent individual—usually some earl or knight—organized people to settle on territory confiscated from the native Irish. The organizer would provide transportation across the Irish Sea and initial provisions, while settlers promised to populate his town or settle on farms in his land grant. It was a migration process that denuded portions of Ireland of natives and Anglicized the townlands with English yeoman farmers.

Judging by their disenchantment, the settlers in the Third Supply expected their plantation in Virginia to follow this pattern. They knew that there would be a governor and that for the first year Gates was the man assigned to that office. They knew that they would owe him a certain obedience. But they also expected that there would be farms and villages, and although life would be hard and labor would be communal, especially at first, as they cleared forests and raised buildings, the settlers expected to be treated as English citizens. Perhaps they expected even more rights than settlers in Ireland, since in this plantation they were part owners in the whole enterprise. They themselves held shares in the very company that was organizing the enterprise.

What was happening in Bermuda bore no relation at all to what they had expected when they adventured their lives. Gates was operating a slave labor camp in Bermuda, which was a good indication of what they would find once they were transported to Virginia. "Their whole life" at Jamestown, Hopkins told people, would be nothing more than "travails and labors" that "serve the turns" of the investors back in London. They would be virtual slaves for the Company. With very good reason, the common settlers became convinced that Gates would work them to death.[11] Trouble times indeed. Cast by calamity into isolation, cut off from rescue, failed by their leaders, Hopkins was convinced (as Elkins and McKitrick would have put it) that he and those he spoke with had the "personal competence" to determine for themselves what to do.

Hopkins's adamantine oratory inspired others with the same belief. As Gates forced the settlers to construct a stone breakwater in Furbusher's building bay, Hopkins preached his gospel of freedom, using "arguments both civil and divine." "God's providence," Hopkins reasoned, gave the settlers "all manner of good food" right there in Bermuda. Why scorn that gift? Moreover, the Company had breached its civil contract, he explained. It was supposed to deliver the settlers safely to Virginia, but the shipwreck had intervened. No one's conscience need be troubled by refusing to bow to the governor's authority. The shipwreck had "freed" each castaway "from the government of any man." Even the "meanest" or poorest laborer among them was bound only by the natural law of self-preservation, which compelled him to "provide for himself and his own family." It was his right and responsibility.

This condition of political detachment, wholly different from the experience of Europeans, depended on the wilderness. Had they wrecked, for instance, somewhere on Britain's coast, their obligations to the Company might have dissolved, but they would have still found themselves under the normal English civil authorities. Likewise, had they been castaways in a Spanish territory in the New World, they would have been obligated to the laws of that place. Hopkins's notion of freedom depended on the desert island, untrammeled even by "savages." Before the shipwreck, the entire Bermuda archipelago was, to borrow Strachey's vocabulary, the "woods," a place outside the law. Gates had no authority there. His authority over the settlers, Hopkins reasoned "ceased when the wrack was committed" and they came ashore. In fact, no one had any authority on these desolate islands, and no man needed to bend to another "except it so pleased themselves." In other words, the settlers were free to light out into the woods and live off God's providence, or they could stay in Gates's camp by the beach under Company law, or they could enter into any other contract that pleased them, a new association that would derive its authority from the freely given consent of its members. And that was what Hopkins proposed they do. Like Namontack and Machumps, like Somers and his sailors, he and his confederates would opt out. They would escape Gates's camp and construct their own settlement on a third island. They felt that was what they had to do to provide for themselves and their families.[12]

Strachey's narrative does not go so far as to describe what society would look like in Hopkins's camp, but we can speculate with reasonable assurance, because consent was the foundation of Hopkins's logic. Government would come into existence as a contract between free people, deriving its authority from the consent of those who joined it. It was a reconception of the relation between the individual and government that the Old World imagined only as outlawry. Rude, thatched huts would keep the rain off their heads. They would hunt swine, fish, or feast on cahow and cahow eggs. If they ever grew "weary of the place," they might choose to do for themselves what Gates was now forcing them to do: "build a small bark." Hopkins persuaded at least one carpenter, Nicholas Bennit, to join the conspiracy, and his skills would give them that option. But if they built their own boat, they would do it in a different spirit than they worked on Gates's pinnace. They would lean into the hard, backbreaking labor in a spirit of mutual consent. And Hopkins promised that they would never sail to Virginia, for the "commander thereof" would take them and their families prisoner and put them to work for the Company. Decisions would be made by mutual consent. Democracy, as Elkins and McKitrick hypothesized, would bloom as a "brutal necessity" of survival.[13]

BROKEN CONTRACTS

Hopkins was before his time. It would be another fifteen years before Hugo Grotius posited the idea that man has a natural right to self-preservation. Thomas Hobbes's *Leviathan* (1651); John Locke's *Two Treatises of Government* (1689); and Jean-Jacques Rousseau's *Discourse upon the Origin and Foundation of Inequality Among Mankind* (1755) and *The Social Contract* (1762) all developed the notion that citizens have the right of self-determination. Their reasoning depended on descriptions of humanity in the "state of nature," a time before societies were developed. Hobbes's described pre-civil condition this way:

> Men live without other security, than what their own strength, and their own invention shall furnish them withal. In such condition, there is no place for Industry; because the fruit thereof is uncertain; and consequently no Culture of the Earth; no Navigation, nor use of the commodities that may be imported by Sea; no commodious Building; no Instruments of moving, and removing such things as require much force; no Knowledge of the face of the Earth; no account of Time; no Arts; no Letters; no Society; and which is worst of all, continuall feare, and danger of violent death; And the life of man, solitary, poore, nasty, brutish, and short.[14]

Locke and Rousseau imagined that pre-civil life was not so grim as Hobbes's perpetual "warre," and consequently their ideas about the social contract are more democratic. But no matter its terms, the very notion of a "social contract" depends on imagining what life was like in the state of nature, before civil society. It is well known (if not well appreciated) that Europeans could only imagine such a state after they beheld America. Again from Hobbes:

It may peradventure be thought, there was never such a time, nor condition of warre as this; and I believe it was never generally so, over all the world: but there are many places where they live so now. For the savage people in many places of America, except the government of small Families, the concord whereof dependeth on naturall lust, have no government at all; and live at this day in this brutish manner . . . [15]

John Locke thought about natives and the American wilderness a lot more than Hobbes did. His library was full of firsthand accounts of the Native Americans, and he, too, drew upon these to develop his notions of private property and civil society.[16] Europeans could hardly even think that civil society *had* an origin until the New World stirred their sluggish minds.

This apparent window into the state of nature was a happy mistake, based as it was on false portraits of Native Americans. Indians might have lived in a society far more egalitarian than Europeans. As we have seen, for example, even a man as exalted as Wahunsonacock spent most of his time doing the same things that every other man in Tsenacomoco did. He hunted like them. He ate the same food they ate. He even made his own shoes. But native society was far more complex than anything Hobbes and Locke meant by the state of nature. Every Indian child was born into a polity that extended over hundreds, sometimes thousands of others. Growing up on the Chesapeake in 1600 meant bending oneself to a role already defined by that society, linking one's thread to a web of relations and structures of power. The Tsenacomocoan had no more choice in the matter than the European. Tsenacomoco was already a "civil" society when the English arrived, no matter the ignorance of many European philosophers. Nor can we point to other Native Americans with societies less extensive and complex than Tsenacomoco and say: There men lived in the state of nature. Anthropologists long ago

exploded the notion that human beings *ever* lived in the kind of preso-
cial condition on which the social contract theory is based.

But maroons did. Castaways on desert islands lived out that theo-
retical epoch before there were social contracts, when individuals
were profoundly and dangerously free. The shock of shipwreck cuts
through the preexisting webs of relations. In the case of the *Sea
Venture*, that was particularly evident because the preexisting web was
defined, literally, in a contract. Bermudan castaways had bound themselves to a government, just as the Virginia Company bound itself to
them. But the salty brine of a Bermuda lagoon dissolved the paper on
which that contract was written. Weary, bewildered, amazed even to
be alive in this Eden, with the salt water still streaming off their
clothes, the survivors did not at first understand the opportunities.
They came to a consciousness of their freedom only slowly. But come
to it they did.

Each and every adult male, Stephen Hopkins explained in secret,
conspiratorial sessions, enjoyed a freedom more absolute than anyone
experienced anywhere else on earth. Just beyond the light of their
campfires was land that no man ruled. It was a wilderness never before
occupied by human beings, not even by "savages." There was no
industry, no farming or culture of the land. No commodities would
come over the sea. There would be no writing, no art, no society at all,
unless they formed it themselves. If they fled to that wilderness, at
first they would live in houses that by civilized standards were rough,
crude, provisional, not "commodious," to borrow Hobbes's language.

Locke barely describes pre-civil man at all in his *Second Treatise*,
other than his crucial point that private property does not exist in the
state of nature. Rousseau spends pages and pages detailing what
human beings were like in the state of nature: they had reason but did
not yet use it. To Rousseau's way of thinking, maroons are a few stages
removed from this hyper-primitive state.[17] But in all of these thinkers
the crucial point is that in nature men do not have government.

Government is created when men begin to cooperate. They enter into agreement with each other, sacrificing some liberties to secure benefits that they cannot obtain in the natural state of isolation. Some might choose to live as the hermit, alone in some isolated glade. But others collaborate—help each other erect shelters, for instance, and hunt. Once the pig is tracked down and killed, the hunters must divide its carcass. Each cannot take the choicest part for himself and his family. They must consent to be governed by some rules. They choose to entangle themselves in new obligations, a web of their own design and construction and freely joined.

It is an incredible misfortune that Strachey did not devote more time to anatomizing his villain's logic. But from this record, brief as it is, we can detect the ideas on which Jefferson erected American independence, especially about tyranny and the rights to life and liberty. Governor Gates had no right to roust the settlers at dawn to muster for a roll call. He had no right to organize them into work gangs and bid them do his will. No right to force them to work on the ship when they wanted to wander the woods or linger at the water's edge fishing or even lounge in the shade of their crude huts in the heat of the day. He had no right to count them at nightfall and whip those who were not there to toe the line. Gates ruled in Bermuda only by virtue of sword and gun and the hangman's noose. If the settlers had but the courage and audacity to escape to their own island, they might regain their natural freedom.

Hopkins planted these ideas like seeds into minds made fertile by the same experiences of being shipwrecked and lost. The roots of his subversive network spread wide underground. The plot to escape was well advanced, nearly ready to burst from beneath this nourishing soil, shoots seeking the light of day. But it seems almost inevitable that by reaching out to include all who might sympathize and all who might benefit, such egalitarian schemes reach too far. John Want had overreached months earlier. Hopkins overreached in January.

On the twenty-second of that month, armed guards seized Hopkins without warning and chained him in irons. The hated bell was rung. The other settlers must have been puzzled, for it was neither the morning nor the evening muster time, but they knew something horrible was to take place when they were herded into urgent assembly. Whether they wanted to or not, the settlers were forced to gather where Gates waited for them like a prison warden. His corps du guard hustled Hopkins into the open where the entire camp could see him, dragged down by his irons, looking, assuredly, like a miserable and frightened man. The settlers were just as frightened. Most of them knew the ideas that Hopkins had been spreading and his plan to escape the dreadful camp. Hopkins had had the courage to encourage them, and they had looked on him with hope. Most were in sympathy with his plans. Many had been ready to follow him into the wilderness. And here was their leader, denuded of his dignity, frightened and alone, crumbled before the power of Governor Gates.

Across the waters at the cove where Somers and his camp were building their pinnace—where the carpenter, Nicholas Bennit, worked alongside the willing sailors—no one had yet heard about the arrest. Too far to hear the summons from the bell, they went on with their work. Nor did the wilderness notice. The waters of the bay, quiet or ruffled by the wind, didn't care. The fish went on swimming in their shoals. On the islets in the bays, the cahows slept in their ground burrows, oblivious, not caring about justice or injustice. The day birds sang as they always sang, in the lush shade of the forests. The tall, stately cedars stood high above the melancholy affair, majestic, silent, as they had stood for thousands of years. They did not look down at the affairs of men. The long umbrella leaves of the palmettos cast generous cooling shadows, as they always had, indifferent to right and wrong.

The corps du guard, a cadre of armed men, kept order among the human beings while Governor Gates formally accused Hopkins of mutiny and rebellion. Hopkins denied the charge. But when two men, Samuel Sharpe and Humfrey Reede, were called forward, Hopkins knew he had been betrayed. He had taken these two into his confidence. He had explained his ideas of personal sovereignty and confided his plans for moving to a third island. Perhaps the three men talked up in the hills overlooking the little building bay, where the men cut stone for the causeway and the surveillance of guards would have been thin. Maybe they whispered under the dark of night, long after the evening muster, with the sounds of cicadas droning in the background. Hopkins sounded them out as he had sounded so many before. Sharpe and Reede listened intently but with growing concern. They were unpersuaded, but they concealed their disapproval, and when the interview concluded, each went their separate ways, Hopkins still cultivating recruits, and Sharpe and Reede turning this intelligence to advantage. They "discovered" or revealed Hopkins's plans to the governor. They explained to him the arguments that Hopkins was using to win the settlers to his side. And now, before the gathered camp, they recited the arguments that Hopkins had made.

Denial was useless. Hopkins saw the faces around him, the condemning eyes of Gates's loyalists and the frightened eyes of his own followers. He was frightened. The shackles, the armed guards, the governor's merciless expression, the sure knowledge of his fate, hacked at his confidence like an ax at a tree. He no longer looked like a leader of men. As Gates continued his interrogation of the prisoner, at least six of the settlers, John Want, Christopher Carter, Francis Pearepoint, William Brian, William Martin, and Richard Knowles, must have been especially worried, for they had been condemned as mutineers before, and Gates only pardoned them when they assured him that their hearts had reformed. Others would have stood dumbstruck and frightened as well. If planning to slip off to another island was mutiny and rebellion, might not they themselves be found out and condemned? All it took was a vague admission from Hopkins—I spoke with so-and-so—and Gates would throw them in shackles too.

Hopkins kept quiet. Such was the extent of his heroism. He named no one. But in truth, Gates did not want to expose the true extent of the conspiracy. Far better to find a scapegoat, terrorize him, strip him of all dignity and credibility in front of his followers, and thereby demonstrate that no one but Gates ruled the castaways. To discover the true numbers of mutineers would be ruinous, unless they salvaged from the *Sea Venture* enough leg-irons and manacles to hobble dozens of people. It benefited Gates to decide that Hopkins was "both the captain and the follower of this mutiny," a happy phrase that Strachey settled upon, although the details of his own narrative contradicted it. A swift verdict and sentence, the final terrorizing blow, broke Hopkins and the adamantine power of his leadership: he was guilty of mutiny, to be paid with "the sacrifice of his life."[18]

No matter how sympathetic his erstwhile followers might have been, this sentence separated them from the condemned man. The sentence of death isolates the condemned from the living more thoroughly than death itself. Looking round at the faces of the castaways, Hopkins saw pity and contempt, sometimes mingled in the same face, but more than anything else a consciousness in those eyes that they would see the sunshine of the next day while he would not. There would be no appeal. On this island there was no authority behind or above Gates. Nothing but the magnificent, ancient trees, which looked indifferently on both the righteous and the wrong. Whatever semblance of composure Hopkins had left was knocked away, and all his feeble resistance collapsed into sobbing and moans. Nothing but abjection might save his life now. A stream of begging issued from the prisoner's mouth. He confessed his error. He regretted his folly. He pled for his life, for another chance, for the all-powerful Gates to let him live. He repented! He repented! What should become of his wife and children, widowed and orphaned? He begged mercy for their sakes. Hopkins was brought low. He repudiated his radical ideas about freedom and consent. It was the final humiliation. The man who had defiantly argued that Gates had no right of authority was reduced to a shackled heap of obedience made to beg Gates to spare his life.

The governor was satisfied. He had been as jealous as the Old Testament God, but now that his challenger subsided in such abject fashion, now that his own power was restored, absolute and inviolable, he was as complacent as a god. He might be merciful if he chose, and he chose to pardon the atoning prisoner.

All this, at least, if Strachey is to be trusted. If Hopkins was able to retain any dignity under the terrible weight of Gates's kangaroo court and his power to execute people at will, Strachey would be unlikely to preserve it in his narrative. Strachey's contempt for Hopkins and for the political theory that Hopkins espoused is so palpable that we should be wary of crediting his account of Hopkins's humiliation. Even so, we also should be wary of our own prejudices, how much we like our heroes to comport themselves with self-possession and high purpose on the scaffold of death. Nathan Hale went to the gallows defiant, the dignity of his self-sacrifice lending dignity to his cause. History would have been better satisfied had Hopkins regretted he had but one life to sacrifice to the cause of liberty. But it must be remembered that if all men stand alone on the scaffold, Nathan Hale at least could borrow courage from Washington's army ranging beyond New York. The American soldiers were not near him when he died, but Hale was cheered by their solidarity. He knew that legions shared his conviction and sense of injury, and that they would praise his memory. By contrast, Hopkins was truly alone. He was the first man to articulate his cause. He had every reason to think that the idea he had pioneered would die with him. We should not wish him to be made of braver stuff than ourselves.

He was an ordinary man in extraordinary circumstances; a man fit to lay down the foundation of democracy; the son of a middle-class farmer; perhaps the clerk of a minister; fortified, perhaps, by his intimate knowledge of the psalter and a sense of the danger Gates posed to all the settlers. He should have feared no evil though he walked in the shadow of the valley of death. But he did fear. Gates broke him. It might have been a failing, but a flaw full of tragedy.

## CHAPTER TEN

# The Kiss-My-Arse Revolution

**The departure of the charismatic** and effective John Smith in October 1609 upended Jamestown yet again. The "place of government," George Percy wrote, was suddenly "void." Power might be expected to have devolved upon Francis West, Lord De La Warr's brother, who had been elected by several of the "gentlemen" of the Third Supply to rival Smith's command. But as soon as Smith was neutralized, West's authority seems to have been swept aside. "Seeing [Smith] gone," the *General History* explains, "they persuaded Master Percy to . . . be their president." According to Percy himself, the persuaders were actually very few: just "three busy instruments" talked him into it. These could have been none other than Ratcliffe, Martin, and Archer, the "unholy triumvirate," to use Philip Barbour's term, of Smith's old rivals. Other than his name, Percy's chief qualifications seems to have been that he was malleable, ill, and weak. As a matter of fact, he accepted the office of president only if the triumvirate promised that they themselves would exercise "the chiefest offices and burthen of government." So the wheel of fortune turned round again, and those who ruled Jamestown before Smith ruled again after Smith. Wafting around this whole episode is a cloud of smoky backroom dealing: You get to enjoy the prestige of the presidency, they must have explained to Percy, and we'll do all the work. Archer, Martin, and Ratcliffe took charge.[1]

Percy's presidency violated all of Jamestown's various constitutions, and Smith's loyalists were disgusted. Their preferred leader, a man of action and courage, had resuscitated the ailing colony and molded it into a paramount chiefdom that dominated the James River. But these Machiavels nearly assassinated him, and now Smith's loyal retinue must suffer the indignity of this illegal transfer of power. By toppling Smith, the triumvirate finally dissolved the First Charter. By usurping West, they severed ties, however tenuous they had been, to the Second Charter. Ratcliffe, Archer, and Martin presented their regime as a fait accompli. Not even the "better sort" were consulted. No one consented. But once it was accomplished, a good number of Jamestown's captains, seeing now which way the wind blew, stumbled over each other to "fawn on those new commanders." Most of these captains probably were greenhorns who had arrived in the Third Supply, but they gave the triumvirate the authority they needed: superiority of arms.[2]

Without anyone having consented to the government, Jamestown descended into anarchy. Those dangerous, disgruntled men who were still loyal to Smith reported that now there were "*twenty presidents with all their appurtenances.*" Percy's legitimacy was that vaporous. His incompetence destabilized the regime even further. Percy himself "was so sick he could neither go nor stand." Men felt no compunction to follow orders that were not backed by the threat of violence.[3] English dominion over the Indians of the James River fell apart. Without Smith, it had the substance of smoke.

The triumvirate's first great blunder was to circulate rumors among the Indians that Smith was dead. Foolishly, Ratcliffe, Archer, and Martin assumed that they would inherit Smith's authority over the Indians. They expected that the tribute the James River districts paid to Smith would now be paid to Percy. The news of Smith's death had the opposite effect. Having been built in the native fashion on Smith's personal prestige, English dominion disappeared when Smith disappeared. His fall left as great a vacuum among the Indians as it did in Jamestown, and Wahunsonacock deftly stepped into the void. Almost instantly, the Indian districts all over the James realized that they had more to fear from Wahunsonacock than from anyone in Jamestown. Almost overnight these districts were restored to Tsenacomoco.

The first to suffer this shift in power was Francis West. Still stationed up at the falls, he felt the full brunt of Powhatan hostility. So many of his of men had been poached by Powhatans that West and his troops completely abandoned the outpost and headed down-river back to Jamestown. Foolishly, they did not keep to the middle of the river. They came ashore at Arsetecke, where the Indians ambushed and killed another eleven men and stole one of the boats. The remainder of the 140 men whom West had at the falls oared their way to Jamestown, beaten, harassed, hungry, tired, decimated, destitute, demoralized. They were hardly welcome. The garrison was already hungry and had little provision for these refugees. But "in charity" Percy felt he could "not deny them to participate with us."

As the harvest months slipped by, the triumvirate realized it had better secure some source of food. Back in September, Martin had been dispatched to the Nansemond district, where he and sixty well-armed men were supposed to plant an English settlement and collect tribute from the natives. As we have seen Martin routed the few Indians he found on a river island and desecrated their temples, but he could do no more than establish a temporary garrison there. He had aroused the enmity of the entire district. The Nansemonds had great piles of food in store, but Martin got none of it. And in the end Martin himself left the outpost, returning to Jamestown in what many considered a cowardly abandonment of his own men. A plot developed among the soldiers he left behind. They had seen enough and had suffered enough under the incompetence of the new regime. They were tired, hungry, and surrounded by a wilderness teeming with Nansemond Indians who were enraged by the smoldering remains of their sacred sites, desecrated and burned by the English. The discontented soldiers probably were Smith veterans, who knew that the Nansemonds had recently been a stable and quiescent client state of Jamestown. Martin's blundering violence had ruined the whole district, and they themselves were on a fool's errand trying to retrieve the loss by shaking a few ineffectual sabers at the numerous and hostile Indians. Here they were fighting their recent allies at the urging of a government they neither respected nor trusted, for a captain who lacked the courage to stand with them. If they stayed in Nansemond, they would likely die. They couldn't return to Jamestown as Martin had: they'd be hanged for desertion. But there was a third option. They could defect to the Indians. It would mean turning their backs on England for the rest of their lives, but at least they'd be alive. It was a course of action contemplated only in the most extreme of circumstances, only when the government of Jamestown proved lethal. Such was now the case. If they wanted to live, they must escape. Seventeen of the soldiers stole the expedition's boat and sailed downriver to Kecoughtan.

Jamestown never heard from them again. They disappeared from the historical record. Percy presumed that "they were served according to their deserts," that they were "cut off and slain by the savages." But that account was hope, not history. There was no evidence, then or now, that these defectors were massacred, and the Indians were not in the habit of hiding their carnage, so it is more likely they survived. If they touched at Kecoughtan, they did not stay long. It was too close to the English. Probably they pushed on farther up the Chesapeake to some district on the Potomac or beyond where Smith had established good relations. Many villages would be happy to have them, for these were skilled soldiers with better arms than the typical native possessed. By this time Wahunsonacock had a good number of English weapons, even muskets; but the villages farther north on the Rappahannock and the Potomac did not, and they would be especially eager to welcome defectors.

The soldiers who kept to their post were doomed. Few in number, led by a novice, they constituted but a feeble, jerry-rigged garrison in the middle of Nansemond territory. They had no ordnance, only small arms. Jamestown did not send aid, for Jamestown expected aid from them. Almost every day Percy expected to see a boat laden with stolen or extorted corn coming on the rising tide from Nansemond. Finally, Percy sent a search party, which trudged across the river island looking for the fort where Martin said he had left his men. They found no signs of life, no fires from their camp, nothing but silence in the long grass. Eventually they stumbled upon Lieutenant Michael Sicklemore's body. His corpse lay on the ground, stripped of all value, surrounded by the plundered bodies of every soldier who had stayed. They were each "slain, with their mouths stopped full of bread," another massacre deliberately meant to be found, an unmistakable message to the English: Thus will the Nansemonds serve anyone who tries to collect Smith's tribute.

Summer was then over. It was the harvest time, and, having failed to sow, Jamestown had no reaping. Right at this moment of distress, when the first pangs of hunger foretold a disastrous winter, a delegation of four or five Indians appeared at the gate of Jamestown. As a token of esteem, this delegation carried a supply of venison, a taste of the plenty that the Indians were enjoying, a sudden gift from Wahunsonacock. Two years earlier, at the end of their first summer, plundered by disease and dissension and beginning to starve, harassed by the Indians, Jamestown had been saved, miraculously, by Wahunsonacock. Percy, Archer, Martin, and Ratcliffe could all remember those times. Now, again, Wahunsonacock, who had so recently been harassing the fort, suddenly sent this token of relief. Just as the James River Indians had reserved their tribute for Smith alone, perhaps Wahunsonacock reserved his hostility for Nantaquod.

Perhaps, Ratcliffe reasoned, Wahunsonacock had made war on Smith, not on the English.

Wahunsonacock included in his delegation the English teenager, Thomas Savage. Savage had been living with Wahunsonacock, first at Werowocomoco and then at Orapax, for about a year and a half, since Newport's first embassy to Wahunsonacock in the spring of 1608. By the fall of 1610, Savage was fluent in Algonquian, and he demonstrated the fluidity of loyalties and identity that obtained in the "middle ground" of the Chesapeake. Savage did not consider his return to Jamestown a homecoming. He looked around at the state of the place, saw the looming hunger, the troubled looks on the faces of the settlers, and promptly told President Percy that he had to return, with the rest of the native delegation, to Orapax. Of course he was not the only European living there: many other defectors had gone there also, and Percy found nothing strange in Savage's haste to get back to his Indian town. He sent another youth, Henry Spelman, to go with him. Spelman was eager to go. The "victuals were scarce" in Jamestown, he later explained, and he knew there would be plenty of food in the Indian town.

This adventure was not Spelman's first. Just a month or two earlier, he had been at the falls when John Smith and Francis West came nearly to blows. Smith left Spelman with "Little Powhatan," Wahunsonacock's son, who was chief of the Powhatan district. Probably, Smith expected Spelman to learn the language and function, eventually, as his liaison with the subordinate district of Indians. But Spelman didn't know this. He had the feeling that Smith had "sold" him to the Indians—that he was abandoned—and he spent his first seven or eight days with the Indians lonesome and uneasy. The Powhatans were kind enough. When Spelman told Little Powhatan that he needed to return to the fort at the falls "to fetch such things," the Indians let him go. Spelman made his visit to the English and then returned, dutifully if reluctantly, to the Indians.

But he found they had decamped in his absence, so there was nothing for him to do but return to the river. Onshore, he was lucky enough to find an English ship just starting down the river to Jamestown. Spelman did not say whether this was Smith's boat, in which case he would have witnessed the flash of Smith's powder bag and his horrible burns, or if it was one of the boats that West used to evacuate his troops in his humiliating retreat from the falls. Either way, Spelman was in Jamestown when Smith was deposed and sent back to England and when the triumvirate installed Percy as president. And now the boy who had connived to evade living with Little Powhatan jumped at the chance to go with Savage to Orapax. His eagerness gives us some sense of how bad things already were in Jamestown.

Like Savage, Spelman integrated into Indian life and learned the Powhatan language and customs. And the Indians began to think of him as part of the middle ground, no longer fully English. Less than a month into his sojourn with Wahunsonacock—it must have been November by this time—the chief sent Spelman back to Jamestown as messenger: if the English "would bring their ship and some copper" to Orapax, Wahunsonacock would freight "her back with corn." Percy saw this offer as the colony's best hope for survival, and he immediately sent orders to the one remaining English outpost, the garrison at the tip of the peninsula, Point Comfort, where Ratcliffe was commander.[4] Ratcliffe launched his embassy "to procure victuals and corn by the way of commerce and trade." In retrospect, Percy blamed Ratcliffe for his rash "credulity," but in truth Percy himself was just as eager to believe that Wahunsonacock was again their friend. Now that Smith was eliminated, Ratcliffe would demonstrate that the English were returning to Captain Newport's policy of forbearance and generosity.[5]

Ratcliffe took an impressive honor guard of fifty men to Orapax. He must overwhelm the Indians with a sense of England's superiority. English technology and wealth must overawe them. Ratcliffe was pleased with his opening gambit. Wahunsonacock's son and daughter met him at the river and willingly came aboard the pinnace. We don't know who the son was. The daughter might have been Pocahontas, for she was present at the bloody sequel. One of the witnesses to this embassy was William Phettiplace, who had been one of John Smith's loyalists and was now, by necessity rather than inclination, a lieutenant under Ratcliffe. Either Phettiplace or someone else warned Ratcliffe that he should keep the two siblings on the ship as hostages. Caution must rule the day. John Smith would have handled things this way. But Ratcliffe did not want to jeopardize Wahunso-nacock's friendship with any unwarranted show of violence. He followed the chief's son and daughter ashore, and thirty of the English trailed along, the rest staying with Phettiplace on the pinnace. The landing party was greeted warmly. Wahunsonacock sent them bread and venison, which took the edge off their hunger. Ratcliffe offered a gift of beads and copper, a courteous prelude to larger trades.[6]

There are two versions of what happened next, and although they differ in particulars, they align in their broad strokes. Ratcliffe and his men tarried inland, about a mile from the river, well beyond the pinnace's cannon range. Savory scents snaked their way out of the houses in plumes of hospitable smoke. One narrative puts the English all together in one house, which Wahunsonacock visited, "slenderly accompanied" by a few warriors. The other story has Ratcliffe's men dividing into various homes by twos and threes, led, probably, by the smells of good food and the customary allures of young women. Either way, Ratcliffe thought the kind welcome promised well, and he expected that he would return to Jamestown with hundreds of bushels of food. The restoration of relations with Wahunsonacock would vindicate the coup d'état and discredit Smith's own Indian policy.

Captain Phettiplace and about twenty men waited on the ship. No word came from the Indian town, no sign at all until a flotilla of canoes approached. Phettiplace did not like the look of things. Quickly he deployed his men in a desperate defense of the ship. Sure enough, the Indians assaulted. Phettiplace beat off the first attack, but the canoes came again in another wave, and then again in yet a third. Phettiplace knew he must retire or fight to the death. He gave up hope, hoisted anchor, dropped sails, and headed out into the deeper water, where the Indians did not follow. With this respite from battle, he assessed the situation. The deck was awash in blood. Several of his men were killed. Sixteen survived. He could not press in close to shore again. But what did it matter? The attack on the ship could only mean one thing: Ratcliffe and his thirty soldiers were all lost. He brought the ship back round the peninsula, past Fort Algernon, and into the James River, riding higher in the water than when it set out.

Only when he came into Jamestown did Phettiplace learn for sure what had happened to Ratcliffe and his company of men. The second day in the village, Wahunsonacock brought the English to a great storehouse of food. To English eyes, the bounty was tremendous, and they felt their troubles were over. Ratcliffe and Wahunsonacock concluded a deal: so much copper for a "proportion of the baskets of corn." But, as Thomas Savage told the story to Henry Spelman, Wahunsonacock tried to cheat the English "by pulling or bearing up the bottom of their baskets with their hands, so that the less corn might fill them." The English took exception to the trick. "Discontentment" rose between the English and the Tsenacomocoans, the Indians pulled out their weapons, and "killed them all," except for three: Ratcliffe was spared for the time being, and William Russell and Jeffrey Shortridge escaped. Shortridge was either a frequent visitor to the York River or he had actually lived among the Indians for a time, because he was well enough "acquainted with the country" to elude capture and make it, eventually, all the way to Jamestown, hiking overland.[7] These details come from Spelman. But he knew them only secondhand, because, before Ratcliffe's arrival, Wahunsonacock had sent him and "the Dutchman," Samuel, one of Jamestown's early deserters, to a town more than twenty miles away, perhaps because he did not fully trust them. Spelman heard the story later, when Wahunsonacock's party joined them at this distant village.[8]

The distinctive feature of Spelman's version of Ratcliffe's massacre was that it included a provocation. An argument about good or bad faith in the trade escalated into a full-pitched battle, where all the odds favored the Indians. Russell and Shortridge told a more gruesome tale. The Indians connived from the very start to kill the English. Rather than keeping his men together in force, Ratcliffe let them "straggle" into the Indian houses by "two and three and small numbers." Wahunsonacock waited until the English had fully let down their guard, and then "the sly old king" sent warriors into the houses and "cut them all off." Only Ratcliffe was taken alive. He was tied to a stake in front of a fire, and the women of the town flayed him. As he stood before the fire, his muscles exposed, they tossed his flesh onto the flames. The smell of its roasting added to his death agony.[9]

Now things were truly desperate. Other than Jamestown Island itself and Fort Algernon at Point Comfort, the English held no territory. No hunting grounds were open to them, and their animals were eaten up. "Our commanders, officers, and savages," the *General History* reported, "daily consumed . . . our hogs, hens, goats, sheep, horse, or what lived." Of this dwindling supply, only "sometimes" did the common settler get to taste "some small portion" of meat. But even this store did not last long. The English kept most of their six hundred pigs on Hog Island in the James River, a water-bound pen for the animals. During Smith's regime, it was a living pantry for Jamestown. But now the colony was demoralized and depleted. More than fifty men had been killed between debacles at the falls, in Nansemond, and another thirty or so in Ratcliffe's massacre. The remnant lacked the will to defend Hog Island, and the Indians got the largest share of swine. Rations in Jamestown were reduced to "half a can of meal for a man a day."[10]

Percy still had one hope of deliverance. About this same time Ratcliffe went up the York River, Captain Francis West, Lord De La Warr's brother, sailed the *Swallow* to the distant Potomac River, where Wahunsonacock had less influence. Thirty-six men accompanied him to "trade for maize and grain." West respected the Indians' right to their own crops about as much as he respected a chicken's claim to its eggs or a pig to its own bacon. *Trade* meant take what he wanted and leave in compensation what he wanted to leave. He could not be troubled by diplomacy or any other such nonsense.

West had been gone for weeks and overdue when Captain James Davis, now commanding Ratcliffe's outpost at the peninsula's tip, saw the *Swallow* making its way round the point. "What's the news?" Davis asked. Percy, who was in Jamestown at the time, claimed that all communication went by shouts across the water, but the complexity of the exchange suggests that West came ashore and talked at length and leisure with Davis. Perhaps they ate a hearty meal of barbecued pork, for the garrison at Point Comfort was so well supplied that they were feeding their pigs the leavings from their feasts of crab and oyster. West warned Davis that no Englishmen would be welcome anytime soon on the Potomac River. Whenever the Indians resisted or hesitated to trade their food, West had imposed "harsh and cruel dealing." He had been obliged to decapitate "two of the savages." The baron's brother regaled his listeners with "other extremities" he used to torture and terrify, which Percy's narrative left to his readers' imaginations. When they learned of West's crimes, the leaders in Jamestown lamented that he had turned the Indians into their "implacable enemies." Nevertheless, West could boast that the *Swallow* was full and riding low in the water, heavy with stolen corn and grain.[11]

This was great news indeed. They were hungry in Jamestown, Davis explained to West, and he told a woeful tale illustrating the situation. The wife in one house died—whether killed or starved none could say for sure, because her husband cut the body into pieces, salted the meat, and stuffed it into various parts of his house, a secret store to draw upon as the hunger pangs demanded. But colonists discovered the husband's macabre practice. Despite the damning evidence, the man, perhaps deranged, refused to confess. So Percy had his thumbs pinioned, and then he was hoisted aloft till his feet left the ground. The prisoner was emaciated, a featherweight, so Percy had to have his ankles anchored to increase the pain on his thumbs. The man held out for fifteen minutes, but he confessed in the end, and Percy bound him to a stake and "burned him for his horrible villainy." The greasy smoke of that barbecue must have mocked the hollow ribs and the sunken, sallow stomachs of his tormentors.[12]

"Make all the speed" you can, Captain Davis told West, "to relieve" the hungry garrison. This exhortation rounded out the interview.

That was a tale to ponder.

The sailors on the *Swallow* and the soldiers who had ravaged the Potomac put their heads together to talk the matter over. If they returned to Jamestown, they would immediately be put under Percy's authority. The food they had gathered would be redistributed. They themselves would be taken off the pinnace and redistributed throughout the camp, to fall prey to all the folly and bumbling of ineffectual Percy and his cabal. That agony awaited them all. The decisive moment had come. West and his soldiers and the sailors on the *Swallow* made "a league amongst themselves." The way Percy would later tell it, West's men put the matter before him and won his consent "by persuasion." West and his fellows deliberated with enough formality to call the result a "league," a new body politic that repudiated their obligations to Jamestown. So sure they were in the propriety of their action that the *Swallow* "hois[t]ed up sails and shaped their course" not for the Caribbean and some pirate cruise but directly for England.[13]

Jamestown seethed in anger. This was "sedition." It was "treason." Winter was running toward them, and the *Swallow* had left the settlers in "extreme misery and want." There would be no rescue till Lord De La Warr's arrival in the next year, and they'd be starved by then. Now might the settlers, the rank and file of Jamestown, truly feel that they were on their own, abandoned, lost. They might not have suffered shipwreck, but they were castaways, marooned on the miserable, swampy, diseased-soaked Jamestown Island. Everyone from Percy on down to the humblest laborer must have cursed the *Swallow*'s crew with bile and venom for stealing their food and so many weapons and the colony's best boat. Cursed them and envied their escape.[14]

## HENRY PAINE

Back in Bermuda, Stephen Hopkins disappeared from the narratives. After his humiliation, Strachey does not mention him again. Jourdain never mentioned him. And his name does not appear in any of the other accounts of Virginia. Hopkins melts back into the anonymity of commoners who make their way onstage in aggregate, like a Greek chorus. He will not reappear in the historical record—in certain official documents, for instance—until he joins the Pilgrims. But if he fell into obscurity among the Bermudan castaways, his ideas did not die.

The boats in Furbusher's and Somers's building bays were racing toward completion. By February 20 the hull and decks of Gates's pinnace were in place, and all it lacked was its caulking, masts, and rigging. For days on end, cramped fingers had worried apart the fibers of "old cables" from the wreck, turning them into heaps of oakum that they would pound into the seams between the boards of the hull and the decking. A barrel of tar and a barrel of pitch, salvaged from the wreck, would caulk Gates's ship watertight.[15] The castaways kept toiling as they had for months. Morning muster, work, evening muster, rest. Meals eaten in messes. Occasionally, something punctuated the monotony of their labor. In early February the cries of a newborn child pierced the dullness. John Rolfe's wife gave birth to a baby girl, whom they named Bermuda. Rolfe was twenty-five years old when he and his wife, married about a year, boarded the *Sea Venture*. The child was conceived before the ships left England, but the mother probably did not discover she was pregnant till after she became a castaway.

In years to come, Rolfe would play a leading role in Jamestown. In 1612 he cultivated a Caribbean strain of tobacco, which set the colony's halting economy on the path to profit. In 1614, Bermuda and her mother having died, Rolfe married Pocahontas, who was then a prisoner of war. That liaison not only symbolized but precipitated a lasting peace between Tsenacomoco and Jamestown. Along with John Smith, Rolfe is sometimes cited as the "first" American. There's a certain logic to that claim. Rolfe's first son, Thomas, being of mixed blood, embodied the "middle ground" between Europe and Native America. In 1616, Rolfe wrote his own brief account of Virginia's early days, his *True Relation of the State of Virginia*—he did not mention Hopkins—and at least one historian thinks it was the first English narrative to exhibit a truly "American" tone. But that gives Rolfe too much credit. In Bermuda he did not much distinguish himself except to provide a singular example of a commoner who stayed loyal to Gates and the Company. He identified with and associated with Gates's party. He chose William Strachey to sponsor his infant child when the Revered Bucke baptized her on the eleventh of February. No one whispered plans of escape or mutiny into John Rolfe's ears. Hopkins's confederates could see plainly that his loyalties lay with the "better" sort. In fact, Rolfe faulted other commoners, whom he called "the vulgar sort," for their lack of "husbandry" and industry, and he had little regard for the self-determination that Stephen Hopkins advocated. He much preferred a "more absolute government," he explained with condescension, in which "men spent not their time idly nor improfitably."[16] To men like Rolfe, the storm and shipwreck and their immersion in the surf (to borrow Steven Mentz's metaphor) did not wash away Old World ways of thinking. The iron-bound joints of Tudor and Jacobean thought did not rust. To John Rolfe, it was virtually unthinkable that some of the castaways might decide that it profited them more to stay in Bermuda than to go to Virginia. They had no right to make such a judgment. The Second Charter defined the terms of "profit." The only way to pursue that goal was to launch the pinnaces that were nearing completion in their building bays. Any work that did not bring them closer to launch was "improfitible" labor: idle and useless.

Yet the idlers "persevered" in their resistance. The embers of dissent, though dampened, did not go out. Their glow smoldered in the long February shadows. The ship was "now in good forwardness and ready to launch in short time," Strachey wrote. They would float it within a couple of weeks, and then all that it lacked was the tackling, which they'd string up in due course. If escape was to be attempted at all, the time had come. The coals flared again. A new group of "associates" was more desperate than Hopkins had been. They would not be satisfied with merely running away. They planned to seize the Company's storehouse and take "what was therein of either of meal, cloth, cables, arms, sails, oars, or what[ever] else" they thought they needed. Not only were their obligations to the Company voided, but the Company owed them a debt, and they would exact their pay in axes, adzes, saws, mallets, and cordage. They would take guns and swords to defend themselves from the governor's own party.[17]

For the third time, rumors of mutiny, at first vague, reached Strachey and others in the corps du guard. Then, just as Sharpe and Reede had betrayed Hopkins, new informers issued forth to reveal "the whole order and every agent and actor" in the conspiracy. The informers said these were desperate men willing to become "martyrs" for the cause before they would go to Virginia. The informers denounced so many "associates," and so many of them were camped with Somers on the main island that the corps du guard could not arrest them all at once. Too many were involved. Shrewder methods were required. Gates called his men together to announce emergency measures. He suspended all communication between his island and the main island. He doubled "the sentinels and nightwarders" and told his men to wear their weapons at all times. They must bear their arms at morning's muster, while supervising work in the high afternoon, even when going to the latrine in the middle of the night. For all they knew, their "next neighbor was not to be trusted," and, as Robert Waters had proven, even a spade or hoe might crack open the skull of the unwary.[18]

This vigilance delayed the mutineers. For their plan to work, they had to surprise a thin and unwary guard at the storehouse. Only then could they could pass weapons out to the settlers. If Gates could maintain this vigilance until the boats were ready to set sail, no one would escape transport to Virginia. But the extra watches put a heavy strain on the corps du guard. Double shifts deprived them of sleep and exhausted their limbs, while the constant fear of being clubbed with a shovel strained their nerves. Pressure had been building for several days when a captain of the guard called upon one Henry Paine to take his scheduled shift on the night-warders. Although he was a gentleman himself and thus part of the soldiery, Paine did not want to sail to Virginia. His experience in Bermuda had convinced him of that folly. He was fed up with the Company and the high-handed nature of Gates's administration.

He had come to the conclusion that it was best to stay in Bermuda, either colonizing that place or waiting to return directly to England, and so he secretly allied himself with the conspirators. Hopkins's political philosophy made sense to him. He might be a man of privilege, one of England's 2 percent, but he was converted to Hopkins's idea that everyone had the right of self-determination. For some time past, Paine had been using his access to the storehouse to steal tools and arms "to make good his own bad end," as Strachey put it. On this particular evening, tension had risen to fever pitch in Paine's own mind. When his captain called him to guard duty, Paine seemed to snap. He served up a dose of "evil language," which he followed with a sound thumping. After cuffing his captain, Paine continued to scoff at the governor's double shifts and precautions. It was the first physical blow against Gates's regime, and it was effective. The captain of the guard put up no hand to stop Paine. His power resided not in the exercise but the threat of force, in the settlers' fear that the corps could and would harm them if they resisted Gates's authority. Paine was calling him out, forcing the captain of the guard to lay his cards on the table and show whether he had a winning hand or had been bluffing all along. The captain did not draw his pistol. He did not pull his blade from its scabbard. Weakly, he told Paine that he had better shape up. If the governor was informed of this insolence, Paine might well forfeit his life.

Paine's composure shattered. "A settled and bitter violence" burst like floodwaters from a breaking damn. Gates had no authority, Paine shouted, none whatsoever, over the lives of the castaways. Gates had no right to boss anyone. Even the lowest born among them might refuse his orders. Torrents of foul and abusive language poured forth, rounded out with the definitive coda: "Gates can kiss my arse!"

The curse had the shocking sound of a slap across the face. Bad enough were the physical blows that Paine had inflicted on the ineffectual captain of the guard, but this oath was decisive. There would be no gainsaying this crime. Paine flouted the governor's authority and insulted his person. The governor must respond to such an affront or lose power altogether. Mutiny, twice threatened, had finally arrived. When the blow fell, it had this air of improvisation, not a carefully planned escape or frontier coup d'état but an impulse bursting out of pent-up frustration. A long-suffering Goliath, provoked beyond endurance, suddenly lashed out.

Flabbergasted, the captain of the guard did nothing. Other guardsmen witnessed the whole thing, yet they also did nothing. They did not try to arrest Paine, nor did any of them turn informer, tattling to Governor Gates. But others also saw, and they spread word of Paine's defiance through the camp. Fear of the governor and his corps du guard seemed to deflate, punctured by Paine's sharp wit. All through the night rumor lionized Henry Paine. But rumor did not rally. Paine himself seemed satisfied, as if his refusal of a direct order and his rash insult were enough to topple a regime. If everyone simply ignored Gates, his "mutiny" seemed to imply, they would reveal the governor's impotence. Paine called no one to take up the arms they had stolen or their shovels and bludgeons, and no one else seized this moment to lead the majority against a dejected minority. The camp was electrified, but without a leader to tap and direct that energy, nothing happened.

Day came. The irresistible tale—Henry Paine told the Governor to kiss his arse!—spread to Gates himself. Gates fully understood the basis of his power. "So notorious a boldness and impudency," he knew, must be checked before its logical "issue" might arise. A general mutiny would defeat him. A few guardsmen might stand by him—might be loyal enough to actually cut down their fellow castaways with swords and musket balls—but if it came to a confrontation with a determined company of mutineers, physical force might not prevail. His power largely rested in the faith people had in his authority. They were watching to see what he would do. He sent his guard to seize Paine. Paine did not try to hide. He had not flown to the woods. He suffered himself to be brought before the governor, and the whole camp again gathered as it had for Hopkins's trial, only this time they came of their own accord.

The captain of the watch who had suffered Paine's cuffing was made to tell the tale. Other members of the corps du guard corroborated his testimony. Paine's words were repeated publicly, only this time as an accusation of his crime. Paine denied nothing. He might have repeated to the governor's face and before the whole assembly what he had said the night before: that even the lowest settler could ignore the Company's authority; that Gates could kiss his arse. Probably he did not, because in this court the accused had no right to speak. He had that right in England, but under the Company's law a man had no more right than what Gates gave him, and Gates's one goal was to prove that his authority was absolute. With "the eyes of the whole colony fixed upon him," he ordered that Paine to be "instantly hanged."

The ladder was brought forth.

When Paine, finally, was allowed to speak, he did not break down, as Stephen Hopkins had. He asked that, as a gentleman, he might be executed by firing squad rather than suffer the indignity of being hanged.

"Towards the evening," Strachey reported, "he had his desire, the sun and his life setting together."

Henry Paine was the first man to die for the human rights declared by Congress in 1776. He could not have articulated it in quite the same language, but with the benefit of Stephen Hopkins's arguments about government and consent and contracts, Paine understood that "when a long train of abuses and usurpations, pursuing invariably the same Object evinces a design to reduce [people] under absolute Despotism, it is their right, it is their duty, to throw off such Government." Henry Paine's fury was undirected and self-destructive.

Yet he answered the highest civic duty in a democracy. The gunshots echoed over the tranquil waters of Gates his Bay, but went no farther. Bermuda was cut off from the outside world. When Strachey told England about Henry Paine, he made him into another villain. Paine's death encouraged no one, as Nathan Hale's would a century and a half later. No one would hear about Henry Paine's rage or the outrage of his swift death, except as the news eventually trickled out, dressed in the guise given by his worst enemy.

## A NEW SOCIAL CONTRACT

But the guns' echo sent a shock wave through Bermuda. The sawyers in Somers' building bay stopped their work. Men leaned on the long shafts of their adzes, standing amid the chips of wood. When the news came, Nicholas Bennit, the carpenter, suspended his work, and everyone at the building bay listened. Gates lined up a squad of guardsmen, they were informed, and they shot Henry Paine to death! This was shocking news. Paine executed! All knew that Gates was capable of doing it; none doubted that the old soldier might someday impose such discipline on the settlers. There was so much disgruntlement and dissension in Bermuda, so much covert resistance, that everyone feared blood might be spilled someday. But till now, although several people had been arrested for fomenting mutiny, no one had actually been executed. Everyone, even Sir George Somers himself, was troubled by this escalation. Several men at work in Somers's building bay were themselves part of the conspiracy. In conversations with Henry Paine they had developed plans for raiding the Company's storehouse and fleeing to another island. Paine had known their names. Robert Waters, who had barely escaped a death sentence, and Christopher Carter, who had been marooned for mutiny, were both involved. Nicholas Bennit. There were many others, both sailors and settlers. For weeks Gates had had in his

possession a long list of names, but only after Paine's execution did
the conspirators realize that their plans had been discovered. If Paine
had named anyone before he died, the corps du guard might be
planning arrests even now. If ever they were to escape, they must act
now. On the Sunday following Paine's execution, probably the one
day of rest from the routine of labor, the conspirators gathered what
they could, no doubt taking all the tools and provisions they had at
hand, whatever they could carry, and "like outlaws betook them to
the wild woods."[19]

Exactly when Sir George Somers discovered that a good body of
his builders had lit out depends on how many were involved. If it was
half a dozen, they might not have been missed until Monday morning,
but if their numbers were higher, as they very likely were, he probably knew soon after they left. Some were sailors, and these surely
had to sneak out of camp. The admiral would never concede that
his sailors had a right to self-determination. But the disposition of
the settlers was more ambiguous, and while Somers clearly felt a
responsibility for their well-being, that sense of duty need not have
translated into autocracy. After all, he was sensible to their grievances against the Governor Gates. He disliked the man himself
and was happy to have relocated to his own island, putting a body of
water between himself and any problems stirred up by the governor's misrule. He understood the settlers' reluctance to trust their
lives and their families' lives to Thomas Gates. And his wide experience of the culture of the West Indies, of pirate rules, of renegades,
slaves, maroons, and masters, may have reduced in Somers's mind
any great horror at what Gates was quick to call "mutiny." In his
youth, the one-armed Captain Newport abandoned ship to escape
a tyrannical captain. Going "outlaw" in the "wild woods" was hardly
shocking to someone used to the Atlantic world. In any event,
Somers did nothing to retrieve the fugitives. In fact, he became their
advocate.

No doubt the fugitives found themselves a convenient spot to build a cluster of huts after the style they had been living in for the last eight months, framed with limbs of cedars, thatched with palmetto fronds. It must have been a defensible position or at least a spot that kept open a route of retreat should Gates try to apprehend them. They could fish. They could hunt wild hogs. But when the fugitives took stock of all the goods they had managed to carry into the woods, the tally was discouraging. They were not quite destitute—surely they had with them a few tools and personal items—but they were not much better off than castaways who swam ashore with just the clothes on their backs. No stock of food. No barrels for storage. Little if any cordage. No change of clothes. They decided to negotiate.

The maroons sketched out a petition. Strachey said they became outlaws "by mutual consent," a formulaic term that seventeenth-century writers used to denigrate the democratic nature of mutinies, as if "mutual consent" (as opposed to assuming one's subservient place in a hierarchy) were ipso facto outlawry. Formula or not, the concept of mutual consent, typically engaged by mutineers and castaways, is important, and we might presume that this petition itself invoked the concept, that it opened with some language to this effect, though probably without the eloquence of the U.S. Constitution's Preamble. More than likely, the formula would have been something prosaic: By mutual consent, we the undersigned . . . Some of these fugitives actually signed the document, an effective sort of declaration of their independence, while the illiterates affixed their signs. However pedestrian its wording, the petition demonstrates that those whom Strachey called "outlaws" had formed a community and had devised a means by which that community could make decisions.

This document, which predates the Mayflower Compact by a decade, did not survive. We know of it only through Strachey's rough and unsympathetic sketch of its outline. Yet even those few details give us wonderful insight into how the fugitives interpreted their own condition. As they were taught by Stephen Hopkins, they said that the wreck of the *Sea Venture* voided their contract with the Company. They thought they had the right to determine whether they would continue on to Virginia or stay in Bermuda. They believed that when Gates solicited their help in building a pinnace, the Company was offering a new agreement with a new set of mutual obligations. They traded their labor for Gates's promise to leave anyone who stayed in Bermuda with a generous supply out of the Company's store of salvage. Back in August, no one imagined that Gates might try to transport people to Virginia against their will, so when he began to talk about *compelling* everyone to leave Bermuda, they felt he was violating the deal to which they had consented. And when Gates forced everyone, whether they consented or not, to stay in his camp to work on the ship, the governor was wielding an absolute power over the castaways. He was acting as if the Company owned their lives and labor.

Their petition asked Gates to do no more than honor the promises he had made back in August. The settlers had kept their part of the bargain. They had helped build Furbusher's ship. Indeed, they had helped to build not one but two pinnaces. Gates and anyone who wanted to go with him could soon sail to Virginia. By all rights, then, Gates should now furnish those who wanted to stay in Bermuda with the means to flourish. Strachey mentioned only two things that the petition demanded: double sets of clothes and fifty-two weekly rations: a pound and a half of meal for each castaway. Probably there were other items: guns, shot, and powder; axes, saws, and adzes; seeds and salt.

Admiral Somers sent this remarkable document across the water to St. George's Island, enveloped in some expression of the admiral's sympathy to its requests. Perhaps Somers went so far as to acknowledge the justice of their claim. These were delivered into Governor Gates's hands. Gates replied in a lengthy, legalistic treatise, trying to persuade Somers to side not with the outlaws but with the Company. There can be little doubt this letter was penned by Strachey. By this time he was acting as Gates's secretary; he was taking notes for his *True Reportory*, our best source of information but also a propaganda piece fulsome in its praise of Strachey's new patron, the governor. No matter how poorly he attended to his studies at Gray's Inn, Strachey knew much of the law, and so he is mostly likely responsible for the byzantine legal phrases and the labyrinth of subordinate clauses. The *True Reportory* usually flows with the steady forward motion of a clear stream. It has its eddies. It digresses, for instance, on the flora of the islands. But when it comes to Gates's answer to the petition, the narrative bogs into a dismal swamp, seven hundred words overflowing the banks of one sentence, and readers are soon mired hip-deep in murky legalese, broken logic, passive constructions, with no clear channel to the other side, where the narrative finally runs downstream again. A cogent summary is nearly impossible, but it must be attempted.

It may be true, Gates told Somers, that back in August he had promised to provision those whom he left behind in Bermuda. But he made that promise when he thought he was "compelled by the tyranny of necessity" to leave some people behind; before he knew that Furbusher was "making a vessel capable and large enough to transport all our countrymen at once." If he promised to provision them out of the common store, that only proved that those he left behind still came "under his command." Though no longer under his direct supervision, those whom he was compelled to leave behind were no less his responsibility than the souls who accompanied him to Virginia. Gates did not intend to "forsake" these people "so as given up like savages" to live in the wilderness. They would not be abandoned, forgotten, and marooned, because he would "leave them all things fitting to defend them from want and wretchedness." He always meant to fetch them as soon as he could and ferry them to Virginia. He had promised them a full year's supply not because he thought that their stay in Bermuda would be permanent but because the "many hazards accompanying the sea" might prevent a speedy rescue. But now it was clear that the two pinnaces together had plenty of space to transport everyone. That fact alone obviated Gates's original "grant or consent" to the castaways. He could not in good conscience leave anyone behind now, even if they wanted to be left behind, as they apparently did. Gates said such an action would be "unanswerable." Should King James, who chartered the Company, or should the investors who paid for the voyage, ask Gates why he allowed settlers to stay behind in Bermuda, he would have no credible answer. Those investors, Gates figured, had invested twenty pounds into each worker. By reason of this debt, the labor of the settlers was an asset, and to leave anyone in Bermuda was to steal that much property from the Company. Gates's reference to king and investors alluded also to his sworn obligation to abide by the instructions that the Company's directors had given him, which said that in cases of "Rebellion and mutiny" Gates must forget about the "niceness of the law." He must exercise a "Summary and arbitrary way of Iustice" that would strike "terror" into the people.[20]

But a current in this swamp of legalese runs deeper even than the governor's and the admiral's contractual obligations to the Company. Here's how Strachey phrased it: "What an imputation and infamy it might be to both their own [Gates's and Somers's] proper reputations and honors, having each of them authority in their places to compel the adversant and irregular multitude at any time to what should be obedient and honest; which, if they should not execute, the blame would not lie upon the people (at all times wavering and insolent) but upon themselves, so weak and unworthy in their command . . ." This knotted passage needs unwinding, because it appeals not so much to their duty to king or Company but to the gentleman's sense of the right order of things. The "people," by which Gates clearly means the "common sort" of settlers and sailors, are by their nature inconstant, incapable of governing their own whims and fancies, always distracted from their proper tasks by temptations. Besides this, they are "insolent": the gentlemen must expect that commoners will resent and chafe at the discipline imposed upon them. Conflict between the better and the common sorts is part of the natural order. It is incumbent, then, upon the better sort to ignore the pleas of the people and stick unwaveringly to their right duty, which is to force the "adversant and irregular multitude" to obey. The "obstinate and precipitate many" must be made to "draw in the yoke of goodness." Though obscured by the legal language, Gates's reply unequivocally repudiated the right of self-determination. The people were as oxen who must be yoked by their betters. Somers should be ashamed, Gates told him, if he should shirk this duty. He would be the farmer yielding to the will of the plow horse. He would make himself unworthy of the honor paid to men of their station.

Gates laid out a strategy. Somers must offer no concession to the fugitives, no promise of provisions, not even the promise to be left alone. But he could grant the rebels one thing: amnesty. He should explain to the "revolted company" that if they "would at length survey their own errors," the Company would reconcile with them. "Whatsoever they had sinisterly committed or practiced against the laws of duty and honesty" would not "be imputed against them." At the same time, Gates suggested that Somers should use some "secret practice," such as bad-faith negotiation, whereby he might "apprehend" the outlaws.

Faced with Gates's intransigence, Somers did talk with the fugitives. He "did so nobly work and heartily labor" that he persuaded most of them to return to camp. More than likely, he convinced them that Gates meant business. The governor would hunt them down, and if he did not hang them to terrorize the rest of the settlers, he would carry them to Virginia in chains. All but two of the fugitives returned to Somers's building bay. Christopher Carter and Robert Waters refused to come back. Waters had been pardoned for killing Edward Samuell back in August. Carter was one those original six mutineers whom Gates had marooned back in the fall, before he pardoned them and let them back into camp. Both probably feared they would be hanged. No matter his promise of amnesty, the execution of Paine convinced them that Gates would never forgive a second offense.

Strachey's account brings Somers into a semblance of subordination to Gates by including a rumor that Somers "commanded his men" to "surprise" any renegade who failed to turn himself in. The rumor is contradicted by the facts: Somers never did hunt down Carter and Waters, even when they declined the amnesty. The *True Reportory* is so eager on this point that it trips itself up with muddled chronology and stumbles into logical incomprehensibility. If anything, it signals by way of contrast the central fact demonstrated by this episode: how thoroughly Somers and Gates were estranged from each other. The two commanders communicated indirectly, at arm's length, with the diffidence and fussiness of opposing lawyers. Their camps, situated on distinct islands, each with its own sources of food, its own building bay, its own habits of command, and, significantly, its own weapons, might as well have been rival tribes. Like two districts in Tsenacomoco, the chiefs were generally friendly but always cautious of each other. When Gates wrote to Somers, he chose his words shrewdly, like a weak paramount chief, discreetly hinting at but also soft-pedaling his superiority lest the admiral be moved to demonstrate that the governor had no real power at all on Somers's island.

These conditions lasted for two more months. Carter and Waters lived in the wild woods, like Namontack and Machumps, but the mutinies were over. From August 1609 to May 1610, four distinct episodes of resistance had developed in Bermuda, each one mounting in tension, the frustration of one contributing grievances that helped spark the next. Five episodes, if we include the sailors' move to the

A replica of the pinnace *Deliverance* in St. George's, Bermuda.

main island. A large number of the settlers, probably most of them, no longer wanted to go to the Company's plantation in Virginia. They wanted to stay in Bermuda to live there or wait for rescue and a return to their homes in England. Most of these were commoners, but some of the gentlemen also developed second thoughts about Jamestown. Meanwhile, a small group of armed gentlemen formed a corps du guard that stayed absolutely loyal to Governor Gates. This force had several functions: it guarded the Company's storehouse of food and supplies; by implicit or explicit threat, it intimidated the settlers to work on Furbusher's pinnace; it imposed the established church on people of all faiths; it discouraged renegades and put down mutinies; and, by right of physical force, it authorized Gates's law and Gates's judgments. The corps du guard won out. After the fourth mutiny failed in March, all dreams of resistance faded. The dispirited castaways resigned themselves to captivity.

Furbusher's pinnace was floated on March 30. Four great buoys made of empty casks were secured low on her hull before the causeway was breached and the spring tide was allowed to rush into the building bay. The water lifted the hull off its stocks, and by poles or ropes they eased it out into the cove. They towed it around to a better-sheltered bay to work on the rigging while the ship rode at anchor. This was no mean craft but a ship of eighty tons, "nineteen foot wide at the bream," with a tween deck four feet high, a forecastle, and in the rear an enclosed room for steering, where the whip staff would be handled. Behind that a cabin narrowed to the stern with a gallery and even little windows on either side. A gun was mounted on the forecastle "to scour the deck with small shot," Strachey wrote, "if at any time we should be boarded by the enemy." Hardly roomy, but with judicious packing of a good supply of provisions, every single settler might be stowed below the main deck, tight and dry and cramped, should they run into foul weather.[21]

At the end of April, Somers's ship, a much smaller vessel, with a beam of fifteen feet and drawing just six feet of water, joined Furbusher's. Rigging the second pinnace for its ocean voyage took another week. The provisioning took time as well, the careful stowing of all of the supplies they had salvaged from the *Sea Venture* as well as smoked pork and fish prepared on the island. Just before Gates closed down the camp where his company had lived for the last ten months, he had a "mighty cedar" lopped off at the top and its branches sheared away so that it became a stout pillar that the storm winds would not topple. This tree stood in the "middest" of "Sir George Summers' garden," that field he planted in their first month on the island. Two giant salvaged timbers unused by the new pinnaces were "screwed in[to the cedar] with strong and great trunnels" in the shape of a cross. A twelve-pence piece of silver bearing King James's image was fastened where the timbers crossed, and on either side of the tree a résumé of the wreck and redemption was "graven in copper" plates, one in English and the other in Latin. It was rather wordy. It named Gates, Somers, and Newport, numbered the "passengers and mariners," and mentioned the circumstances and date of the wreck. Strangely, it did not mention that they were sailing away in ships they had built themselves or where they were headed. If they were lost at sea, their disappearance would be as mysterious today as the loss of the Roanoke colonists.

On the tenth of May, Somers and Newport went out in the long-boats and fixed buoys to mark the safe channel between shoals and rocks. It was but sixty yards wide, too narrow to risk sailing through, and so they tried to tow the pinnaces out to the open sea. Pulling hard on the oars in the longboats, they aimed for the heart of the channel, but despite their efforts one pinnace was driven toward a buoy, and suddenly they felt a great shudder as it struck rock. Luckily, the rock or coral was so soft that it pulverized, and soon the ship was in twenty feet of water, running clean. They labored against a steady wind all that day into the next till finally, after so much time, hardship, and strife, they "got clear of the islands." According to Strachey, this was "to the no little joy of us all." It's a strange thing to claim, so clearly contradicted by the foregoing text. But Strachey's easy elision into *us* and *we*—as if the company of men and women were unanimous in their emotion; as if there were no great divide between the Company men and the ordinary settlers—is a habit historians have found hard to break. The victors get to write the history, and Strachey was the voice of the victors.

Machumps came out of the woods before the ships sailed, but he was alone. It is not so clear what happened to Namontack. The only evidence we have is John Smith's story, told much later, that Machumps killed him, chopped him up, and hid the body, a tale that most historians ignore and one discredits. Hobson Woodward, who has sifted the matter more thoroughly than anyone else, is sure only that Namontack disappeared in Bermuda. Thomas Gates, he specu-lates, suspected foul play but had no evidence to justify executing Machumps. Carter and Waters were left behind, marooned, as they had hoped to be. The two ships, then, carried between 130 and 140 people, settlers and sailors together.[22]

"When she began to swim," Strachey wrote about Furbusher's pinnace, the governor "called her the *Deliverance*." The name invoked solemnity and reverence among the Company's loyalists, who saw the ship as the instrument by which God finally delivered them from the devilish hurricane that had cast them away on Bermuda nearly a year before. But when the common settlers were brought on board under the keen watch of the corps du guard, the name was cruel irony. They did not feel that they were being rescued. They felt delivered up, as captives are to their fate. In truth, the English did not yet have a word to express what was happening to them. Not until the 1670s would the language incorporate the term, *transportation*, and not until 1717 was the practice regularized: the shipping of prisoners over the ocean to a penal colony. In the eighteenth century the typical sentence was roughly equal to the term that the Company meant to extract from the castaways when they finally made it to Jamestown: seven years. But whatever one called what was happening to those settlers, they knew it was not deliverance.

## CHAPTER ELEVEN

# *Rescue*

**The wind from Bermuda was** "sometimes fair and sometimes scarce." After only seven days they all sensed a change in the water. "Rubbish" swam by the sides of the ships. Their lead plumb found the ocean's bottom at a little more than two hundred feet. A day later and the water was barely a hundred feet deep, and on the ninth day, May 19, 1610, in the dead of night a "marvelous sweet smell from the shore" suddenly scented the water. At dawn a sailor spying from aloft cried, "Land!"

William Strachey, Thomas Gates, and the Company's loyal men felt that their rescue was accomplished. Virginia was perfumed with the "strong and pleasant" smells they associated with southern Spain. Strachey's narrative conveys the relief, gratitude, and great sense of anticipation as they approached, after so much delay and so many trials, "the famous Chesipiacke Bay." "God be ever praised for it," he thought. Their long sojourn was over, they thought. They believed they were about to step out of the eddy of oblivion back into history's stream to take up the work they had intended to undertake almost a year before. They expected to find more than five hundred English men and women settled at four locations: Jamestown Island, Point Comfort, the falls, and Nansemond. A few of Bermuda's survivors, the loyal Company men, looked keenly on the shoreline as the symbol of their redemption, and their hearts stirred with visions of their future.[1]

Most of the travelers had more complicated emotions. They had not drowned. They had survived another sea adventure. That was something. But the common folk who stood on the deck of the *Deliverance* knew they were not rescued. They were still lost. Their eyes looked on the trees of the shore, and pictures of labor and disease troubled their minds. This passage did nothing more than shift the site of their captivity. They had signed on to this adventure with visions of owning land. Now they understood that they were virtual prisoners exiled to work under threat of lash and gun. They had been dragooned against their wills to this pestilent place where they would be fed and drilled as if they were soldiers and worked as if they were slaves. The nine-day crossing from Bermuda was a sort of respite. They had little if anything to do, a vacation from their hard labor on Bermuda, a prelude before their misery resumed. Their hearts did not lighten with anticipation. Dread weighed them down.

Miles away on their right-hand side, a point on the riverbank flashed, and then a puff of smoke, and many seconds later the sound of a cannon boomed across the water. It was the garrison at Point Comfort guarding the mouth of the James River. Four bulwarks made of earth faced the mouth of the river. "Stockades and posts" were made of wood, and thirty men could handle the seven iron guns pointed at the river.[2] A few preliminary hails, and Governor Gates was invited to the fort, where he would find the current president of Jamestown. Gates climbed down into the skiff, accompanied by Strachey and, no doubt, a personal guard. They were rowing past Kecoughtan, the Indian town, when a fierce storm—one of those sudden squalls that frequent the Chesapeake—conjured itself out of the waters of the bay. They got to the fort just as rain, thunder, and lightning exploded in the air. The happy faces of the thirty or so men greeted him, as did the fort's captain, James Davis. Then came the Earl of Northumberland's brother, George Percy, the current president of the colony.

Percy had a small, neatly trimmed moustache in the middle of a melon-shaped face, and clean-shaven cheeks and chin. There was nothing sharp about him, no angles, only convex curves. The eyes were sensitive, curious, almond-shaped, and dark. They look out of his portrait as if Percy were caught by surprise, which is a strange expression to have while posing for a painter. But it matches the personality that emerges in Percy's own memoirs: a delicate, aristocratic man, bewildered by the New World's beauty and bewildered by the immense suffering of the colony under his command.[3] The man was ineffectual, unequal to circumstances, nonplussed.

The benevolence of his father, then an older brother, then a nephew, allowed Percy to live at one of the family's several grand houses, the magnificent, palatial Petworth in Sussex, not far from Southampton and the southern coast. He was a sickly child and a sickly man, "troubled . . . by epilepsy and other ailments," including some "grievous" illness. He went to Eton and Oxford, studied law at the Middle Temple in London, and tried (unsuccessfully) to live on an annuity that amounted, eventually, to a comfortable one hundred pounds a year. Whenever his health allowed it, Percy was active. In the summer of 1602, when he was twenty-two years old, he sailed on a cruise to the West Indies.[4] Ironically enough, he might have gone to Virginia in 1607 to improve his health, for he felt that the "fits" he suffered in England diminished the closer he got to the equator. His brother, the ninth earl of Northumberland, may have pushed the twenty-seven-year-old George into going to Jamestown.[5] He encouraged him with provisions, like a "jerkin and hose," twenty-four "silk points," "sweet gloves," and other items, packed them in "a littell Chest with lock and key," which the earl had delivered to Captain Newport's lodging. Newport carried them to Jamestown in the First Supply in fall 1607.[6]

Percy was a great equivocator. "Cautiously," his biographer writes, and "somewhat ambiguously" he sided with the anti-Smith faction of Archer, Martin, and Ratcliffe. Nevertheless, he was so circumspect that Smith describes him, with careful equanimity, as having "bold and resolute spirits." Percy was neither a coward nor a backstabbing conspirator. He was not as bad as Ratcliffe, for instance. Nevertheless, he was a horrible snob. In one particularly unflattering letter he pleaded with his brother to send more resources, not to relieve the hunger or deprivations of the colony, but because "my reputation," Percy wrote, compelled him "to keep a continuall and dayly Table for Gentlemen of fashion aboute me." One historian wrote that Percy held an "aristocratic contempt" for those who had no "claim to gentility." Another says that he "despised" commoners, which might exaggerate the point a bit unfairly, but in general it is true that Percy was too proud of his name.[7]

At the fort near Point Comfort, Gates listened as Percy told him about the "starving time."

### PERCY'S REGIME

After Smith's departure in October 1609, the new president Percy told Captain Tucker to "calculate and cast up our store." His tally was alarming. As Percy remembered it years later, Jamestown had enough to feed each colonist only "half a can of meal" per day. The recipients of that allowance remembered the rations being a little more generous. Their testimonial, written fourteen years later, recalled "eight ounces of meal and half a pint of peas for a day," which would have been slim but better fare had not "the one and other been moldy, rotten, full of cobwebs, and maggots, loathsome to man and not fit for beasts." The exact timing of this reckoning is unclear, but probably as early as November the colonists were on strict rations. Their hogs were stolen or slaughtered by the Indians. They had little means to fish:

few if any nets and only "one boat and a canoe." With no other food source, they might hold out for only three or four months. That would get them through the winter at least, perhaps into March. But they had no idea when Lord De La Warr and the Fourth Supply might bring relief.[8]

Francis West and the *Swallow* had absconded with the corn extorted from Indians on the Potomac. As a result, trade with the upper Chesapeake was ruined. The other pinnace—the one that William Phettiplace had managed to salvage from Ratcliffe's massacre—had presumably transported Captain Davis to Fort Algernon, where the thirty to forty soldiers garrisoned there were living well on roast pig and shellfish. Throughout the entire spring of 1610, this outpost was strangely out of communication with Jamestown.[9] The two settlements were forty miles apart but they might as well have been a thousand. The last contact we can be sure of is when Captain Davis informed Percy that Francis West had deserted in the *Swallow*. Although Percy could have found food downriver, and although he could have used the second pinnace to look for more, he did neither for months and months.[10]

In a brilliant article reconstructing the psychology of the early settlers in Jamestown, the historian Karen Ordahl Kupperman drew a convincing analogy with American prisoners in the Korean War, "who became so apathetic that they ceased to care about their bodily needs." Held by the North Koreans, these soldiers "retreated further into themselves, refused to get any exercise, and eventually lay down as if waiting to die." They were lucid and sane and seemed "willing to accept the prospect of death rather than to continue fighting a severely frustrating and depriving environment." Malnutrition, its attendant diseases and infections, as well as the psychological stresses of imprisonment combined to inflict upon many captives what the soldiers called "give-up-itis." Eugene Kincaid discussed the phenomenon in a controversial book, using that term pejoratively to censure what he considered a dangerous "softness" among Cold War Americans. Kincaid's thesis pricked other scholars into more research, and they refuted the notion that the "softness" engendered by American prosperity in the 1950s had anything to do with the phenomenon. They found similar behavior among captured soldiers in World War II and even in the American Civil War. They preferred the morally neutral terms *fatal withdrawal* and *prisoner of war syndrome*. People surrendered the very will to live, stopped caring about self-preservation, withered, and died. Jamestown's settlers were like these prisoners. Percy marveled that sometimes people "going to bed," as he imagined, in good health were "found dead the next morning."[11]

If the settlers in Jamestown suffered prisoner of war syndrome, we must ask: Who were their jailers? Most histories of Jamestown assert, not without reason, that the Tsenacomocoans laid siege to the town. The occasional ambush does demonstrate that the settlers faced some danger if they wandered outside the pen of the fort. But the image of a siege gives a false impression. There was no siege as Europeans practiced that stratagem of war. No army ringed the fort in a permanent cordon. Not a single foray of raiders probed the defenses of the fort, looking for weak places to breach the wall. Nevertheless, when Thomas Gates arrived with the *Sea Venture* castaways, sections of the palisade were down. For weeks if not months, Jamestown had no more than a skeletal defense, and apparently by mid-May even those bare bones were gone. Jamestown might have been toppled with the slightest breath of wind. If Wahunsonacock had wanted to storm the fort, kill the inhabitants, and obliterate the colony, by April he could have done so with the slightest casualties. What's more, he *knew* this. His intelligence on the English was far greater than the English intelligence on the Indians. Yet the Indians never attacked. Even in April and May, when several dozen determined Indians might have conquered the town, not a single Indian seems to have attempted to infiltrate the fort.

Nor did they surveil it from the woods with a permanent encampment of warriors. Sometimes, when the English settlers foraged in the woods, they came back with wild roots. Some people were shot down but others disappeared, melted into the wilderness, apparently escaping into Indian villages, cashing in on friendships they had already established or merely trusting to the kindness of strangers. Far from waging war, Wahunsonacock seems to have ordered the people of Tsenacomoco to leave the fort alone. The depredations reported by Percy, the occasional body riddled with arrows, suggests that Wahunsonacock left matters to Jamestown's neighbors, the Paspahegh and the Kecoughtan. They might do as they wished, absorb some settlers, kill others, discriminate among the English according to their own lights. Back in 1607, Percy wrote that the Paspaheghs had as many as a hundred warriors, which was easily enough to carry the thinly guarded walls of Jamestown. The chief of the Paspaheghs, Wowinchopunck, might have killed the settlers on his own authority, plundered the town of its tools and weapons, and burned it to the ground. That he did not explodes the notion of siege.[12]

If the Indians were not the jailers, who were? And if the Indians did not damage the fort in several attacks, what accounts for its broken defenses? Neglect and bad weather might have ruined parts of the curtain wall. But Virginia was in the midst of a drought that lasted from 1606 to 1612, so it is unlikely that sustained rains weakened the foundation of the palisade.[13] The ruination of the walls parallels the ruin of Jamestown's houses, which the settlers themselves dismantled for firewood. That the Indians did not exploit breaches in the walls suggests that they didn't make them. The most likely explanation is that people inside the fort pried loose weak spots in the palisade. The hallmark of John Smith's presidency was a vigilant and effective guard, both on the walls of the fort and the blockhouse overlooking the causeway to the mainland. Percy meant to continue that regime of control and surveillance. The jailers who imposed on the settlers a prison mentality were not besieging Indians; they were Percy and his guard. To run away to the Indians was considered mutinous and treasonous, a capital crime. But Percy could not prevent it, and the palisade became a sieve. Damaged joints in the wall were repaired "weakly and unwillingly," and they were widened surreptitiously. The fort's derelict gate and porous walls allowed people under watch to slip free.

"Many of our men," Percy admitted, "did run away unto the savages." As the settlers themselves put it, Percy's policies "forced many to flee for relief to the savage enemy." Both accounts say hunger motivated their flight. These were people who did not suffer from "give-up-itis." Faced with near-certain death inside the fort, they fled toward the only sure source of food they knew. But they also fled *from* something. One incident in particular demonstrates the enmity that settlers felt for Percy and his regime. In Percy's version of the tale, some settlers "robbed the store" of food "to satisfy their hunger." For this crime, Percy writes, "I caused them to be executed." That punishment might be forgiven by the extremity of their situation. If thieves broke into the store, everyone's ration of half a can of meal and some moldy peas would be reduced even further. But the other settlers had more sympathy than antipathy for the perpetrators. In their account, some people were "forced by famine to filch for their bellies," and so they stole from the store "2 or 3 pints of oatmeal." Percy simply reports the thieves were "executed." The people remembered how Percy killed them: one man's tongue was "thrust through" with a dagger, and then the poor soul was chained to tree, immobilized there till he starved to death. His agonies were meant for display. Even though the settlers were no strangers to the use of public humiliation—stocks, for instance, were common—they found something sinister in Percy's love of torture. Hanging people by their thumbs? Burning people alive? Daggers through tongues? The president seemed to have been motivated by more than the desire to maintain public order. He seemed to have become unhinged. The levelling of class disturbed his mind. In Virginia, men who had been footmen or carpenters or tailors assumed a freedom in their manners. Where was the deference that must be paid to the brother of an earl? The ferocity of his punishments suggest that Percy felt a deep injury, as if he personally were insulted by every act of resistance. And so he would chain a man to a tree and force his friends to watch him starve to death, force them to hear his prayers for a morsel of food, and he would prevent them from answering the pleas. By the razor edge of his sword, Percy made the settlers participate in this obscene punishment. Percy was profoundly insecure. The world he knew was gone. Virginia was an altogether different place.[14]

The old hierarchy of aristocrat and commoner was replaced by another, divided along similar lines: jailers and prisoners. The section of Smith's *General History* that deals with the starving time was written by a Smith partisan who, under Percy's regime, was among the unfavored. Each word is charged with bitterness against "these governors" who forced him to endure what was "too vile to say." Virginia, he wrote, was an abundant "paradise" that, properly managed, would have provided for everyone. Under incompetent leadership, the land provided nothing. They ate only what they had taken off the ships, and those provisions were not equally shared. Everyone might have gotten their measure of moldy peas, but the "hogs, hens, goats, sheep, horse, or what lived" went exclusively to the plates of "commanders [and] officers." Sometimes the common settlers tasted "[s]ome small proportions" of these meats, the leavings of the better sort. Otherwise the commoners had to live as best they could on "roots, herbs, acorns, walnuts, berries, now and then a little fish." Percy had been ill when he accepted the presidency. He grew stronger as the colony weakened, which tells us much about inequality in Jamestown.[15] Percy and his men ate well enough during the common settlers' famine.

One day the colony's boat "did accidentally break loose and did drive four miles down the river." The loss was important enough to Captain Martin, who ordered some men to get into Jamestown's one remaining vessel, a canoe, and paddle downriver to retrieve the lost boat. Martin was particularly disrespected by the settlers. His cowardice at Nansemond had earned general scorn. On this occasion, the settlers outright refused his order. What was the boat to them? No fish came of it. Martin remonstrated. The settlers ignored him. They were unarmed, threatened no one, and simply refused to do what he bid them to do. It was like Henry Paine's rebellion in Bermuda. Martin went to the president's house to complain, and Percy rushed out in a fury, drew his sword, and threatened to cut down any man who refused to obey their commanders. "Happy was he," Percy wrote years later, fondly recalling his own role in the affair, who "could ship himself into the canoe" before the edge of the earl's brother's sword came down on his head. Percy's narrative oozes with the smugness of the aristocrat facing down the presumptions of the common sort. He had his day. The men got into the canoe. They retrieved Martin's boat. But the incident probably represents a hundred lesser cases of passive resistance. The settlers followed the Company's orders, as they themselves would later testify, "weakly and unwillingly."[16]

Eventually, Percy's narrative explains, "all of us at James Town beg[an] to feel that sharp prick of hunger, which no man truly [can] describe but he which hath tasted the bitterness thereof." The English who had not fled to the Indians ate their horses. They ate "other beasts"—perhaps deer taken near the palisade—"as long as they lasted." They ate dogs and cats before proceeding to rats and mice. Soon these disappeared, either eaten up or eluding the weakened settlers. They looked for snakes in the woods and dug up "wild and unknown roots." Their ration of meal did not help much. A corn diet leaves one susceptible to several diseases. A niacin deficiency causes pellagra, the symptoms of which include anorexia, skin lesions, diarrhea, muscle weakness, insomnia, mental confusion, even dementia. The famous lethargy among Jamestown's settlers, their seeming inability to stir themselves to work to prevent their own starvation, might have been caused by their eating little more than corn. A lack of protein will compound the symptoms, as does scurvy, which we know the colonists suffered: "anorexia, weakness, aching in the joints and muscles." To compound the problem, Percy withheld food from those who grew too weak to work. "Being weary of life," the survivors reported bitterly years later, these outcasts "digged holes in the earth and there hid themselves till they famished." Soon they were eating their clothes: cloth for the starch and their own boots and "any other leather they could come by," boiled to squeeze from them the least bit of nutrition.[17]

And then, perhaps by March or April, there was nothing left to eat. The rats had abandoned the fort as if it were a sinking ship. The barrels that had stored meal were empty, and even the mice had no crumbs. Famine turned the faces of the settlers "ghastly and pale." They were walking ghosts, skeletons with a little flesh. It was then that they resorted to "those things that seemed incredible." They "licked up blood that had fallen from their weak fellows."[18] Finally, came the last resort of the starving. They ate each other.

For four hundred years, people have argued heatedly about cannibalism in Jamestown: the scope of the practice, the exact form it took, even whether it happened at all. Thomas Gates denied it, and the Company used his denial to contradict the rumors circulating in England as early as December 1609. The titillating story first came from the crew of the *Swallow*. To justify their own flight, the sailors retold the story they had heard from the garrison at Fort Algernon and related previously in these pages about the man who cut his wife into pieces and salted those steaks and stashed them in various parts of his house. The council subtitled their eleven-thousand-word denial "a confutation of such scandalous reports as have tended to the disgrace of so worthy an enterprise." The *Swallow* had witnessed no destitution, no desperation, in Jamestown. Why, the ship's master, the tract insists, stated that when they left the colony had in store "three months' victuals." That point was disingenuous. It must have referred to Captain Tucker's survey of supplies and his judgment that the allowance of half a can of meal per man per day would last ninety days. An honest dealing with this evidence proved rather than refuted accounts of Jamestown's hunger and desperation.

The Company insisted that the story of the wife-eating husband, which was thrilling all of England, was not what it seemed. It did happen. That was true enough. And the husband may have claimed that he chopped up his wife to "satisfy his hunger." But the council had in their hands a report from Governor Gates that denied the implications of this story. The authorities found "a good quantity of meal, oatmeal, beans, and peas" in the man's house. It was a case of insanity, not famine. Again, on the bare facts, the tract was accurate enough. When this particular case of cannibalism occurred, colonists were not yet eating clothes. But by the time that the council received Gates's version of the event, it also had in its hands reports of the horrible months: March, April, and May of 1610. Although none of the eyewitness accounts we have today—in Smith's *General History*, in the Virginia General Assembly's "Answer," and in Percy's *True Relation*—were yet written, the Company's directors *must* have heard eyewitness accounts of the starving time.[19]

These eyewitness testimonies are confusing and sometimes more suggestive than explicit, but there can be no doubt that settlers were eating people. Though Smith's *General History* is generally eager to fault Percy's regime, it is the least damning account. The "poorer

| Skull of an unidentified young woman, "Jane," exhibiting evidence of cannibalism. | Forensic reconstruction of "Jane's" face from skeletal remains. |

sort" of settler, Smith reports, dug up a dead Indian and "ate him." In Percy's account, settlers resorted to "dig[ging] up dead corpse[s] out of graves and to eat[ing] them . . ." The Virginia General Assembly's account, which is the corporate testimony of survivors of the starving time, insists that "many" people "fed on the corpse' of dead men." One settler developed such a taste for human flesh that he made a "custom" of it. Surely this was someone driven out of his wits by stress and starvation. Particularly interesting in this account is that the other colonists first tried to restrain the cannibal, and only when that proved impossible did they put him to death. A first offense, though abhorrent, was tolerated and excused.[20]

Modern archaeologists at Jamestown have confirmed the stories of cannibalism. In 2012, William M. Kelso and his team were digging in a refuse pit on the Jamestown site, unearthing the remains of butchered dogs and horses, when they came across some human teeth. Further excavation revealed a "partial human skull," and eventually about a quarter of the skeleton of a fourteen-year-old girl emerged from the rubbish heap. The strokes of a butcher's knife gouged her face, jaws, and shins. Kelso brought the remains to

Douglas Owsley, a physical anthropologist with the Smithsonian and an expert on cannibalized remains. "The clear intent," remarked Owsley, "was to remove the facial tissue and the brain for consumption." Someone prized open the girl's skull with a knife and scooped out its contents. Her tongue and cheeks were scraped from the bone. The butchering was inexpertly done, Owsley added: he saw "hesitancy" in the cuts, "trial, tentativeness and a total lack of experience." Whoever ate the girl's leg did a cleaner job.[21]

Hunger drove people into "furious, distracted mood[s]." One Hugh Price, "pinched with extreme famine," ran into the marketplace raving "that there was no God." If God existed, he cried aloud to all who would listen, "He would not suffer His creatures, whom He had made and framed, to endure those miseries . . ." Christopher Columbus had felt these same pangs of abandonment when he was cast away in Jamaica, wounded above all else by the sense that God had abandoned him. They were truly "lost." Price could not stand to stay in Jamestown any longer, so he burst out of the fort and ran into the woods. That same afternoon, "a corpulent fat" butcher also fled into the woods. Sometime later a party from the fort found them both just five yards apart, dead, the feathered ends of arrows stuck out of them at several angles. "[W]olves or other wild beasts" had torn Price apart, while the fat butcher's body was unmolested. "God's indignation," Percy claimed, "was showed upon Pryse's corpse." Here was proof positive that God was yet in Jamestown.[22]

The settlers grew to hate Percy and the whole damn Company. They thought Thomas Smythe, who had signed them up for the American adventure, was a huckster and a liar. They might have signed his contract, but he had tricked them into it. No one had understood the true terms of government. No one had signed up for the prison camp that Jamestown proved to be. One day, as they recalled, one of the horses, a mare, was butchered. That was "the happiest day that ever some of us then hoped to see," they said, not so much for

the taste of meat but because "whilst she was a-boiling" they imagined "that Sir Thomas Smith were upon her back in the kettle."[23]

By early May, all hope died. Those with the strength and courage
to run away to the Indians had long since gone. The Indians killed a
few people, but by May even the ambushes were over. The environs
were stripped of acorns, walnuts, berries, anything even remotely
edible. No one foraged anymore. That's when Percy decided to sail
downriver to the outpost, Fort Algernon. He and several able-bodied
men got into the boats. Many of those left behind had no energy left
to witness the departure or to care. They lay in their beds awaiting
death. Whoever watched must have done so with grim irony as the
boats pulled away from the shore out into the steam. They were finally
rid of their jailors, the Company's president and all his men. But
of course it was too late. The sixty or so who remained, crippled by
hunger and fatigue, turned back to the ruin that was Jamestown. In
ten days, they thought, they would all be dead.

That's when Gates and the castaways from Bermuda arrived.
Percy had just left Jamestown and had recently arrived at Fort
Algernon. To account for his abandoning the settlement, Percy
summoned up two excuses. The first was that he wanted "to understand how things were there ordered" at Fort Algernon. That he did
not already know the conditions there indicates how incredibly
negligent he was as president, especially when we consider that all
through the starving time Captain Davis and his men enjoyed a rich
diet of roast pork and shellfish. Davis himself seems to have been
remarkably incurious about the long silence from Jamestown. No
doubt he knew that the whirlpool of Jamestown's hunger would
suck in him and his men, so he avoided contact. Percy's second
reason for leaving Jamestown was "to have been revenged of the
savages" at Kecoughtan. Revenged for what, Percy did not mention,
so the urgency of that mission seems contrived. But the claim,
however dubious, further demonstrates that a two-class system

obtained: Percy still had about his person a company of soldiers fit enough to attack a populous Indian town defended by able-bodied warriors. His excuses are unconvincing. When Governor Gates and the Bermudan survivors arrived in their miraculous pinnaces, Percy claimed that he was about to bring half the population of Jamestown to Fort Algernon to be fed until they recovered their health and strength, at which time they would be swapped out for the other half. That, too, sounds like a hastily invented excuse. It's more likely that Percy had waited in Jamestown for Lord De La Warr and the Fourth Supply as long as he could, and he decamped when he and his own favorites started to starve. The captain and officers left a sinking ship in the last lifeboat. When he was sure that no one could survive, President Percy and his privileged coterie of able-bodied, well-armed soldiers left the wretched to their fate.

It is impossible to say exactly how many people died under Percy's administration. Most historians have used the rough numbers supplied by John Smith: "Within six months," the *General History* reports, "of five hundred [settlers] . . . there remained not past sixty men, women, and children (most miserable and poor creatures!)."24 James Kelso suggests that about 215 people were living in Jamestown when Francis West and the *Swallow* sailed for England. Another thirty or so served under Captain Davis at Fort Algernon. When Gates arrived from Bermuda in May, he counted about ninety people living in the two places. So we can calculate with some confidence that about 155 people were gone, a casualty rate of over 60 percent. The misery recorded in all three eyewitness accounts suggest that most of the dead starved. A few settlers were killed by Indian ambushes. Many settlers *did* go outside the fort, but most met not hostile but friendly Indians eager to trade. During the first months of the starving time, January and February, colonists were stealing swords, guns, and anything else they could find of value from the Company's stores: hatchets, scissors, and the like. They smuggled these past Percy's guards and traded with their Indian contacts. Eventually, perhaps by March, there was nothing left to trade. A number of colonists escaped the fort, hoping to exploit the relationships they had cultivated among the Indians. How many is impossible to determine. Counting those who defected from Martin's command in Nansemond, we might guess that under Percy's presidency two or three dozen English marooned themselves in the villages of Tsenacomoco. They were numerous enough to be mentioned in all three eyewitness accounts, but not so numerous as to reappear in the record of subsequent events. Like the Roanoke colonists, they stepped out of the visible, historical record, swallowed by the woods. They disappeared in the middle ground, and within a generation the outlines of their previous existence faded except, perhaps, traced in the fair hair or light eyes of an Indian child.[25]

But we should not forget them. Their rebellion, such as it was, might not have amounted to much of a political act. Probably it was a simple calculation of self-preservation. They could stay in Jamestown under the tyranny of Percy, where they would almost certainly die, or they could flee to the Indians. Nevertheless, that so many did flee "civilization" and found refuge among those whom Percy called "savages" indicates that they were changed. They were no longer the same Englishmen and Englishwomen who had set out from London but a year earlier. The trauma of Jamestown, like the experience of shipwreck in Bermuda, was transformative, especially for those who arrived on the Third Supply. When they sailed from London, they knew they were going toward a wilderness, but none could have fully understood what that meant. As they watched people die, one after another, from starvation—as they buried the dead, turning from the fresh graves, feeling the constant pain of an empty stomach—they could not help but feel abandoned. No help was coming from England. For all intents and purposes, they were lost. The ties that bound them to their old lives, their old habits of duty and loyalty and even citizenship, had come unwound. They were stripped bare. Their old world was irretrievable. The Company had no regard for their welfare. As so many later put it, under the Company's regime it was "as if they had been slaves!"[26] Their contract had been a sham. They had been tricked into coming to Virginia. Some died in earthen holes. Some waited in their beds to die. Others took their lives into their own hands. In a willful act of self-creation, they ran away.

### RESCUE

When Gates had learned all he could at Fort Algernon, he and the two Bermudan pinnaces slid up the river toward Jamestown Island. The melancholy journey took two days, for there was no wind at all and they moved only on the incoming tides. Even if he kept Percy's story to himself, Gates's own "grievous" mood must have been communicated to everyone on the ships. His hopeful sanguinity had become grim. No crowd of prosperous settlers would welcome the pinnaces. No bumpers of rich foods would be passed around. The truth could be read on his troubled face. Stephen Hopkins and all those who had conspired to stay in Bermuda were right all along. The sailors' harrowing stories of toil and deprivation in Virginia did not go far enough, not by half.

The boats approached the wharf, but no one hailed them from the fort. No sentries could be seen at their posts. Silence. It was as if they approached a ghost town. At the height of its prosperity, during Smith's reign, the fort had been the stout and impregnable center of a growing empire that ran fifty miles up and fifty miles down the river. Now, parts of the palisade were down. The gates of the fort hung at angles off their hinges. Useless. Inside the curtain wall, no activity stirred the streets. No one and no fire at the forge. The armory was vacant, stripped of all weapons. The church was eerily silent and dilapidated. No human sound. Only clouds of fat flies, those denizens of the dead and dying, filled the air with a vibrating buzz. Most of the houses were empty, unroofed, stripped for firewood. Some had corpses, unburied, attended only by the flies. Perhaps a carrion bird or two was startled from its grotesque work, black wings flying out of gaping doors. Other houses, they soon found, were haunted by vague spirits, bodies that were nearly ghosts, not quite dead but not quite living.

Gates made his way to the church. He ordered that the bell be rung. Clanging iron circles wakened the dead air. Too weak to struggle out of bed, some lingered in the shadows of their houses. But a few emaciated bodies had strength enough to raise themselves from the threshold of the grave. They stumbled into the blinking sunlight. They saw stout Englishmen in the streets.

"We are starved!" these skeletons cried plaintively. "We are starved!"[27]

"All things," William Strachey wrote, were "so contrary to our expectations, so full of misery," that everyone, even Governor Gates himself, was "disheartened and faint."[28] Everyone knew how precarious the situation was. The pinnaces carried only a small supply of food. They might have packed in more supplies from Bermuda, but Gates hadn't suspected Virginia would be in distress. When Gates took inventory, Jamestown yielded next to nothing, "only mushrooms and some herbs" that those inhabitants with any strength left were cooking into a "thin and unsavory broth." The concoction had little to no nourishment, and it "swelled them much." Such fare might have kept the least weak of the survivors on this side of death for about four more days.[29]

Reluctantly, Gates convened a general meeting. The survivors of the starving time came with all their hopelessness, standing on one side. On the other side were all of the castaways, those seething with discontent and those still loyal to Gates. Gates saw his danger. The weight of numbers tilted dangerously against him. A misstep at this point might trigger a spontaneous and general mutiny. Now was not the time for the iron fist. He must choose his words carefully.

"What provisions I have," he told everyone, "you shall equally share." This was good news to one side of the crowd, the starving people of Jamestown. Still, they eyed him silently. They were wary, cautious, listening for what would come next. Gates continued: he would use the able-bodied men who came from Bermuda, he roared out, to try the country for food. This statement pleased no one. But Gates held back their mutinous sentiment, at least for the time being. If he should find it not possible, he continued, to supply them with something from the countryside, he would make ready and transport them all into their native country.[30]

Back to England. That meant a final end to the ordeal: release from their contract with the Company. They would have their lives back. A "general acclamation" rumbled from the crowd. It grew into a "shout of joy on both sides." Even the Company men were cheering.

The boats went down to Point Comfort and across the bay to Cape Henry and Cape Charles, dragging nets behind them, but the sturgeon that should have been plentiful by this time could not be found. The nets never hauled in more than a few fish—too few, even, to feed the fishermen themselves, let alone the whole colony. As word of the newcomers spread throughout the peninsula, Indians began to appear at the fort offering to trade. This unlooked-for development might forestall disaster, Gates knew, but it might hasten their demise. At all costs, he had to monopolize trade. He could not allow any private transactions, not from the settlers or from the sailors. But Jamestown was a sieve, and the Indians had such easy access to European goods that a piece of copper that fetched a bushel of corn in John Smith's day would bring Gates no more than "a pottle," or half a gallon. The Indians seemed to be poking around like spies, measuring English weakness. No rescue came from them.

In the end, Gates's efforts did no more than postpone starvation by a month. So the governor consulted with the "gentlemen of the town," Percy's chosen class, who assured him that, based on their experience, they could squeeze no food from the country, not even by raiding Indian villages. He talked with Captain Newport and Admiral Somers. These seasoned mariners advised him that "with all speed convenient" they should make for Newfoundland, which they might reach before their provisions ran out. At those rich fishing grounds, they should find long-range English fishing ships "into which happily they might disperse most of the company."[31]

In the last days before the evacuation, talk of burning the place circulated among the settlers. From Gates's point of view, "intemperate and malicious people" threatened to set fires that would consume everything, every building and every bit of fortification that three years of toil had raised. On their way out the door, so to speak, the veterans of Jamestown, backed by the discontents from Bermuda, wanted to raze the broken palisade and its dilapidated houses and the armory and the storehouse and the church. There must be no going back. They must never return to Jamestown, and the only guarantee of escape was to wipe the town from the face of the earth. They would not be satisfied till their prison were reduced to a heap of smoldering charcoal. Their removal must have this finality, this devoutly wished-for conflagration.

None of the Company men penetrated the cabal that threatened to torch the buildings. Whispers came to them vaguely and unattached to particular mouths. Ideas without authors. Gates knew that such ideas had "infected minds." But he did not know whom he should terrorize. So he had to guard everything. Everything of value that could be carried onto a boat had been loaded. Every small arm not already traded to or stolen by the Indians was packed and taken aboard ship. The last morsel of food had been stored in barrels that were tightly sealed for an ocean voyage. The provisions, not more than sixteen days' worth of rations, were distributed between the vessels. The platform at the triangular fort's bastioned corners were bare, stripped of their cannon, which the colonists buried before the gate, entombing those symbols of English superiority. It was a complete withdrawal. On the morning of June 7, 1610, Gates commanded the drummers to beat their tattoo. He posted guards, and the people assembled and began filing into the boats. A little over two hundred souls were divided between the colony's four pinnaces—the *Patience* and *Deliverance*, which had been made in Bermuda, and the *Discovery* and *Virginia*, which had been moored at Fort Algernon. There was no fire. The armed corps du guard were the last to embark.

Gates's boat drifted from Jamestown Island and took its place in the line riding downstream. Then the governor made his final, somewhat pathetic salute, attempting to define as a noble effort what nearly everyone on the other three boats considered an ignoble, despotic dystopia. He ordered his guard to let fly "a peal of small shot" in tribute to the fort.[32] The fort said nothing back. Fresh earth showed where the cannons were buried. The yawning gate was silent. No one saluted in return, only the pale echo of their own musket fire met their ears. Jamestown's only tenants were the dead, all buried now, hidden even from the flies.

The evacuation had taken all morning, and they got no farther downriver than Hog Island. They threw out their anchors and spent the night on the rising tide, waiting for it to ebb again the next morning. One more day of food consumed. Fifteen days of rations left.

It didn't matter. They were too late, too late by several days. There would be no escape. They did not yet know it, but the prison gate, opened by Gates, was sliding shut again. Beyond sight of the refugees, sails appeared in the mouth Chesapeake Bay.

## POMP, SLAVERY, TRIBUTE

The four pinnaces lay at anchor off Mulberry Island when they spied a longboat pulling toward them up the James River. They waited and watched till the strange skiff came among them, and one Captain Bruster scrambled aboard the *Deliverance* carrying official-looking papers. Lord De La Warr was in the bay with a fleet of ships. At that moment he was anchored off Fort Algernon, where he was shocked to hear of Gates's decision to abandon the colony. The boat had been dispatched to prevent their removal. Gates barked orders to the captains, Somers in the *Patience*, Percy in the *Discovery*, and Captain Davis in the *Virginia*. Although night was falling, the wind came from the east, perfect for sailing upriver, and the little squadron headed back to Jamestown. They arrived in darkness, and the settlers who thought they were finally headed back to England were made to trundle ashore again, filing through the main gate into the fort they had wished they had burned.[33]

Gates had one day to set the fort in as good order as they might, digging up the cannons and assigning people to their houses, which ran in rows parallel to the palisades. On the tenth of June, the sight of great sails came into view, fluttered, and then furled, and the ships hove to. There must have been a good bit of scurrying back and forth from ship to fort and fort to ship as the protocol was sorted out, for this was no mere knight or captain but a peer of England come to take command: Lord De La Warr waited in his ship while all the pomp of his disembarkation could be arranged.

As a young Oxford graduate—he earned a master's degree—a twenty-two-year-old Thomas West, the future third Baron De La Warr, had accompanied his father, the second Baron De La Warr, to Ireland as part of the Earl of Essex's expeditionary force. They did not succeed in subduing Hugh O'Neill, the Earl of Tyrone, but Essex did pass out knighthoods rather promiscuously, and one of the many

deserving whose shoulders felt the weight of the earl's beneficent
sword was the younger West, promoted to Sir Thomas, in Dublin in
1599. When Essex's 1601 coup d'état fizzled in London, Sir Thomas
West was among the suspects rounded up by Sir Robert Cecil, Queen
Elizabeth's secretary of state. He was imprisoned briefly, but when
the queen died, King James made him a member of his privy council.
By the time the Virginia Company was organized, Sir Thomas's
father was dead and he had become the Baron De La Warr.

The baron was the most eminent English aristocrat to have come
to Virginia, and he must receive the appropriate ceremony. The gates
of the fort were flung open, displaying the governor's corps du guard
standing "in order," with a proud William Strachey at their head
bearing the company's colors. Beyond stood the grim commoners.
When he stepped ashore, Lord De La Warr bent his knee and lowered
his head, and for a great long pause everyone watched him. Then he
stood and marched through the gate into town. In salute, Strachey
lowered the colors of the corps du guard. De La Warr proceeded into
the chapel, where a sermon commenced. Drilled as he was in lessons
of obedience and duty, Reverend Bucke did not have to dig deep into
his repertoire for something suitable. At the conclusion of the pieties,
the baron's ancient, or standard-bearer, read the lord's commission
aloud to the whole colony assembled, and Thomas Gates with all
proper subordination surrendered "his own commission, both patents
and the council seal." The man who had commanded so despotically
in Bermuda was demoted to lieutenant general. Then the pompous
baron condescended to speak to the gaunt-cheeked men of Jamestown
and the sunbaked survivors of the Bermuda shipwreck. These people,
who had endured stranding or starvation, adventure and misery
almost beyond description, had no choice but to listen to the lecture.
They must stop being vain, the baron told them. They must stop being
idle. He "earnestly" wished they would give up their lazy ways, their
presumptuous manners. They must do what their betters told them

to do. Anyone found wanting would be summarily "cut off" by Lord De La Warr's sword. He was the sword of justice, and he would hack to death the "delinquents." If they behaved themselves, he would draw his sword "in their defense to protect them from injuries." His threats were taken seriously. Fifty silent guardsmen fresh from England and armed with poleax halberds and dressed in De La Warr's own scarlet livery flanked the lane. Lieutenant General Gates's corps du guard, ill-clad and irregularly armed, backed them up.[34]

The baron appointed an advisory council (Gates, Somers, Newport, Percy, and Sir Ferdinando Wainman), a "secretary and recorder" (Strachey), a commander of the halberdiers (Bruster), captains of four militia companies of fifty men each, and a captain for the Bermudian corps du guard (George Yeardley), and Martin was put in charge of "the battery works for steel and iron." Clerks were appointed to administer the Company's council and store. Every settler became a militia footman. The second day after his arrival, De La Warr made "every particular member of the colony" down to the lowliest laborer swear to be faithful to the Company, to be of good assistance to the colony, and to keep its secrets. One could hardly be said to have sworn freely to these terms. This ceremony was nothing like the contract made at the table in Thomas Smythe's house in London. In Jamestown, consent could not be refused. Fifty sharpened halberds stood ready to chop off the head of anyone the "lord governor" considered "idle." Years later Thomas Hobbes wrote that oaths such as this, given under duress or threat of violence, were no less valid than consent freely given. But Jamestown's settlers were not Hobbesians. While it was expedient to let on to be faithful, later events prove that many settlers did not feel bound by any oath compelled by the sword.[35]

Under the advice of the council, De La Warr decided that the first priority was to secure a source of meat. The Fourth Supply had brought meal and peas and the like to feed four hundred people for twelve months, but the Company had planned for the swine multiplying in Virginia to supply the colony's meat. De La Warr discovered that Wahunsonacock's warriors had long since poached or wantonly destroyed Jamestown's hogs. But there were thousands in Bermuda, Somers explained, not more than ten days' sailing, and enough fish to salt and dry and pack into as many barrels as their ships could carry. De La Warr dispatched the admiral in the *Patience* and Captain Argall in the *Discovery* to salt and dry six months' supply of fish and pork, and to bring back enough live animals to repopulate Hog Island. On the fifteenth of June, 1610, Somers sailed down the James River and out of the tale. He and Argall made it to Bermuda without incident, but Somers never made it back. He died there of natural causes, and his heart was left there, buried like Rolfe's infant child, Bermuda; the butchered body of Namontack; the bludgeoned Edward Samuell; and the victim of Gates's firing squad, Henry Paine. The rest of Somers's body returned to England pickled in vinegar, so it might not rot before it was interred near his home in Lyme Regis. His reputation has been preserved: Bermudians still celebrate Somers Day each year, second in reverence only to Emancipation Day. But the remainder of men on the *Patience*, realizing they might finally free themselves of Jamestown, and having found a good supply of "ambergris and other commodities" in Bermuda, decided to ignore the hogs and fish and their obligations to the Company. They packed their pinnace with what they thought they could sell back home, and sailed for England. Captain Argall eventually returned to Virginia with salted and dried fish.[36]

The routine in Virginia quickly came to resemble the routine in Bermuda, only with more pomp, more spectacle of power, and many, many more men devoted largely if not entirely to surveillance and guard duty. When the baron went to church, half of his uniformed halberdiers marched in front of him and half behind, followed by a parade of all the "councilors, captains, officers," and the whole train rounded out by "all the other gentlemen." In the chapel, the baron sat on a "green velvet chair," and when he knelt to pray he knelt on a "velvet cushion." When church was over, the whole train led the baron back to his house. The common sort were required to witness such spectacles, because Baron De La Warr wanted to put into their heads a proper respect for the unassailable authority of an English peer.

As Gates had done in Bermuda, the baron organized work gangs. Some men were assigned to revive the glassworks. Situated beyond the blockhouse near the foot of the isthmus that connected Jamestown Island to the mainland, this factory was dangerously close to Indian territory, and the workers there suffered the occasional ambush. Some people were put to work rebuilding the dilapidated church. Some were sent with Robert Tyndall and the ship *De La Warr* to fish in the bay. The sawing of clapboard was resumed. Cedar and black walnut timber were prepared for shipment to England. Iron ore was mined, packaged, and stowed on the ships.[37]

Lord De La Warr put into practice Article 19 of Gates's secret instructions. Each Indian district of Tsenacomoco must supply Jamestown "so many measures of Corne at euery Harvest, soe many basketts of Dye[,] so many dozens of skins, [and] so many of [their] people to worke weekely" for Jamestown. Each weroance would be assessed "according to his p[ro]porcion in greateness of Territory and men." "Feare," not trade, would feed Indian corn to Jamestown. The Indians must be terrorized. This scheme would establish an annual stream of "revennue of euery Commodity growing in that Countrey."[38] In the fantasy world of the Company's directors, Gates would simply replace Smith as the new paramount chief on the James River. Slavery and tribute: England was no longer a beacon of liberation in America.

But in the Company's contorted reasoning, it pretended to be. Subordination to Jamestown would "free" Tsenacomocoans from the "Tirrany" of Wahunsonacock. Eventually, the Company's instructions explained, freeing the Indians might require kidnapping or killing all of their chiefs. "Upon landing," the new governor must "fly vp into the Countrey and . . . seise into [his] custody half there corne and harvest" and each district's weroance and all "their knowne successors at once." The Indian priests should be kidnapped and kept from speaking to the people. Stubborn weroances would be imprisoned. Indian children kidnapped, raised in English house-holds, and indoctrinated into English "Manners and Religion," would be installed as the new chiefs. Only then would "their people . . . easily obey" the English and "become in time Civill and Christian" themselves. Dominion over the Chesapeake, the Company's direc-tors realized, would require a decisive fight with Wahunsonacock. Take him prisoner if you can, the Company advised, but, one way or another, Jamestown's governor "must make" Wahunsonacock his "tributary."[39]

Hostilities began almost at once. One Humphrey Blunt was in the Nansemond district when he was ambushed and killed. In retri-bution, Lieutenant General Gates and his corps du guard sailed down river to sack Kecoughtan, a different district on the opposite side of the river. They came as if friends, and the Kecoughtans welcomed them as such. At the head of Gates's troop was a drummer boy whose playing and dancing "allure[d] the Indians to come unto him." Then Gates gave a signal, and his men drew their weapons and started murdering the townspeople indiscriminately. Five were "put . . . to the sword" and many others were wounded in the first moments. Several Indians, with blood pouring from great gashes, made it into the woods, running as hard as they could. When the English finally found their corpses, they marveled that people with such wounds "could fly so far." This bloodletting did not make it into the official account, written by Strachey, who was now Virginia's official "recorder." "Kecoughtan," Strachey wrote almost casually, was "soon taken . . . without loss or hurt of any of [Gates's] men." As for the Indians, all he said was that the women had fled, leaving "their poor baggage and treasure to the spoil of our soldiers." The Indians abandoned their town, and the English took possession of the houses, the fields, and the "baggage," which consisted of a few baskets of wheat, peas, beans, and tobacco. Those soldiers who had learned their trade in the scorched-earth policies of the last Irish war began applying those methods to the James river valley. Natives were routed from their land and turned into destitute, starving refugees. English settlers were put to work in Kecoughtan's cornfields, the new breadbasket of Jamestown. Some Frenchmen in the Fourth Supply planted grapevines. The Kecoughtan district seems to have been particularly prized by the English as fertile ground.[40]

Trying to secure the entire peninsula, the English turned their attention to Paspahegh and Chickahominy, their northern neighbors. A kangaroo court found two Paspahegh warriors guilty of having "attempted upon many in our fort"—that is, of having assaulted Englishmen. The arm of one of the unfortunates was stretched across a block of wood and his right hand was struck off. He and his stub were sent as a blunt demand to the paramount chief. Wahunsonacock must return all of the English settlers who had run away to the Indians over the years, and he must return all the English weapons they had taken when they escaped and all the weapons that the Indians had managed to steal in their ambushes or had traded for food. If not, the second Paspahegh hostage would be executed; the English would kill each Indian who happened to cross their path; and the scourge of fire and sword would rain on the Indian "cornfields, towns, and villages" that neighbored Jamestown.[41]

The "subtle" chief considered all of the intelligence he had received regarding the new strength of the English, including the counsel of Machumps, and decided to give "proud and disdainful answers." Lieutenant General Gates was "much incensed." The savage mocked the civilized man. It was as shocking to his sense of right order as the mutinies in Bermuda. But Gates was sick, so he "commissioned" George Percy to lead seventy soldiers against the Paspaheghs and Chickahominys. They boarded boats on the ninth of August, traveled upstream in the dark, and put ashore three miles from town. Strangely, Percy did not know where Paspahegh was, exactly. Nor did anyone else, for it seems that all of these raiders were newly arrived men of the Fourth Supply, soldiers who could be relied upon. Percy was obliged to use his Paspaheghan prisoner, the one whose hand had not been chopped off, to show them the way to the Indian town.[42]

The man's name was Kempes, and he was still shackled when the provost marshal pushed him forward. Kempes knew that he was leading the English to his own countrymen, perhaps to his own family, and the scourge of fire and sword promised by De La Warr was about to fall upon Paspahegh. So he led the English "out of the way" until even Percy suspected the misdirection. The commander whipped out his truncheon and severely beat Kempes, the blows coming with no mercy until the mutilated native finally gave in. The expedition continued in several files, each headed by a lieutenant or captain, creeping in the darkness. The surprise attack, coming before dawn, was effective. Captain William West gave the signal, a pistol shot, and the columns fell upon the town from different directions. Several Indians rushed out in the forefront and absorbed the fury of the English charge. Fifteen, Percy tells us, were killed outright. These few slowed the charge long enough for everyone else to escape. "Almost all the rest," Percy reported, fled the village and made it into the woods, everyone but the town's unfortunate "queen and her children and one [male] Indian prisoner." These were spared by Percy's lieutenant, who, apparently, was still tied to his humanity by a filament.

Percy was perplexed. It would have been better had the man killed the woman and her children in the heat of the battle. What was Percy to do with them now, he wanted to know, in the cold aftermath?

The lieutenant answered sharply that Percy might do whatever he pleased with the prisoners, for he washed his hands of them.

Ineffectual Percy lashed out. He ordered the Indian man beheaded, and it was done in an instant. Fire the town, he ordered, and trails of acrid smoke drew charcoal lines on the dawning sky. When it was light enough, Percy's men cut down all the corn standing in the fields. They gorged themselves on destruction till their bellies were full of it, and then they marched back the three miles to their boats, dragging the grief-stricken mother and her children with them. This woman must have been terrified by the barbarity. She knew little of war. In the heart of Tsenacomoco, under Wahunsonacock's rule, Paspahegh had lived in peace and security for a generation. But she knew that in war women were not supposed to be killed, and children were adopted and became part of the victor's people. These English slaughtered everyone, women and children too. Their barbarity would have been incomprehensible to a Tsenacomocoan woman.

In the boats, Percy was losing control of his command. Why had they spared this woman and her children? the soldiers wanted to know. And here proceeds one of the most difficult passages in all of the Jamestown narratives. The soldiers perceived Percy's indecision, his lack of natural authority, and like pirates they convened a council to discuss the Indians' fate. "It was agreed upon," Percy wrote, speaking in the passive voice of a decision that ought to have been his alone, "to put the children to death, the which was effected by throwing them overboard and shooting out their brains in the water." This was the old conquistador spirit, worthy of Spanish soldiers pacifying Hispaniola. Only the English had no Bartolemé de las Casas to record the evil deeds. The fate of these Paspaheghan Indians was written with little notice. Neither Smith nor Strachey told the story. Only George Percy thought it of much significance, probably because he was there and felt the heat of violence and smelled the smoke from the ruins. By afternoon even the lines of smoke were erased from the sky, and the town, which had been leveled, smoldered, its winter supply of food gone, the survivors of the massacre, now refugees of war, peeping from the woods.

Percy congratulated himself for shielding the "queen" from the sport that killed her children. But the prisoner they ferried away must have been all but dead already, her heart hollowed out by the sight of her children murdered by such devils. The raiders hit another town, this one after a fourteen-mile march from the river, perhaps a Chickahominy town, with "houses, temples, and idols, and amongst the rest a spacious temple, clean and neatly kept," a building of note in Tsenacomoco. The soldiers walked unopposed through the deserted lanes of the town as they set fire to each building and cut down the crops in the field. At the end of the day Percy brought his command back down to Jamestown, and he found that Gates was "discontent" because Percy had spared the Paspaheghan queen.

"It was my lord's pleasure," Davis told him somewhat officiously, "that we should see her dispatched." Gates thought that burning was the appropriate method of execution. Even Percy, who had led the early morning raid on Paspahegh and had directed the killing of so many of the town's innocents, balked at this barbarity.

"Having seen so much bloodshed [already] that day," Percy replied, "now in my cold blood I [desire] to see no more." It would be best not to burn the poor wretch, but to "give her a quicker dispatch . . . by sword or shot."

Davis conceded this much humanity. Two soldiers brought the woman into the woods, where Davis hacked her to death.[43]

Captain Samuel Argall headed another raiding party against yet a third town, across the river. By this time it was impossible for the English to surprise any village. They burned down the houses and ruined the fields, pacifying the district as English armies had recently pacified Ireland. But they killed no Indians. It was a disappointing day.

## THE FALLS CAMPAIGN

The Fourth Supply was divided into the now-familiar two classes. There were those we might describe as an officer class, a group used to military discipline, which remained implicitly loyal to the Company's hierarchy of command. They were headed by gentlemen, who had purchased shares in the Company, identified with Company's interests, and were accustomed to being treated with deference by their inferiors, either as officers in Ireland or the Netherlands or merely as gentlemen walking the lanes of their hometowns and the streets of London. They had constituted Gates's corps du guard in Bermuda. With the arrival of Lord De La Warr's fleet, they were augmented by a fresh cadre of gentlemen soldiers, and they were backed now by the baron's personal guard of fifty halberdiers. The halberdiers seem to have been men that the baron himself recruited, mustered, and drilled the way an aristocrat might raise a company of soldiers to join a typical English expedition to Ireland or the Netherlands. Very likely the baron had borrowed the cash for this private army from his wife. The recruits might have joined the adventure on such terms—as mercenaries. The baron financed a considerable portion of the Fourth Supply, banking on a king's ransom in return, and it is likely that many of the commoners living in Jamestown in the summer of 1610 were essentially his employees. They were similar to the wage-earning sailors.[44]

The other group, who would more properly be called "settlers," came to Jamestown with the expectation of becoming landowning yeomen. These were the people who were disappointed to find they were prisoners urged to their tasks by the threat of the sword.

Although most of these were drilled into the militia for emergencies, they were not professional soldiers. They had no regular access to weapons, and under normal circumstances they were mere workers. Like their counterparts in Bermuda, who came to think of themselves more as prisoners of a labor camp than partners—albeit junior partners—in a plantation, this class of people showed signs of discontent almost right away.

"About this time," Percy reported again, almost wearily, "there was a conspiracy."

Hardly three years into its history, Virginia was convulsed by no fewer than twelve separate instances of mutiny, from singular refusals of direct commands to widespread conspiratorial plans for escape. The regularity of these eruptions indicate the discontent that percolated all the time in Jamestown. It was a perpetual condition. The common settlers were in a more or less constant state of resistance, even when it was not evident, like the pressure constantly building beneath a volcano.

This thirteenth eruption manifested itself among those who had been assigned to dig for iron ore. None of the narratives describe the mining operation in any kind of detail, but a letter from 1621 speaks of "great stones" near the falls "lying on the place, as though they had been brought thither to advance the erection of those [iron] Workes." Probably this "mine" consisted of men who were ferried up to an open-air camp near the falls, where they fell to work breaking up stones, filling barrels with the broken rock, and loading them on boats for transportation back to the smelter at Jamestown. It was heavy, difficult work, and probably very few settlers had imagined their plantation of Virginia would be in this kind of labor camp. The mine was a torment, but it was also an opportunity, for it was forty miles away from De La Warr's halberdiers.[45]

Percy's narrative is sketchy, saying only that the conspirators planned to "run away with a bark." Their "bark" was probably no more than an oared barge or other open boat, and they probably meant to maroon themselves among Indians on the north bank of the James River. The plot went the way of all conspiracies: "discovered" by some loyal Company man, who reported it to the authorities, who reported it to the lord governor, who ordered a number of men arrested. One of these prisoners was sentenced to death. A rope was slung over a gallows and a ladder set up, which the prisoner was made to mount. He was flung from that height, but when the rope snapped tight, "what with the swinge and weight of his body," the rope broke, and the half-choked, unfortunate prisoner fell all the way to the ground. The baron was a pious Church of England man and saw something of God's hand in this reprieve, so he issued a pardon. Little good it did the would-be maroon: it took two days, but he eventually succumbed to the jerk of the rope and the "extremity of the fall," an anonymous martyr to the cause of liberty.[46]

The baron was suffering from ague, flux, cramps, gout, and scurvy, but sick as he was he realized that the disturbance at the mines required his own attention. Captain Bruster, who preceded him overland, was harassed all along the way by Indians in territory that was supposed to have been pacified by the raids on Paspahegh and Chickahominy. De La Warr, who traveled on the water, discovered the mine in a shambles. This was near where his younger brother, Francis West, had tried to build a fort, and now the older brother, the baron, starting again from scratch, caused "a fort to be builded there both for their defense and shelter." The baron's presence and, no doubt, the presence of his guard were enough to put a lid on discontent, but it kept percolating.

Lord De La Warr intended to spend the winter in the fort and with the coming spring launch yet another search for better mines closer to the mountains. It was not to be. His incessant illnesses forced the baron to retire from this outpost and then to retire from Virginia altogether, first sailing for Nevis and thence for England.

His last act was to choose Percy, feeble Percy, "to execute marshal law or any other power and authority as absolute as himself."[47]

### CALIBAN'S GABERDINE

As the ships of the Fourth Supply were loading their timber, clapboard, and ore for the return to England, William Strachey scribbled a hasty end to his *True Reportory of the Wreck and Redemption of Sir Thomas Gates, Knight, upon and from the Islands of the Bermudas.* Despite his prejudices, Strachey's narrative remains our most thorough source of the eventful Third Supply—from its departure from England, the hurricane and shipwreck, the months in Bermuda, and the events in Jamestown through the first weeks of Baron De La Warr's reign. His narrative had its practical elements, its lists of marketable commodities, and its cartographic features, but Strachey wrote to stir the heart. He knew that this adventure was more than so many sea tales, however incredible those were. He witnessed the germ of empire, as Joseph Conrad would put it three hundred years later, and Strachey sensed that these were epic events. They settled on "this fair river . . . the Kings River," Strachey told his readers, "as Virgil writeth Aeneas did, arriving in the region of Italy called Laitum, upon the banks of the River Tiber." It was the birth of a nation that would rival Rome.[48]

The *True Reportory* was not published until 1625, but as was typical in the early seventeenth century, the manuscript raced from eager hands in aristocratic drawing rooms to the desks of commerce and policy, until it touched nearly every aristocrat interested in Virginia.

One of those was William Shakespeare.

The playwright was near the end of his remarkable career in the fall of 1610, and he was writing what fans have for centuries considered his swan song: *The Tempest.* My book began with the opening scene of that play, the hurricane and shipwreck, which Shakespeare clearly borrowed from Strachey's moving tale of the *Sea Venture*'s foundering. Here, at the end, we return to this play, for it represents the first truly popular interpretation of America's genesis. In the fiction of Shakespeare's play, Prospero's island is situated in the Mediterranean, where England owned no territory. But the play really is a parable of British empire.

Caliban's rude, gigantic cloak resembles Tudor descriptions of the distinctive "mantle" used by the "natives" of England's first colony, the Gaels of Ireland, while his very name recalls the cannibals who (in the European imagination) populated so many parts of the New World. Prospero brings sweetness and light to the native Caliban. But Caliban's residual, bestial sex drive breaks through this thin gilding of civilization, and he tries to rape Prospero's daughter. The shipwrecked wizard gives up on his program of reclamation and decides to enslave the islander. Shakespeare probably did not intend it, but his story parallels England's first bright hope to liberate a hemisphere, its disillusionment, and its resorting to tyranny.[49]

The character of Caliban has been rehabilitated in the last century. We can see him as Shakespeare did not, for the machinery of Europe's empires, rusted into ruin, exposes itself as it decomposes. Modern productions treat the island's "monster" as a complex figure deserving of more sympathy than blame. In some productions, Caliban is the tragic hero, the emblem of American races subjugated or annihilated by European conquistadors.

A couple of other ne'er-do-wells in the play have never gotten their due. Certainly they have never been reinterpreted the way Caliban has. Shakespeare made them the butt of all jokes in 1611, and they have been stage buffoons ever since: the "drunken butler" called Stephano, and Trinculo the idling jester. They are the very embodiment of Strachey's "common sort," the ordinary settler as seen through the prejudicial eyes of the gentleman. After the shipwreck,

"The Scene, an vn-inhabited Island

Names of the Actors.

Alonso, K. of Naples.
Sebastian his Brother.
Prospero, the right Duke of Millaine.
Anthonio his brother, the vsurping Duke of Millaine.
Ferdinand, Son to the King of Naples.
Gonzalo, an honest old Councellor.
Adrian, & Francisco, Lords.
Caliban, a saluage and deformed slaue.
Trinculo, a Iester.
Stephano, a drunken Butler.
Master of a Ship.
Boate-Swaine.
Marriners.
Miranda, daughter to Prospero.
Ariell, an ayrie spirit.
Iris
Ceres
Iuno                } Spirits.
Nymphes
Reapers

"The Names of the Actors," showing Stephano as the "Drunken Butler."

The "Chandos" portrait of William Shakespeare in the National Portrait Gallery, London.

Trinculo comes across Caliban hiding under his cloak. The jester muses that had he been in England, he could make money off the creature, because Londoners who "will not give a doit to relieue a lame Begger . . . will give out ten to see a dead Indian." Eventually the jester thinks, "My best way is to creep under his gaberdine." To protect himself from the coming storm, he goes native, taking cover in the savage mantle. The action symbolizes what the Company's captains feared so much: that the settlers might turn renegade. Stephano is less susceptible. Having "scaped drowning," he would never fear "Savages and men of Ind . . ." He brings the gift of alcohol to Caliban, who worships him as a god, but in truth Stephano and Trinculo do not elevate the native: they stoop to his ways, and Caliban, marching with the drunk and the jester, sings, "Freedom, hey-day, hey-day, freedom!" Such is Shakespeare's view, which was the same as Strachey's view: when practiced by commoners, liberty means license to become savage. This conspiracy of dunces plots to sneak upon the sleeping Prospero so they can "knock a nail into his head." Stephano would then possess the island's "nonpareil" (the word reminds us of Pocahontas), the fair Miranda, and fancy himself lord or king. Their plot unravels when Stephano and Trinculo are distracted by the fine clothes in Prospero's closet, as if their rebellion were nothing more than the desire to enjoy the luxuries of gentlemen. The rebellion ends with a hangover and a confession: "I am not Stephano," the drunken butler admits, "but a Cramp."

Prospero asks contemptuously, "You'ld be King o' the Isle, Sirha?"

"I should have been a sore one then," Stephano concedes. With such laughs shaken from his audience, Shakespeare demonstrated how unfit the commoner is to rule over himself, let alone an entire island kingdom. At the play's end, the aristocrats are restored to their perch of privilege.[50]

Whether or not Shakespeare called his rebel "Stephano" after Stephen Hopkins, he read about Hopkins in Strachey's narrative, and the subplot of his play is a cautionary tale about how easily colonization could destabilize England's caste system. Shakespeare was a relatively recent admission to the "made" men of England. Like Strachey's father, he bought a coat of arms. Like both Strachey and John Smith, he adhered to the political orthodoxy with the zealotry of the convert. *The Tempest* presumes the superiority of the 2 percent and imagines the chaos that would result if the other 98 percent did not do what they were told but what they wanted.[51] In a distant, isolated place such as Bermuda or Virginia, where the structures of authority were vulnerable, the poor might readily conspire to "knock a nail" into their governor's head.

Shakespeare's version of the shipwreck narrative has proven so seductive that even today historians of Jamestown perfume their narratives with an air of disapproval. Virginia's failures, so the histories tell us, derive from the greed, lethargy, indolence, and downright mutinous impulses of the settlers. To be fair, sometimes the idleness is blamed on gentlemen unused to physical work and unwilling to change. But the common settlers take their share of the blame. Nearly all of the histories of Jamestown impugn their indiscipline, their mutinous impulses, their ungovernability, their self-destructive and irrational refusal to take orders.

The reality is quite different. Colonists abandoned Jamestown by the dozens and defected to the Indians, and some even helped the Tsenacomocoans try to push the little English garrison back into the ocean. Not one of these mutineers looked like Shakespeare's Stephano, the drunken butler. No commoner designed to kill the Company's president or governor. None of the discontents hoped to don the rich, embroidered garb of a man like Percy. They preferred Caliban's gaberdine. They wanted nothing more than to light out for the woods and maroon themselves. Like the slaves of Panama, they wanted to determine for themselves how to live. They wanted to dissolve their contract with the Company and start over with a new compact of mutual consent. Jamestown's earliest history, it turns out, was not the germ of empire but the trampled seed of democracy.

A fourteenth mutiny erupted in August or September of 1611. It came under the government of Sir Thomas Dale, a new arrival and yet another veteran of the wars in the Low Countries, who took over command from Percy.[52] In a third attempt to plant a permanent English settlement at the strategic falls, Dale took about two hundred men upriver, many of them already unwilling, disillusioned, and sick of the Company. When the new fort was nearly finished, as Percy tells the story, "divers of his men, being idle and not willing to take pains, did run away unto the Indians." Some got clean away, but many were recaptured by Dale's guardsmen, and the interim governor punished them "in a most severe manner." He wanted to "terrify" the other settlers, and he took to the task with enthusiasm and creativity. The lucky were merely hanged. Dale burned to death a few others. Some he fastened upon wheels "to be broken," a slow and excruciating way to die. Others were "staked," although exactly what that means is unclear, while others were shot. A few whom he accused of robbing the storehouse were "bound fast unto trees and so starved . . . to death." The sadistic nature of these punishments underlines the tyrannical terms of the Company's contract with its settlers. That this Leviathan could feed upon so many victims further suggests how wide discontent had spread throughout the colony. About this time, back in London, at the luxurious Whitehall Palace, an audience laughed at their ridiculous mutiny. On All Saints Day, Shakespeare's Stephano and Trinculo strutted their antics before the rich patrons of the king's private theater.

William Strachey might have been in Shakespeare's audience, for he was back in England in late October or early November, preparing a slim volume for publication. The *Articles, Lawes, and Orders, Diuine, Politique, and Martiall for the Colony in Virginea* was a compilation of Company rules then enforced in Jamestown, employed first by Governor Gates in Bermuda, then formally promulgated by him when he assumed command of Jamestown in May 1610, then augmented by the Baron De La Warr when he arrived a month later, and perfected finally by Dale when he was interim governor. The book was designed to explode the rumors that Jamestown was a lawless place. It accomplished that task admirably, for these were draconian regulations. "No man shal commit the horrible, and detestable sins of Sodomie vpon pain of death," while mere whipping would serve fornicators. Settlers must attend prayers twice a day, and must not disrespect the minister. To possess without permission any edged tool; to butcher one's own cow or pig; to "bargaine, for any apparrell, linnen, or wollen, householdstuffe, bedde, bedding, sheete, towels, napkins, brasse, pewter or such like"; merely to speak ill of the Company or its officers were all crimes, most bearing the penalty of death. To sneak over the walls of the palisade, to speak with Indians without the approval of the "General, or chiefe officer," to "truck, or trade with the Indians," were all crimes. "No man or woman," the laws indicated, "(vpon paine of death) shall runne away from the Colonie, to Powhatan [Wahunsonacock], or any sauage Weroance else whatsoever." Nearly all property—down to every ear of corn they cultivated in the fields and every fish taken out of the river—belonged to the Company. All labor belonged to the Company. At the sounding of the drum in the morning, people mustered into their assigned work gangs and toiled all day till the drum beat again in the evening. Anyone who failed to appear at muster or left work early had to "lie vpon the Guard head and heeles together all night." The repeat offender was whipped, and the inveterate idler would be "condemned to the Gally for three years." "[O]verseers of workmen" must be zealous, or they would suffer a court-martial. These were not the laws of an English town or village. They were the rules of a slave labor camp. Anyone who resisted, disobeyed, or merely murmured against a Company officer would be "whipt three seuerall times, and vpon his knees . . . acknowledge his offence, with asking forgiuenesse vpon the Saboth day in the assembly." He who murmured twice could join the idlers as a galley slave. All conspirators would be put to death; anyone with knowledge of a conspiracy who did not report it would be put to death.

Although all were made to swear to this new contract, the settlers had no choice, and few then living in Virginia could be said to have consented to them. The government of Virginia had turned into a monster. "O brave new world!" Miranda crowed to the well-heeled audience at Whitehall, while in Virginia buzzards plucked the unburied dead.

# CONCLUSION

*Genesis*

**The war between Tsenacomoco and Jamestown** dragged on for another two years, delaying but not halting England's advance on the Chesapeake and debilitating though never defeating the native alliance. Violence was neither constant nor universal. Pocahontas, for instance, trusted the English well enough when she was visiting her Patawomeck relatives on the Potomac River in April 1613. An English ship happened to be in the river, and its captain, Samuel Argall, played the gracious host to the young woman until it came time to leave, when Pocahontas discovered that she was not a guest but a prisoner. At Argall's request, Wahunsonacock released seven English prisoners and returned a few weapons and tools, but Governor Gates did not release his native hostage.[1] Pocahontas converted to Christianity and married John Rolfe, and the mixed-race couple had a child, Thomas, in 1615.

The Pocahontas-Rolfe liaison smoothed tensions between the two peoples, and for several years the English did not need to fear ambushes throughout the Chesapeake. Settlements at Kecoughtan (near the peninsula's point), Henrico (near the falls), and Bermuda Hundred (between Jamestown and Henrico) prospered. The economy improved, not only because Rolfe had discovered a strain of tobacco that flourished in the Virginia climate and soil, but also because by 1616 the Company was beginning to abandon its communal,

1616 engraving of
Pocahontas during her visit
to England.

labor-camp method of colonization. People began settling on, clearing, and improving individual landholdings in units of fifty acres.

Pocahontas died in England in 1617. Wahunsonacock died the following year, succeeded by his brother, Opitchapam. And the following year, 1619, marked the end of Thomas Smythe's reign as treasurer of the Company. His faction at the Company was replaced by a more liberal group, who sent a new governor, George Yeardley, to Jamestown along with new "instructions." These abolished the heavy-handed martial law that had more or less reigned for a dozen years. In fact, they departed so dramatically with past practice that they are known today as "the Great Charter." Most significantly, they called for an assembly of representatives—the colony had grown to eleven different districts—to approve the rules and write new ones. The general assembly was still subject to the governor, who was subject to the Company's council back in London. Nevertheless, with a few large reservations we can date representative government in America to July 1619, when the assembly of elected burgesses met in the church at Jamestown. After six days of examining and revising the "instructions," these burgesses formally consented to the laws under which they would live.

The reservations are important, because this assembly replicated the mistake that the Company made the first day that settlers disembarked on Jamestown Island. On that day President Wingfield gathered only the gentlemen to witness the swearing in of the councillors, leaving the commoners aside. In 1619, anyone who owned land was allowed to vote for representatives, which did expand the ranks of the "better sort," but captive laborers were again excluded. Indentured servants did not vote, and so they clearly did not "consent" to the new laws and new officials who would govern their lives. And within weeks Governor Yeardley and the colony's cape merchant purchased the first African captives in English America: twenty Angolans sold by the captain of the privateer *White Lion*. These two groups—indentured servants and slaves— inherited the position of the discontents of Jamestown's first settlement, and their grievances, simmering for generations, erupted eventually in Bacon's Rebellion of 1676, the first truly *American* revolution. Although the causes of that uprising are complex and although the rebels were hardly without blame, they are remarkable today for repudiating the white supremacy that came to define the South. Black slaves and white servants made common cause.

Under the Great Charter, the colony grew steadily for three years, till nearly 1,200 Europeans were living on the Chesapeake. But the expansions increased pressure on Tsenacomoco, and the Indians lashed back. On March 22, 1622, Opechancanough launched an all-out war to push the English out of Virginia once and for all. Like most frontier wars, the violence was savage, both sides committed inhuman atrocities, and casualties ran very high. A third of the English settlers were killed, many others fled their homesteads, and disease settled among the refugees.

The war precipitated another crisis in governance, and Thomas Smythe threatened to regain control of the Company. The ensuing struggle precipitated some of our richest sources for events in the colony's early years as the two sides debated the effectiveness of the Company's initial policies. Thomas Dale's "reign of terror" at the falls, for example, was remembered as a particularly vicious but characteristic example of Smythe's regime. Many of the survivors from those days, self-styled the "Ancient Planters now remaining alive in Virginia," collaborated on *A Brief Declaration of the plantation of Virginia during the first twelve years*, while the General Assembly itself produced its own lengthy corroborating testimony.[2] John Smith's *General History* and George Percy's *True Relation* both appeared in the midst of this controversy. Although Strachey wrote his *True Reportory* fifteen years earlier, this unequivocal endorsement of the Company's wisdom under Smythe was first published during this public controversy.

### THE CITY ON A HILL

In a 1954 issue of the *Saturday Evening Post*, a disgruntled Southern apologist named Herbert Ravenel Sass complained that "in the mass American consciousness . . . Plymouth Rock and the Pilgrims have simply obliterated Jamestown and the Virginia colonists, who preceded them by thirteen years." Sass, the Southern gentleman, insisted that "[t]he strong but terrifying zealotry which ruled Massachusetts with an iron hand, the hangman's noose and Beelzebub's brimstone" did not come close to representing the "liberal philosophy" that Americans held dear. The eminent historian Bernard DeVoto immediately wrote up a rebuttal from his book-crammed study in West Newton, Massachusetts. "Now Charleston is a beautiful and gracious city," he wrote with condescension, "[b]ut it has certain ways of looking at the world which suggest defects of vision." If the American consciousness remembers the Pilgrims, it's because the Puritans produced "remarkable writers," like William Bradford, "whose *Of Plimoth Plantation* is one of the masterpieces of American literature." According to the Yankee historian, that narrative "was so graphic, so charged with emotion, so alive with homely details of Plymouth's daily life that it created images and symbols which have delighted people ever since."

The *Saturday Evening Post* was right to frame the rivalry as a competition between versions of American identity. Long before this spat between Sass and DeVoto, Jamestown and Plymouth had been jostling for the right to tell America's origin story. In the early Republic, Jamestown might have had the edge. Bradford's *Of Plimoth Plantation* had not yet been discovered, and the lively character of Pocahontas engaged the public in a way no Pilgrim could. In 1994 the scholar Robert S. Tilton published his study of all of the many texts representing Pocahontas, from travel narratives to scientific treatises (for example, in 1787, *An Essay on the Causes of the Variety of Complexion and Figure in the Human Species* by the Reverend Samuel Stanhope Smith) to stage plays and novels. Tilton's bibliography includes twenty-seven different eighteenth-century texts, including four by Thomas Jefferson, that retold the Pocahontas story. In the nineteenth century, there were hundreds. As early as 1800, Tilton writes, "Pocahontas was already beginning to take on a mythic significance." She was the "heroic rescuer and the savior" of Jamestown. Her marriage to John Rolfe, and the ever-widening spread of their progeny among Virginia's gentry, symbolized the "merging of the two peoples." Most nineteenth-century commentators admitted that this marriage was "a model that, to the detriment of both Indians and whites, had not been followed." Nevertheless, the myth was important, for it confirmed the difference between the American and the European. In confrontation with natives, the European metamorphosed by absorbing much of the culture (if not the blood) of those he fought. The hugely popular Southern novelist William Gilmore Simms painted a fine example of this mystical process of absorption through obliteration in his 1835 novel, *The Yemassee*. It is a historical novel dramatizing the Yemassee War of 1715, which was his native South Carolina's equivalent of Opechancanough's war in 1622. The Indians, of course, lose

"Marriage of Pocahontas," engraved by
John McRae in 1855.

the war, but in the process of their extermination they become
mythic progenitors of white America. Embodied in Native Americans, our heroic age closed yesterday, not thousands of years ago, as
it did for Europeans. Although this tendency is evident in novelists
of the middle states, such as Washington Irving and James Fenimore
Cooper, by the 1850s it became a Southern version of the American
Genesis.

"The Pocahontas narrative," Tilton argues, became the "recol-
lection of the founding moment of a particularly southern culture."
Eventually this Jamestown story helped Southern nationalists
distinguish themselves from Northerners.[3]

Northern scholars, mostly from Massachusetts, began attacking
John Smith's credibility in order to demythologize Pocahontas and
thereby delegitimize the Southern version of the American genesis.
The first salvo came obscurely enough in 1860 in the *Transactions and
Collections of the American Antiquarian Society*, a publication of a Massa-
chusetts organization. The most famous of the demythologizers was
Henry Adams, scion of the famous Massachusetts political family,

who, in 1862, considered his historical argument "a flank, or rather a rear attack, on the Virginia aristocracy . . ." The ideological nature of the dispute cannot be mistaken: it was an intellectual version of the battles fought at Gettysburg and Antietam, and the result, although it came more gradually and long after the Civil War, was as decisive as Lee's surrender at Appomattox. We must remember that the first time Thanksgiving was celebrated as a "national" holiday was in 1863, with a proclamation thanking God for (among other things) the "advancing armies and navies of the Union." For generations after, white Southerners must have felt that the festooning of the "national" holiday with images of New England was a slap in the face. The Pilgrim holiday no longer signifies Northern triumph and Southern defeat, but when exactly it stopped doing so is impossible to say. Surely it was not until the twentieth century, probably not till the First World War. Herbert Sass's pique indicates that in some hearts the sentiment lasted a long time.[4]

The Pilgrims' eclipsing Pocahontas began with the discovery (in the 1840s) of Bradford's *Of Plimouth Plantation*. The first edition of the narrative was edited and privately published in 1856 by none other than Charles Deane, the same Massachusetts scholar who initiated the attack on John Smith's *General History*. The influence of this discovery on American identity cannot be overemphasized. As Bernard DeVoto rightly noted, that narrative brought vivid color to the spare charcoal lines that, until then, had sketched the Puritan colony. The Puritans finally had characters who could rival the vivid and charming Smith and Pocahontas. Two years later Henry Wadsworth Longfellow composed his epic *The Courtship of Miles Standish*, and the romantic poem became an instant bestseller. The Union victory in the Civil War gave New England a decisive moral advantage: for the next several generations, no one would look to the antebellum, rebellious South for an acceptable story of America's birth.

In 1915 the Boston literary scholar Van Wyck Brooks published an impassioned polemic, "On Creating a Usable Past," which called for the formation of a canon of American literature, the loamy soil in which contemporary writers might plant their roots. Within about a generation, scholars of New England's culture and history—many of them (including Brooks himself) either trained or teaching at Harvard University—established the Puritans as this font of American identity. Even the famous Frederick Jackson Turner, whose "frontier thesis" helped turn historians' gaze westward, was recruited to the cause. Harvard lured him from the University of Wisconsin in 1910, and four years later, when he applied his thesis to the earliest years of colonial America, he chose Massachusetts, not Virginia, as the object of his study.[5]

So matters stood when Herbert Sass complained to the *Saturday Evening Post* that the Pilgrims hardly embody the "liberal" values of twentieth-century Americans. Sass did not elaborate those values: he took it for granted his readers understood what they were. And probably they did. Henry Luce probably spoke for most Americans when, back in 1939, he famously wrote in *Life* magazine that the twentieth century should be the "American century." He urged the nation not only to join England's fight against Germany but to accept the role that was thrust upon it two years later when the Japanese bombed Pearl Harbor: leader of the free world. "We have some things in this country," Luce wrote, "which are infinitely precious and especially American—a love of freedom, a feeling for the equality of opportunity, a tradition of self-reliance and independence and also of co-operation. In addition to ideals and notions which are especially American, we are the inheritors of all the great principles of Western civilization—above all Justice, the love of Truth, the ideal of Charity."[6]

Herbert Sass thought anyone honestly reading Bradford's Pilgrim epic would look in vain for these ideals. Of course he was right, but by the mid-fifties the Pilgrims proved useful again. We were fighting not fascists but atheistic communists, and Pilgrim piety became a very useful referent. In 1953, in his first inaugural address, Dwight Eisenhower turned Luce's ideals into an "abiding *creed* of our fathers." Where Luce tried to convince Americans to consent to the responsibility of leading the free world, the new president attributed our international role to divine election.[7] By the 1960s our culture was using the Pilgrims, as Nathaniel Philbrick puts it, to "symbolize all that is good about America." John Kennedy was the first to use John Winthrop's "city set upon a hill" as a national metaphor, and since then the religious discourse of "covenants," "promised land," and "chosen people" have provided sustenance to both Democrats and Republicans. On the shrill and rocky peaks of partisan politics, footing may be uncertain, but the Pilgrim myth has become common ground, the solid bottomland of bipartisan cultural belief.[8]

Growing from that soil is the conviction that God chose Americans for special blessings, and to deserve these blessings we must keep pure and cleave to a romanticized vision of a more righteous past. According to this myth, the foundational contract of the United States is this covenant with God first articulated on the *Arbella* in 1630. The Puritan myth of Exodus provided a very useful origin tale, helping us combat Eastern Bloc communism. For several generations, then, the Pilgrims helped to spread rather than diminish liberty and equality around the globe.

But the Exodus myth always tends towards tyranny. People imperil their own sovereignty the longer they use such myths of origin. The deep narrative of the Pilgrims is about resisting temptation, enforcing obedience, excluding outsiders, clinging to doctrine when contradicted by scientific truth, suppressing dissent, and expelling or executing the dissenter. Fidelity to orthodoxy or simply to the tyrant will eventually, inevitably, mark the good citizen. Some Jeremiah is sure to rise up and promise to lead America back to its original greatness. Orthodoxy need not be the theocratic government beloved by William Bradford. The tyrant can adopt any face— whichever version of purity most excites the zealots. This book means to repudiate the logic underlying Exodus and provide an alternative to this tale of national origin.

Jamestown is a better place to look for the genesis of American ideals. The sectional prejudice of the nineteenth-century attacks on Jamestown are now generally acknowledged, and Philip Barbour's definitive biography of Captain John Smith, first published in 1964, has done much to restore belief in most of Smith's testimony.[9] But restoring the importance of Virginia does not mean returning to those early days of the Republic, when Southern nationalists appropriated Pocahontas as the mythical progenitor of Virginia's slaveocracy. If we are to readopt Jamestown narratives as the foundational texts of American identity, we must read them in a new way, subversively, with sympathy for the idlers, discontents, and mutineers.

## THE MAYFLOWER COMPACT

According to Thomas Jefferson, governments derive their powers from the "consent of the governed," and when government becomes tyrannical, the people should withdraw their consent and write up a new contract. More importantly, the American people themselves asserted these principles when their representatives, assembled in Congress, adopted the Declaration of Independence in 1776. The United States Constitution asserts that the government instituted therein is the will of "the people" themselves. The most celebrated precursor to the Declaration and the Constitution is the remarkable document signed by forty-one men on the *Mayflower*, then riding at anchor off the coast of what they would name "Plymouth" in Massachusetts.

The importance of the Mayflower Compact cannot be denied. "We whose names are underwritten . . ." So begins the document, using the standard form of mutual consent that the Constitution would use nearly 170 years later: *We the People.* Historians have long credited the Pilgrims with writing the compact. As I mentioned in the Introduction, James Truslow Adams's 1931 *Epic of America* asserted that "the Pilgrims . . . even before they landed from the *Mayflower* . . . [realized that] some government was needful . . . They simply avoided the possible dangers of anarchy or an iron dictator by agreeing to abide by the expressed *common* will." And more recently: "Just as a spiritual covenant had marked the beginning of their congregation in Leiden," wrote Nathaniel Philbrick in his *Mayflower*, "a civil covenant would provide the basis for a secular government in America."[10] It is, perhaps, natural that historians should leap to this conclusion, because the Compact comes to us in the narratives written by the Pilgrims themselves. It was first published in England in 1622 in a part of *Mourt's Relation* that was penned by Plymouth Plantation's governor, William Bradford, and today it is usually framed as part of Bradford's *Of Plimouth Plantation.* The Compact has belonged, so speak, to the Pilgrims, the folk Bradford calls the "Saints," those who belonged to his congregation of Separatists. But was it their work? Was it modeled, as Philbrick claims, on *spiritual* covenants?[11]

If we read Bradford's narrative with the same level of suspicion that we have regarded Strachey's *True Reportory* and John Smith's *General History*, another possibility presents itself: that the real credit for the Compact belongs with the outsiders, those on the *Mayflower* who were not among the chosen people. From Bradford's point of view, these people were "Strangers." Rarely do readers question Bradford's point of view, but any dispassionate examination of the *Mayflower*'s manifest will surely undermine his terminology. Bradford's "strangers" are much more like us than the *Mayflower's* self-styled *chosen* people.

The "first foundation of their government," Bradford explained, was "occasioned partly by the discontented & mutinous speeches that some of the strangers amongst them had let fall." The strangers argued that the "patente" for the colony designated a spot in "Virginia," while the *Mayflower* was hovering off the coast of "New-england, which belonged to an other Government, with which the Virginia Company had nothing to doe." In other words, "when they came a shore," the contract binding them to government by the Company would be voided. The Strangers threatened to "use their owne libertie; for none had the power to comand them."[12] The Strangers' argument, yet another insistence on the right of self-determination, predicated as it is on a notion of free men living in a wilderness, sounds remarkably like Stephen Hopkins's political discourse in Bermuda. The words are almost identical to those attributed to Hopkins in Strachey's indictment of the yeoman farmer. The resemblance should not surprise us: Stephen Hopkins was one of the "stangers" on the *Mayflower*.

Hopkins did not die, as he feared he would, laboring in the swampy lowlands of Virginia. During perhaps five or more years of slave-like labor, he learned considerable woodcraft and the Algonquian language. By the time the Company granted him permission to return to England, he was an accomplished frontiersman. He was living in London when he heard the promotions for a new colony to be established on the Hudson River. He knew that his skills made him one of the adventure's most valuable recruits, and in September 1620 he, his wife, and their three children embarked on the *Mayflower*. The difficult passage—the storm, the near foundering of the ship—must have brought to his mind the fate of the *Sea Venture*, just as what he observed of the colony's leadership might have reminded him of Gates, De La Warr, and Dale.

"We whose names are underwritten," the compact reads, "do by these presents mutualy in the presence of God, and one of another, covenant & combine our selves togeather into a civill body politick."

It was the Strangers—not the Saints—who insisted this contract would "be as firme as any patent" granted by the Virginia Company, "and in some respects more sure." The new body politick would be empowered to "enacte, constitute, and frame such just & equall lawes, ordinances, acts, constitutions, & offices, from time to time, as shall be thought most meete & convenient for the general good of the Colonie." It seems very likely that these civil protections and the legitimizing emphasis on mutual consent were carefully drafted by someone who had suffered when those same powers of government were put into the hands of a single man. The "just & equall lawes" of Plymouth certainly promised to serve the common good more than the *Articles, Lawes, and Orders* published by Strachey in 1611, which were drafted to serve the Company's bottom line. The signatories of the Compact promised "all due submission and obedience" to the body politick they themselves created. What Stephen Hopkins had hoped to accomplish in Bermuda seemed to be coming to fruition.[13]

John Carver, the man elected governor—"or rather," as Bradford put it, "confirmed" governor—did not manage colonial matters much better than Percy had managed Jamestown. More than half the settlers in Plymouth died the first winter. Trouble times had come. In the midst of the disaster, "discontents & murmurings ar[o]se amongst some, and mutinous speeches & carriags in other." But the governor and the "better part" of settlers "quelled & overcame" these dissensions. Bradford's *better part* is a curious phrase. He did not use it, as Strachey used *better sort*, to mean gentlemen as opposed to commoners. He might have meant the "better part" of the whole, that is, the majority, which would mean that the survivors in Plymouth had established a healthy democracy. But it seems likely that Bradford's "better part" was the Saints, "which clave faithfully togeather in the maine," as they should in an Exodus tale. They "clave" together so faithfully that the Puritans ruined the body politick imagined by Stephen Hopkins. Government in Plymouth did not serve the common good as well as it served the theocratic aims of its elites. In Virginia, the interests of the Company's investors dictated policy. In Plymouth, the "Saints" were the dictators. Very quickly a strict, authoritative, oppressive theocratic government reigned.

Hopkins lived another quarter century in Plymouth Plantation, making his living as the publican of a tavern on Leyden Street. His rebel days were over. He toed the line for a while and was even elected to the governor's council, a body that settled civil disputes between settlers. But he did not become one of the chosen people. Men drank liquor in his place on Sundays, and they played games that annoyed pious men like Bradford. Hopkins had the temerity to serve alcohol to servants in his tavern the same as he served their betters, which also got him in trouble. Apparently he dabbled in a black market, undermining the government's monopolies on trade. In 1636 he fell afoul of the law for fighting with a twenty-one-year-old newly arrived settler, and he never recovered his public stature.[14]

He was a survivor. In 1644, at sixty-three years of age, Hopkins, then a widower, had five children, aged nineteen to thirteen, still living in his house, while the two oldest lived elsewhere in Plymouth and already had given him more than half a dozen grandchildren. The family was multiplying rapidly, and Hopkins was a man of some material substance as well. He owned two bulls, four cows, and several calves, pigs, and chickens. The house was well furnished, with rugs, beds, bolsters, and a kitchen fully stocked with "pans, porringers, funnels, salt shakers, basins, dishes, spoons, graters, candels and baking tubs." He was not rich, but he was certainly living comfortably when he succumbed to the quiet death of a middle-class innkeeper.

The real origin story of America is not embodied in the myth we cherish of the Pilgrims. It resides in the lives of innkeepers, the servants who drank at the inns, the diggers-up-of-roots, the card players, the fornicators, those who trucked with Indians, the defiers of tyranny, the idlers, the disobedient, the victims of witch hunters, the deserters and exiles and escapees and all the great variety of maroons who demanded of the world the right of self-determination. Eventually, they won out. By the end of his narrative Bradford has already morphed descended into a screechy Jeremiah. He decries Plymouth's failure to cleave to the true faith. He rants against the sinners. He forewarns the colony that breaking their covenant with God will end in retribution.

In a little over a year, we will celebrate the four hundredth anniversary of the *Mayflower* crossing, the landing at Plymouth Rock, the suffering of the first winter, the first Thanksgiving dinner, and the erection of civil society. That anniversary is sure to trigger a dozen new histories of the Pilgrims' plantation. It is right and fitting that it should, so long as the new histories pay more attention to those who did not write the narratives. As in Jamestown, the truly American story is the lives of the discontents. We need to discard that image of a city shining on a hill, because it is populated by a pure and uncontaminated chosen people cleaving to doctrine. Our city does not shine. It is messy. It is the nature of a free society. We are castaways in the twenty-first century, where we must salvage what is valuable from the old world and adapt to the new. Each new generation must remake its sovereignty by pledging mutual consent, for we are always marooned.

## ACKNOWLEDGMENTS

**When writing a book like this,** one tends to see maroons not only in the obvious channels, like *Pirates of the Caribbean* and *Peter Pan*, but in episodes of *Seinfeld* and *Doctor Who*. My family—Susan, Spencer, Owen, and Hannah—have endured five years of maroon sightings, and they have done much to keep me honest and tried hard to keep me humble.

The argument of this book, that the idea of America came from the Atlantic maroon experience, percolated in a course that the historian Richard Bodek and I taught over three different semesters at the College of Charleston's Honors College, and the framing discussion of Exodus and jeremiads evolved in an early American literature course. I am especially grateful to the sixty or seventy undergraduates who tested the argument in several parts of the book, and to Richard Bodek, who I must give equal credit for the idea on which the book is founded.

Coming at a subject outside my own previous areas of expertise required a lot of help. For thirty years, my brother, Timothy Kelly, has tutored me in the methods of social history. Whatever is praiseworthy in my treatment of true maroons—escaped slaves—derives from the unflinching criticism of Richard and Sally Price, who examined key parts of the early manuscript. I hope that this final, completed manuscript will render proper credit to those brave people, the first Americans, who were not cast away in the wilderness but sought it as a place of liberty. Other participants in a conference on Marronage and Maroonage, sponsored by the Carolina Lowcountry and Atlantic World Program at the College of Charleston, were invaluable. In particular, I want to thank the scholar of early American literature, Steven Mentz; and the historian of absent-law communities in the Caribbean, Isaac Curtis.

At Historic Jamestowne, both William Kelso (director of archaeology) and James Horn (president and chief officer of the Jamestown Rediscovery Foundation) very generously contributed their time and encouragement to this project. It goes without saying but ought to be said anyway that any scholar who writes about Jamestown owes a debt to these two, whether or not they quote directly from their books. Helen Rountree's work has been extraordinarily helpful in understanding Tsenacomoco. I have never met her, but I could not have written this book without her. At the National Museum of Bermuda, Jane Downing provided invaluable help, as did Peter Frith of the St. George's Foundation in St. George, Bermuda. For help in finding and securing images, Roger Green and Melanie Pereira at the National Parks Service; Daisy Njoku at the Smithsonian Institute; Jamison Davis at the Virginia Historical Society; and most especially, Christopher Grimes, who painted several particularly beautiful and useful historic scenes concerning the *Sea Venture*.

Michael Casamento and Conor Synnett, both graduate students at the College of Charleston, contributed to my research, especially in its early stages.

I want to thank my colleagues at Bloomsbury Publishing, especially Anton Mueller. This book was once nearly twice as big as it is now, and if the finished product is at all readable, it is because Anton showed me where to take hammer and chisel to stone. I want to thank Grace McNamee and Barbara Darko, also at Bloomsbury. And a very warm and grateful acknowledgment for Jacqueline Flynn at Joelle Delbourgo Associates, who helped shape the book in its first, amorphous conception.

Finally, I want to thank my parents, Bill and Mary Lou Kelly, the unacknowledged progenitors to whom this book is dedicated. Creative scholarship begins in the garden of childhood. The roots of my work are still there.

## IMAGE CREDITS

Page x: Map by Gary Antonetti

Page 19: Royal Netherlands Institute of Southeast Asian and Caribbean Studies and Leiden University Library / Wikimedia Commons.

Page 24: Painted by Christopher Grimes and used with his permission.

Page 43: Courtesy National Park Service, Colonial National Historical Park

Page 63: By Internet Archive Book Images, via Wikimedia Commons

Page 71: Library of Congress.

Page 76: U.S. National Archives and Records Administration, via Wikimedia Commons.

Page 83: By John White, explorer and artist (British Museum, London), via Wikimedia Commons.

Page 97: Houghton Library, Harvard University, 007033465-METS.

Page 100: By Architect of the Capitol (Architect of the Capitol information webpage), via Wikimedia Commons.

Page 108: Houghton Library, Harvard University. 007033465-METS.

Page 142: *Group of cannibal Indians dismembering and cooking captive*, 1591. Library of Congress.

Page 166: Virginia / discovered and discribed [*sic*] by Captan [*sic*] John Smith, 1606; graven by William Hole. Library of Congress.

Page 191: Theodore de Bry's 1598 "Illustrations de Narratio regionum Indicarum per Hispanos quosdam devastattarum." Joos van Winghe, via Wikimedia Commons.

Page 193: Portrait of Sir Francis Drake; contained in *The World Encompassed by Sir Francis Drake, Being His Next Voyage to That to Nombre de Dios Formerly Imprinted: Carefully Collected out of the Notes of Master Francis Fletcher, Preacher in This Imployment*, 1628. Wikimedia commons.

Page 209: Baptista Boazio (fl. 1588–1606), Cartagena [Colombia], Hand-colored engraving, 1589. Jay I. Kislak Collection Rare Book and Special Collections Division, Library of Congress (25.4).

Page 222: University of Pennsylvania.

Page 256: Courtesy of the National Museum of Bermuda.

Page 292: Virginia / discovered and discribed [*sic*] by Captan [*sic*] John Smith, 1606; graven by William Hole. Library of Congress.

Page 321: By Samuel Purchas, 1577?–1626, via Wikimedia Commons.

Page 383: Photographed by Donald E. Hurlbert, Smithsonian Institution.

Page 383: Sculpted bust by Jiwoong Cheh. Coif head covering by Aimee Kratts. Photograph by Donald E. Hurlbert, Smithsonian Institution.

Page 408: The Bodleian First Folio, digital facsimile of the First Folio of Shakespeare's plays, Bodleian Arch. G c.7, http://firstfolio.bodleian.ox.ac.uk/.

Page 408: Wikimedia Commons.

Page 414: Simon van de Passe, via Wikimedia Commons.

Page 418: Library of Congress.

# BIBLIOGRAPHY

**CW**

Smith, John. *The Complete Works of John Smith (1580–1631)*. Philip Barbour, ed. 3 vols. Chapel Hill: University of North Carolina Press, 1986.

**GH**

Smith, John. *The General History: The Third Book—The proceedings and accidents of the English colony in Virginia, extracted from the authors folloing by William Simons, Doctor of Divinity*. London: Printed by I. D. and I. H. for Michael Sparkes, 1624. Republished in Haile, *JN*, 215–349.

**JN**

Haile, Edward Wright, ed. *Jamestown Narratives Eyewitness Accounts of the Virginia Colony The First Decade: 1607–1617*. Champlain, VA: Roundhouse, 1998.

**JV**

Barbour, Phillip, ed. *The Jamestown Voyages Under the First Charter 1606–1609*. 2 vols. Published for the Hakluyt Society. London: Cambridge University Press, 1969.

**TR**

Strachey, William. *A True Reportory of the wrack and redemption of Sir Thomas Gates, knight, upon and from the Islands of the Bermudas; his coming to Virginia, and the estate of that colony then, and after under the government of the Lord La Warre. July 15 1610*. In Haile, *JN*, 381–443.

**TRUE RELATION**

John Smith, *A True Relation of such Occurrences and Accidents of Note as hath hap'ned in Virginia since the First Planting of that Colony which is now resident in the South Part thereof, till the Last Return* (1608), in *JN*, 141–82.

**TWCJS**

Barbour, Phillip. *The Three Worlds of Captain John Smith*. Boston: Houghton, Mifflin: 1964.

Adams, Henry. "Captain John Smith." *North American Review* 104, no. 214 (January 1867): 1–30.

——. *The Letters of Henry Adams.* J. C. Levenson et al., eds. 2 vols. Cambridge, MA: Harvard University Press, 1982.

Adams, James Truslow. *The Epic of America.* Boston: Little, Brown, 1934.

——. *The March of Democracy: A History of the United States. Volume I: The Rise of the Union.* New York: Charles Scribner's Sons, 1965. First published in 1932.

——. *The Rise of the Union.* Vol. 1 of *The History of the United States.* New York: Charles Scribner's Sons, 1965; original copyright 1932.

de Aguado, Fray Pedro. *Historia de Venezuela.* Jerónimo Beckier, III, ed. Madrid: Imprenta y Editorial Maestre, 1950.

Alexander, Michelle. *The New Jim Crow: Mass Incarceration in the Age of Colorblindness.* New York: New Press, 2010.

"The American Dream." Library of Congress. No date. Online. Accessed December 27, 2014.

Anderson, David L., ed. *The Columbia History of the Vietnam War.* New York: Columbia University Press, 2011.

Aneil, Morag Barbara. *"All the World Was America": John Locke and the American Indian.* Dissertation. University College London, 1992.

Aptheker, Herbert. *American Negro Slave Revolts.* New York: International Publishers, 1969.

——. "Maroons Within the Present Limits of the United States," in Price, *Maroon Communities,* 151–67. First published in *Journal of Negro History* 24 (1939): 167–84.

Ascraft, Richard. "Leviathan Triumphant: Thomas Hobbes and the Politics of Wild Men." In *The Wild Man Within: An Image in Western Thought from the Reaissance to Romanticism.* Edward Dudley and Maximillian E. Novak, eds. Pittsburgh: University of Pittsburgh Press, 1972, 141–82.

Axtell, James. "Colonial America Without the Indians," in *Major Problems in the history of the American West: Documents and Essays.* Clyde A. Milner, II, ed. Lexington, MA: D. C. Heath, 1989, 70–83.

——. *The Invasion Within the Contest of Cultures in Colonial North America.* New York: Oxford University Press, 1985.

——. "The White Indians of Colonial America." *William and Mary Quarterly* 32, no. 1 (January 1975): 55–88.

Baker, James W. *Thanksgiving: Biography of an American Holiday.* Hanover: University Press of New England, 2009.

Baker, Kevin. "Vanished Americans," *New York Times,* October 9, 2005, Section 7; Column 1; Book Review Desk; 21. LexisNexis. Web. Accessed October 13, 2016.

Barbour, Phillip L. "The Honorable George Percy, Premier Chronicler of the First Virginia Voyage." *Early American Literature* 6, no. 1 (Spring 1971): 7–17.

———, ed. *The Jamestown Voyages Under the First Charter 1606–1609*. 2 vols. Published for the Hakluyt Society. London: Cambridge University Press, 1969.

———. *The Three Worlds of Captain John Smith*. Boston: Houghton, Mifflin: 1964.

Beer, A. R. *Sir Walter Raleigh and His Readers in the Seventeenth Century: Speaking to the People*. Macmillan: Basingstoke, 1997.

Bercovitch, Sacvan. *The American Jeremiad*. Madison: University of Wisconsin Press, 1978.

———. "A Model of Cultural Transvaluation: Puritanism, Modernity, and New World Rhetoric." Keynote address. CUNY Renaissance Studies Conference, "Early Modern Trans-Atlantic Encounters: England, Spain, and the Americas," March 7, 1997.

"Bermuda's Cahow Recovery Program." Department of Environment and Natural Resources (Bermuda). Online, n.d. Accessed August 11, 2017. http://environment .bm/cahow-recovery-programme.

"Bermuda Cedar (*Juniperus bermudiana*)." Department of Environment and Natural Resources (Bermuda). Online, n.d. Accessed August 7, 2017. http://environment .bm/bermuda-cedar/.

"Bermuda Palmetto (*Sabal Bermudana*)." Department of Environment and Natural Resources. Online, n.d. Accessed August 7, 2017. http://environment.bm/bermuda -palmetto/.

"Bermuda Petrel (*Pterodroma cahow*)." Department of Environment and Natural Resources (Bermuda). Online, n.d. Accessed August 11, 2017. http://environment .bm/bermuda-petrel-cahow/.

Bernard, Virginia. *A Tale of Two Colonies: What Really Happened in Virginia and Bermuda*. Columbia: University of Missouri Press, 2011.

Blackwood, B. G. *The Lancashire Gentry and the Great Rebellion, 1640–1660*. Chetham Society, 3rd series, vol. 25 (1978).

Blanton, Dennis B. "Drought as a Factor in the Jamestown Colony, 1607–1612." *Historical Archeology* 34, no. 4 (2000): 74–81.

Bradford, William. *Bradford's History "Of Plimouth Plantation" from the Original Manuscript*. Boston: Wright & Potter, 1898. Electronic version prepared by Ted Hildebrandt, 2002.

Boss, Judith E. "The Golden Age, Cockaigne, and Utopia in *The Faerie Queene* and *The Tempest*." *Georgia Review* 26, no. 2 (Summer 1972): 145–55.

Bowman, George Ernest. *The Mayflower Compact and Its Signers with Facsimiles and a List of the Mayflower Passengers 1620–1920*. Boston: Massachusetts Society of Mayflower Descendents, 1920.

Bradford, John W. *The 1607 Popham Colony's Pinnace Virginia: An In-Context Design of Maine's First Ship*. Maine Authors Publishing: Rockville, 2011.

"braue English Iipsie, the." Anonymous. London: John Trundle, c. 1597–1626. English Broadside Ballad Archive. University of California, Santa Barbara. Online. Accessed April 21, 2017.

Brown, Alexander. *The Genesis of the United States*. 2 vols. Boston: Houghton, Mifflin, 1891.

Buchanan, Judith. *"Forbidden Planet* and the Retrospective Attribution of Intentions." In *In Film/fiction*, Deborah Cartmell, I. Q. Hunter, and Imelda Whelehan, eds. London: Pluto Press, 2001, 148–62.

Campbell, Joseph. *The Power of Myth*. With Bill Moyers. Betty Sue Flowers, ed. Doubleday: New York: 1988.

Canny, Nicholas. "The Ideology of English Colonization: From Ireland to America." *William and Mary Quarterly* 30, no. 4 (October 1973): 575–98.

Carey, Vincent. "'As lief to the gallows as go to the Irish wars': Human Rights and the Abuse of the Elizabethan Soldier in Ireland, 1600–1603." *Journal of the Historical Association* 99, no. 336 (July 2014), 468–86.

Charlton, Kenneth. "Liberal Education and the Inns of Court in the Sixteenth Century." *British Journal of Educational Studies* 9, no. 1 (1960): 25–38.

Cliff, Michelle. "Caliban's Daughter." *Journal of Caribbean Literatures* 3, no. 3 (Summer 2003): 157–60.

Cliffe, J. T. *The Yorkshire Gentry from the Reformation to the Civil War*. London: Athlone Press, 1969.

Coleman, William Macon. *The History of the Primitive Yankees; or, The Pilgrim Fathers in England and Holland*. Washington, D.C.: Columbia, 1881.

Colón, Fernando. *The History of the Life and Deeds of the Admiral Don Christopher Columbus*. Ilaria Caraci Luzzana, ed. Geoffrey Syncox and Blair Sullivan, trans. Vol. 13 of the Repertorium Columbianum. Turnhout, Belguim: Brepols, 2004.

Cook, Noble David. Reviewed Work: *1491: New Revelations of the Americas before Columbus*, *Journal of Latin American Geography* 5, no. 1 (2006): 130–31.

Cronon, William, George Miles, and Jay Gitlin, eds. *Under an Open Sky: Rethinking America's Western Past*. New York: W.W. Norton, 1991.

Crosby, Alred W. *The Columbian Exchange: Biological and Cultural Consequences of 1492*. Westport, CN: Praeger, 2003. (First published 1972.)

———. *Ecological Imperialism: The Biological Expansion of Europe, 900–1900*.

Csicsila, Joseph. *Canons by Consensus: Critical Trends and American Literature Anthologies*. Studies in American Literature and Realism series, Gary Scharnhorst, ed. Tuscaloosa: University of Alabama Press, 2004.

Culliford, S. G. *William Strachey, 1572–1621*. Charlottesville: University of Virginia Press, 1965.

Cummins, John. *Francis Drake: The Lives of a Hero*. New York: St. Martin's Press, 1995.

Curtis, Isaac. "Masterless Peoples: Maroons, Pirates, Commoners," in *The Caribbean: A History of the Region and Its Peoples*, Stephen Palmié and Francisco A. Scarano, eds. Chicago: University of Chicago Press, 2011, 149–62.

Dampier, William. *Voyages and Descriptions*. 3rd edition. London: James Knapton, 1705. Eighteenth Century Collections Online. University of Michigan Library, September 2008. Accessed July 18, 2016.

Davis, John Patterson. *Corporations: A Study of the Origin and Development of Great Business Combinations and of their Relation to the Authority of the State*. 2 vols. New York: G. P. Putnam's Sons, 1905.

Davis, Kenneth C. *America's Hidden History: Untold Stories of the First Pilgrims, Fighting Women, and Forgotten Founders Who Shaped a Nation*. New York: Harper, 2008.

de las Casas, Bartolemé. *A Short History of the Destruction of the Indies*. Nigel Griffen, ed. and trans. London: Penguin, 1992.

Denevan, W. M. "Pristine Myth," in the *Encyclopedia of Cultural Anthropology*, D. Levinson and M. Ember, eds. New York: Holt, 1996, vol. 3, 1034–36.

———. "The Pristine Myth: The Landscape of the Americas in 1492," *Annals of the Association of American Geographers* 82, no. 3 (1992): 369–85.

Desbarats, Catherine. "Following *The Middle Ground*." *William and Mary Quarterly* 63, no. 1 (January 2006), 81–96.

Denning, Michael. "Class and Culture: Reflections on the Work of Warren Susman," *Radical History* Review 36 (1986): 110–13.

"Description of a Great Sea-Storm, / That happened to some Ships in the Gulph of FLORIDA, in September last [1670]; Drawn up by one of the / Company, and sent to his Friend at London." London: Thomas Milbourn, 1671. English Broadside Ballad Archive. University of California, Santa Barbara. Online. Accessed April 21, 2017.

Diamond, Jared. "In Conversation with Jared Diamond: "Traditional Societies Are Not Frozen Models of the Past." Interview with Peter Christoff. *Conversation*. March 1, 2013. Online. Accessed September 28, 2017.

———. *The World Until Yesterday: What Can We Learn from Traditional Societies?* New York: Penguin, 2012.

Dillon, John. "Plato and the Golden Age." *Hermathena* 153 (Winter 1992): 21–36.

Dobyns, Henry F. *Their Number Become Thinned: Native American Population Dynamics in Eastern North America*. University of Tennessee Press, 1983.

Doherty, Kieran. *Sea Venture: Shipwreck, Survival, and the Salvation of the First English Colony in the New World*. New York: St. Martin's Press, 2007.

Douthwaite, William Ralph. *Gray's Inn, Its History & Associations*. London: Reeves and Turner, 1886.

Dudley, Edward, and Maximillian E. Novak, eds. *The Wild Man Within: an Image in Western Thought from the Reaissance to Romanticism*. Pittsburgh: University of Pittsburgh Press, 1972.

Edwards, David, Pádraig Lenihan, and Clodagh Tait, eds. *Age of Atrocity: Violence and Conflict in Early Modern Ireland*. Dublin: Four Courts, 2007.

Eisenhower, Dwight David. Inaugural Address, January 20, 1953, delivered in person at the Capitol. Eisenhower Presidential Library, Museum and Boyhood Home. N.d. Online. Accessed December 27, 2014.

Eliade, Mircea. *Myth and Reality*. Willard R. Trask, trans. New York: Harper & Row, 1963.

Elizondo, Virgil. "The New Humanity of the Americas." In Leonardo Boff and Virgil Elizondo, eds., *1492–1992: The Voice of the Victims*. London: SCM Press, 1990.

Elkins, Stanley, and Eric McKitrick. "A Meaning for Turner's Frontier: Democracy in the Old Northwest." In George Rogers Taylor, ed., *The Turner Thesis: Concerning the Role of the Frontier in American History*. Boston: D.C. Heath, 1956, 144–60.

Virginia Foundation for the Humanities. *Encyclopedia Virginia*. Virginia: Virginia Humanities and Library of Virginia, 2002–. www.encyclopediavirginia.org.

Escalante, Aquiles. "Palenques in Colombia," in Richard Price, ed., *Maroon Societies: Rebel Slave Communities in the Americas*. 3rd edition. Baltimore: Johns Hopkins University Press, 1996, 74–81. From Aquiles Escalante, "Notas sobre el palenque de San Basilio, una communidad negra en Colombia," *Divulganciones Ethnologicas* 3, no, 5 (1954): 207–359. The selection in Price is translated from 225–31.

Fantina, Robert. *Desertion and the American Soldier, 1776–2005*. New York: Algora, 2006.

Faragher, John Mack. Introduction to Frederick Jackson Turner, *Rereading Frederick Jackson Turner: "The Significance of the Frontier in American History" and other Essays*. New York: Henry Holt, 1994.

Fielder, Leslie. *The Stranger in Shakespeare*. New York: Stein and Day, 1972.

"Forget the 1%; Free exchange." *Economist*, November 8, 2014, 79 (US). *Academic OneFile*. Online. Accessed February 25, 2015.

Francis, Richard. *Judge Sewall's Apology: The Salem Witch Trials and the Forming of an American Conscience*. New York: HarperCollins, 2005.

Franco, José L. "Maroons and Slave Rebellions in the Spanish Territories," in Richard Price, ed., *Maroon Societies: Rebel Slave Communities in the Americas*. 3rd edition. Baltimore: Johns Hopkins University Press, 1996, 35–48.

Frazer, Sir James George. *The Golden Bough: A Study in Magic and Religion*. New York: Macmillan, 1922, 1950.

Fuchs, Barbara. "Contextualizing *The Tempest*." *Shakespeare Quarterly* 48, no. 1 (Spring 1997): 45–62.

Gamble, Richard M. *In Search of the City on a Hill: the Making and Unmaking of an American Myth*. New York: Bloomsbury, 2012.

Gleach, Frederick W. *Powhatan's World and Colonial Virginia: A Conflict of Cultures*. Lincoln: Unversity of Nebraska Press, 1997.

*Global Wealth Data Book 2013*, Credit Suisse Research Institute, October 2013.

Glover, Lorri. and Daniel Blake Smith. *The Shipwreck that Saved Jamestown: The Sea Venture Castaways and the Fate of America*. New York: Henry Holt, 2008.

Goldberg, Dror. "Money, Credit, and Banking in Virginia: 1585–1645." Unpublished part of the forthcoming book, *How Americans Invented Modern Money: 15851692*. University of Chicago Press. On-line. Accessed May 16, 2017. http://economics.yale .edu/sites/default/files/goldberg-paper.pdf.

Gradie, Charlotte M. "The Powhatans in the Context of the Spanish Empire," in Helen C. Rountree, ed. *Powhatan Foreign Relations, 1500–1722*. Charlottesville: University Press of Virginia, 1993, 154–72.

———. "Spanish Jesuits in Virginia: The Mission That Failed." *Virginia Magazine of History and Biography* 96, no. 2 (April 1988): 131–56.

Greenblatt, Stephen. "Shakespeare's Montaigne." In Stephen Greenblatt and Peter G. Platt, eds., *Shakespeare's Montaigne: The Florio Translation of the Essays—A Selection*. New York: New York Review Books, 2014, ix–xxxiii.

Grizzard, Frank E., and D. Boyd Smith. *Jamestown Colony: A Political, Social, and Cultural History*. Santa Barbara, CA: ABC Clio, 2007.

Guasco, Michael. "'Free from the Tyrannous Spanyard'? Englishmen and Africans in Spain's Atlantic World." *Slavery and Abolition* 29, no. 1 (March 2008): 1–22.

Gunn, Giles. *Early American Writing*. New York: Penguin Books, 1994.

Haile, Edward Wright, ed. *Jamestown Narratives Eyewitness: Accounts of the Virginia Colony—The First Decade: 1607–1617*. Champlain, VA: Roundhouse, 1998.

———. *John Smith in the Chesapeake*. Champlain, VA: Roundhouse, 2008.

Hakluyt, Richard. *Discourse Concerning Western Planting Written in the Year 1584*. Charles Deane, ed. Cambridge, MA: Maine Historical Society, 1877.

———. *The Original Writings and Correspondence of the Two Richard Hakluyts*. Vol. 1. E. G. R. Taylor, ed. Hakluyt Society, 2nd Series, no. 71. London, 1935.

———, collector. *Principle Navigations, Voyages, Traffiques, and Discoveries of the English Nation. Vol. 1: Northern Europe*. Edmund Goldsmid, ed. Edinburgh, E. & G. Goldsmid, 1885. First published in 1589.

Hamlin, William M. "Florio's Montaigne and the Tyranny of 'Custome': Appropriation, Ideology, and Early English Readership of thye *Essayes*." *Renaissance Quarterly* 63, no. 2 (Summer 2010): 491–544.

Hammer, Paul E. J. "A Welshman Abroad: Captain Peter Wynn of Jamestown." *Parergon* 16, no. 1 (July 1998): 59–92.

Harrison, William. *Harrison's Description of England*. F. J. Furnivall, ed. 6th series, no. 1. London: 1877.

Hartle, Ann. *Michel de Montaigne: Accidental Philosopher*. New York: University of Cambridge Press, 2003.

Hayes-McCoy, G. A. "The Tudor Conquest: 1534–1603," in *The Course of Irish History*, T. W. Moody, F. X. Martin, and Dermot Keogh, eds. 5th edition. New York: Roberts Rinehart, 2011, 151–63.

———. "The Completion of the Tudor Conquest, and the Advance of the Counter-Reformation," chapter IV of *A New History of Ireland, III, Early Modern Ireland 1534–1691*, T. W. Moody, F. X. Martin, and F. J. Byrne, eds. Oxford: Clarendon Press, 1976, 94–141.

Hening, William Waller, ed. *Statutes at Large; Being a Collection of All the Laws of Virginia from the First Session of the Legislature*, in the Year 1619. Vol. 1. New York: R. & W. & G. Bartow, 1823.

Herrmann, Rachel. "The 'Tragicall Historie': Cannibalism and Abundance in Colonial Jamestown. *The William and Mary Quarterly* 68, no. 1 (January 2011): 47–74.

Herzogenrath, Bernd. *An American Body/Politic: A Deleuzian Approach.* Lebanon, NH: Dartmouth College Press, 2010.

Hobbes, Thomas. *Leviathan.* C. B. MacPherson, ed. Baltimore: Penguin Books, 1968.

Hodges, Margaret. *Hopkins of the Mayflower Portrait of a Dissenter.* New York: Farrar, Straus and Giroux, 1972.

Hodgkins, Christopher. "Stooping to Conquer: Heathen Idolatry and Protestant Humility in the Imperial Legend of Sir Francis Drake" *Studies in Philology* 94, no. 4 (Autumn 1997): 428–64.

[Holinshed, Raphael]. *The First and Second Volume of Chronicles. (The Third Volume) Newlie Augmented and Continued by J. Hooker Alias Vowell, Gent, and Others* (1587). H. Denham at the expense of J. Harrison, G. Bishop, R. Neweberie, H. Denham and T. Woodcocke.

Hoobler, Dorothy, and Thomas. *Captain John Smith: Jamestown and the Birth of the American Dream.* Hoboken, NJ: Wiley & Sons, 2006.

Horn, James. *A Kingdom Strange: The Brief and Tragic History of the Lost Colony of Roanoke.* Philadelphia: Basic Books, 2010.

——. *A Land As God Made It: Jamestown and the Birth of America.* Basic Books, 2006.

Horwitz, Tony. *A Voyage Long and Strange: On the Trail of Vikings, Conquistadors, Lost Colonists, and Other Adventurers in Early America.* New York: Picador, 2008.

Hulme, Peter. *Colonial Encounters: Europe and the Native Caribbean 1492–1797.* London and New York: Routledge, 1992.

Humber, John L. *Backgrounds and Preparations for the Roanoke Voyage, 1584–1590.* Raleigh, NC: America's Four Hundredth Anniversary Committee, 1986.

Innes, Paul. *Epic.* New York: Routledge, 2013.

Jarvis, Michael. *In the Eye of All Trade: Bermuda, Bermudians, and the Maritime Atlantic World, 1680–1783.* Chapel Hill: University of North Carolina Press, 2010.

Johnson, Caleb. *Here I Shall Die Ashore Stephen Hopkins: Bermuda Castaway, Jamestown Survivor, and* Mayflower *Pilgrim.* Xlibris: no location, 2007.

Jones, H. G., ed. *Raleigh and Quinn: The Explorer and:is Boswell.* North Caroliniana Society Imprints No. 14. Chapel Hill: North Caroliniana Society, 1987.

Jourdain, Sylvester. *A Discovery of the Bermudas,* in *a Voyage to Bermuda in 1609: Two Narratives.* 2nd edition. Louis B. Wright, ed. Charlottesville: University of Virginia Press, 2013, 103–16. First published as *A Discovery of the Bermudas, Otherwise Called the Isle of Devils.* London: John Windet, 1610.

Karp, Lauren. *Truth, Justice, and the American Way: What Superman Teaches Us About the American Dream and Changing Values within the United States.* Thesis. Oregon State University. June 4, 2009.

Keeler, Mary Frear, ed. *Sir Francis Drake's West Indian Voyage, 1585–86.* Burlington, VT: Ashgate, 2010. First published in 1975 as Works Issued by the Hakluyt Society, Second Series No. 148.

Kelly, Joseph. "The Evolution of Slave Ideology in Simms's *The Yemassee* and *Woodcraft*," *Simms Review* 20 (Summer/Winter 2012): 51–66.

Kelly, William, ed.*Docwra's Derry: A Narration of Events in North-west Ulster, 1600–1604*. Belfast: Ulster Historical Foundation, 2003.

Kelsey, Harry. *Sir Francis Drake: The Queen's Pirate*. New Haven, CT: Yale University Press, 1998.

Kelso, William M. *Jamestown, the Buried Truth*. Charlottesville, VA: University of Virginia Press, 2008.

Kennedy, John F. "City Upon a Hill" Speech (January 9, 1961). Miller Center University of Virginia. No date. Online. Accessed February 27, 2017. http://millercenter .org/president/kennedy/speeches/speech-3364.

Kessler-Harris, Alice. "From Warren Susman to Raymond Williams and Allen Ginsburg: Moving Towards a Future with Illusions." *European Contributions to American Studies* 43 (1999): 129–41.

Kingsbury, Susan Myra, ed. *The Records of the Virginia Company of London*. Vols. I–III. Washington, DC: US Government Printing Office, 1906.

Kupperman, Karen Ordahl. "Apathy and Death in Early Jamestown," *Journal of American History* 66, no. 1 (June 1979): 24–40.

———. *The Jamestown Project*. Cambridge: Harvard University Press, 2007.

———. *Roanoke: the Abandoned Colony*, 2nd edition. New York: Rowan and Littlefield, 2007.

———, ed.*Captain John Smith: A Select Edition of His Writings*. Chapel Hill: University of North Carolina Press, 1988.

Lacey, Robert. *Sir Walter Ralegh*. New York: Atheneum, 1974.

Leckie, Ross. "1491: The Americas Before Columbus," *Times* (London), November 11, 2006, Features; Books; 14. LexisNexis. Online. Accessed October 12, 2016.

Lee, Sidney. *Elizabethan and Other Essays*. Oxford: Clarendon Press, 1927.

Lemay, J. A. Leo. *The American Dream of Captain John Smith*. Charlottesville: University Press of Virginia, 1001.

———. "Captain John Smith: American(?)," *University of Mississippi Studies in English*, n.s. 5 (1984–1987): 288–96.

———. *Did Pocahontas Save Captain John Smith?* Athens: University of Georgia Press, 1992.

Lenman, Bruce. *England's Colonial Wars, 1550–1688: Conflicts, Empire and National Identity*. London: Routledge, 2001.

Lewis, Clifford M., and Albert J. Loomie, *The Spanish Jesuit Mission in Virginia, 1570–1572*. Chapel Hill: University of North Carolina Press, 1953.

Lyttleton, James and Colin Rynne, eds. *Plantation Ireland: Settlement and Material Culture c. 1550-c. 1700*. Dublin: Four Courts, 2009.

Lockley, Timothy James, ed., *Maroon Communities in South Carolina: A Documentary Record*. Columbia: University of South Carolina Press, 2009.

Lodge, Henry Cabot. "An American Myth." *Outlook* (August 26, 1911): 952–60.

Loewen, James. *Lies My Teacher Told Me*. New York: Norton, 1995.

Luce, Henry. "The American Century," *Life* (February 17, 1941): 61–65.

Madicott, J. R. "The Birth and Setting of the Ballads of Robin Hood," *English Historical Review* 93, no. 367 (April 1978): 276–99.

Maginn, Christopher, and Steven G. Ellis. *The Tudor Discovery of Ireland*. Dublin: Four Courts Press, 2015.

Major, R. H., ed. *Select Letters of Christopher Columbus: With Other Original Documents Relating to His Four Voyages to the New World*. 2nd edition. Digital. Burlington, VT: Ashgate, 2010. First published by the Hakluyt Society, London, 1870.

Malone, Edmund. *An Account of the Incidents, from Which the Title and Part of the Story of Shakespeare's* Tempest *Were Derived; and Its True Date Ascertained*. London: C. and R. Baldwin, 1808.

Maltby, William S. *The Black Legend in England: The Development of Anti-Spanish Sentiment, 1558–1660*. Durham, NC: Duke University Press, 1971.

Mancall, Peter. *Hakluyt's Promise: An Elizabethan's Obsession for an English America*. New Haven, CT: Yale University Press, 2007.

Mann, *1491: New Revelations of the Americas before Columbus*. New York: Knopf, 2005.

Marx, Karl, and Friedrich Engels. *The Communist Manifesto*. Jeffrey C. Isaac, ed. Rethinking the Western Tradition Series. New Haven, CT: Yale University Press, 2012.

Marx, Leo. "Shakespeare's American Fable." *Massachusetts Review* 2 (1960): 40–71.

McGinn, Christopher, and Stephen G. Ellis. *The Tudor Discovery of Ireland*. Dublin: Four Courts Press, 2015.

McGurk, John. *The Elizabethan Conquest of Ireland: The 1590s Crisis*. New York: Manchester University Press, 1997.

McMichael, George, et al., eds. *Anthology of American Literature*. 8th edition. Prentice-Hall, 2003.

McShane, Joseph M. S. J., "Winthrop's 'City Upon a Hill' in Recent Political Discourse." *America* (October 1, 1988): 194–98.

Mentz, Steven. *Shipwreck Modernity Ecologies of Globalization, 1550–1719*. Minneapolis: University of Minnesota Press, 2015.

Menzer, Paul, ed. *Inside Shakespeare: Essays on Blackfriars*. Cranbury, NJ: Associated University Presses, 2006.

Miller, Lee. *Roanoke: Solving the Mystery of the Lost Colony*. New York: Arcade, 2000, 2011.

Mills, Charles W. *The Racial Contract*. Ithaca, NY: Cornell University Press, 1997.

Montaigne, Michel. *The Essays of Montaigne Done into English by John Florio, Anno 1603*. John Florio, trans. George Saintsbury, ed. London: David Nutt, 1892.

——. *Shakespeare's Montaigne: The Florio Translation of the Essays—A Selection*. John Florio, trans. Stephen Greenblatt and Peter G. Platt, eds. New York: New York Review Books, 2014.

Morgan, Edmund S. *American Slavery American Freedom: The Ordeal of Colonial Virginia*. New York: W. W. Norton, 1975.

——. *The Pilgrim Dilemma: The Story of John Winthrop*. New York: Pearson Longman, 2006.

Mossiker, Frances. *Pocahontas: The Life and Legend*. New York: Knopf, 1976.

"Moving On Up Why Do Some Americans Leave the Bottom of the Economic Ladder, but Not Others?" Economic Mobility Project. Pew Charitable Trusts. November 7, 2013. Online. Accessed January 22, 2015.

Neill, Edward D. *History of the Virginia Company of London with Letters to and from the First Colony Never Before Printed*. Albany, NY: Joel Munsell, 1869.

Nelson, Richard J. "On the Geology of the Bermudas." *Transactions of the Geological Society of London*. Second series. 1837. Vol. 5, Part 1, 103–25.

Newton, John. *An Authentic Narrative of Some Remarkable and Interesting Particulars in the Life of John Newton Communicated in a Series of Letters to the Rev. Mr. Haweis. Rector of Aldwinckle, Northamptonshire*. New York: Evert Duyckinck, 1806.

Nicholls, Mark. "George Percy's 'Trewe Relacyon': A Primary Source for the Jamestown Settlement." *Virginia Magazine of History and Biography* 113, no. 3 (2005): 212–75.

Nicholls, Mark, and Penry Williams. *Sir Walter Raleigh: In Life and Legend*. London: Continuum, 2011.

Nichols, A. Bryant, Jr. *Captain Christopher Newport Admiral of Virginia*. Newport News, VA: Sea Venture, 2007.

Norton, Anne. *Alternative Americas: A Reading of Antebellum Political Culture*. Chicago: University of Chicago Press, 1986.

*Nova Britannia Offering Most Excellent Fruits by Planting in Virginia, Exciting All Such As Be Well Affected to Further the Same*. London: Samuel Machum, 1609. Reprinted in *American Colonial Tracts Monthly* 6 (October 1897).

Obama, Barack. "Remarks of the President at Fourth of July Celebration." The White House. Office of the Press Secretary. July 4, 2013. Online. Accessed January 7, 2015.

Oberg, Michael Leroy. *The Head in Edward Nugent's Hand: Roanoke's Forgotten Indians*. Philadelphia: University of Pennsylvania Press, 2010.

O'Grady, Standish, ed. *Pacata Hibernia, or A History of the Wars in Ireland During the Reign of Queen Elizabeth, Especially Within the Province of Munster and Under the Government of Sir George Carew and Compiled by His Directions and Appointment*. Vol. 1. London: Downey, 1896.

Onuf, Peter. Review of *Freedom Bound: Law, Labor, and Civic Identity in Colonizing English America* by Christopher Tomlins. *Journal of Legal Education* 61, no. 2 (November 2011): 316–24.

*Oxford English Dictionary*, 3rd edition, December 2000. Online.

Padget, Cindy D. "The Lost Indians of the Lost Colony: A Critical Legal Study of the Lumbee Indians of North Carolina." *American Indian Law Review* 21, no. 2 (1997): 391–424.

Palmer, Patricia. *Language and Conquest in Early Modern Ireland: English Renaissance Literature and Elizabethan Imperial Expansion*. New York: Cambridge University Press, 2004.

Parks, George Bruner. *Richard Hakluyt and the English Voyages*. 2nd edition. James A. Williamson, ed. New York: Frederick Ungar, 1961. First edition 1928.

Pattee, Fred Lewis. *Century Readings for a Course in American Literature*. New York: Century Co., 1919.

Percy, George. *A True Relation of the proceedings and occurents of moment which have hap'ned in Virginia from the time Sir Thomas Gates was shipwrack'd upon the Bermudes, anno 1609, until my departure out of the country, which was in anno Domini 1612*. In Edward Haile, *Jamestown Narratives*, 497–519. (A transcription of the only original copy, now at the Elkins Collection of the Free Library in Philadelphia: Nicholls, Mark. "George Percy's 'Trewe Relacyon': A Primary Source for the Jamestown Settlement." *Virginia Magazine of History and Biography*, vol. 113, no. 3, 2005, 212–75. *JSTOR*, www.jstor.org/stable/4250269.

Peterson, Douglas L. "A Probable Source for Shakespeare's Sonnet CXXIX." *Shakespeare Quarterly* 5, no. 4 (1954): 381–84.

Pettegree, Andrew. *The Invention of News: How the World Came to Know About Itself*. London: Yale University Press, 2014.

Philbrick, Nathaniel. *Bunker Hill: A City, a Siege, a Revolution*. New York: Viking, 2013.

———. *Mayflower: A Story of Courage, Community, and War*. New York: Penguin, 2007.

Pike, Ruth. "Black Rebels: The Cimarrons of Sixteenth-Century Panama." *Americas* 62, no. 2 (October 2007): 243–66.

Piketty, Thomas. *Capital in the Twenty-first Century*. Cambridge, MA: Harvard University Press, 2014.

Pollard, A. J. "Political Ideology in the Early Stories of Robin Hood," in *Outlaws in Medieval and Early Modern England: Crime, Government, and Society, c. 1066–c. 1600*. John C. Appleby and Paul Dalton, eds. Burlington, VT: Ashgate, 2009: 148–71.

Potter, Stephen R. *Commoners, Tribute, and Chiefs: The Development of Algonquian Culture in the Potomac Valley*. Charlottesville: University Press of Virginia, 1993.

Powell, William S. "Who Were the Roanoke Colonists?" in *Raleigh and Quinn: The Explorer and his Boswell*. H. G. Jones, ed. North Caroliniana Society Imprints No. 14. Chapel Hill: North Caroliniana Society, 1987, 51–68.

Price, David A. *Love and Hate in Jamestown: John Smith, Pocahontas, and the Heart of a New Nation*. New York: Knopf, 2003.

Price, Richard, *First-Time: The Historical Vision of an African American People*. Chicago: University of Chicago Press, 1983, 2002.

———. ed. *Maroon Societies: Rebel Slave Communities in the Americas*. 3rd edition. Baltimore: Johns Hopkins University Press, 1996.

"Publishing Shakespeare." Folger Shakespeare Library. No date. Online. Accessed April 24, 2017. http://www.folger.edu/publishing-shakespeare.

Quinn, David Beers, ed. *The Lost Colonists Their Fortune and Probable Fate*. Raleigh: North Carolina Division of Archives and History, 1984.

———. *The Roanoke Voyages, 1585–1590: Documents to Illustrate the English Voyages to North America under the Patent Granted to Sir Walter Raleigh in 1584*. Vol. 1. Works Issued by Hakluyt Society. Second Series, 114. Lessingdruckerei Wiesbaden: Hakluyt Society, 1952.

———. *Set Fair for Roanoke Voyages and Colonies, 1584–1606*. Chapel Hill: University of North Carolina Press, 1985.

Quitt, Martin H. "Trade and Acculturation at Jamestown, 1607–1609: The Limits of Understanding." *William and Mary Quarterly* 52, no. 2 (April 1995): 227–58.

Raine, David F. *Sir George Somers: A Man and His Times*. St. George's, Bermuda: Pompano, 1984.

Raleigh, Sir Walter. *The History of the World*. London: Walter Burre, 1614.

Raleigh, Walter Alexander. "The English Voyages of the Sixteenth Century." Introduction to Richard Hakluyt, *The Principle Navigations Voyages Traffiques & Discoveries of the English Nation*. vol. 12. Glasgow: James MacLehose & Sons, 1905–1907.

Ramsberger, Peter F., and D. Bruce Bell. *What We Know About AWOL and Desertion: A Review of the Professional Literature for Policy Makers and Commanders*. Alexandria, VA: U.S. Army Research Insititute for the Behavioral and Social Sciences, 2002.

Rapple, Rory. "Gilbert, Sir Humphrey (1537–1583)." *Oxford Dictionary of National Biography*. H. C. G. Matthew and Brian Harrison, eds. Oxford: Oxford University Press, 2004. Online edition, David Cannadine, ed. Accessed January 2012.

Reagan, Ronald. "Remarks at a Dinner Marking the loth Anniversary of the Heritage Foundation," October 8, 1983. Online by Gerhard Peters and John T. Woolley, *The American Presidency Project*. Accessed March 3, 2018. http://www.presidency.ucsb .edu/ws/?pid=40580.

Rediker, Marcus. *Between the Devil and the Deep Blue Sea: Merchant Seamen, Pirates and the Anglo-American Maritime World, 1700–1750*. New York: Cambridge University Press, 1987.

Reising, Russell. *The Unusable Past: Theory & the Study of American Literature*. New York: Methuen, 1986.

Richter, Daniel. Review of *Their Number Become Thinned*, in *William and Mary Quarterly* 41, no. 4 (October 1984): 649–53.

———. *Trade, Land, Power: The Struggle for Eastern North America*. Philadelphia: University of Pennsylvania Press, 2013.

———. "Tsenacommacah and the Atlantic World," in *The Atlantic World and Virginia, 1550–1624*. Peter C. Mancall, ed. Chapel Hill: University of North Carolina Press, 2007, 29–65.

Roberts, Neil. *Freedom as Marronage*. Chicago: University of Chicago Press, 2015.

Robinson, Paul, and Sarah Robinson. *Pirates, Prisoners, and Lepers: Lessons from Life Outside the Law*. N.p.: University of Nebraska Press, 2015.

Rochefort, Charles de. *The history of the Barbados, St. Christophers . . . and the rest of the Caribby-islands.* John Davies, trans. London: J.M., 1666.

Rose, Arnold M. "The Social Psychology of Desertion from Combat." *American Sociological Review* 16, no. 5 (1951): 614–29. Online.

Rountree, Helen C. *Pocahontas' People: The Powhatan Indians of Virginia Through Four Centuries.* Norman: University of Oklahoma Press, 1996.

———. *Pocahontas, Powhatan, and Opechancanough: Three Indian lives changed by Jamestown.* Charlottesville: University of Virginia, 2005.

———. *The Powhatan Indians of Virginia: Their Traditional Culture.* Norman: University of Oklahoma Press, 1989.

———, ed. *Powhatan Foreign Relations, 1500–1722.* Charlottesville, VA: University Press of Virginia, 1993.

Rountree, Helen C., and E. Randolph Turner. *Before and After Jamestown: Virginia's Powhatans and their Predecessors.* Gainesville: University Press of Florida, 2002.

Said, Edward. *Orientalism.* New York: Vintage Books, 1979.

Schaffer, Edward R. "The Myth of American Exceptionalism and Global Peace," in *Mythology: From Ancient to Post-Modern.* Jürgen Kleist and Bruce A. Butterfield, eds. New York: Peter Lang, 1992, 87–94.

Shakespeare, William. *The Tempest.* In *Mr. William Shakespeares Comedies, Histories, & Tragedies.* London: 1623. Digital facsimile of the Bodleian First Folio of Shakespeare's plays, Arch. G c.7. http://firstfolio.bodleian.ox.ac.uk/ff/tem/1/1.

Sidgwick, Frank, ed. *Ballads of Robin Hood and Other Outlaws.* Popular Ballads of the Olden Time Fourth Series. London: Sidgwick and Jackson, 1912. The Project Gutenberg Ebook of *The Ballads of Robin Hood and Other Outlaws* by Frank Sidgwick, 2009.

Singman, Jeffrey L. *Daily Life in Elizabethan England.* Daily Life Through History Series. Westport, CT: Greenwood Press, 1995.

Simmons, William S. "Cultural Bias in the New England Puritans' Perception of Indians." *William and Mary Quarterly* 38, no. 1 (January 1981): 56–72.

*Sir Francis Drake Revived. Who is or may be a Pattern to stirre up all Heroicke and active Spirits of the these Times, to benefit their Countrey and eternize their Names by like Noble ATTEMPTS. Being a Summary and true Relation of foure severall VOYAGES made by the said Sir FRANCIS DRAKE to the WEST-INDIES.* London: Nicholas Bourne, 1653 (1652).

Smith, John. *The Complete Works of John Smith, 1580–1631.* 3 vols. Philip Barbour, ed. Chapel Hill: University of North Carolina Press, 1986.

Smith, Sir Thomas. *The State of England, A.D. 1600 [De Republica Anglorum].* 3 vols. F. J. Fisher, ed. London: Offices of the Camden Society, 1936.

Snow, David R. "Picturing the Pre-Columbian Americas," *Science,* New Series, vol. 312, no. 5778 (June 2, 2006): 1313. LexisNexis. Online. Accessed October 12, 2016.

Southern, Ed, ed. *The Jamestown Adventure: Accounts of the Virginia Colony, 1605–1614.* Winston-Salem, NC: John F. Blair, 2004.

Spivak, Gayatri Chakravorty. "Three Women's Texts and a Critique of Imperialism." *Critical Inquiry* 12, no. 1 (Autumn 1985): 235–61.

Spurling, Sir Stanley. *Sir Thomas Smythe, knt., 1558?–1625, Governor of the East India Company and patron of Bermuda.* New York: Newcomen Society, 1955.

Stade, Hans. *The Captivity of Hans Stade of Hesse, in A.D. 1547–1555.* Albert Tootal and Richard F. Burton, eds., Farnham, UK: Ashgate, transferred to digitial printing 2010; originally published by the Hakluyt Society, 1874.

Stannard, David E. *American Holocaust: Columbus and the Conquest of the New World.* New York: Oxford University Press, 1992.

Stebbins, Sarah J. "Meet the State-Recognized Virginia Indian Tribes." Historic James-towne. The National Park Service. August 11, 2016. Online. Accessed September 29, 2017.

Stedman, John Gabriel. *Narrative, of a Five Years' Expedition, Against the Revolted Negroes of Surinam, in Guiana, on the Wild Coast of South America; from the Year 1772, to 1777: Elucidating the History of that Country, and Describing Its Productions . . . with an Account of the Indians of Guiana, & Negroes of Guinea.* 2nd edition, vol. 2. London: J. Johnson, 1813.

Stevens, Peter F. *The Rogue's March: John Riley and the St. Patrick's Battalion, 1846–48.* Washington, D.C.: Potomac Books, 2005.

Stick, David. *Roanoke Island: The Beginnings of English America.* Chapel Hill: University of North Carolina Press, 1983.

Strachey, William. *A true reportory of the wracke, and redemption of Sir THOMAS GATES Knight; vpon, and from the Ilands of the Bermudas: his comming to Virginia, and the estate of that Colonie then, and after, vnder the gouernment of the Lord LA WARRRE, Iuly 15. 1610.* In Edward Haile, *Jamestown Narratives,* 381–442. Originally published in Samuel Purchas, *Hakluytus posthumus; or, Purchas his pilgrimes.* Vol. 4. London: William Stansby, 1625. 1734–58.

Stromberg, Joseph. "Starving Settlers in Jamestown Colony Resorted to Cannibalism." Smithsonian.com. April 30, 2013. Accessed July 13, 2017.

Susman, Warren. *Culture as History: the Transformation of American Society in the Twentieth* Century. New York: 1984.

——. "History and the American Intellectual: Uses of a Usable Past" *American Quarterly* 16, no. 2 (Summer 1964): 243–63.

Symonds, William. *A Sermon Preached at White-Chappell, In the Presence of the Adventurers and Planters for Virginia.* London: I. Windet, 1609.

Taylor, George Rogers, ed. *The Turner Thesis: Concerning the Role of the Frontier in American History.* 3rd edition. Lexington, MA: D. C. Heath, 1972.

Tillyard, E. M. W. *Shakespeare's History Plays.* Harmondsworth, UK: Penguin, 1944.

Tilton, Robert S. *Pocahontas: The Evolution of an American Narrative.* New York: Cambridge University Press, 1994.

Todd, Jack. *Desertion in the Time of Vietnam.* New York: Houghton Mifflin Harcourt, 2001.

**BIBLIOGRAPHY**

Tomkins, Jane. *Sensational Designs: The Cultural Work of American Fiction, 1790–1860*. New York: Oxford University Press, 1985.

Turner, E. Randolph. "A Reexamination of Powhatan Territorial Boundaries and Population, ca. A.D. 1607," *Quarterly Bulletin of the Archeological Society of Virginia* 37 (1982): 45–64.

Turner, Frederick Jackson. *The First Official Frontier of the Massachusetts Bay*. Cambridge, MA: John Wilson and Son, 1914.

——. *The Frontier in American History*. With a forward by Ray Allen Bullington. New York: Holt, Rinehart and Winston, 1962. First copyright 1920.

——. *Rereading Frederick Jackson Turner: "The Significance of the Frontier in American History" and other Essays*. John Mack Faragher, ed. New York: Henry Holt, 1994.

Usner, Daniel H., Jr. *Indians, Settlers, and Slaves in a Frontier Exchange Economy: The Lower Mississippi Valley Before 1783*. Chapel Hill: University of North Carolina, 1992.

Vanderbilt, Kermit. *American Literature and the Academy: Roots, Growth, and Maturity of a Profession*. Philadelphia: University of Pennsylvania Press, 1988.

Van Rossum, Matthias and Jeannette Kamp. *Desertion in the Early Modern World: A Comparative History*. London: Bloomsbury, 2016.

Vaughan, Alden T. *American Genesis: Captain John Smith and the Founding of Virginia*. Boston: Little, Brown, 1975.

——. "The Americanization of Caliban." *Shakespeare Quarterly* 39, no. 2 (Summer 1988): 137–53.

——. *Captain John Smith*. Revised edition. New York: Twayne, 1993.

——. *New England Frontier: Puritans and Indians, 1620–1675*. Norman, OK: University of Oklahoma Press, 1965, 1979, 1995.

——. *Transatlantic Encounters: American Indians in Britain, 1500–1776*. Cambridge: Cambridge University Press, 2006.

——. "William Strachey's 'True Reportory' and Shakespeare: A Closer Look at the Evidence." *Shakespeare Quarterly* 59, no. 3 (2008): 245–73.

Vest, Jay Hansford C. "'Love You Not Me?' Pocahontas and the Virginia Masque: A Jacobean Drama in the Glade," *Journal of Intercultural Disciplines* 10 (Spring 2012): 9–22.

Vorallo, Daniel R. "Lincoln, Stowe, and the 'Little Woman/Great War' Story: The Making, and Breaking, of a Great American Anecdote" *Journal of the American Lincoln Association* 30, no. 1 (Winter 2009): 18–34.

Wallace, Willard M. *Sir Walter Raleigh*. Princeton, NJ: Princeton Univ. Press, 1959.

Waters, Tony. "Why Students Think There Are Two Kinds of American History." *History Teacher* 39, no. 1 (November 2005): 11–21.

Watts, Gordon Payne, Jr. *Shipwrecked: Bermuda's Maritime Heritage*. Bermuda: National Museum of Bermuda Press, 2014.

Weaver, Jace. *Red Atlantic: American Indigenes and the Making of the Modern World, 1000–1927*. Chapel Hill: University of North Carolina Press, 2014.

Weber, David J. *The Spanish Frontier in North America*. New Haven, CT: Yale University Press, 1992.

Weber, Max. *The Protestant Work Ethic and the Spirit of Capitalism: The Talcott Parsons Translation Interpretations.* New York: W. W. Norton, 2009.

West, Thomas. *The Relation of the Right Honorable the Lord De-La-Warre, Lord Governor and Captain Generall of the Colonie, planted in Virginia* (London: William Hall, 1611). Reprinted in London by C. Wittingham, 1858. Unpaginated pamphlet. Online at Archive.org. Accessed September 12, 2017.

White, Hayden. "The Forms of Wildness: Archeology of an Idea." In *The Wild Man Within: An Image in Western Thought from the Renaissance to Romanticism.* Edward Dudley and Maximillian E. Novak, eds. Pittsburgh: University of Pittsburgh Press, 1972, 3–38.

White, Richard. *The Middle Ground: Indians, Empires, and Republics in the Great Lakes Region, 1650–1815.* New York: Cambridge University Press, 1991.

Whitehead, Neil L. *Of Cannibals and Kings: Primal Anthropology in the Americas.* University Park: Pennsylvania State University Press, 2011.

Whitt, David, and John Perlich, eds. *Myth and the Modern World: Essays on Intersections with Ideology and Culture.* Jefferson, NC: MacFarland, 2014.

Wilberforce, Samuel. *A History of the Protestant Episcopal Church in America.* London: James Burns, 1844.

Wilderness Act. Public Law 88-577 (16 U.S. C. 1131–1136), 88th Congress, Second Session, September 3, 1964.

Willard, Pat. *The Secrets of Saffron: The Vagabond Life of the World's Most Seductive Spice.* Boston: Beacon Press, 2001.

Wingfield, Edward Maria. *A Discourse of Virginia.* Charles Deane, ed. In vol. 4 of *Transactions and Collections of the American Antiquarian Society.* Worcester, MA: American Antiquarian Society, 1860, 67–103.

Wingfield, Jocelyn R. *Virginia's True Founder: Edward Maria Wingfield and His Times 1550–1631.* 2nd edition. North Charleston, SC: Booksurge, 2007.

Wintrhop, John. "A Modell of Christian Charity." In Giles Gunn, *Early American Writing,* 108–112.

Wolfe, Brendan. "Sir Thomas Smythe (ca. 1558–1625)." *Encyclopedia Virginia.* Virginia Foundation for the Humanities, October 27, 2015. Online. Accessed August 16, 2016.

Woodward, Hobson. *A Brave Vessel: The True Tale of the Castaways Who Rescued Jamestown and Inspired Shakespeare's* The Tempest. New York: Viking, 2009.

Woolf, Virginia, *A Room of One's Own.* New York: Harcourt, Brace, Jovanovich, 1929, 1957.

Wright, Irene A. *Documents Concerning English Voyages to the Spanish Main, 1569–1580.* Works issued by the Hakluyt Society, 2nd series, 71. London: 1932.

Wright, Kaye. "*Crocus sativus* (saffron): A monograph," *Australian Journal of Herbal Medicine* 26, no. 1 (2014): 18–21.

Wrightson, Keith. *English Society: 1580–1680.* London: Routledge, 1993.

Zinn, Howard. *A People's History of the United States.* New York: HarperPerennial, 2003.

# NOTES

## INTRODUCTION: IN THE BEGINNING

1   For a very readable historical account of news circulation in seventeenth-century Europe, see Andrew Pettegree, *The Invention of News: How the World Came to Know About Itself.*

2   Shakespeare, *The Tempest*, I, i, 14–64, 1. Quotations from the Bodleian Library's online facsimile edition of the First Folio.

3   Bernhard, *Tale of Two Colonies*, 19.

4   See *Mayflower* for sailing in bad weather. For other details, Doherty, *Sea Venture*, 21. After Edmund Downing discovered the wreck's remains in 1958, and using shipbuilding standards of 1600, archaeologists were able to model the size and shape of the vessel. Cf. Watts, *Shipwrecked*, 102–5.

5   Strachey, *TR*, in Haile, *JN*, 384.

6   See Warren Susman, "History and the American Intellectual: Uses of a Usable Past," 264. Susman's self-description: *Culture as History*, 192; quoted in Michael Denning's assessment of Susman's influence, "Class and Culture: Reflections on the Work of Warren Susman," 110. Encomiums to Susman's "transformative" influence on the study of American history and culture fill the generation that followed him. See for example, Alice Kessler-Harris, "From Warren Susman to Raymond Williams and Allen Ginsberg: Moving Towards a Future with Illusions"—one memoir chosen almost at random. I am aware of the long list of scholars who have refined, modified, or even disputed Susman's essay. Nevertheless, neither this concept of the uses to which we put the past nor even the phrase "usable past," which did not originate with Susman, is disputed. The relation between cultural myth and the coherence of nations has been long acknowledged and studied, not only in American studies but in postcolonial studies and studies of nationalism in general. A bibliography of studies of the cultural work performed by myth in relation to forming and sustaining national identities would be far too long to include here, but would range across texts as disparate as Henry Cabot Lodge's essay "An American Myth" and Edward Said's *Orientalism*. The "sociological function" of myth: Joseph Campbell, *The Power of Myth*, 31. This is a type of myth that is shallower, so to speak, than those universal stories found by Campbell's method (and Sir James Frazer's before him) of "comparative mythology."

Sociological myths are specific to a culture. I realize this is a somewhat specialized use of the word *myth*, which is, for example, similar to but ultimately at vari-
ance with Mircea Eliade's definitions in *Myth and Reality*, 5–10. However, it must
be borne in mind that Eliade describes the function of myth in "archaic societies"
(18), not in complex, modern nation-states. Cultural studies that treat myth in the
modern world use the term much more loosely, more or less following Campbell's
lead. (See, for example, the essays collected by David Whitt and John Perlich in
*Myth and the Modern World: Essays on Intersections with Ideology and Culture*.)

7    In the ninth edition of the McMichael *Anthology of American Literature* the Iroquois
League and Christopher Columbus are represented. But the Puritans and Massachusetts still dominate the opening section, "Literature of Early America": twelve
of fifteen selections. One is from New Jersey and two are from Virginia: John Smith
and William Byrd II. And half of the twenty pages allowed Smith come not from
his three years living in Virginia but his three months sailing the coast of New
England. Of the 260 pages in this section, all but 60 come from Massachusetts.
The Norton, the Heath—nearly all of the standard anthologies—tell the same
story. They include the voices of a few "others," but the Puritans are still presented
as the progenitors of American literature, culture, and values. Penguin is the worst
offender. The 2004 Penguin Anthology of *American Literature* (Vol. 1) excludes all
mention of Virginia. John Smith gets three pages, but that selection comes from
his description of New England. The Penguin classic edition of *Early American
Writing* tells students that William Bradford's "vivid and moving account of the
Pilgrims' arrival in America . . . planted some of the most durable images in terms
of which Americans have defined themselves and their cultural project: of America
itself as a kind of last chance for mankind; of the American adventure as a voyage
into the unknown and the untried; of the American people as a community knit
together by suffering and upheld by a sense of hope tempered with an understanding of always threatening defeat; and of the American experience itself as a
grappling with adversity and dissension" (Giles Gunn, *Early American Writing*, 120).
Here is everything but divine selection, which I suppose Gunn left out because
that concept would too overtly violate the decorum of scholarship.

8    For a short, readable discussion of the place of Pilgrims in American K–12 education, see Tony Waters, "Why Students Think There Are Two Kinds of American
History."

9    Ronald Reagan used the "city on a hill" motif from 1974 through his farewell speech
from the White House in 1989. The quotation is from a speech he gave in 1983 to
the Heritage Foundation (see Richard M. Gamble, *In Search of the City on a Hill*,
150). John F. Kennedy, "City Upon a Hill" Speech. For a fuller discussion of the
image in political rhetoric, see Joseph M. McShane, "Winthrop's 'City Upon a Hill'
in Recent Political Discourse." Sacvan Bercovitch, for instance, calls the motif of
the city on a hill "key to the social-symbolic game through which the United
States has perpetuated itself as America" ("A Model of Cultural Transvaluation:

Puritanism, Modernity, and New World Rhetoric," keynote address, March 7, 1997, CUNY Renaissance Studies Conference, "Early Modern Trans-Atlantic Encounters: England, Spain, and the Americas"). Often cited, this speech seems to be unavailable online. (See, for instance, Bernd Herzogenrath's bibliography in *An American Body/Politic: A Deleuzian Approach*.)

10 James Truslow Adams, *The Epic of America*, 29, 45. Adams attributes the image of a city on a hill, which is most often associated with John Winthrop's sermon on the *Arbella*, to another source. The originating role of the Pilgrims' landing at Plymouth, the Mayflower Compact, and Puritan New England is even more evident in the first volume (*The Rise of the Union*) of Adams's monumental, multivolume *The History of the United States*, 1–63. Demonstrating Adams's influence, the Library of Congress instructs teachers to use *The Epic of America* to define the American Dream ("The American Dream"). Although several critics have tackled the issue of canonicity in American literature, and many of these have studied the history of the college anthology, surprisingly few discuss the all-important issue of origins. Joseph Csicsila's *Canons by Consensus: Critical Trends and American Literature Anthologies*, for instance, does not concern itself with when the Puritans Bradford, Bradstreet, Mather, or Winthrop became the supposed origin of American literary culture. Sacred texts: As far back as the 1870s, Matthew Arnold suggested that the national anthology functions in the modern, post-Darwinian world the same way the Bible functioned in the pre-Darwinian world ("The Study of Literature").

11 Philbrick, *Mayflower*, xiii–xiv. Nathaniel Philbrick, *Bunker Hill: A City, a Siege, a Revolution*. "The City on the Hill" is the title of the first chapter.

12 Bradford, Ch. 32; Winthrop, "A Modell of Christian Charity," 112.

13 Karen Ordahl Kupperman, *The Jamestown Project*, 8–9.

14 Karen Ordahl Kupperman, *The Jamestown Project*, 8–9. Other recent books include Virginia Bernard, *A Tale of Two Colonies: What Really Happened in Virginia and Bermuda* (2011); Kieran Doherty, *Sea Venture: Shipwreck, Survival, and the Salvation of the First English Colony in the New World* (2007); Lorri Glover and Daniel Blake Smith, *The Shipwreck That Saved Jamestown: The Sea Venture Castaways and the Fate of America* (2008); and Hobson Woodward, *A Brave Vessel: The True Tale of the Castaways Who Rescued Jamestown and Inspired Shakespeare's The Tempest* (2009). The exception to this tendency to apologize for Jamestown has to be the first in this recent explosion, James Horn's *A Land as God Made It: Jamestown and the Birth of America*, which came out two years before the four hundredth anniversary.

15 This volume is the most complete collection easily accessible to today's readers, and, speaking generally, it contains most of the historical texts anyone cites in their histories of Jamestown. It runs to 1,300 pages. Philip Barbour's two-volume *Jamestown Voyages*, published by the Hakluyt Society, contains several sources unselected by Haile (especially Spanish sources), is more scholarly, and is less readily available to the general reader. Because of its accessibility, I have chosen to use Haile's edition when I can and Barbour's when I cannot. For the reader

looking only for the most important narratives, I highly recommend Horn's Library of America edition. For the last couple of generations, the only new evidence has been the artifacts unearthed by William Kelso's team of archaeologists at the Jamestown site (see *Jamestown, the Buried Truth*).

16  One commoner in particular, Henry Spelman, left behind an important record of his thoughts and impressions.

17  John Davies, translator of Charles de Rochefort, *The History of the Barbados, St. Christophers . . . and the Rest of the Caribby-islands*, 202. Noted in the entry on "Maroon" in the *Oxford English Dictionary*.

18  Richard Price provides a succinct historiography of the term in *Maroon Societies*, 1n1.

19  Herbert Aptheker, *American Negro Slave Revolts*, 163. Quoted by Price, *Maroon Societies*, 149. See also Aptheker's "Maroons Within the Present Limits of the United States." Nearly all we know of these early maroons we learn from the Europeans from whom they escaped. In other words, their own point of view has almost never been recorded. A rare exception is Richard Price's remarkable *First-Time: The Historical Vision of an African American People*, which in 1983 recorded oral traditions three hundred years old. Those traditions—often corroborated by colonial records—confirm both the initial hostility that "the forest" posed for escaped slaves, and role played by American indegenes. (See especially "Lánu's Escape" [45] and Price's commentary on "Ayakô's Flight" [48]). For a remarkable collection of historical evidence regarding maroons in South Carolina, see Timothy James Lockley, ed., *Maroon Communities in South Carolina: A Documentary Record* (Columbia: University of South Carolina Press, 2009). Unfortunately, Lockley's records cover only the English settlement, beginning in 1711.

20  Cf. Price, *Maroon Societies*, 5.

21  Price, *First-Time*, 11–12.

22  Neil Roberts, *Freedom as Marronage*, 11, 181. Isaac Curtis, "Masterless People: Maroons, Pirates, and Commoners," 152. Paul Robinson and Sarah Robinson's speculative essay, *Pirates, Prisoners, and Lepers: Lessons from Life Outside the Law*, discusses in similar terms pirates, castaways, and other "absent-law" communities; quotation regards eighteenth-century Nassau: 28. Diouf, *Slavery's Exiles*, 2.

23  The story of Drake's Panamanian campaign occupies most of Kelsey's third chapter, 40–67. The main primary source of information is *Sir Francis Drake Revived*.

24  See *OED*, "marooned, v."; William Dampier, *Voyages and Descriptions*, 84.

25  See for example, William S. Simmons, "Cultural Bias in the New England Puritans' Perception of Indians." Even Alden T. Vaughan's classic *New England Frontier: Puritans and Indians, 1620–1675*, which paints the Puritans more favorably than previous histories, focusing on the Puritans' attempts to deal with Native Americans according to their own lights of justice, acknowledges their European abhorrence of American culture.

26  Strachey, *TR*, in Haile, *JN*, 384–85.

## CHAPTER 1: RENEGADES

1   Percy, *Discourses*, in Haile, *JN*, 90; Barbour, *JV1*, 133–34, 170.

2   Percy, *Discourses*, in Haile, *JN*, 90–94; Barbour, *JV1*, 132–38.

3   Alexander Brown's sketch of Smythe, compiled from a variety of documents and composed in the late nineteenth century, is still the foundation of most accounts of Smythe's life (*Genesis*, vol. 2, 1012–18). Brown thinks that among Smythe's accomplishments was being a soldier; that he was with Robert Devereux, Earl of Essex, in his 1596 raid on Cádiz; and that Essex knighted him for gallantry in that engagement. However, the *Encyclopedia Virginia* casts credible doubt on that episode. King James's conferral of knighthood in 1603 lends weight to the *Encyclopedia*'s position. "Pierpont Morgan": Parks, *Richard Hakluyt and the English Voyages*, 207.

4   On Popham's role, see Barbour, *JV*, vol. 1, 14. King James's patent or what is commonly called the "First Charter" is reprinted in the same volume, 24–34, as are his "instructions." For "constitutions": 43. The "most part" was stipulated in relation to the assignment of land (33). "Major part" appears several times in the November instructions. Company's councilors' oath: 44. London colony's councillors' oath: 47–48.

5   "iron hatchets": Barbour, *JV*, vol. 1, 159; copper: 130; "Storehouse": 53.

6   "tiplinge": Barbour, *JV*, vol. 1, 59; the December 10, 1606 "Orders": 46–47.

7   The Company's instructions divided a supposed 120 colonists into three squads of forty men: one to build the fort, one to start a farm, and one to explore the rivers. Only ten men of the farming squad were specifically designated as sentinels. Presumably, the forty explorers would have been armed and ready for a fight. See Barbour, *The Jamestown Voyages*, vol. 1, 51.

8   We know the occupation of most settlers because John Smith published them in the 1612 *Proceedings of the English Colonie in Virginia*.

9   Nichols, *Captain Christopher Newport*, 5–8.

10  Nichols, *Captain Christopher Newport*, 24–27. John White's *Narrative*, in Quinn, *Roanoke Voyages*, II, 619. See also Nichols, *Captain Christopher Newport*, 29.

11  Nichols, *Captain Christopher Newport*, 42, 46.

12  Nichols, *Captain Christopher Newport*, 44.

13  Nichols, *Captain Christopher Newport*, 46, 53, 62; see 182–85 for a chronology of his life that includes all of his West Indian cruises.

14  Nichols, *Captain Christopher Newport*, 64.

15  Jocelyn R. Wingfield, Edward Maria Wingfield's apologetic biographer, eagerly blames Newport, insisting that Wingfield has been wrongfully charged with enmity toward Smith. But he is the outlier. Most biographers use Smith's arrest and near execution to establish his credentials as a foe of elitism and aristocratic privilege: a pragmatic man who believed in meritocracy. Vaughan says that Smith annoyed the pride of the gentlemen, who plotted against him and persuaded Newport to arrest him, even if they could not persuade the old sea captain to hang him. The Hooblers believe that it was Wingfield who charged Smith with

plotting mutiny against the Company and planning to set himself up, pirate fashion, as king of Virginia. Barbour, the nearly unquestioned authority on Smith, held Wingfield accountable, speculating that the old man was piqued at not receiving the "proper respect" for his rank. This "most trivial pretext," Barbour wrote, "served Wingfield to rid himself of nuisance." Wingfield, *Virginia's True Founder*, 177–78; Vaughan, *Captain John Smith*, 26; Hoobler and Hoobler, *Captain John Smith*, 86; Barbour, *TWCJS*, 114.

16  Spanish ambassador: Barbour, *JVI*, 68; Percy, *Discourse*, in Haile, *JN*, 86 and Barbour, *JV*, 130.

17  Percy, *Discourse*, in Haile, *JN*, 87 and Barbour, *JV*, vol. 1, 130–32.

18  Percy, *Discourse*, in Haile, *JN*, 94 and Barbour, *JVI*, 138.

19  Percy, *Discourse*, in Haile, *JN*, 92–94 and Barbour, *JVI*, 135–38; Smith, *True Relation*, in Haile, *JN*, 145. See also Barbour's summary of the extant sources in his biography of Smith, *TWCJS*, 124–26.

20  "principal persons": Barbour, *JVI*, 47.

21  For the bringing ashore of provisions and initial work on the fort: Smith, *True Relation*, in Haile, *JN*, 145; for the first night ashore, see Percy, *Discourse*, in Haile, *JN*, 138.

22  Although we have accounts of these days from Percy, Wingfield, and Smith himself, the fullest narrative and the only one that mentions the following proceedings is Gabriel Archer's *A Relation of Our Discovery*, in Haile, *JN*, 116–17.

23  Smith, *True Relation*, in Haile, *JN*, 146.

24  See Archer's account (in Haile, *JN*, 115) and Smith's account (in *True Relation*, in Haile, *JN*, 147).

25  Archer, *A Relation*, in Haile, *JN*, 116–17. The emphasis on *gentleman* is in the original (see *JVI*, 95).

26  See Alexander Brown, *The Genesis of the United States*, vol. 1, 73.

27  "take and leade": Barbour, *The Jamestown Voyages*, vol. 1, 29. For Newport's powers, see 46; for the crimes, see 37–38; sawing clapboard: 96–97.

28  William Kelly, *Docwra's Diary*, 7. For Spenser, see Fuchs, "Contextualizing *The Tempest*," 49. For general English view of the Gaels, see Canny, "The Ideology of English Colonization," 584–94. For O'Neill, see Hayes-McCoy, "The Tudor Conquest," 158–59. The description of O'Neill's entourage quotes Camden's *Annales Rerum*.

29  These insights about Tudor attitudes toward the Irish are commonplace among historians. See, for example, Maginn and Ellis, *The Tudor Discovery of Ireland*, 17.

30  McGurk, *The Elizabethan Conquest of Ireland*, 204–9.

31  McGurk, *The Elizabethan Conquest of Ireland*, 204–8, 241.

32  Hayes-McCoy, "The Completion," 125–26. See also Wingfield, *Virginia's True Founder*, 114–19.

33  See McGurk, *The Elizabethan Conquest of Ireland*, 213. In 1600 the English authorities relented and issued mantles to their soldiers.

34  Ramsberger, *What We Know*, 7.
35  This paragraph draws nearly from Rose, "The Social Psychology of Desertion from Combat," 616–26.
36  Unfortunately, no one has really studied combat desertions in that war. There is plenty of literature, especially memoirs, on desertion before deployment and on draft avoidance, but very little on deserters in Vietnam. See, for instance, Jack Todd's *Desertion in the Time of Vietnam*. Desertion is not even indexed in *The Columbia History of the Vietnam War*. By any estimate, only a tiny fraction of the hundreds of thousands of soldiers went "over the hill" in Vietnam and naturalized themselves as Vietnamese. Despite voluminous folklore among servicemen, it seems that only about 250 deserted permanently in country (Robert Fantina, *Desertion and the American Soldier*, 149). Even so, psychological conditions in Vietnam were somewhat comparable to the Nine Years War in Ireland: "By every conceivable indicator," one colonel reported in the *Armed Forces Journal*, "our army that now remains in Vietnam is in a state approaching collapse, with individual units avoiding or having refused combat, murdering their officers and noncommissioned officers, drug-ridden, and dispirited where not near mutinous" (quoted in Fantina, 156). By far, the richest literature on combat desertion concerns the American Civil War. But the shared culture between combatants makes that war less analogous to Ireland circa 1600. In some ways, more instructive would be the desertions of Irish American Catholic soldiers fighting for the United States in the Mexican American War. Peter F. Stevens's *The Rogue's March: John Riley and the St. Patrick's Battalion, 1846–48* documents the psychological and physical abuse that precipitated unprecedented numbers of U.S. soldiers taking refuge amongst their erstwhile enemies. Most apropos is Matthias van Rossum and Jennette Kamp's comparative study of *Desertion in the Modern World*. Though it deals almost exclusively with the Dutch empire, their collection of essays connects maroons to deserters of other bound labor, including mariners, soldiers, and contracted laborers.
37  Hayes-McCoy, "The Completion," 125.
38  Percy, *Discourse*, in Haile, *JN*, 95–96.
39  Jocelyn R. Wingfield, *Virginia's True Founder*, 107.
40  See Karen Ordahl Kupperman, "Apathy and Death in Early Jamestown." Percy and Smith both briefly describe these events (Percy, *Discourse*, in Haile, *JN*, 99–100; Smith, *True Relation*, in Haile, *JN*, 147–49). For the descriptions of symptoms, see Percy, *Discourse*, in Haile, *JN*, 99.
41  Wingfield's *A Discourse of Virginia*, in Haile, *JN*, 185–86.
42  Percy, *Discourse*, in Haile, *JN*, 100; Wingfield, *Discourse of Virginia*, in Haile, *JN*, 186; Smith, *True Relation*, in Haile, *JN*, 149.
43  Smith, *True Relation*, in Haile, *JN*, 146; Percy, *Discourse*, in Haile, *JN*, 95.
44  Barbour, *JVI*, 79.
45  Archer, *A relation*, in Haile, *JN*, 117.

46 "runagates": Wingfield, *Discourse of Virginia,* in Haile, *JN,* 186. "Renegade" and "Pasportes," see the *Oxford English Dictionary.* For examples of passports, see Standish O'Grady, *Pacata Hibernia*; "Fugitiues": Barbour, *JVi,* 150.

47 Percy gives us the clue to the date of his return (Barbour, *JVi,* 145). White's testimony comes to us secondhand through Smith, and thirdhand through Percy (see *JVi,* 147–50). Seeming to rely on White, Samuel Purchas suggested that most renegades in that first summer "were cruelly and treacherously executed" by the Indians. He cites the example of one George Casson, whom the Indians backed against a fire, staked his arms and legs to two poles, and gutted him alive. His bowels were thrown into the flames, while his flesh slowly "dried . . . to the bone." But in fact Casson was not a deserter. The Indians captured him much later, in December, as part of John Smith's famous adventure, which I'll discuss below. None of the writers who were in Jamestown—Archer, Percy, Wingfield, and Smith—said that deserters were tortured or executed by the Indians. By 1614, when Purchas's account was published, the Company knew full well that desertion was a huge problem, so tales of devil-worship and human sacrifices served their need to control their own people. In fact, Wingfield admitted that their Indian hosts treated the renegades with hospitality and kindness, and, despite the misinformation about Casson's death, White very likely was the one who first disputed the claim that the Algonquians were cannibals. See *JVi,* 150, 216.

48 Percy, *Discourse,* in Haile, *JN,* 100.

49 Wingfield, *Discourse of Virginia,* in Haile, *JN,* 186.

50 Percy, *Discourse,* in Haile, *JN,* 100; Smith, *True Relation,* in Haile, *JN,* 149.

51 Axtell, 82.

52 Wingfield, *Discourse of Virginia,* in Haile, *JN,* 188.

53 Smith, *True Relation,* in Haile, *JN,* 149–51.

54 Smith, *True Relation,* in Haile, *JN,* 149.

55 "Apathy and Death in Early Jamestown."

56 Smith, *True Relation,* in Haile, *JN,* 154–56.

57 Smith, *True Relation,* in Haile, *JN,* 154.

58 Smith, *True Relation,* in Haile, *JN,* 155–56.

## CHAPTER 2: TSENACOMOCO

1 See John Smith, *A Map of Virginia,* in Barbour, *CWCJS,* 173.

2 John Smith, *A Map of Virginia,* 173.

3 See Helen C. Rountree, *Pocahontas, Powhatan, and Opechancanough,* 31–32.

4 For a discussion of council procedure, see Rountree, *The Powhatan Indians of Virginia,* 119–20. For Winganuske, see Rountree, *Before and After Jamestown,* 112–17.

5 Wilderness Act.

6 "Columbian Exchange" was coined by Alfred W. Crosby in his 1972 book of the same name. See also his *Ecological Imperialism: The Biological Expansion of Europe, 900–1900.* "Humanized landscape": Mann, *1491,* 11. Mann is actually quoting

W. M. Denevan's 1996 article, "Pristine Myth," in the *Encyclopedia of Cultural Anthropology*. For a fuller account, and see Denevan's "The Pristine Myth: The Landscape of the Americas in 1492," in the *Annals of the Association of American Geographers*. "In 1750": Denevan, *Annals*, 369. Williams and Cronin quoted by Denevan, *Annals*, 371–72.

7   See Mann, *1491*, 353–62; for Audubon and Schorger: Mann, *1491*, 354–55.

8   Kevin Baker in *The New York Times* called *1491* a "marvelous new book" that was "rarely . . . less than enthralling." The *London Times* called it "important" and "challenging," with provocative implications for "modern environmentalism" (Ross Leckie, "1491: The Americas before Columbus"). In *Science* magazine, Dean R. Snow pointed out "overstatements, errors, and speculations," including "Henry Dobyns's wildly inflated [Indian] population estimates." Dobyns, the anthropologist who was among the first to realize that pre-Columbian North America was well populated, estimated that about eighteen million people lived above the Rio Grande. Daniel Richter, among others, panned Dobyns's methods in *William and Mary Quarterly*, opining that "we simply do not know enough yet to make reliable guesses—let alone estimates—of pre-Columbian population for most areas in North America" (Review, 653). See also Noble David Cook, Reviewed Work, 130–31.

9   For a discussion of the Empire's boundaries, see Helen Rountree, "Who Were the Powhatans and Did They Have a Unified 'Foreign Policy,'" in *Powhatan Foreign Relations, 1500–1722*, 1–20. For population figures, see Rountree, *The Powhatan Indians*, 15.

10  Richter, Review, 653. E. Randolph Turner, "A Reexamination of Powhatan Territorial Boundaries and Population" (cited in Rountree, *The Powhatan Indians*, 15). "Probably fewer": Rountree and Turner, *Before and After Jamestown*, 15.

11  According to Daniel Richter, as early as 1546 the Indians of the Chesapeake were acquainted with European goods ("Tsenacommacah," 38). For a discussion of Powhatan/Spanish relations, see Charlotte M. Gradie, "The Powhatans in the Context of the Spanish Empire."

12  Rountree discusses Powhatan ingenuity in many places, for example, *Pocahontas' People*, 7, and *Powhatan Indians*, 30–38, 42, 62–69. "Tempered": Rountree, *Powhatan Indians*, 63.

13  Rountree, *Powhatan Indians*, 34.

14  Rountree and Turner, *Before and After*, 85. Rountree cites several examples of how clear the woods were (*The Powhatan Indians of Virginia*, 60n10); see Morgan *American Slavery American Freedom*, 55.

15  Rountree discusses the scant direct evidence of Powhatan family and village organization, as well as analogous examples, in *The Powhatan Indians of Virginia*, 91–94. The quotation is from Spelman, quoted by Rountree, *The Powhatan Indians*, 93.

16  *The Powhatan Indians of Virginia*, 9.

17  Our geography of Tsenacomoco derives from the map drafted by John Smith. (See page 166). Rountree includes another map derived from Smith's in her

*Pocahontas, Powhatan, Opechancanough*, which includes known hamlets as well as chiefs' towns. It clearly indicates the uneven distribution of Powhatans over Tsenacomoco. Density increases significantly as one travels upstream to fresher waters. Jamestown itself was situated at the threshold between thinly populated saltier areas and thickly populated fresher waters (54).

18  See Rountree, *The Powhatan Indians*, 79–82, and Gleach, *Powhatan's World*, 39–40. Quotations from Beverly, cited in Gleach, 39.

19  Diamond studies such societies that still exist today despite the pressures of contact with modern societies, and admits in the modern world these are more "transitional" than the "traditional" societies that existed before modern contact. For his definition, see *The World Until Yesterday*, 6.

20  Whether traditional societies throughout the ages were more cooperative or warlike is not without controversy, although Diamond claims that "all the studies surveying" the scholarship agree: modern societies are far less violent than traditional societies. See Diamond, "In Conversation with Jared Diamond."

21  For simplicity's sake, I most often use the modern names of these rivers. When the English arrived in Virginia, and on John Smith's first map, the James River was called the Powhatan and the York was called the Pamunkey. Modern names for the two northern rivers of Tsenacomoco, the Rappahannock and the Potomac, retain their Indian origins.

22  See Sarah J. Stebbins, "Meet the State-Recognized Virginia Indian Tribes."

23  Ralph Hamor, *A True Discourse of the present estate of Virginia, and the success of the affairs there till the 18 of June, 1614*, in *Jamestown Narratives Eyewitness Accounts of the Virginia Colony The First Decade: 1607–1617*, in Haile, *JN*, 811.

24  Contemporary accounts of Don Luís's life contradict each other. Charlotte M. Gradie, who sifts the reports, believes this is the likeliest sequence of his travels (see "Spanish Jesuits in Virginia: The Mission That Failed," 142n32. Many of the primary documents are collected in Clifford M. Lewis and Albert J. Loomie, *The Spanish Jesuit Mission in Virginia*.

25  Lewis and Loomie, *The Spanish Jesuit Mission in Virginia*, 119, 140. Even as late at the 1950s, Lewis and Loomie, American Jesuits who published a collection of the primary documents concerning the affair, suggested that the "neophyte" Christian succumbed to the "grave temptations" of pagan life. See Gradie, "Spanish Jesuits," 140, 146.

26  Gradie discredited those old, prejudicial notions of natives' moral degeneracy by explaining how the very presence of the Jesuits, and their presumptuous proffer of a superior culture, would have been obnoxious to the Paspaheghs. The priests might not have threatened with swords and bullied with guns the way Spanish soldiers did, but their *culture* posed danger, and at a moment when the Paspaheghs felt particularly vulnerable. See Gradie, "Spanish Jesuits," 146–49. See also Gradie's "The Powhatans in the Context of the Spanish Empire," 154–72. Gradie was influenced largely by Rountree's view that the Jesuits had set themselves up in

competition with the Powhatan priesthood, who were powerful in Indian culture and would have felt threatened (Rountree, *Powhatan Indians*, 101, 133).

27 Some stories have Alonso swimming out to the ships, climbing aboard naked and dark as an Indian, and finding his own father among the Spanish soldiers. Several accounts insist that Alonso had nearly forgotten how to speak Spanish, so thoroughly accustomed was he to Paspahegh ways. Alonso lived many years after these events in St. Elena, what is now Beaufort, South Carolina, as a soldier, and he told his maroonage tale for years to anyone who would listen. And so several different accounts are preserved, some written down thirty and forty years later. The most authoritative seems to be the August 1572 "Letter of Juan Rogel to Francis Borgia," written from the Chesapeake during Menéndez's mission of revenge (Lewis and Loomie, *The Spanish Jesuit Mission in Virginia*, 103–18). Daniel Richter plausibly attributes the Jesuits' failure in Paspahegh to their misunderstanding of the prestige-goods economy in Tsenacomocoan chiefdoms (*Trade, Land, Power*, 19–24).

28 For details on the raising of children, see Rountree, *Pocahontas, Powhatan, Opechancanough*, 31–33; for social distinctions, see Rountree, *The Powhatan Indians*, 100–113.

29 "Conduit" and "breadbasket": Rountree, *Pocahontas, Powhatan, and Opechancanough*, 41.

30 Rountree reconstructs this fascinating history in *Pocahontas, Powhatan, Opechancanough*, 42–46 (quotations from 44). See also Gleach, *Powhatan's World*, 22, 28.

31 For a thorough and fascinating study of the prestige-goods economy that supported Wahusnonacock's dominion over Tsenacomococo, see the first chapter of Daniel Richter's *Trade, Land, Power: The Struggle for Eastern North America*, 13–41.

32 Rountree, *Pocahontas, Powhatan, Opechancanough*, 35–39. For parent-child affections, see Rountree, *The Powhatan Indians of Virginia*, 96. Mossiker, *Pocahontas*, 41.

33 Scholars once proposed that Paquiquineo was Powhatan's younger brother and one of his heirs, Opechancanough, though experts discard the notion today. Daniel Richter thinks he was "almost certainly a member of a chiefly lineage" if not brother, father, or uncle to the paramount chief ("Tsenacommacah and the Atlantic World," 37). See also Clifford M. Lewis and Albert J. Loomie, *The Spanish Jesuit Mission in Virginia*.

34 For a discussion of Powhatan-Spanish relations, see Charlotte M. Gradie, "The Powhatans in the Context of the Spanish Empire." As early as 1546, Daniel Richter notes, the Indians of the Chesapeake were well acquainted with European goods, although the relatively little direct contact with Europeans kept such goods far rarer there than they were farther south ("Tsenacommacah," 38). See also, Rountree's chapter, "The Powhatans and the English: A Case of Multiple Conflicting Agendas," in *Powhatan Foreign Relations*, especially 177–80, for Wahunsonacock's considerations in 1607.

35 See Rountree, *The Powhatan Indians of Virginia*, 119.

36 See Rountree and Turner, *Before and After Jamestown*, 15 and 96–97.

37 John Smith, *True Relation*, in Haile, *JN*, 151.

38 Rountree, *Pocahontas, Powhatan, Opechancanough*, 30 and 190.

39 All historical accounts of this story derive from two main sources, both penned by John Smith: his 1608 *True Relation* and his 1624 *General History*.

40 "Moacasseter": Smith, *General History*, in Haile, 236. "Chawnzmit": Rountree, *Pocahontas, Powhatan, Opechancanough*, 6.

41 Smith, *General History*, in Haile, 237.

42 Smith, *General History*, in Haile, 239; in Barbour, *CWCJS*, vol. 2, 151.

43 See Haile, *John Smith in the Chesapeake*, 30. Wahunsonacock, Haile argues, "hope[d] that through ritual adoption and a promise of generous rewards he [could] turn Smith's allegiance from Jamestown." Smith gave him "desperate assurances," after which Wahunsonacock turned him loose.

44 "A few miles" is Barbour, *CWCJS*, Smith, vol. 2, 151n4; "Nantaquod": *General History*, in Haile, 239; in Barbour, *CWJS*, vol. 2, 151.

## CHAPTER 3: NANTAQUOD ON THE JAMES

1 "Forty in all" Smith reports in his *General History*, in Haile, *JN*, 241.

2 So Smith described Kecoughtan town when he visited there in December 1608 (*GH*, in Haile, *JN*, 297).

3 Smith, *GH*, in Haile, *JN*, 225.

4 Most of our knowledge of these intrigues come from Smith's brief account in *GH*, in Barbour, *CWCJS*, vol. 2, 151–53; and are corroborated in some places by Wingfield.

5 Hoobler and Hoobler, *Captain John Smith*, 247 and 249; Barbour, *TWCJS*; *David A. Price, Love and Hate in Jamestown: John Smith, Pocahontas, and the Heart of a New Nation*, 4–5; Vaughan, *American Genesis*, viii; Lemay, "Captain John Smith: American," 288 (quoted in Vaughan, *Captain John Smith*, x); J. A. Leo Lemay, *The American Dream of Captain John Smith*, especially 32–37.

6 Barbour, *TWCJS*, 4 and 10. Unless otherwise indicated, the details of Smith's life are gleaned from Barbour, who, despite his old-school prejudices (for instance, about Native Americans), remains the highest authority on the facts of Smith's life.

7 "Fat": Barbour, *TWCJS*, 6. This paragraph summarizes 6–13.

8 Barbour, *TWCJS*, 14–16.

9 Barbour, *TWCJS*, 24.

10 Barbour, *TWCJS*, 26–29.

11 Barbour, *TWCJS*, 45–46.

12 Barbour, *TWCJS*, 49.

13 Cf. Barbour, *TWCJS*, 2, 206; cited in Lemay, *The American Dream*, 107.

14 "Up and down": Barbour, *TWCJS*, 53; Smith quoted in Barbour, *TWCJS*, 57.

15 See, for instance, Lemay's *American Dream*, 190–91.

16  Smith, *GH*, in Haile, *JN*, 334. Lemay severely disputes Kupperman and barely mentions the Willoughbys at all in his own study of Smith. In general, historians tend to fall into one or another "camp" in their treatment of Smith: those who deprecate his character and contribution to history (at first, these were northern partisans of a Puritan-founded America, as I'll discuss in the Conclusion, but more lately they are the historians who seek to elevate the role of Indians in the foundation of the nation); and those apologists who see in Smith the prototype of the self-made American frontiersman. On this particular issue—that of Smith's dependence—good sense favors Kupperman.

17  This is a section of his *General History* (chapter 12) written by Richard Pots, William Phettiplace, and William Tankard (in Haile, *JN*, 334).

18  Lemay's discussion of Anas Todkill is particularly instructive on this point (*American Dream*, 100–101).

19  Cf. Smith, *GH*, in Haile, *JN*, 284–85.

20  Perhaps the best list of the qualities Smith admired in a man are found in Lemay's index under the rubrics "Smith, Captain John" and "respect for:" (*The American Dream of Captain John Smith*, 285).

21  Smith, *GH*, in Haile, *JN*, 243.

22  Francis Perkins, "Letter from Jamestown to a Friend, 28 March 1608," in Haile, *JN*, 133–34.

23  Smith, *GH*, in Haile, *JN*, 245–46.

24  See Smith, *GH*, in Haile, *JN*, 243–44.

25  Smith, *GH*, in Haile, *JN*, 248.

26  Cf. Smith, *GH*, in Haile, *JN*, 250.

27  Smith, *GH*, in Haile, *JN*, 249.

28  Smith, *GH*, in Haile, *JN*, 248.

29  Smith, *GH*, in Haile, *JN*, 249–50. "Spades": Smith, *TR*, in Haile, *JN*, 178.

30  Smith, *GH*, in Haile, *JN*, 250 and Smith, *TR*, in Haile, *JN*, 179.

31  Smith, *TR*, in Haile, *JN*, 181.

32  Smith, *TR*, in Haile, *JN*, 182.

33  Smith, *GH*, in Haile, *JN*, 258–59. The reputation of the Massawomeks may have derived from their possession of iron hatchets, which they had obtained from the French, and the nimbleness of their birchbark canoes, a technology unknown in Tsenacomoco (see Rountree, *Pocahontas, Powhatan, Opechancanough*, 42).

34  Smith, *GH*, in Haile, *JN*, 259. James Horn believes that in his two "discoveries" of the Chesapeake in the summer of 1608, Smith, like Newport, was looking for gold as well as passage to the South Sea (*A Land as God Made It*).

35  "Rewrote": Haile, *JN*, 215. Smith, *GH*, in Haile, *JN*, 260.

36  Smith, *GH*, in Haile, *JN*, 263–64.

37  Smith, *GH*, in Haile, *JN*, 260.

38  Stephen R. Potter, *Commoners, Tribute, and Chiefs*, 11.

39  Smith, *GH*, in Haile, *JN*, 271–74.

40 Smith, *GH*, in Haile, *JN*, 260.
41 Smith, *GH*, *JN*, 278.
42 Smith, *GH*, *JN*, 278.

## CHAPTER 4: CALL OF THE WILD

1 Paul Hammer, "A Welshman Abroad": tall, imposing, 84; "embodiment," 61; "pardon," 68; "old hand," 86.
2 Smith, *GH*, in Haile, *JN*, 293. Newport sustained the suspension of Ratcliffe's seat on the council, voiding his votes.
3 "Wit": Smith, *TR*, in Haile, *JN*, 181.
4 Smith, *GH*, in Haile, *JN*, 281. This episode has earned its share of attention from historians, biographers, anthropologists, and literary critics. Some describe it as a native "bacchanal," treating by analogy with sacred Greek rituals of fertility and sex. Some go so far as to suggest it has no ethnographic value at all—that Smith's description so closely copies English Renaissance theatrical conventions that it cannot be based on what really happened that night in Virginia. What is important for our purposes, and what seems to me impossible to deny, is that the English interpreted the event as a sexual invitation. For a summary of these interpretations, see Jay Hansford C. Vest, "'Love You Not Me?' Pocahontas and the Virginia Masque: A Jacobean Drama in the Glade."
5 Greenblatt, "Shakespeare's Montaigne," xii.
6 Hartle, *Michel de Montaigne*, 174–75.
7 For Bacon, see Hamlin, "Florio's Montaigne and the Tyranny of 'Custom,'" 516.
8 For a summary of Montaigne's treatment of custom, or habit, as "hampering perception and judgment" and depriving us "of liberty," see Hamlin, "Florio's Montaigne," 499, especially n24.
9 Greenblatt, "Shakespeare's Montaigne," xi.
10 Greenblatt, "Shakespeare's Montaigne," xi. Montaigne, *Shakespeare's Montaigne*, 70. Weaver, *Red Atlantic*, 190–91.
11 The full text of this narrative is reprinted in Hans Stade, *The Captivity of Hans Stade of Hesse, in A.D. 1547–1555*. "brew drinks": 53; "his brains": 158.
12 See Hamlin, "Florio's Montaigne," 505–7.
13 Montaigne, "Of Cannibals," in *The Essays of Montaigne*, 221.
14 Plato did not. He satirized this fetish of simplicity; Montaigne surely had Pindar and Hesiod in mind when he praised the cannibals' tribal life above Plato's utopian Republic. See John Dillon, "Plato and the Golden Age," 28. Dillon discusses also the psychological impulse that might account for myths of a golden age, and a theory posited by Lewis Mumford about the transition societies experience as they develop from villages to cities. "Harsh, corrupt": Judith E. Boss, "The Golden Age, Cockaigne, and Utopia in *The Faerie Queene* and *The Tempest*," 145.
15 Montaigne, *The Essays of Montaigne*, 222.
16 James Axtell, *The Invasion Within*, 169–70.

17 Axtell, *Invasion Within*, 278, 5; Richard White, *Middle Ground*, 61 and 63. See also Axtell's "The White Indians of Colonial America."

18 Symonds, *Virginia. A Sermon Preached at White-Chappell*, 25.

19 Quitt, "Trade and Acculturation at Jamestown," 231.

20 For the timing of Pocahontas's coming of age, see Rountree, *Pocahontas, Powhatan, Opechancanough*, 142.

21 For Capahoasick, see Haile, *JN*, 162 and 240; Rountree, *Pocahontas, Powhatan, Opechancanough*, 142.

22 Smith, *GH*, in Haile, *JN*, 281–82.

23 Daniel Richter offers a different interpretation of these events, which undermines Smith's humor and suggests that Newport's gifts—and his whole Indian policy—was more sophisticated and successful than Smith's (see *Trade, Land, Power*, 3335).

24 Smith, *GH*, in Haile, *JN*, 283–84.

25 Letter, Peter Winne to Egerton, 26 November 1608, in Haile, *JN*, 203.

26 Smith, *GH*, in Haile, *JN*, 285, 287.

27 Smith, *GH*, in Haile, *JN*, 287.

28 Smith, *GH*, in Haile, *JN*, 286.

29 Smith, *GH*, in Haile, *JN*, 287; Nansemond, 293

30 Smith, *GH*, in Haile, *JN*, 298–99.

31 Smith, *GH*, in Haile, *JN*, 293–94; "Adam": 304.

32 Smith, *GH*, in Haile, *JN*, 294

33 Smith, *GH*, in Haile, *JN*, 296.

34 Smith, *GH*, in Haile, *JN*, 297. The following account is drawn from Smith's own record of the events, in Haile, *JN*, 298–313.

35 Smith, *GH*, in Haile, *JN*, 307, 310.

36 Smith, *GH*, in Haile, *JN*, 310.

37 Or this episode might signal a shift in Smith's thinking about the Indians. The singular historian Edward Haile thinks Smith was undergoing a "change of heart" and that his Indian policy in spring was considerably more sympathetic than it was in winter. Haile puts the decisive moment a few weeks later. See Haile, *John Smith in the Chesapeake*.

38 *GH*, in Haile, *JN*, 317.

39 *GH*, in Haile, *JN*, 316, 320.

40 *GH*, in Haile, *JN*, 325 and 323.

41 Smith, *GH*, in Haile, *JN*, 304.

42 Smith, *GH*, in Haile, *JN*, 310.

43 *GH*, in Haile, *JN*, 312.

44 *GH*, in Haile, *JN*, 314–15.

45 *GH*, in Haile, *JN*, 314.

46 *GH*, in Haile, *JN*, 319.

47 *GH*, in Haile, *JN*, 314, 319.

48 *GH*, in Haile, *JN*, 320.

49 *GH*, in Haile, *JN*, 322.

50 *GH*, in Haile, *JN*, 322.

51 *GH*, in Haile, *JN*, 322.

52 *GH*, in Haile, *JN*, 322–23.

53 *GH*, in Haile, *JN*, 323–24.

54 *GH*, in Haile, *JN*, 324.

55 *GH*, in Haile, *JN*, 324–25; Gabriel Archer, "Letter from Jamestown, 31 August 1609," in Haile, *JN*, 352. Details of Argall's passage: *A True and Sincere* Declaration, in Haile, *JN*, 361; "natural and primary": *A True and Sincere* Declaration, in Haile, *JN*, 363.

## CHAPTER 5: MAROONS

1 We know that Newport was in London by January 23, 1609, because he is referenced in a letter from John Chamberlain to Dudley Carleton at Eton. (See Brown, *Genesis*, I, 205; and Barbour, *JVI*, 246–47.) For the iron ore, see Nicholls, *Captain Christopher Newport*, 109.

2 For Newport's influence on Company policy, see Gabriel Archer's "Letter from Jamestown, 31 August 1609," in Haile, *JN*, 352. For a succinct summary of the council's gathering of intelligence under Thomas Smythe's leadership, see Horn, *A Land as God Made It*, 131–35.

3 For a "court" session at Thomas Smythe's house, see Kingsbury, I, 211. John Smith's famous letter is reprinted in Haile, *JN*, 287–91 and Barbour, *JVI*, 241–45.

4 Smith, "Copy of a Letter," in Haile, *JN*, 287; Barbour, *JVI*, 244.

5 For the expansion of the colony, see Zúñiga's letter to King Phillip, November 8, 1608, in Brown, *Genesis*, I, 196. *Nova Britannia* alludes to a meeting in late January or early February (3); "solemne": Brown, I, 206; Egerton: quoted by Zúñiga, in Brown, I, 259; eight hundred settlers: "A Letter from His Majesty's Council of Virginia to the Corporation of Plymouth," in Brown, I, 239. For Sandys's biography, see Brown, II, 992–93.

6 Karl Marx and Friedrich Engels, *The Communist Manifesto*, 74.

7 Harry Kelsey, *Sir Francis Drake*, 6.

8 Harry Kelsey, *Sir Francis Drake*, 17.

9 See John Cummins, *Francis Drake*, 149.

10 *Sir Francis Drake Revived*, 19. The text was first published in 1626, compiled and edited by "Philip Nichols, Preacher" from "the Reporte of Mr. Christopher Ceely, Ellis Hixon, and others, who were in the same voyage with him." As do most modern versions of the text, I am using the 1652 edition, which bundled Nichols's book with accounts of other voyages.

11 Despite our continued reverence for Columbus, the historiography on his crimes against humanity is pretty robust and irrefutable. Popular accounts include Howard Zinn's *People's History of the United States* and James Loewen's *Lies My Teacher Told Me*. David E. Stannard's *American Holocaust: Columbus and the Conquest*

*of the New World* is a fairly definitive treatment of the subject, and the facts in this paragraph derive from that book's section, "Pestilence and Genocide" (57–148). The greater part of Stannard's descriptions of Hispaniola comes from Bartolemé de las Casas's eyewitness account.

12  Bartolemé de las Casas, *A Short History of the Destruction of the Indies*, 14–15.

13  Bartolemé de las Casas, 14.

14  Stannard, *American Holocaust*, 73.

15  José L. Franco, "Maroons and Slave Rebellions in the Spanish Territories." For an excellent, brief overview of maroons in the Caribbean, see Isaac Curtis, "Masterless Peoples: Maroons, Pirates, Commoners."

16  Unless otherwise indicated, what follows derives from Ruth Pike, "Black Rebels," whose main source for Bayano's regime is Fray Pedro de Aguado, *Historia de Venezuela*. See Pike, 245–46.

17  Pike, "Black Rebels," 244.

18  *Sir Francis Drake Revived*, 48.

19  *Sir Francis Drake Revived*, 46. Kelsey notes conflicting records about the manner and date of John Drake's death (*Sir Francis Drake*, 60).

20  *Sir Francis Drake Revived*, 50–52.

21  *Sir Francis Drake Revived*, 54.

22  *Sir Francis Drake Revived*, 54.

23  Kelsey, *Sir Francis Drake*, 216.

24  Kelsey, *Sir Francis Drake*, 82, 217, 80.

25  For discussions of Hakluyt's early life, see George Bruner Parks, *Richard Hakluyt and the English Voyages*, 56–74; and Peter Mancall, *Hakluyt's Promise*, 8–24. Quotations from Parks, 57–58.

26  Mancall, *Hakluyt's Promise*, 24.

27  Richard Hakluyt, *The Principle Navigations*, 4.

28  Mancall, *Hakluyt's Promise*, 31. See also Taylor's account in *Original Writings*, vol. 1, 7–11.

29  *Principle Navigations*, 4.

30  Hakluyt, "A Discourse of the Commodity of the Taking of the Straight of Magellanus," in *Original Writings*, vol. 1, 142–43. Historians tend to dismiss this scheme, but they fail to take into account that Drake knew the *Symerons* better than any European then and better than all of us today. He lived with them intimately for months under harsh conditions. He slept under their roofs. He followed their lead in the trackless jungles. He had listened to their hopes and learned of their anxieties. Nor was Richard Hakluyt given to fantasy; that fact distinguishes him even today as an astute judge of rumor and exaggeration. He always did his homework and published only those narratives he considered credible. Parks praises "the empirical method of the two Hakluyts." Parts of *Divers Voyages* might "look pretty dubious now," but we must remember that if Hakluyt's authorities were "not unimpeachable, [they] were yet unimpeached" (*Richard Hakluyt*, 72).

31  For a full account of English publications decrying Spanish crimes, see William S. Maltby, *The Black Legend in England*. Hakluyt was only one of several writers who helped shape the ideology of Elizabethan and early Stuart England. See Macall, *Hakluyt's Promise*, 29.

32  According to E. G. R. Taylor, Hakluyt's modern editor, he "was evidently possessed with a burning desire to witness the destruction of the sea-supremacy and monopoly of Spain" (*Original Writings*, vol. 1, 17). Peter Mancall, *Hakluyt's Promise*, 110. Morgan, *American Slavery American Freedom*, 13. Sir Walter Raleigh, *The History of the World*, A2 and B2. Because Raleigh's *History* was written under James I, not Elizabeth, when relations with Spain were much improved, the version of history soft-pedals the ideological divisions, and Raleigh dispraises Phillip II and other Spanish royalty more for defects of character than belief. See Christopher Hodgkins's interpretation of Drake's *The World Encompassed*, a firsthand account first published (in condensed form) in Hakluyt's *Principle Navigations* (1589) ("Stooping to Conquer: Heathen Idolatry and Protestant Humility in the Imperial Legend of Sir Francis Drake," 432).

33  From his Preface to *Divers Voyages*, vol. 1, 175. See Taylor's "Introduction" to Hakluyt's *Original Writings*, 15–17.

34  See "Document 38," two letters from Walsingham to Hakluyt, in *Original Writings*, vol. 1, 196–97.

35  See Taylor, in Hakluyt's *Original Writings*, 31–34. Parks's account of these events in Hakluyt's life and of his *Discourse*, though now nearly a hundred years old, is still by far the most informed and insightful. Parks devotes an entire chapter to the *Discourse* (*Richard Hakluyt*, 87–98) and two others to Hakluyt's five-year investigations in Paris (99–122); "trumpet" (85).

36  *A Discourse Concerning Western Planting*, 159.

37  *A Discourse Concerning Western Planting*, 159. This point concludes Edmund Morgan's argument in the first two chapters of his provocative *American Slavery American Freedom*. I find myself in agreement with Morgan; I am somewhat at odds with the interpretation of Michael Guasco, who concludes that Elizabethan English by and large did "not really" think about Africans any differently than did the Spanish, who used them as slaves. (See "'Free from the tyrannous Spanyard'?" 16n28).

38  How sincere was England's commitment to liberating slaves is not without controversy, and the doubtful historian can cite much evidence if not of English perfidy than certainly of expediency. Given the later history of slavery in America, it might be hard to believe that the English could ever claim to be the saviors of black Africans. So wrote Michael Guasco in 2008 in the journal *Abolition and Slavery*. Drake's most current (and highly cynical) scholarly biographer, Harry Kelsey, agrees. He finds little evidence of English altruism in the West Indies, even in the 1570s and 1580s. On the face of it, Guasco and Kelsey have a plausible case. "English mariners," Gausco writes, "were prepared to treat Africans with

either benevolence or cruelty depending, most often upon mere expediency" ("'Free from the tyrannous Spanyard'?" 14).

39   "Fortie or fiftie": Quinn, *The Roanoke Voyages*, I, 98; "white skin," etc.: 112. According to Quinn, Roanoke Island was occupied by a tribe of that same name; that conclusion has been disputed, most recently by Lee Miller, *Roanoke: Solving the Mystery of the Lost Colony* (see Miller's Appendix A). Miller suggests that Roanoke was part of the Secotan chiefdom.

40   According to the *Encyclopedia Virginia*, "Little is known about Barlowe's life" before 1784, except that he was a "gentleman-soldier attached to Walter Raleigh's household in London." "In the sweate": *Genesis*, 3:19; "most pleasant, and fertile": Quinn, *The Roanoke Voyages*, I, 114–15; "the Earth": Quinn, *The Roanoke Voyages*, I, 108.

41   "White moors": Michael Leroy Oberg, *The Head in Edward Nugent's Hand*, 52. For Herriot's interaction with Manteo and Wanchese, see Quinn, *The Roanoke Voyages*, I, 16.

42   See Oberg's *The Head in Edward Nugent's Hand: Roanoke's Forgotten Indian*.

43   Elizabeth had already granted Sir Humphrey Gilbert a license to plant North America, which expired shortly after his death at sea. But that enterprise, had it ever succeeded, was aimed much farther north, where it was less likely to trouble Spain. Raleigh's proposal was more provocative by far. It's also true that England had been entangled with Ireland for a long time—several centuries if we begin counting with the twelfth-century Norman invasion. But Ireland was always a special case. Colonization was nearly a domestic affair because it was always part of Britain's home defense. This strategic consideration meant that English occupations of Ireland did not commit the country to empire. This fact is reflected in the swift and unequivocal way Elizabeth made decisions about Ireland compared to her sloth regarding America.

44   See Quinn, *Roanoke Voyages*, I, 22; and Morgan, *American Slavery*, 29–31. James Horn, taking his cue from Kelsey and Quinn, agrees, calling Raleigh's and Drake's separate expeditions a grand-scale, "double-edged attack" on Spain (*A Kingdom*, 60). Nearly every commentator on Roanoke agrees that the colony was designed as a naval base or what Spain would consider a pirate's haven. See also Irene Wright, *Documents concerning English voyages to the Spanish Main*, 8.

45   For authoritative but very readable, fuller accounts of these and the following events, see David Beers Quinn, *Set Fair for Roanoke*, 130–54, and Karen Ordahl Kupperman's *Roanoke: the Abandoned Colony*, 75–94.

46   Harriot's "A briefe and true report" is republished in Quinn, I, 314–87. "They are a people": 368–69.

47   Quinn, *Set Fair for Roanoke*, I, 370–76.

48   Keeler, *Sir Francis Drake's West Indian Voyage*, 12, 54. Three documents recording the venture's finances have survived (see Keeler, 51–63).

49   David Quinn, *The Roanoke Voyages*, I, 144–45, 151–52.

50    Keeler, *Sir Francis Drake's West Indian Voyage*, 45, 255. Morgan, *American Slavery*, 13. Crusade: the Spanish certainly considered it as such. According to one report from Santo Domingo, the English committed "a thousand abominations, principally in the temples and with the images. They broke these all to pieces, heaping ignominy and vituperation upon our religion, profaning everything" (Wright, 34). "Corsair," Wright, 134.

51    Wright, *Documents Concerning English Voyages to the Spanish Main*, 31; Morgan, *American Slavery*, 13, 24.

52    See Keeler, *Sir Francis Drake's West Indian Voyage*, 191–93, 237.

53    This convenient précis of the cruise can be found in Keeler, *Sir Francis Drake's West Indian Voyage*, 63–69.

54    Wright, *Documents concerning English Voyages to the Spanish Main*, 26, 35; 150 rowers, 78; for blacks fighting Drake, 31; presents: 46; fifty slaves, 51; Cartagena galley slaves, 54; de Busto, 55; "they carried," 135; ransom, 159.

55    Wright, *Documents concerning English Voyages to the Spanish Main*, 30, 35, 52. For "plenty of wyne," see Keeler, *Sir Francis Drake's West Indian Voyage*, 112.

56    Keeler, *Sir Francis Drake's West Indian Voyage*, 246n2.

57    Keeler, *Sir Francis Drake's West Indian Voyage*, 196, 242.

58    See Wright, *Documents Concerning English Voyages to the Spanish Main*, 143, 173. For four hundred thousand ducats, see 54. For the value of a ducat, see Keeler, *Sir Francis Drake's West Indian Voyage*, 259.

59    Wright, *Documents Concerning English Voyages to the Spanish Main*, 52.

60    *Summarie*, Keeler, *Sir Francis Drake's West Indian Voyage*, 254. For seven hundred effectives, see Keeler, 254n4.

61    *Summarie*, Keeler, *Sir Francis Drake's West Indian Voyage*, 255–57n4.

62    *Summarie*, Keeler, *Sir Francis Drake's West Indian Voyage*, 255–57n4. For the Irishman, 243. For the thirty or forty violators, 151. For the soldiers' oath, 140. The complex details of the expedition's accounts can be found on 50–62.

63    See David Beers Quinn, *Set Fair for Roanoke*, 130–54, and Karen Ordahl Kupperman's *Roanoke: the Abandoned Colony*, 75–94.

64    John L. Humber, *Backgrounds and Preparations for the Roanoke Voyage*, 55.

65    Quinn, *Set Fair*, 141, 371.

66    Kupperman, *Roanoke*, 137.

## CHAPTER 6: THE AMERICAN ADVENTURE

1    See Mancall, *Hakluyt's Promise*, 252, and Parks, *Richard Hakluyt*, 203.

2    "Mad": Brown, *The Genesis of the United States*, I, 248; for the fishmongers, see 280–82; members of Parliament: 229n10.

3    Eight hundred settlers: "A Letter from His Majesty's Council of Virginia to the Corporation of Plymouth," in Brown, *The Genesis of the United States,* I, 239; Archbishop of York: Neill, *History of the Virginia Company of London*, 26; *Nova Britannia*: 4–6, 13–14, 18–19, 21. For the fall 1609 recruitment drive, see "A True & Sincere

Declaration," in Haile, *JN*, 371; Symonds in Brown, I, 288–89; "rankness": Haile, *JN*, 358; Lord Mayor: quotations are Neill's summary, *History of the Virginia Company*, 25. Willing volunteers: See Article XVI of the Second Charter, in Hening, *Statutes at Large*, 93. Broadside: Brown, I, 248–49.

4   Stephen Hopkins's genealogy and childhood are reconstructed here from Caleb Johnson's *Here Shall I Die Ashore*, 15–25. The ingenuity of a few researchers—Caleb Johnson, Ernest Martin Christenson, and Simon Neal—squeeze enough marrow from the dry bones to sketch Hopkins's life.

5   Johnson, *Here I Shall Die Ashore*, 26–29.

6   Broadside: Brown, *The Genesis of the United States*, I, 248–49.

7   Brown, *The Genesis of the United States*, I, 248; "strange interesting trophies": Sir Stanley Spurling, *Sir Thomas Smythe, knt., c. 1558–1625*, 15–16.

8   *Nova*, 23–25. "Special service": *The Second Charter*, Brown, *The Genesis of the United States*, I, 231; "Implements": Second Charter, in Hening, *Statutes at Large*, 93. Unfortunately, Smythe's ledger is lost (see Kingsbury).

9   Broadside: Brown, *The Genesis of the United States*, I, 248–49; *Nova*, 23; mayor: Brown, I, 253.

10  Hening, *Statutes at Large*, 98. For the text of Oaths of Supremacy and Allegiance, see Kingsbury, *The Records of the Virginia Company of London*, III, 4–6.

11  "Such person": Brown, *The Genesis of the United States*, I, 248.

12  The first earliest recorded use of the term dates from 1466. (See "adventurer, n," at OED Online Oxford University Press, June 2014, accessed June 23, 2014.)

13  "Enjoy": Hening, *Statutes at Large*, 95; "disfranchise": 92.

14  Brown, *The Genesis of the United States*, I, 239–40.

15  "Forget the 1%; Free exchange."

16  Thomas Piketty, *Capital in the Twenty-First Century*, 21.

17  A large amount of study has gone into the minutiae of the English aristocracy and their privileges of regalia, beginning with the source most cited by historians, William Harrison's *Harrison's Description of England*. The best modern discussion of all classes in the Elizabethan age is Keith Wrightson, *English Society: 1580–1680*. Much of this description is based on Wrightson's first chapter. The phrase "race and blood," is Harrison's, quoted by Wrightson, 4.

18  *Global Wealth Data Book 2013*, 119, 146. "Moving On Up: Why Do Some Americans Leave the Bottom of the Economic Ladder, but Not Others?" Ironically, American society comes closer to Old England's caste system than England does today. The richest 10 percent of British citizens today own 53.3 percent of their nation's wealth, and in France the figure is just below 52 percent. One might object that the important factor is not the concentration of wealth in one small segment of society but the ease with which people move into and out of their "caste." High socioeconomic mobility is a better indicator of a meritocracy; just as immobility indicates inherited castes. But economic mobility is much more difficult to measure than wealth. Usually, economists express it as a

tendency for people to move from one quintile of income to another—for example, someone from the lowest fifth of a nation's income level moving up to another quintile, or someone in, say, the 60 percent to 80 percent range dropping down a notch to the middle quintile. Mobility studies, of course, are longitudinal, examining data over time, sometimes over thirty or even sixty years, to determine the heritability of class. Such measures indicate that developing countries like China and India have the greatest mobility, not only because of their rapidly growing economies, but because they are starting from a position of widespread poverty. What in the United States would seem to be a tiny improvement could launch one's income up two or three quintiles in the developing world. Developed countries, which have wider differences between each quintile, naturally show less mobility. And within these developed nations, it's clear that the super-rich Americans, the few billionaires at the very top, retain their position at higher rates than their fellows in Europe. Lower down, the strata evidence is equivocal, and conservatives and liberals argue over the its meaning. Nevertheless, the preponderance of evidence suggests that if you are born into the bottom or the top quintile in the United States, you have a high chance of staying there. The PEW Charitable Trusts Economic Mobility Project, for instance, has found that it's especially hard for the poorest fifth of Americans, whose income is below $20,000 a year, to ever rise up the ladder. Over 40 percent never move out of the lowest quintile, and 70 percent never make it to the middle. The icon of the self-made American moving "from rags to riches" is a Hollywood fantasy. Similarly, the very rich stay very rich. The U.S. may be, as some fear, moving toward an "inheritance" society. See "Moving On Up: Why Do Some Americans Leave the Bottom of the Economic Ladder, but Not Others?"

19  Wrightson, *English Society*, 10. Wrightson bases his conclusions on B. G. Blackwood, *The Lancashire Gentry and the Great Rebellion, 1640–1660* and J. T. Cliffe, *The Yorkshire Gentry from the Reformation to the Civil War.*

20  S. G. Culliford, *William Strachey*, 23.

21  S. G. Culliford, *William Strachey*, 12–19; "and the residents": 14. See also, 23, 29–30.

22  Culliford, *William Strachey*, 31.

23  Culliford, *William Strachey*, 31, 41–46.

24  Culliford, *William Strachey*, 46, 57.

25  William Ralph Douthwaite, *Gray's Inn, Its History & Associations.*

26  Douthwaite, *Gray's Inn*, xiv, 183.

27  Douthwaite, *Gray's Inn*, 230.

28  Kenneth Charlton, "Liberal Education and the Inns of Court in the Sixteenth Century," 26 and 37. For Sir Walter Raleigh, see Douthwaite, *Gray's Inn*, 185.

29  Culliford, *William Strachey*, 32, 3. *Twelfth Night*: II.v.40.

30  Culliford, *William Strachey*, 40–42.

31  Sir Thomas Smith, *The State of England*, vol. 3, 52 (quoted in Jeffrey L. Singman, *Daily Life in Elizabethan England*, 12). "Classic . . ." is Singman.

32  Virginia Woolf, *A Room of One's Own*, 43.

33  Culliford, *William Strachey*, 51.

34  The Second Charter is in Hening, *Statutes at Large*, 80–98; partially published in Brown, *The Genesis of the United States*, I, 208–37; and fully published in Kingsbury, *The Records of the Virginia Company of London*, III.

35  Just about all we know about Gates was first gathered in by Brown, *The Genesis of the United States*, II, 892–93.

36  Kingsbury, *The Records of the Virginia Company of London*, III, 15.

37  See Articles 24–27.

38  David Edwards, *The Age of Atrocity: Violence and Conflict in Early Modern Ireland*, 11. See also the essays in James Lyttleton, *Plantation Ireland: Settlement and Material Culture, c. 1550–1700*.

39  Four well-researched books about the *Sea Venture* came out near the four hundredth anniversary of Jamestown's founding. From a scholar's perspective, the most useful of these is Hobson Woodward's *A Brave Vessel* (Viking, 2009), followed by Virginia Bernhard's *A Tale of Two Colonies* (University of Missouri Press, 2011). Glover and Smith's *The Shipwreck That Saved Jamestown* (Henry Holt, 2008), though well documented, is aimed at a less expert readership; readers less concerned with following facts to their sources will find Kieran Doherty's *Sea Venture* (St. Martin's, 2007) an engaging narrative. "Butter": Strachey, *TR*, in Haile, *JN*; lemon juice: Woodward quoting John Smith, 24. For ballast, cabins, etc., see Woodward, who does a fine job detailing the fitting out of vessels such as these for a transatlantic journey (24–26). Six horses . . . : Letter, Gabriel Archer, August 31, 1609, in Haile, *JN*, 350. For the quarrel: Bernard, 20.

40  Gabriel Archer, "Letter from Jamestown," in Haile, *JN*, 351.

41  Strachey, *TR*, in Haile, *JN*, 384–90.

**CHAPTER 7: LOST**

1  "No phenomenon," etc.: Peter Hulme, *Colonial Encounters*, 94. Hulme discusses the novelty of hurricanes and the inadequacy of English language and consequently English thought to cope with them at some length (94–101); "the experience": Hulme, 97. Eden is quoted from Hulme, 95.

2  Acts, 27:1–44.

3  "hurlecano": Hulme, *Colonial Encounters*, 95; "where God": 97–98.

4  "Description of a Great Sea-Storm." "prayers": in Haile, *JN*, 385; Glover and Smith imagine that the doomed passengers thought of the storm using familiar formulae: "Was God testing their faith or punishing them for their sins?" (*The Shipwreck*, 96). But this is almost certainly a misinterpretation. Such questions did not seem to obtain in Atlantic hurricanes.

5    "A Letter written by Don Christopher Columbus . . ." in Major, *Select Letters of Christopher Columbus*, 179.

6    "A Letter," in Major, *Select Letters of Christopher Columbus*, 184.

7    "A Letter," in Major, *Select Letters of Christopher Columbus*, 198. The quotation comes from Fernando Colón, *The History of the Life and Deeds of the Admiral Don Christopher Columbus*, 194.

8    "A Letter," in Major, *Select Letters of Christopher Columbus*, 197.

9    "A Letter," in Major, *Select Letters of Christopher Columbus*, 193.

10   Fernando Colón, *The History of the Life and Deeds of the Admiral Don Christopher Columbus*, 217.

11   See Fernando Colón, *The History of the Life and Deeds of the Admiral Don Christopher Columbus*, 219, 417.

12   "A Letter," in Major, *Select Letters of Christopher Columbus*, 210. Nearly 250 years after Columbus ran the sinking *Bermuda* aground in Jamaica, an English ship returning from the African coast sailed into a storm. She sprang leaks everywhere. The mariners tried to plug the seams with bits of their own clothing. They nailed spare boards into the planking to hold the bits of cloth in place. The story is familiar. Days and nights toiling at the pumps, the men on deck were kept from washing overboard into the surging waves by means of lifelines. "Every time the vessel descended in the sea," recalled one sailor, they feared "she would rise no more." But this ship never sank. Although the water rose steadily in the hold, and the bow of the vessel sank in the foam with every wave, she rose again every time. One of the sailors, John Newton, had lived a life as licentious and adventurous as Robinson Crusoe. He had been both slaver and slave. He had been lashed to the grating of a navy ship and whipped by the cat-o'-nine-tails, and he had carried Africans across the ocean to die working the West Indian sugar plantations. He had meted out and suffered much, a hardened man. But this storm broke him. All was lost. Without conviction, without believing there was any God to hear him, he began to pray, *Lord have mercy*. The ship did not go down. The pumps gained on the water in the hold. The clouds broke. They made port. The direction of Newton's life changed as if it had turned on a pivot. Miraculously saved, he acted as if he believed, and then he did believe. His life was a miracle. He became an evangelical Christian, a minister, an abolitionist, and a hymnist. He is best remembered today for that singular anthem "Amazing Grace." Thinking back on his lonely experience in the cold ocean storm, he wrote those lines that echo in the cathedrals of memory: *I once was lost, but now am found*. See John Newton, *An Authentic Narrative*, 76. "Lost to the world," meaning ignored or forsaken or forgotten by society, dates as far back as 1638, half a century after the "lost" colony of Roanoke, when it appeared in a now obscure English play by James Shirley. It is from this use that we have our phrase "lost to history." Gone from the written record. Gone from archaeology. Not even a shard of pottery or a rusted blade or so much as a golden signet ring, crusted in centuries of soil, to tell us the story of someone's life, to

testify where and how they once lived or tell us where they died. The trace of their lives was erased from the earth as if they had never been born.

13    Fernando Colón, *The History of the Life and Deeds of the Admiral Don Christopher Columbus*, 220. The Italian for signed up: "*si sottoscrissero*," 417.

14    Strachey, *TR*, in Haile, *JN*, 391.

15    Strachey, *TR*, in Haile, *JN*, 394. As described in the *Transactions of the Geographical Society of London*, the "principal islands are generally separated by channels, from ten to twenty feet deep, and many of the spaces between the smaller islands are fordable." See Nelson, "On the Geology of the Bermudas," 104.

16    See Doherty, *Sea Venture*, 45, 259n19. Strachey, *TR*, in Haile, *JN*, 394.

17    Kieran Doherty convincingly speculates that social class would have dictated the first to "flee the doomed ship" (*Sea Venture*, 47, 259n20). Woodward disputes the notion, speculating that Somers and Newport would have been the last to leave the wreck (49).

18    Woodward, *A Brave Vessel*, 49; "ere night": Strachey, *TR*, in Haile, *JN*, 390.

19    "by the mercy": Strachey, *TR*, in Haile, 390; Devil's Islands, etc.: Strachey, *TR*, in Haile, *JN*, 391. "navigator": Jourdain, *A Voyage to Virginia in 1609*, 108.

20    Watts, *Shipwrecked*, 11–12.

21    For the sixteenth-century wrecks, see Watts, *Shipwrecked*, 49–56; "gold, pearls": Watts, 100; for 1603 and 1605 wrecks, see Watts, 90.

22    See Watts, *Shipwrecked*, 50–51.

23    Steven Mentz, *Shipwreck Modernity*, xxv–xxvi, 2.

24    Jourdain, *A Voyage to Virginia in 1609*, 108.

25    Jourdain, *A Voyage to Virginia in 1609*, 110. See also Woodward, *A Brave Vessel*, 23.

26    "Bermuda Cedar." In later centuries, the rich, dark red cedars supported a flourishing industry of carved objects. The National Museum of Bermuda is filled with objects fashioned by generations of prisoners of war held captive on the islands, from Irish rebels in 1798 to crewmen from a German U-boat in the 1940s. By the 1650s, Bermuda was exporting "chairs, desks, and tables to Barbados, Jamaica, and other Caribbean colonies." Bermudian shipwrights in a flourishing industry considered local cedars better than Yucatán mahogany. The greater height of mahogany trees allowed for longer keels, which had to be carved in one piece from a single tree, but even in the eighteenth century shipwrights were still using Bermudan cedar for ship's ribs. For shipbuilding properties, see Michael Jarvis, *In the Eye of All Trade*, 232. For palmettos, see "Bermuda Palmetto."

27    "daily hunted": Strachey, *TR*, in Haile, *JN*, 403.

28    Strachey, *TR*, in Haile, *JN*, 394.

29    Strachey, *TR*, in Haile, *JN*, 413. Somers's absence is inferred by his later intervention on Waters's behalf.

30    Strachey, *TR*, in Haile, *JN*, 413.

31    Strachey, *TR*, in Haile, *JN*, 413.

32    Strachey, *TR*, in Haile, *JN*, 400.

33 For all of these and subsequent details of the islands, see Strachey, *TR*, in Haile, *JN*, 394–401.

34 Strachey, *TR*, in Haile, *JN*, 410–11.

35 Interview with Jay Caffee, August 5, 2014, Bath, Maine. See also John W. Bradford, *The 1607 Popham Colony's Pinnace Virginia*, 7, 20.

36 Strachey, *TR*, in Haile, *JN*, 397, 403.

37 For the boat's dimensions, see Strachey, *TR*, in Haile, *JN*, 414–15; "friends and country," etc.: 404–405. The narrative of this mutiny occurs on those same pages.

38 Strachey presents the events in the first few months after the shipwreck—Waters's trial, the launching of the longboat, Want's mutiny, and the sailors' removal to the main island—in definite sequence. Strachey does not attempt to organize them in chronological order, and some events come with vague references to time. (Strachey puts this mutiny at the beginning of September, which seems to be impossible. That would mean these six were tried, convicted, and banished at almost exactly the same time the longboat was launched. But the narrative also implies that their refusal to work was triggered by labor on the pinnace, which could hardly have begun at all before work on the longboat was completed. The *True Reportory* is very confused as to timing and sequence of events in the first few months of their maroonage. Any reconstruction, including my own, requires an uncomfortable amount of speculation, and must be accompanied by a disclaimor.

39 Strachey, *TR*, in Haile, *JN*, 406.

## CHAPTER 8: THE FIRST FRONTIER

1 Richard White, *Middle Ground*, 51–60 and x. See also Daniel H. Usner's *Indians, Settlers, and Slaves in a Frontier Exchange Economy*; and *Under an Open Sky: Rethinking America's Western Past*, edited by William Cronon, George Miles, and Jay Gitlin. Fifteen years after White's book was published, the *William and Mary Quarterly* used an entire issue to assess White's contribution to American history. Six historians, including White himself, evaluated the book's considerable influence. (See *William and Mary Quarterly* 63, no. 1 [January 2006].) See especially Catherine Desbarats's "Following *the Middle Ground*," 81–96.

2 John Mack Faragher, "Introduction" in *Rereading Frederick Jackson Turner*, 1-3.

3 "Alumni": Faragher, "Introduction," 3.

4 Turner, *The Frontier in American History*, 1–4. The essay, "The Significance of the Frontier in American History," is available in a dozen convenient printed forms, and the casual reader will have little trouble finding its text on the Internet. I am using the 1962 Holt version because it includes another Turner essay elaborating his theory, "The First Official Frontier of the Massachusetts Bay," to which I will refer in the last chapter of this book. That chapter will consider the other great origin myth, which seems to be ascendant in popular culture, which is embodied in the Pilgrim story. I said White "resurrected" the frontier thesis, but it might be more proper to say he made it respectable again. Turner's thesis at first nearly

revolutionized American history, as "the whole center of gravity of American historical writing and teaching shifted" toward the West. But by the 1920s, when Turner himself was wooed from the University of Wisconsin and moved to Boston to teach at prestigious Harvard, the backlash began, and historians of Eastern culture made a comeback. Nevertheless, as late as 1972, in his introduction to yet another reprint and reconsideration of Turner's work, George Rogers Taylor would report that, although "scholars have been arranging a decent burial for the Turner thesis" since the 1920s, "the hypothesis . . . has refused to die and is today as much alive as it was" in 1893. See George Rogers Taylor, *The Turner Thesis*, viii and vii. Turner, *The Frontier in American History*, 4. Massachusetts: See Turner's "The First Official Frontier of the Massachusetts Bay," in *The Frontier in American History*, 39–66.

5   Francis Maguel, "Report," in Haile, *JN*, 448.

6   For houses, see Strachey, *TR*, in Haile, *JN*, 430. Smith, *GH*, in Haile, *JN*, 320–24. For the market, see Maguel, "Report," in Haile, *JN*, 450.

7   Smith, *GH*, in Haile, *JN*, 225.

8   For these numbers, see Smith, *GH*, in Haile, *JN*, 320–21.

9   Smith, *GH*, in Haile, *JN*, 320.

10  For the cannon at Jamestown, see Maguel, "Report," in Haile, *JN*, 448.

11  For Smith's leadership qualities, see *GH*, in Haile, *JN*, 334.

12  Archer, "Letter from Jamestown," in Haile, *JN*, 351.

13  We might presume that the Indians used the same tactics to oppose this supposed Spanish raid as they used on the upper Chesapeake to oppose Smith's landings the previous year. See Smith, *GH*, in Haile, *JN*, 257.

14  Smith, *GH*, in Haile, *JN*, 290.

15  We have two accounts of this standoff: Smith, *GH*, in Haile, *JN*, 327–29, and Archer, "Letter," in Haile, *JN*, 352–53.

16  Archer's and Smith's accounts do not contradict each other, but they are each so sketchy as to require some speculation by the historian. The exact order of these events, for instance, is not clear. I have reasoned that Smith resigned his commission to Martin before Ratcliffe arrived on the *Diamond*. It seems likely that West's election occurred *after* Ratcliffe's arrival, just as it seems unlikely that Martin would have resigned his commission back to Smith after so many colonists elected West to be their president. Both Barbour and Haile have pointed out the illegality of West's election. See Smith, *GH*, in Haile, *JN*, 329, and Archer, "Letter," in Haile, *JN*, 353. "frontier coup d'état": Vaughan, *American Genesis*, 64.

17  Archer, "Letter," in Haile, 352–53; see also Smith, *GH*, in Haile, *JN*, 331.

18  Archer, "Letter," in Haile, *JN*, 353; Smith, *GH*, in Haile, *JN*.

19  "how greedy": *GH*, in Haile, *JN*, 331; for the length of a trip to the falls: See Haile, *John Smith in the Chesapeake*, 8–9. Ratcliffe and Archer's presence at the falls is implied rather than stated definitively in *GH*, in Haile, *JN*, 331.

20  Spelman, *Relation of Virginia*, in Haile, *JN*, 482.

21 See Rountree, *The Powhatan Indians of Virginia*, 11.

22 *GH*, in Haile, *JN*, 330. For a fascinating discussion of money in the Indian economy, including a reference to this peculiar transaction, see Dror Goldberg, "Money, Credit, and Banking in Virginia: 1585–1645," 15. Dewey's Island and Orapax: Haile, *John Smith in the Chesapeake*, 87.

23 Percy, *TR* in Haile, *JN*, 501–2.

24 For Martin's failures, see Smith, *GH*, in Haile, *JN*, 329–30.

25 Spelman, *Relation of Virginia*, in Haile, *JN*, 483; Percy, *A True Relation*, in Haile, *JN*, 502; Smith, *GH*, in Haile, *JN*, 332; "more profound": Haile himself thinks Smith gave the order to attack; see *John Smith in the Chesapeake*, 88.

26 *GH*, in Haile, *JN*, 332.

27 Smith, *GH*, in Haile, *JN*, 332–33. For the proper distance between the falls and Jamestown, see Haile, *John Smith in the Chesapeake*, 87.

28 Barbour, *TWCJS*, 276; Vaughan, *American Genesis*, 64–65; Lemay, *John Smith's American Dream*, 104; Horn, *A Land as God Made It*, 169.

29 *GH*, in Haile, *JN*, 333. Horn: *A Land as God Made It*, 169. Kupperman does not raise the issue (*The Jamestown Project*, 251).

30 Dyer or Coe: Barbour, *TWCJS*, 278. Barbour does not give his reason to finger these two, but the *General History* mentions in another context that they "should have murdered" (in Haile, *JN*, 336).

31 Ratcliffe, "Letter," in Haile, *JN*, 354.

32 For a discussion of these charges, see Barbour, *TWCJS*, 278–79.

33 *GH*, in Haile, *JN*, 334–45.

34 Percy, "A True Relation," in Haile, *JN*, 502.

35 *GH*, in Haile, *JN*, 334–45 and 338.

36 *GH*, in Haile, *JN*, 333, 335. Smith's final days in Virginia are a bit murky. Barbour's speculations are still the most credible (*TWCJS*, 277–80).

## CHAPTER 9: TROUBLE TIMES

1 "ringing of a bell," etc.: Strachey, *TR*, in Haile, *JN*, 412–13; "kind of web-footed": Strachey, 398–99. For the cahow, see "The Bermuda Petrel (*Pterodroma Cahow*)." The subsequent history of these birds is fascinating. When the English settled the islands in greater numbers, they poached these birds mercilessly and ravaged their remaining breeding grounds. The inevitable introduction of dogs and cats and rats resulted in their feasting on the eggs in the cahows' burrows. The colonial government tried to halt the animal's decline with what might be the first environmental laws in Western history, but it didn't help. The cahows disappeared by the 1620s, and for over three hundred years none were seen. But in the 1950s, they reappeared, miraculously, and the government set aside some small islands in Castle Harbour, the biggest being Nonsuch Island, as protected habitat. With great difficulty, predatory and competing species were eradicated from these islands, and since the 1970s the extinct cahows have reemerged, one of the few

"Lazarus" species seemingly risen from the dead ("Bermuda's Cahow Recovery Program").

2   Elkins and McKitrick, "A Meaning for Turner's Frontier, Democracy in the Old Northwest," 146–47.

3   Elkins and McKitrick developed their idea by analyzing three frontiers: the Old Northwest of Ohio, Indiana, and Illinois; "the Southwest frontier of Alabama and Mississippi"; and "the Puritan frontier of Massachusetts Bay" ("A Meaning," 151).

4   Strachey, *TR*, in Haile, *JN*, 403–4.

5   "Sir George's men": Jourdain, in *A Voyage to Virginia in 1609*, 110. Curiously, we have no indication about which camp Captain Newport chose. As vice admiral, he was subordinate to Somers, but the plan was that he would stay in Virginia, subject to Gates's orders.

6   Louis B. Wright, "Introduction" to *A Voyage to Virginia in 1609*, xxvii.

7   As Douglas Peterson observed over half a century ago in *Shakespeare Quarterly*, the sentiment expressed here, that "lust" can enslave "reason and will," is "a commonplace theme throughout the literature of the Renaissance" (381).

8   "devilish disquiets": Strachey, *TR*, in Haile, *JN*, 404; Hopkins's mutiny is on 406–7.

9   Strachey, *TR*, in Haile, *JN*, 414.

10  See Strachey, *TR*, in Haile, *JN*, 412. It is likely that Strachey inflated the value of the Company's investment: his point was to demonstrate the debt that each settler owed to the Company.

11  "their whole life": Strachey, *TR*, in Haile, *JN*, 407.

12  Strachey, *TR*, in Haile, *JN*, 406. It is certainly worth noting here that Hopkins thought wives and children were bound naturally to the authority of husbands and fathers. The brief précis of his arguments that Strachey cared to record does not address the case of unmarried adult women, although we know some were among the castaways.

13  Strachey, *TR*, in Haile, *JN*, 406.

14  Hobbes, *Leviathan*, 186.

15  Hobbes, *Leviathan*, 187. Traditional scholarship on Hobbes tended to treat his "state of nature" as a "hypothetical construct" and deny any connection to real "savages." Richard Ashcraft demolishes that facile notion. (See "Leviathan Triumphant: Thomas Hobbes and the Politics of Wild Men," 144–54.)

16  See Arneil, 20. For a critique of how fully the "classic" social contract theory depended upon misrepresentations of Native Americans, see Charles Mills, *The Racial Contract*.

17  Rousseau's *Origins of Inequality* rightly points out that when Hobbes describes the state of nature, he takes civilized man, with all his habits of thought, and strips him of government. More than a hundred years later, Rousseau attempted a much subtler approach, which we would describe today as anthropological, imagining

how human society really developed, from isolated human beings in a pre-linguistic state through many stages of increasing cooperation and complexity.

18 Strachey, *TR*, in Haile, *JN*, 407.

## CHAPTER 10: THE KISS-MY-ARSE REVOLUTION

1 Percy, "A True Relation," in Haile, *JN*, 502–3. Barbour, *TWCJS*, 278.
2 Smith, *GH*, in Haile, *JN*, 333–34.
3 Smith, *GH*, in Haile, *JN*, 339.
4 Spelman, *Relation of Virginia*, in Haile, *JN*, 483.
5 Percy, *TR*, in Haile, *JN*, 504. Smith's *GH* interprets Indian "revolt" on the James River as support for him in the internecine struggle to control Jamestown (339).
6 Spelman, *Relation of Virginia*, in Haile, *JN*, 483.
7 Spelman, *Relation of Virginia*, in Haile, *JN*, 484–85.
8 Haile, *JN*, 482.
9 All of these reversals are narrated by Percy, "A True Relation," in Haile, *JN*, 503–4.
10 *General History*, in Haile, *JN*, 339; Percy, "A True Relation," in Haile, *JN*, 504.
11 "Created": Strachey, *TR*, in Haile, *JN*, 439.
12 Percy, "A True Relation," in Haile, *JN*, 504–5. "burned him": Strachey, *TR*, in Haile, *JN*, 440. Strachey relates this tale to discredit the story of starvation: the man is described as insane. But subsequent evidence, especially William Kelso's archaeological discoveries, suggest the story was true.
13 In somewhat contradictory accounts, Percy and Strachey both tell versions of these events (in Haile, 439–40 and 504–5). Percy *TR*, in Haile, *JN*, 505.
14 Percy *TR*, in Haile, *JN*, 505.
15 Strachey, *TR*, in Haile, *JN*, 414.
16 John Rolfe, *A True Relation of the State of Virginia*, in Haile, *JN*, 868.
17 Unless otherwise indicated, these details and those in the following paragraphs are from Strachey, *TR*, in Haile, *JN*, 408–12.
18 Strachey's narrative is inconsistent here. Some phrases imply that settlers could walk from Gates's camp to Somers's building bay as if they were both on St. George's Island (408–9), while earlier he unequivocally stated that Somers moved across the water to the main island. Until some archaeological evidence is discovered and resolves these inconsistencies, we must remain unsure of exactly where Somers's people were encamped.
19 Strachey, *TR*, in Haile, *JN*, 410. Unless otherwise indicated, the details of this mutiny are drawn from Strachey, 410–12.
20 Kingsbury, *The Records of the Virginia Company of London*, III, 15.
21 A replica of this remarkable vessel is on display in St. George's Island, maintained by the St. George's Foundation.
22 Woodward's résumé of the accounts of Namontack's death, elaborated on in his notes, is the best summary available; however, his own narrative is quite speculative,

going so far as to assert such details (with no evidence) as that the Indians constructed a canoe and explored the archipelago.

## CHAPTER 11: RESCUE

1   Strachey, *TR*, in Haile, *JN*, 416–17.
2   "Report of the Voyage to the Indies," in Haile, *JN*, 539. See also Percy, *A True Relation*, in Haile, *JN*, 507.
3   See Nicholls, "Percy's 'Trewe Relacyon,'" 220.
4   Philip Barbour, "The Honorable George Percy," 7.
5   Such advice came from the Tower of London, for the Percy name was connected again to treasonous activity in 1605. He was implicated in the infamous Guy Fawkes gunpowder plot to blow up the king and House of Lords in 1605. The earl's connection to the conspirators was tenuous enough to spare him the agony of being drawn and quartered, but it was credited enough to keep him in the Tower, whence he attended to his financial affairs and indulged his love of geography. At the family's lowest point of prestige and influence, George sailed into a sort of self-imposed exile that not only removed him from the family's intrigues but also might have helped redeem the Percy name, if intrigues had not followed the ships across the ocean.
6   "thinly documented," as well as all of these biographical details: Mark Nicholls, "George Percy's *Trewe Relacyon*," 214–19; "jerkin and hose," Nicholls, 215–16.
7   "aristocratic contempt": Nicholls, 236; "despised": Barbour, "The Honorable," 12; "my reputation," quoted in Barbour, 12. Both Nicholls and Barbour discuss Smith's assessment of Percy's character.
8   "calculate": Percy, *True Relation*, in Haile, *JN*, 504; "eight ounces": Virginia General Assembly, "The Answer," 913; "one boat": Percy, *True Relation*, 505.
9   Years later, Percy inexplicably wrote of "two pinnaces" moored at Fort Algernon through the entire starving time (*True Relation*, in Haile, *JN*, 506). This must be a mistake, for the *Swallow* had by then returned to England.
10  Percy, *True Relation*, in Haile, *JN*, 504–5; for the lack of fishing nets, see Strachey, *TR*, in Haile, *JN*, 419.
11  Kupperman, "Apathy and Death"; "so apathetic": Edgar Schein in the *Journal of Social Issues* and the *American Journal of Psychiatry*, quoted by Kupperman; Percy, *True Relation*, in Haile, *JN*, 507.
12  Percy, "Discourses," in Haile, *JN*, 94.
13  Dennis B. Blanton, "Drought as a Factor in the Jamestown Colony, 1607–1612," 76.
14  Percy, 505; Virginia General Assembly, 913.
15  For a discussion of Percy's aristocratic snobbery, see Nicholls, "George Percy's *Trewe Relacyon*," 236. Smith, *GH*, in Haile, *JN*, 339–40.
16  Percy, *True Declaration*, in Haile, *JN*, 505–6. "Weakly": General Assembly, "The Answer," in Haile, 915. The General Assembly also corroborated the desertions to Indians, 913.

17   Virginia General Assembly, "The Answer," in Haile, *JN*, 913. For disease, see Kupperman, "Apathy and Death in early Jamestown," 32–33.

18   "famine"; "those things"; "licked": Percy, 505.

19   Council of Virginia, "A True Declaration," in Haile, *JN*, 468, 473, 474. Fairly recently, Rachel Herrmann ("The tragicall historie") attempts to discredit the idea that settlers resorted to cannibalism, largely on Gates's testimony. For a good historiography of skepticism, see page 48n7.

20   Smith, *GH*, in Haile, *JN*, 340; Percy, in Haile, *JN*, 505; Virginia General Assembly, in Haile, *JN*, 913.

21   Joseph Stromberg, "Starving Settlers." According to Stromberg, Owsley consulted with the FBI on the Jeffrey Dahmer case.

22   Percy, *True Relation*, in Haile, *JN*, 507.

23   Virginia General Assembly, "The Answer," in Haile, 913.

24   Smith, *GH*, in Haile, *JN*, 339.

25   "swords": Smith, *GH*, in Haile, *JN*, 339.

26   Virginia General Assembly, "The Answer," in Haile, *JN*, 913.

27   Percy, *True Relation*, in Haile, 507.

28   Strachey, *TR*, in Haile, *JN*, 418–19.

29   Strachey, *TR*, in Haile, *JN*, 420, 424.

30   Strachey, *TR*, in Haile, *JN*, 420.

31   Strachey, *TR*, in Haile, *JN*, 420, 426–27.

32   Strachey, *TR*, in Haile, *JN*, 427.

33   Strachey, *TR*, in Haile, *JN*, 426–27; Percy, *A True Relation*, in Haile, *JN*, 508.

34   Strachey, *TR*, in Haile, *JN*, 432; for the halberdiers, see 429.

35   Strachey, *TR*, in Haile, *JN*, 432–33. For the new appellation, *lord governor*, see, for example, 434.

36   Strachey, *TR*, in Haile, *JN*, 433–34; Percy, in Haile, *JN*, 509.

37   Strachey, *TR*, in Haile, *JN*, glassworks: 429; church: 429.

38   "Instructions, Orders, and Constitutions to Sr Thomas Gates Knight Governor of Virginia," in Kingsbury, *The Records of the Virginia Company of London*, III, 18–19.

39   Kingsbury, *The Records of the Virginia Company of London*, III, 19.

40   Strachey, *TR*, in Haile, *JN*, 435.

41   Strachey, *TR*, in Haile, *JN*, 437.

42   Haile, *JN*, 435.

43   Percy, in Haile, *JN*, 510–11.

44   Years later, when she was made a widow, the baroness Cecily laid a claim upon the colony to recover her own money, and King James granted her an annuity of five hundred pounds to be paid for thirty-one years, as some partial compensation for her loss. So it seems very likely that Lord De La Warr contributed in excess of sixteen thousand pounds to the Virginia enterprise. All of this sum need not have been poured into the money pit that was the Fourth Supply. See

Alexander Brown's biographical sketch of Thomas West in *The Genesis of the United States*, vol. 2, 1048.

45  "conspiracy": Percy, *True Relation*, in Haile, *JN*, 511. For iron mining, see "Falling Creek Iron Works," in Frank E. Grizzard and D. Boyd Smith, *Jamestown Colony: A Political, Social, and Cultural History*, 73.

46  Percy, in Haile, *JN*, 511.

47  For these illnesses, see Thomas West, *The Relation of the Right Honorable the Lord De-La-Warre, Lord Governor and Captain Generall of the Colonie, planted in Virginia.* Percy, in Haile, *JN*, 512–13.

48  Strachey, *TR*, in Haile, *JN*, 428.

49  *The Tempest*'s connection to the *Sea Venture* and Bermuda was first noted in 1808, when Edmund Malone traced the parallels between the play and Sylvester Jourdain's *Discovery of the Bermudas* and one of the Virginia Company's propaganda pamphlets (*An Account of the Incidents, From Which the Title and Part of the Story of Shakespeare's* Tempest *Were Derived.* It took another hundred years before the English scholar Sidney Lee explicitly based his interpretation of the play on the identification of Prospero's island with Bermuda and Caliban with American indigenes (*Elizabethan and Other Essays*). The interpretation we take for granted today—that Caliban is an Indian—was more or less settled by the 1960s and 1970s by Leo Marx ("Shakespeare's American Fable") and Leslie A. Fiedler (*The Stranger in Shakespeare*). For a summary of this scholarship, see Alden T. Vaughan, "The Americanization of Caliban," 138. Shakespeare's reliance on Strachey is not without its controversy, and some critics have proposed other sources. See Vaughan's "William Strachey's 'True Reportory' and Shakespeare: A Closer Look at the Evidence."

50  Shakespeare, *Tempest*, II, ii, 9–10; and III, ii, 12.

51  In 1905 an English critic with the improbable name, Walter Alexander Raleigh, took the allegory further, connecting Stephano to "Virginia's disreputable early settlers" (to quote Vaughan, 141) and Miranda to Virginia Dare ("The English Voyages of the Sixteenth Century," 112–13). The principal editor of John Smith's papers, Philip Barbour, links Miranda to Pocahontas and Caliban to Rawhunt (*CWCJS*, 1, 93).

52  See Brown, *The Genesis of the United States*, 2, 869–74 for Dale's biography. Although significantly longer than most of Brown's sketches, it yields little of real interest about the man and nothing of his personality.

## CONCLUSION: GENESIS

1  See Argall's "Letter to Hawes, June 1613," in Haile, *JN*, 754–55.

2  "reign of terror" is Edward Haile's phrase (*JN*, 891). The General Assembly's document, officially adopted by that body, was called *The Answer of the General Assembly in Virginia to a "Declaration of the state of the colony in the 12 years of Sir Thomas Smith's government"—exhibited by Alerman Johnsone and others, 20 February 1624.* This is item 58 and the *Brief Declaration* is item 57 in Haile, *JN*, 891–915.

3   "Pocahontas was already": Tilton, *Pocahontas: The Evolution of an American Narrative*, 11–12. For a discussion of miscegenation in these New York writers, see Tilton, 66–69. "Pocahontas narrative": Tilton, *Pocahontas*, 149. Pocahontas came to thoroughly represent the Southern view of American character. As early as 1820, for example, William Hillhouse, a Northern abolitionist, wrote a lengthy satirical manifesto purportedly in the voice of Pocahontas, which concludes with the eager anticipation of the day when "every [Northern] neck shall bow, and every knee shall bend, in token of their submission" to Southern aristocrats (quoted in Tilton, *Pocahontas*, 151). See also Anne Norton's *Alternative Americas*. For the full argument about Simms's treatments of Native Americans, see Joseph Kelly, "The Evolution of Slave Ideology in Simms's *The Yemassee* and *Woodcraft*."

4   The 1860 attack came in Charles Deane's edition of Edward Maria Wingfield's *A Discourse of Virginia*. Adams made this remark, quoted by Tilton (*Pocahontas*, 173), in a letter to John Gorham Palfrey (*Letters of Henry Adams*, I, 287). Adams's decisive attack came after the war in the *North American Review*. "Advancing armies": Abraham Lincoln's Proclamation of Thanksgiving.

5   For a full treatment of the "city on a hill" motif in American identity, see Richard T. Gamble, *In Search of the City on a Hill: the Making and Unmaking of an American Myth*.

6   Turner, *The First Official Frontier of the Massachusetts Bay*.

7   Henry Luce, "The American Century," *Life*, February 17, 1941. Readers of my own generation probably hear the echoing phrase, "Truth, Justice, and the American Way," coined for the *Superman* television series in 1951, when Americans fully identified themselves with the role of international beacon (see Lauren N. Karp, *Truth, Justice, and the American Way: What Superman Teaches Us About the American Dream and Changing Values Within the United States*, 45).

8   Dwight Eisenhower, Inaugural Address, emphasis added.

9   Barbour argues that Smith did not lie about being rescued by Pocahontas, although the Englishman might have misunderstood Pocahontas's intervention, which was probably scripted, not spontaneous. Barbour was actually equivocal about the theory ("whether it was an adaptation of an annual puberty rite . . . or whether [Wahunsonacock] really decided to risk executing" Smith cannot be determined [167]), although most of the important scholars in the last generation, including Mossiker, Kupperman, and Lemay, favor it. Rountree and Vaughan are unconvinced (Tilton, *Pocahonatas*, 5). Like Rountree, I think the anthropological evidence for a puberty rite is so slim that it must be rejected. I think Barbour's theory is attractive mostly because it is congenial to the prejudices of today's historians. Unlike Rountree and Henry Adams, I see little reason to dispute Smith's claim that Pocahontas did in fact rescue him. The first public reference to Bradford's narrative came in Samuel Wilberforce's *A History of the Protestant Episcopal Church in America* (1844), which used the text extensively as a source (55–61).

10    Page 41.

11    Our oldest text of that document is the version printed in England in 1622 now
      called *Mourts Relation*, mainly written by John Winslow and partly by Bradford,
      which was reprinted in 1625 in *Purchas his Pilgrims*, the same volume that first
      printed Strachey's *True Reportory*. I take my text here from the facsimile of the 1622
      version, reprinted in George Ernest Bowman's *The Mayflower Compact and Its
      Signers*, 6.

12    Bradford, *Of Plimouth Plantation*, 180.

13    So far as I know, Hopkins's biographer, Caleb Johnson, is the only one to
      suggest that Hopkins played any significant role in composing the Mayflower
      Compact. Even Johnson assigns greatest credit to the Pilgrims: "With Stephen's
      consultation no doubt, the Pilgrims arrived at a very novel solution" (*Here I Shall
      Die Ashore*, 67).

14    See Johnson, *Here I Shall Die Ashore*, 130–31.

## A NOTE ON THE AUTHOR

Joseph Kelly is a professor of literature at the College of Charleston. He is the author of *America's Longest Siege*: *Charleston, Slavery, and the Slow March Toward Civil War* and *Our Joyce: From Outcast to Icon* and the editor of the Seagull Reader series. He lives in Charleston, South Carolina.